THE HISTORY OF AL-ṬABARĪ

AN ANNOTATED TRANSLATION

VOLUME XV

The Crisis of the Early Caliphate

THE REIGN OF ʿUTHMĀN

A.D. 644–656/A.H. 24–35

The History of al-Ṭabarī

Editorial Board

Ihsan Abbas, University of Jordan, Amman

C. E. Bosworth, The University of Manchester

Franz Rosenthal, Yale University

Ehsan Yar-Shater, Columbia University(*General Editor*)

SUNY

SERIES IN NEAR EASTERN STUDIES

Said Amir Arjomand, Editor

The preparation of this volume was made possible in part by a grant from the National Endowment for the Humanities, an independent federal agency.

Bibliotheca Persica
Edited by Ehsan Yar-Shater

The History of al-Ṭabarī
(Ta'rīkh al-rusul wa'l mulūk)

VOLUME XV

The Crisis of the Early Caliphate

translated and annotated
by

R. Stephen Humphreys

University of Wisconsin, Madison

State University of New York Press

Published by
State University of New York Press, Albany

Printed in the United States of America

For information, address the State University of New York Press,
90 State Street, Suite 700, Albany, NY 12207
Library of Congress Cataloging in Publication Data
Tabarī, 838?–923.
The crisis of the early caliphate.
(The history of al-Tabarī = Ta'rīkh al-rusul wa'l
mulūk ; v. 15) (Bibliotheca Persica) (SUNY series in
Near Eastern studies)
Translation of extracts from: Ta'rīkh al-rusul
wa-al-mulūk.
Bibliography: p.
Includes index.
1. Islamic Empire—History—622-661. 2. 'Uthmān
ibn 'Affān, Caliph, d. 656. I. Humphreys, R. Stephen.
II. Title. III. Series: Tabarī, 838?-923. Ta'rīkh
al-rusul wa-al-mulūk ; 15. IV. Series: Bibliotheca
Persica (Albany, N.Y.) V. Series: SUNY series in Near
Eastern studies.
DS38.2.T313 1985 vol. 15 909'.1 s 88-35555
[DS38.1] [909'.097671]
ISBN 0-7914-0154-5
ISBN 0-7914-0155-3 (pbk.)
10 9 8 7 6 5 4 3 2 1

Preface

The History of Prophets and Kings (*Ta'rīkh al-rusul wa'l-mulūk*) by Abū Ja'far Muḥammad b. Jarīr al-Ṭabarī (839–923), here rendered as the *History of al-Ṭabarī*, is by common consent the most important universal history produced in the world of Islam. It has been translated here in its entirety for the first time for the benefit of non-Arabists, with historical and philological notes for those interested in the particulars of the text.

Ṭabarī's monumental work explores the history of the ancient nations, with special emphasis on biblical peoples and prophets, the legendary and factual history of ancient Iran, and, in great detail, the rise of Islam, the life of the Prophet Muḥammad, and the history of the Islamic world down to the year 915. The first volume of this translation will contain a biography of al-Ṭabarī and a discussion of the method, scope, and value of his work. It will also provide information on some of the technical considerations that have guided the work of the translators.

The *History* has been divided here into 38 volumes, each of which covers about two hundred pages of the original Arabic text in the Leiden edition. An attempt has been made to draw the dividing lines between the individual volumes in such a way that each is to some degree independent and can be read as such. The page numbers of the original in the Leiden edition appear on the margins of the translated volumes.

Al-Ṭabarī very often quotes his sources verbatim and traces the chain of transmission (*isnād*) to an original source. The chains of transmitters are, for the sake of brevity, rendered by only a dash

(—) between the individual links in the chain. Thus, According to Ibn Ḥumayd—Salamah—Ibn Isḥāq means that al-Ṭabarī received the report from Ibn Ḥumayd who said that he was told by Salamah, who said that he was told by Ibn Isḥāq, and so on. The numerous subtle and important differences in the original Arabic wording have been disregarded.

The table of contents at the beginning of each volume gives a brief survey of the topics dealt with in that particular volume. It also includes the headings and subheadings as they appear in al-Ṭabarī's text, as well as those occasionally introduced by the translator.

Well-known place names, such as, for instance, Mecca, Baghdad, Jerusalem, Damascus, and the Yemen, are given in their English spellings. Less common place names, which are the vast majority, are transliterated. Biblical figures appear in the accepted English spelling. Iranian names are usually transcribed according to their Arabic forms, and the presumed Iranian forms are often discussed in the footnotes.

Technical terms have been translated wherever possible, but some, such as dirham and imām, have been retained in Arabic forms. Others that cannot be translated with sufficient precision have been retained and italicized as well as footnoted.

The annotation aims chiefly at clarifying difficult passages, identifying individuals and place names, and discussing textual difficulties. Much leeway has been left to the translators to include in the footnotes whatever they consider necessary and helpful.

The bibliographies list all the sources mentioned in the annotation.

The index in each volume contains all the names of persons and places referred to in the text, as well as those mentioned in the notes as far as they refer to the medieval period. It does not include the names of modern scholars. A general index, it is hoped, will appear after all the volumes have been published.

For further details concerning the series and acknowledgments, see Preface to Volume I.

Ehsan Yar-Shater

Contents

Preface / v

Abbreviations / xi

Translator's Foreword / xiii

Transliteration and Editorial Conventions / xxi

Table 1. ʿUthmān's Lineage / xxii

The Events of the Year 24 (644/645) / 1

The Sermon of ʿUthmān and the Slaying of al-Hurmuzān by ʿUbaydallāh b. ʿUmar / 3
The Governorship of Saʿd b. Abī Waqqāṣ in Kūfah / 5
The Letters of ʿUthmān to His Officials and Governors and to the Common People / 5
The Campaign of [al-Walīd b. ʿUqbah in Ādharbayjān and Armenia] / 8
The Gathering of Byzantine Forces against the Muslims and the Muslims' Call for Aid from the Kūfans / 9
The Account of That Event / 9

The Events of the Year 25 (645/646) / 12

The Events of the Year 26 (646/647) / 14

The Reason Why ʿUthmān Removed Saʿd from Kūfah and Named al-Walīd His Governor There / 15

The Events of the Year 27 (647/648) / 18

The Conquest [of Ifrīqiyah] and the Reason for the Appointment of ʿAbdallāh b. Saʿd b. Abī Sarḥ as Governor of Egypt and ʿUthmān's Removal of ʿAmr b. al-ʿĀṣ from (That Province) / 18

The Events of the Year 28 (648/649) / 25

Muʿāwiyah's Attack on Cyprus / 26

The Events of the Year 29 (649/650) / 33

The Reason for ʿUthmān's Removal of Abū Mūsā [al-Ashʿarī] from Baṣrah / 34
[ʿUthmān's Alterations to the Pilgrimage Rites] / 38

The Events of the Year 30 (650/651) / 41

The Campaign of Saʿīd b. al-ʿĀṣ in Ṭabaristān / 42
The Reason for ʿUthmān's Removal of al-Walīd and His Appointment of Saʿīd as Governor [in Kūfah] / 45
How the Signet Ring Fell from ʿUthmān's Hand into the Well of Arīs / 62
The Reports Concerning Abū Dharr [al-Ghifārī] / 64
[The Flight of Yazdagird from Fārs to Khurāsān] / 69

The Events of the Year 31 (651/652) / 71

The Account of the Battles [of the Masts and against the Blacks] / 72
The Reason Why (Syria) Was Unified under [Muʿāwiyah] / 72
Return to al-Wāqidī's Account of the Two Battles Mentioned Above / 74
The Cause of [Yazdagird's] Murder / 78
[ʿAbdallāh b. ʿĀmir's Campaign in Khurāsān] / 90

The Events of the Year 32 (652/653) / 94

[The Disaster at Balanjar] / 95
The Account of the Death of [Abū Dharr al-Ghifārī] / 100
[ʿAbdallāh b. ʿĀmir's Conquests in Northeastern Iran] / 102
[The Peace between al-Aḥnaf and the People of Balkh] / 106

The Events of the Year 33 (653/654) / 111

The Exile of the Kūfans Whom [ʿUthmān] Sent [to Syria] / 112
ʿUthmān's Exile of Certain Baṣrans to Syria / 125

The Events of the Year 34 (654/655) / 131

The Character of the Meeting [to Confront ʿUthmān] and [the Day of] al-Jaraʿah / 131

The Events of the Year 35 (655/656) / 145

An Account of the Egyptians Who Went to Dhū Khushub, and the Reason Why Certain Iraqis Went to Dhū al-Marwah / 145
The Account of the Murder [of ʿUthmān] / 181
The Conduct of ʿUthmān b. ʿAffān—May God Be Pleased with Him / 223
The Reason Why ʿUthmān Ordered ʿAbdallāh b. ʿAbbās to Lead the Pilgrimage in This Year / 236
ʿUthmān's Burial Place, and Those Who Led the Prayer for Him and Took Charge of His Funeral Rites / 246
The Date of ʿUthmān's Murder / 250
ʿUthmān's Life Span / 252
ʿUthmān's Personal Appearance / 252
The Date of His Conversion to Islam and of His Seeking Refuge / 253
The Kunyah of ʿUthmān b. ʿAffān / 253
ʿUthmān's Lineage / 254
His Children and Wives / 254
The Names of ʿUthmān's Provincial Governors during This Year / 255
Citations from ʿUthmān's Sermons / 256

Abbreviations

BSOAS: *Bulletin of the School of Oriental and African Studies, University of London*
EI²: *Encyclopaedia of Islam, New Edition*
IJMES: *International Journal of Middle East Studies*
JSS: *Journal of Semitic Studies*
SEI: *Shorter Encyclopaedia of Islam*
WKAS: *Wörterbuch der klassischen arabischen Sprache*

Translator's Foreword

Ṭabarī as Narrator and Interpreter of ʿUthmān's Regime

When ʿUthmān b. ʿAffān acceded to the caliphate in 24/644, he inherited a new but already imposing empire. The main field armies of Byzantium and Sasanian Iran had been crushed, and a rudimentary administration had been established in the newly conquered territories of Arabia, Egypt, and the Fertile Crescent. The struggle to bring Anatolia and the Iranian plateau under Islamic domination continued and was bitterly contested, but Muslim Arab forces retained the offensive on all fronts. Not only wartime booty but also vast tax and tribute revenues were flowing into Medina and the provincial capitals of Kufah, Basrah, Damascus, and al-Fusṭāṭ. Nevertheless, the new Islamic state was already afflicted by serious internal stresses. The caliphate had very little control over its provincial governors and field commanders; the proud tribal leaders (the *ashrāf*) were loath to submit to government authority of any kind. There were resentments over the benefits lavished on some men and not others; there was even rivalry within the inner circle of the Prophet's Companions. Altogether, it is hardly surprising that ʿUthmān governed in an atmosphere of growing tension, and ultimately of crisis.

Political crisis degenerated into open rebellion by troops from Egypt and Iraq, and rebellion ended in the murder of the aged caliph. ʿUthmān's bloody death opened nearly a century of civil war, Muslim set against Muslim, as a host of factions and sects struggled to reestablish the government of God within the Islamic community. In these struggles, there were momentary victors who succeeded in seizing control of the apparatus of government, but the underlying conflicts and issues were never fully resolved—nor have they been even to this day. One could make a case that the murder of ʿUthmān was the single most formative event in early Islamic history. It was not only a matter of the host of immediate and long-term consequences that flowed from this act. Rather, ʿUthmān's death compelled Muslims to confront crucial questions not only about the mutual claims and obligations of rulers and subjects in Islam, but also about the fundamental nature of the relationship between God and His community. The disparate and conflicting answers that they evolved to these questions became the very substance of Islamic political thought, theology, and law.

In this light, it is no surprise that early Muslim historians devoted extraordinary attention to the caliphate of ʿUthmān, and especially to its final phase. Nor is it surprising that Ṭabarī's account is in some sense the definitive one—not only the largest and most comprehensive, but also the one that most accurately reflects the many controversies surrounding this tragic figure. More fully and precisely than in any other source, we find in Ṭabarī the irreconcilable differences of interpretation and judgment that ʿUthmān's reign engendered among Muslims. As to his own opinion, he remains as always a master of cunning. The naive reader sees a sympathetic and even laudatory portrayal of a rightly guided caliph; the critical reader must confront ambiguity, internal contradiction, and the impossibility of reaching a definitive judgment.[1]

Ṭabarī does not present us with a unified narrative. His text is a complex mosaic of verbatim citations from older sources, most of them compiled in the late second/eighth and early third/ninth centuries. Through the careful juxtaposition of self-contained anecdotes and reports, Ṭabarī is able to present many different perspectives on any given incident or topic. A reader (whether Ṭa-

1. M. G. A. Hodgson, *The Venture of Islam* (Chicago and London: 1974), I, 352–53.

barī's contemporary or a modern one) might well suppose that he is thereby obtaining independent testimony on these events, but here caution is in order.

I am persuaded that we cannot accept these texts as direct and authentic (albeit partisan) accounts of the events themselves. Rather, we should regard them as literary constructions that tell us not what actually happened, but rather what 'Uthmān meant to men living a century or more after him. I do not mean that Ṭabarī's narratives are mere inventions; clearly they are in some way rooted in real things that happened to real people. On the other hand, it is not at all clear that we can penetrate to the core of fact that lay behind these stories. On some level, 'Uthmān's reign will always remain veiled in the controversies and values of the later generations who compiled the sources that Ṭabarī used. Ṭabarī's relationship to the reign of 'Uthmān is rather like the relationship of Tolstoy to the Napoleonic Wars. If we had nothing but the novel *War and Peace,* what would we really know about Alexander I, Kutuzov, and Napoleon himself?[2]

Ṭabarī uses a formidable array of sources for his account of 'Uthmān, but three historians provide the bulk of his material. His narrative of the wars in Iran is drawn mostly from 'Alī b. Muḥammad al-Madā'inī (d. 855), either directly or through the transmission of 'Umar b. Shabbah. Al-Madā'inī is himself a compiler and editor of much older materials, but he has imposed a considerable degree of clarity and coherence on his sources. Most remarkable, no doubt, is the long series of narratives on the death of Yazdagird III, the last Sasanian king of Iran.

For events in Iraq and Arabia—the real key to the crises of 'Uthmān's caliphate—Ṭabarī relies chiefly on Muḥammad b. 'Umar al-Wāqidī (d. 823) and the mysterious Sayf b. 'Umar (d. ca. 800). Both of these authorities raise real problems. Al-Wāqidī writes well-organized, concrete narratives, full of telling detail and significant conversations. His informants are for the most part identifiable and even well known. His accounts are in fact a

2. These statements are of course influenced by the arguments of Petersen and Noth, though I am perhaps a degree less skeptical than they. E. L. Petersen, *'Alī and Mu'āwiya in Early Arabic Tradition* (Copenhagen: 1964); Albrecht Noth, *Quellenkritische Studien zu Themen, Formen, und Tendenzen frühislamischen Geschichtsüberlieferung* (Bonn: 1973).

little too good—too well crafted, too pointed. It is clear from other contexts (e.g., the wars of the Prophet) that al-Wāqidī was not above elaborating on older and more austere narratives, and he may be suspected of the same thing here. In addition, he displays a detectable pro-ʿAlid bias, though that in itself should not disqualify his testimony. In any case, medieval Muslim commentators did not regard him as wholly reliable; perhaps they had better reason for this than we sometimes think.[3]

It is Sayf b. ʿUmar who is most troubling, however. Ṭabarī shows a unique fondness for him, in two senses. First, Sayf is the source most heavily used by Ṭabarī for the whole period from the Riddah Wars to the Battle of Ṣiffīn (A.H. 11–37). Second, no one beside Ṭabarī appears to use Sayf at all. There is no obvious way to explain Ṭabarī's preference. It is certainly not explained by the formal characteristics of Sayf's narratives, for he relies on informants who are usually obscure and often very recent. Likewise, he makes heavy use of the "collective report," which blends together in unspecified ways the accounts of several transmitters.[4]

I would suggest that Sayf appealed to Ṭabarī for two reasons. First, Sayf presents a "Sunday school" interpretation of ʿUthmān's caliphate. In his presentation, one sees a profound unity and harmony within the core community of Muslims, a unity and harmony founded on strict fidelity to the legacy of Muhammad. It is unthinkable that men such as those portrayed by Sayf could have been moved by worldly ambition or greed. On the contrary, in Sayf's presentation most conflicts are illusory, a reflection of malicious misinterpretations by later commentators. Where real conflicts did arise among sincere Muslims, they were instigated by outsiders like the notorious ʿAbdallāh b. Sabāʾ, a converted Jew from the Yemen.

On this level, at least, Sayf's version of events is obviously a very naive one, and no doubt Ṭabarī perceived that as clearly as we do. Even so, it served a very useful function for Ṭabarī. By making Sayf's reports the visible framework of his narrative, he could slip in the much less flattering interpretations of early

3. I wish to thank Dr. Lawrence Conrad for drawing this issue to my attention.

4. Martin Hinds, "Sayf b. ʿUmar's Sources on Arabia," *Studies in the History of Arabia*, I, part 2 (1979), 3–16.

Islamic history presented by his other sources. Ordinary readers would dismiss this dissident testimony as irrelevant, and only a few critical readers would catch his hint and pursue the issues raised by such secondary accounts. In this way, Ṭabarī could say what needed to be said while avoiding accusations of sectarianism. Accusations of this kind were of course no small matter in view of the enormous social and religious tensions in Baghdad during the late ninth and early tenth centuries.[5]

Ṭabarī, I think, found something else almost equally valuable in Sayf's narratives. Sayf is seldom content merely to give a bald account of events. Rather, he uses events as a springboard for overt reflection on religious and moral themes, expressed through the mouths or pens of his protagonists. These reflections tend to be filled with sentimental piety, and I would argue that they were strongly influenced by popular preaching, by the art of the *quṣṣāṣ*, who were so esteemed by ordinary people and so suspect in the eyes of scholars. Such elements of popular piety allowed Sayf's protagonists to emerge as larger-than-life heroes of the faith. More than that, such heroes sanctified the very events in which they were involved, removing these events from the gritty realm of profane strife and bloodshed, transforming them into sacred history.

The events of ʿUthmān's reign could be profoundly disheartening to Ṭabarī's own contemporaries, beset as they were by violence and sectarian conflict on every side. It was easy to lose all hope, to imagine that the venture of Islam had been for nothing. The events of ʿUthmān's caliphate might well suggest that Islam had in fact been betrayed even in the lifetime of the Prophet's Companions. In such a milieu, Sayf's account of ʿUthmān was an antidote to cynicism and despair, for it proclaimed that in the face of schism and rebellion, there were true Muslims who had remained faithful to the covenant that they had assumed under Muḥammad. And whatever evils had since befallen, the deeds of these early heroes stood as a symbol of hope, and a call to steadfastness, even in the gloom of Ṭabarī's troubled age.

5. Cf. Hodgson, *Venture,* I, 353.

The State of the Text

I have based this translation on the text established by Eugen Prym in the Leiden edition directed by M. J. de Goeje. I have also consulted the recent Cairo edition prepared by Muḥammad Abū al-Faḍl Ibrāhīm. However, for this part of the text Ibrāhīm used no manuscripts unknown to Prym. To all intents and purposes, then, his text is the same as that of the Leiden edition, though he does incorporate many of the corrections suggested in vol. 14 (*Introductio, Glossarium, Addenda et Emendanda*). In addition he supplies punctuation, which is often helpful in unscrambling convoluted passages, as well as a very few emendations of his own.

Prym's text is based on four manuscripts, none of them complete:

1. Istanbul, Köprülü 1041 (C in the apparatus): pp. 2845–2851. According to the colophon, copied in Cairo in 651/1253.[6]
2. Istanbul, Köprülü 1043 (Co): pp. 2799–2892, 2914–2926. A very handsome volume, probably copied for the library of the Ayyubid prince of Mayyāfāriqīn, al-Muẓaffar Ghāzī (618–641/1221–1244).
3. Oxford, Bodleian Marsh 394 (O): pp. 2799–2923, 2940–2944, 2953–2980.
4. Berlin, Sprenger 41 (B): pp. 2897–3065. A very old manuscript, copied in 447/1055.

It should be noted that Prym could not see the important Istanbul manuscripts for himself, but had to depend on transcripts of varying reliability made for the Leiden project. Unfortunately, a trip to Istanbul in the autumn of 1984 only confirmed that no new manuscripts for this part of Ṭabarī are to be found, though the Köprülü volumes would certainly demand direct scrutiny in any

6. De Goeje (*Introductio*, liii ff.) erroneously identifies this volume as Köprülü 1042. In fact, K. 1041 covers the period from A.H. 5 to 65, but with very long gaps between 21 and 61. The pages in this volume are frightfully scrambled, as if they had been tossed into the air and rebound in the order in which they fell to the ground. K. 1042 is a volume of the same size and format, but it is written in a different (and far clearer) hand, and covers the years A.H. 158–302.

future edition.[7] More important, perhaps, is that we are dependent on a single witness (namely, the Berlin manuscript) for long stretches of the text, especially the crucial last eighty-five pages. No doubt many of the textual difficulties in this section of Ṭabarī are connected with that fact.

In order to confirm or clarify the text, as well as to fill in a few missing lines and words, Prym drew on as many parallel texts as were available to him, and de Goeje refers to others in the *Addenda et Emendanda.* Of these Ibn al-Athīr's *al-Kāmil fī al-Ta'rīkh* is clearly the most important. In fact, however, Ibn al-Athīr is seldom of much help, since the more obscure passages are either reproduced verbatim or omitted altogether. This fact might suggest that he did not understand them either. In using Ibn al-Athīr, we need to recall that our oldest and best manuscripts were produced in Egypt, Syria, and Mesopotamia between the late twelfth and mid-thirteenth centuries—that is, precisely when Ibn al-Athīr was composing his own chronicle. The manuscript tradition available to us is therefore probably the very same one that he used.

A great many relevant texts have been published since the turn of the century, of course, and in an ideal world I would have brought all these to bear. For reasons of practicality, however, I drew only on the *Ansāb al-Ashrāf* of Aḥmad b. Yaḥyā al-Balādhurī (d. 892), which gives us the longest and most important account of 'Uthmān's reign after that of Ṭabarī himself. Balādhurī draws chiefly on Wāqidī, and he therefore provides a useful check on Ṭabarī's use of this important source. However, we cannot expect exact textual parallels, because Balādhurī gives us paraphrases of his sources, whereas Ṭabarī favors verbatim citations.

To sum up, this translation is based on a serviceable Arabic text—certainly the best that could have been produced in de Goeje's day. There is, however, room to try again. A direct examination of the Istanbul manuscripts and the use of parallel texts

7. I wish to acknowledge the generous support of the American Philosophical Society, which funded my trip to examine the Ṭabarī manuscripts in Istanbul, London, and Oxford in autumn 1984. I hope to publish elsewhere a fuller discussion of the problems raised by these manuscripts.

published since 1900 (e.g., Balādhurī, Ibn Abī al-Ḥadīd, Ibn Ḥubaysh, Ibn Aʿtham al-Kūfī, Ḥassān b. Thābit) would probably resolve some of the puzzles in the existing text; at the very least, they would provide a broader context for them.

R. Stephen Humphreys

Transliteration and Editorial Conventions

In transliterating Arabic names and terms, I have followed the usage of the *The International Journal of Middle East Studies*, which has become standard in North America.

Two editorial conventions in this translation call for comment:

1. Square brackets [] are used to enclose words and phrases which do not appear in the Arabic text. I have either added such words and phrases for the sake of clarity, or else I have taken them from a parallel text. In the latter case, the source of the words is identified in a footnote.
2. Parentheses () are used for two purposes: (a) to indicate Arabic technical terms or particularly significant expressions in the passage being translated; (b) to specify proper names or other words which are expressed by pronouns in the Arabic text. The antecedents to these pronouns are often very uncertain, especially in the narratives of Sayf b. ʿUmar; parentheses allow me to propose a reconstruction of Ṭabarī's meaning while alerting the reader to the ambiguity of the original.

Table 1. ʿUthmān's Lineage

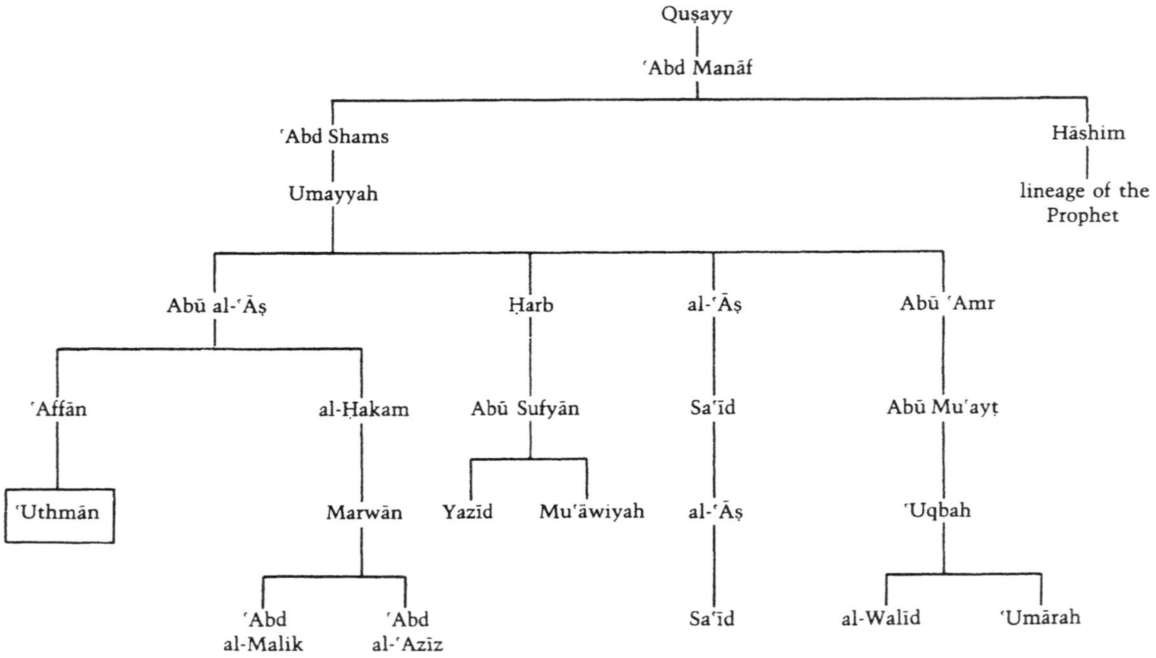

The Events of the Year

24

(November 7, 644–October 27, 645)

[2799]

In (this year) the oath of allegiance was rendered to ʿUthmān b. ʿAffān as Caliph. There is disagreement as to when the oath was rendered to him. Some authorities (*baʿḍuhum*) follow the account related to me by al-Ḥārith—Ibn Saʿd—Muḥammad b. ʿUmar (al-Wāqidī)—Abū Bakr b. Ismāʿīl b. Muḥammad b. Saʿd b. Abī Waqqāṣ—ʿUthmān b. Muḥammad al-Akhnasī. He [Ibn Saʿd] says: according to Muḥammad b. ʿUmar—Abū Bakr b. ʿAbdallah b. Abī Sabrah—Yaʿqūb b. Zayd—his father: The oath of allegiance was rendered to ʿUthmān b. ʿAffān on Monday, the next to last day of Dhū al-Ḥijjah of the year 23 (November 5, 644).[1] He accepted the Caliphate in al-Muḥarram of the year 24 (November 7–December 6, 644).

1. This implies that al-Muḥarram would begin on Tuesday at sunset. There is a discrepancy between the day of the week and the date of the month here. According to Caetani's tables (*Annali*, VII, 2), Muḥarram 1, 24 should have fallen on Sunday (= November 7); hence the oath of allegiance to ʿUthmān would have taken place on Friday rather than Monday. In this case, I have followed the Julian-Hijri equivalents for the day of the month, disregarding the day of the week. However confused these dates may seem, Ṭabarī appears to have transcribed his

Others follow the account related to me by Aḥmad b. Thābit al-Rāzī—someone who mentioned it[2]—Isḥāq b. ʿĪsā—Abū Maʿshar: The oath of allegiance was rendered to ʿUthmān in the Year of Nosebleeds, the year 24. It is said [by certain authorities]: This year was called the Year of Nosebleeds only because nosebleeds were a common occurrence among the people during this time.[3]

Others follow the account transmitted to me in writing by al-Sarī—Shuʿayb—Sayf—Khulayd b. Dhafarah and Mujālid: ʿUthmān was named Caliph on al-Muḥarram 3 of the year 24 (November 9, 644); then he went out and led the people in the afternoon prayer. He increased [their stipends] and permitted delegations to be sent [to him from the provinces];[4] this was established as a precedent.

---

source (al-Wāqidī) accurately, for Balādhurī, *Ansāb,* V, 23, who also follows al-Wāqidī, gives the same ones. The dates of ʿUthmān's election and assumption of office are subjects of considerable confusion, as will become evident below; on this issue see Caetani, *Annali,* VII, 7–8.

2. *ʿamman dhakarahu.* The phrase could also be rendered, "on the authority of someone whom he has mentioned." But cf. the *isnād* of Aḥmad b. Thābit below, p. 25. *Dhakara* normally indicates a written, not an oral, source: "he mentioned in a book."

3. I have consistently rendered *al-nās* as "the people" in this translation. Unfortunately there are other terms (e.g., *qawm, ahl*) that appear to be near-synonyms and which for the sake of English idiom sometimes must be translated as "people," though I have tried to find other equivalents wherever possible. In this section of Ṭabarī, *al-nās* is consistently used to refer collectively to the Muslims, either as a whole or (more commonly) to those involved in a particular incident. The term has strongly positive connotations; normally it is applied to a group that is morally upright and devoted to the ideals of the Community. *Qawm* in contrast is usually negative in tone, implying a group acting in opposition to Islam or (if made up of Muslims) subverting the unity and integrity of the Community. *Qawm* is commonly used in the Qur'ān and elsewhere to mean "a people, nation," and its root meaning is "the fighting men of a tribe." In this section of Ṭabarī, however, *qawm* almost always refers to a small, voluntary association. I have normally translated it as "group" or "band." *Ahl* is a morally neutral term that refers simply to the populace of a certain locality or to the partisans of a given religio-political tendency. Hence, an expression like *ahl al-Baṣrah* can appropriately be translated as "the Baṣrans," though occasionally "the inhabitants/people of Baṣrah" seems better.

4. Presumably in order to swear the oath of allegiance to him on behalf of the officials and troops of the frontiers, and to receive accession donatives from the new Caliph. This and the succeeding text repeat (with identical *isnāds*) reports already cited in connection with the account of ʿUmar's death above: I, 2727, 2728. The latter reads *"wa-waffada ahla al-amṣāri wa-ṣaniʿa fīhim"*—"He permitted the inhabitants of the garrison towns to send delegations, and treated them generously."

It was transmitted to me in writing by al-Sarī—Shuʿayb—Sayf—ʿAmr—al-Shaʿbī: The men of the *shūrā*[5] agreed on ʿUthmān on al-Muḥarram 3 (November 9). It was now midafternoon, and the muezzin of Ṣuhayb[6] had called the prayer. They reached [2800] agreement between the call to prayer and its actual inception. Then (ʿUthmān) went out and led the people in prayer. He increased [the stipends of] the people by 100 [dirhams] and permitted the inhabitants of the garrison towns (*ahl al-amṣār*) to send delegations; he was the first to do these things.

Others follow the account of Ibn Saʿd—al-Wāqidī—Ibn Jurayj—Ibn Abī Mulaykah: The oath of allegiance was rendered to ʿUthmān on al-Muḥarram 10, three nights after the murder of ʿUmar.

The Sermon of ʿUthmān and the Slaying of al-Hurmuzān by ʿUbaydallāh b. ʿUmar

It was transmitted to me in writing by al-Sarī—Shuʿayb—Sayf—Badr b. ʿUthmān—his paternal uncle: When the men of the *shūrā* had rendered the oath of allegiance to ʿUthmān, he went out more distressed than any of them. He came to the pulpit of the Messenger of God and preached to the people, praising and extolling God and asking His blessing upon the Prophet. He said: "Verily you are in a transitory abode and in the flower of life, so set forth until the time appointed for your death and aim for the best which you can attain, for you may be met [by your end] morning or evening. Surely this world harbors deceit, 'so let not the present life delude you,' and 'let not the deceitful one delude you

5. The *shūrā* was the electoral council of six men (ʿAbd al-Raḥmān b. ʿAwf, Ṭalḥah, Zubayr, Saʿd b. Abī Waqqāṣ—who was not actually present—ʿAlī b. Abī Ṭālib, and ʿUthmān b. ʿAffān) named by ʿUmar on his deathbed in order to choose his successor from among their own number. The *shūrā*'s deliberations and choice of the aged ʿUthmān were matters of intense controversy. See Vol. 14 of the present translation (text, I, 2776–2797).

6. Ṣuhayb al-Rūmī was a freedman, presumably of Greek Christian origin, whom the stricken ʿUmar had appointed to lead the prayers while the *shūrā* met *in camera* to determine his successor. The text reads "*muʾadhdhin Ṣuhayb*," so it is clear that Ṣuhayb himself was not the muezzin.

concerning God.'[7] Consider those who have gone before you, then be in earnest and do not be neglectful, for you will surely not be overlooked. Where are the sons and brothers of this world who tilled it, dwelt in it, and were long granted enjoyment therein? Did it not spit them out? Cast aside this world as God has cast it aside and seek the hereafter, for verily God has coined a parable
[2801] for it and for that which is better. The Almighty has said: 'And strike for them the similitude of the present life: it is as water that We send down out of heaven, [and the plants of the earth mingle with it; and in the morning it is straw the winds scatter; and God is omnipotent over everything. Wealth and sons are the adornment of the present world; but the abiding things, the deeds of righteousness, are better with God in reward, and better in] hope.' "[8] Then the people came forward to render the oath of allegiance to him.

It was transmitted to me in writing by al-Sarī—Shuʿayb—Sayf—Abū Manṣūr: I heard al-Qumādhbān speaking about the murder of his father. He said: The Persians (*al-ʿAjam*) in Medina were taking their ease with one another when Fayrūz[9] passed by my father with a two-bladed dagger. (My father) took it from him and said, "What are you doing with this around here?" Fayrūz said, "I like having it."[10] Now a man saw him, and when ʿUmar was struck down, he said, "I saw this (dagger) with al-Hurmuzān; he gave it to Fayrūz." Then ʿUbaydallāh came up and killed (al-Hurmuzān). When ʿUthmān took office, he summoned me and put (ʿUbaydallāh) in my hands. Then he said, "My son, this man is the murderer of your father; it is your duty rather than ours to take vengeance upon him, so go and kill him." I went out with him, and there was no one in the land who did not support me and demand that [I take action] against him. I said to them, "Is it up to me to kill (ʿUbaydallāh)?" They answered, "Yes." And they reviled ʿUbaydallāh. Then I said, "Is it your place to protect him?"

---

7. Qur'ān 31:33; 35:5.
8. Qur'ān 18:42–44. The words in brackets are supplied to complete the passage, cited here (as is usual in medieval Arabic texts) in abridged form.
9. Fayrūz Abū Lu'lu'ah, the murderer of ʿUmar.
10. Reading *"ānasū bihi"* in accordance with Ibrāhīm's text and the mss (Oxford Marsh 394, Köprülü 1043), rather than *"abussu bihi,"* a conjectural restoration by the editor (E. Prym) of the Leiden text.

They answered, "No," and they reviled him. Then I left ['Ubaydallāh] to God's hands and theirs, and they bore me away. By God, I only reached my home carried upon the heads and hands of these men.[11]

The Governorship of Sa'd b. Abī Waqqāṣ in Kūfah

In this year, 'Uthmān removed al-Mughīrah b. Shu'bah from Kūfah and appointed Sa'd b. Abī Waqqāṣ as governor there, according to the account transmitted to me in writing by al-Sarī—Shu'ayb—Sayf—al-Mujālid—al-Sha'bī. He says: 'Umar had said, [2802]
"I enjoin the Caliph after me to name Sa'd b. Abī Waqqāṣ as governor, for I did not remove him on account of any evil action, and I fear that something of that kind may be attributed to him." The first governor (*'āmil*) whom 'Uthmān appointed was Sa'd b. Abī Waqqāṣ in Kūfah. He removed al-Mughīrah b. Shu'bah from office, al-Mughīrah being in Medina at that time. Sa'd acted as governor in (Kūfah) for one year and part of another. ('Uthmān) retained Abū Mūsā (al-Ash'arī) in office for a number of years.[12]

According to al-Wāqidī—Usāmah b. Zayd b. Aslam—his father: 'Umar enjoined that his governors (*'ummāl*) should be maintained in office for a year. When 'Uthmān came to power, he kept al-Mughīrah b. Shu'bah in Kūfah for a year and then removed him, naming Sa'd b. Abī Waqqāṣ as his governor [there]. Then he removed him and appointed al-Walīd b. 'Uqbah. If al-Wāqidī is correct about that, then Sa'd's governorship in Kūfah on behalf of 'Uthmān fell in the year 25.

The Letters of 'Uthmān to His Officials ('ummāl*) and Governors (*wulāt*) and to the Common People (*al-'āmmah*)*

It was transmitted to me in writing by al-Sarī—Shu'ayb—Sayf—Muḥammad and Ṭalḥah—their usual chain of authorities (*bi-*

11. Other versions of this story portray 'Ubaydallāh and 'Uthmān in a far more hostile light: see Vol. 14 of the present translation (I, 2795–2797); Ya'qūbī, *Ta'rīkh*, II, 188; Ibn al-Athīr, *Kāmil* (Beirut), III, 75–76.

12. As governor of Baṣrah; see below, p. 34.

isnādihimā): When ʿUthmān took office, he dispatched ʿAbdallāh b. ʿĀmir to Kābul—that is, the province of Sijistān. He stayed in Kābul until he had captured all of it. Now the province of Sijistān was larger than Khurāsān until Muʿāwiyah died; then the inhabitants of Kābul resisted stubbornly.

According to some authorities (*qālū*), the first letter which ʿUthmān wrote to his officials was [as follows]: "To proceed: God has commanded the imāms to be shepherds; He did not direct them to be tax collectors. Indeed at the inception of this Community they were made shepherds and not tax collectors. But your imāms are surely on the verge of becoming tax collectors rather
[2803] than shepherds. If they turn out thus, then modesty of manners, integrity, and good faith will be at an end. Verily, the most just conduct is for you to examine the affairs and obligations of the Muslims, so that you may give them what is properly theirs and take from them what they owe. Do likewise as regards the Pact of Protection;[13] give to them what is theirs and take from them what they owe. As to the enemy whom you encounter, faithfully seek God's aid against them."

According to some authorities, the first letter that he wrote to the commanders of the armies in the frontier passes was [as follows]: "To proceed: Verily you are the guardians and protectors of the Muslims, and ʿUmar laid down for you [instructions] that were not hidden from us; on the contrary, they were in accordance with our counsel. Let me hear of no change or alteration on the part of any one of you, lest God change your situation and replace you with others. So examine your conduct, for I shall examine what God has required me to examine and watch over."

According to some authorities, the first letter that he wrote to the tax officials (*ʿummāl al-kharāj*) was [as follows]: "To proceed: Verily God created mankind in truth, and he accepts naught but

13. *al-dhimmah.* The treaty made with non-Muslims at the time of the Conquest, guaranteeing them security of life and property and limited freedom of worship in return for submission to Muslim rule. Some of the vast literature on this complex subject is surveyed in the translator's *Islamic History: A Framework for Inquiry* (Minneapolis: 1988), 233–39. A recent general reference is C. E. Bosworth, "The Concept of Dhimma in Early Islam," in B. Braude and B. Lewis, eds., *Christians and Jews in the Ottoman Empire* (2 vols., New York: 1982), I, 37–51.

the truth. Take what is right and give for it what is right. Strive for integrity! Uphold it and be not the first to violate it, so that you may share what you have acquired with those who come after you. Keep faith, keep faith! Do not wrong the orphan nor one with whom you have made a pact, for God is the opponent of him who wrongs them."

According to some authorities, his letter to the common people was [as follows]: "To proceed: You have attained so much only by strict adherence to sound models [of conduct]. Let not this world turn you away from your proper concerns (*amrikum*), for this Community will become involved in innovation after three things occur together among you: complete prosperity, the attainment of adulthood by the children of captive women, and the recitation of the Qur'ān by both Arabs and non-Arabs (*al-a'ājim*). [2804]
The Messenger of God has said, 'Unbelief stems from speaking Arabic badly; if something seems foreign to them, they will do it awkwardly and [thereby] bring about innovation.'"

It was transmitted to me in writing by al-Sarī—Shu'ayb—Sayf—'Āṣim b. Sulaymān—'Āmir al-Sha'bī: 'Uthmān was the first Caliph to increase the stipends paid to the people by a hundred [dirhams]; this became the usual practice. 'Umar used to pay to every living person among the authorized recipients of stipends (*ahl al-fay'*)[14] one dirham per day during Ramaḍān, and stipulated for the wives of the Messenger of God two dirhams each. He was told, "You should have prepared food for them and brought them to one place to get it." He replied, "Feed the people in their homes." 'Uthmān confirmed what 'Umar had done, but increased [the amount]. He established the [grants of] food for Ramaḍān, saying, "[This is] for the devout worshiper who lingers in the mosque, for the wayfarer, and for the destitute among the people during Ramaḍān."

In this year—that is, the year 24—al-Walīd b. 'Uqbah raided

14. *Ahl al-fay'*, literally "the people of booty." In the context of the Conquest years, it means those Muslims who were entitled to a regular stipend from the public treasury, whose revenues came from taxes and tribute levied against the "immovable booty" (*fay'*) constituted by the conquered territories and their inhabitants. These stipends were paid to Muslims who had joined the new religion in the time of Muḥammad and to the Arab soldiers who had accepted Islam and participated in the wars of conquest. See F. Løkkegaard, "Fay'," *EI*[2], II, 869–70.

Ādharbayjān and Armenia, because their inhabitants had repudiated the terms to which they had agreed with the Muslims during ʿUmar's reign. [That is] according to the account of Abū Mikhnaf, but other authorities relate that this took place in the year 26.

[2805]

The Campaign of [al-Walīd b. ʿUqbah in Ādharbayjān and Armenia]

According to Hishām b. Muḥammad—Abū Mikhnaf—Farwah b. Laqīṭ, of the clan of Ghāmid in the tribe of Azd:[15] The campaigns of the Kūfans took place in Rayy and Ādharbayjān; in the two frontier zones there were 10,000 Kūfan warriors, 6,000 in Ādharbayjān and 4,000 at Rayy. In Kūfah itself, there were at that time 40,000 warriors, and every year 10,000 of them would go on campaign to these two frontier zones, so that a man would be subject to one campaign every four years. During his governorship in Kūfah during the reign (*sulṭān*) of ʿUthmān, al-Walīd b. ʿUqbah campaigned in Ādharbayjān and Armenia. (Al-Walīd) summoned Salmān b. Rabīʿah al-Bāhilī, sending him ahead as his vanguard, while al-Walīd set out with the body of the people, with the intention of devoting every effort to [the conquest of] the land of Armenia. He proceeded with the people until he entered Ādharbayjān. He sent ʿAbdallāh b. Shubayl b. ʿAwf al-Aḥmasī with 4,000 (troops), and he attacked the inhabitants of Mūqān, al-Babar, and al-Ṭaylasān. He seized some of their wealth and cattle, but these people (*qawm*) were on guard, and he took only a few captives from among them before turning back to meet al-Walīd b. ʿUqbah.

[2806] Then al-Walīd made peace with the inhabitants of Ādharbayjān, in return for [a tribute] of 800,000 dirhams, these being the terms which Ḥudhayfah b. al-Yamān had negotiated in the year 22, one year after the battle of Nihāwand.[16] With the death of ʿUmar, they had stopped payment. When ʿUthmān took office and

15. Text: *al-Azdī thumma 'l-Ghāmidī.* See Wright, *Arabic Grammar,* I, 293C.

16. The battle of Nihāwand (21/642) was the Arab victory in the mountain passes leading from Iraq to Hamadhān over Sasanian forces commanded by the king Yazdagird III. This victory opened the Iranian plateau to Arab attack, and brought an end to centrally controlled Iranian resistance to the Arab invaders. It was not the end of the fighting in Iran, which stretched on for more than a decade

al-Walīd b. ʿUqbah became governor of Kufah, (the latter) campaigned until he had trampled them underfoot with (his) army. When they saw that, they submitted to him, beseeching him to maintain for them [the terms of the original] treaty. He did so, taking from them the sums due. He also dispatched a series of expeditions against the enemies of the Muslims roundabout (those who had just submitted). When ʿAbdallāh b. Shubayl al-Aḥmasī returned unharmed and bearing plunder from his raid, (al-Walīd) dispatched, in the year 24, Salmān b. Rabīʿah al-Bāhilī against Armenia with 12,000 (troops). He went into the land of Armenia killing and taking prisoners and booty. Then, his hands laden [with plunder], he left and returned to al-Walīd. Al-Walīd now departed, having triumphantly achieved his aims.

The Gathering of Byzantine Forces against the Muslims and the Muslims' Call for Aid from the Kūfans

In this year, according to Abū Mikhnaf, the Byzantines mobilized their forces to such a level that the Muslim armies in Syria sought reinforcements from ʿUthmān.

The Account of That Event

According to Hishām—Abū Mikhnaf—Farwah b. Laqīṭ al-Azdī: When—during the year 24 according to (Abū Mikhnaf's) chronology—al-Walīd achieved his aims in Armenia in the campaign discussed above, and then entered Mosul, making camp at al- [2807]
Ḥadīthah, he received a letter from ʿUthmān, [as follows]: "To proceed: Muʿāwiyah b. Abī Sufyān[17] has written to inform me that the Byzantines have mobilized vast forces against the Mus-

and was often very bitter, but this was henceforth a matter of local sieges, regional campaigns, guerilla resistance, and the like.

17. At this time governor of Syria, having succeeded his elder brother Yazīd in 639 when the latter had perished during an outbreak of the plague. Muʿāwiyah was the son of the Prophet's most obdurate opponent and had accepted Islam only with the occupation of Mecca in 8/630. In spite of this taint, however, his great talents were recognized by Muḥammad himself and—somewhat reluctantly—by the Caliph ʿUmar.

lims; therefore, I have thought it fit that their Kūfan brothers should assist them. When my letter reaches you, send to them, [directly] from the place where my emissary shall find you, a man whose courage, steadfastness, valor, and [devotion to] Islam satisfies you, along with eight or nine or ten thousand (troops). Peace!"

Then al-Walīd stood up amidst the people. He praised and extolled God, then he said: "To proceed: O People, God has in this manner conferred a great blessing upon the Muslims. He has restored to them lands of theirs that had reverted to unbelief and has opened up lands that had not been conquered [before], sending them back safe and sound and fully compensated [for their struggles]. Praise be to God, Lord of the Worlds! The Commander of the Faithful has written, commanding me to dispatch between eight and ten thousand of you to reinforce your brothers in Syria, for the Byzantines have gathered their forces against them. In that there will be a mighty recompense and manifest bounty.[18] Go forward then—may God be merciful to you—with Salmān b. Rabī'ah al-Bāhilī."

(Abū Mikhnaf) says: So the people pressed forward, and a third
[2808] day had not elapsed before 8,000 men from among the Kūfans departed, marching until they entered Byzantine territory together with the Syrians. Commanding the Syrian army was Ḥabīb b. Maslamah b. Khālid al-Fihrī, while the Kūfan army was under Salmān b. Rabī'ah al-Bāhilī. They launched attacks against the Byzantine territory; the people seized as many captives as they desired, filled their hands with plunder, and captured numerous fortresses there.

Al-Wāqidī claims that Sa'īd b. al-'Āṣ was the one who sent Salmān b. Rabī'ah to the aid of Ḥabīb b. Maslamah. He says: the reason is that 'Uthmān had written to Mu'āwiyah, ordering him to send Ḥabīb b. Maslamah with the Syrians to attack Armenia, and he did so. Then Ḥabīb learned that al-Mawriyān al-Rūmī had set out to meet him with 80,000 Byzantines and Turks.[19] Ḥabīb

18. Qur'ānic allusions to the rewards (both now and hereafter) given by God to those who serve Him faithfully. Cf. Qur'ān 27:16.

19. Al-Mawriyān al-Rūmī: probably the strategos Maurianos or Mavrianos, a Byzantine general in Armenia. Other sources (Sebeos, Theophanes, and Balādhurī's *Futūḥ al-Buldān*) state that he was defeated (and perhaps killed) by Ḥabīb b. Maslamah at the Armenian city of Dvin in 653–655—that is, about a decade later

wrote to Muʿāwiyah about this, and Muʿāwiyah [in turn] wrote to ʿUthmān. Thus, ʿUthmān wrote to Saʿīd b. al-ʿĀṣ, ordering him to support Ḥabīb b. Maslamah. (Saʿīd) then sent Salmān b. Rabīʿah with 6,000 [troops] to aid him. Ḥabīb was a master of military ruses, and he decided on a night attack against al-Mawriyān. His wife—[known as] Umm ʿAbdallāh bt. Yazīd al-Kalbiyyah—heard him mentioning this, and she said to him, "Where is your rendezvous?" He answered, "At the pavilion of al-Mawriyān or in Paradise." Then he attacked them by night, killing whoever came within his sight. He reached (al-Mawriyān's) pavilion and discovered that his wife had preceded him; she was the first woman among the Arabs to whom a pavilion was assigned [as her share of the booty]. Ḥabīb died and she survived him; al-Ḍaḥḥāk b. Qays [2809] al-Fihrī took his place as her husband, and she was the mother of his child.

There is disagreement as to who led the pilgrimage in this year. According to some authorities, ʿAbd al-Raḥmān b. ʿAwf led the pilgrimage this year by order of ʿUthmān; Abū Maʿshar and al-Wāqidī follow this opinion. According to others, however, ʿUthmān b. ʿAffān made the pilgrimage this year.

As regards disagreement concerning those conquests, which some people ascribe to the time of ʿUmar and others to the reign of ʿUthmān, I have previously mentioned in this book such differences of opinion under the date of each conquest at issue.

---

than Abū Mikhnaf's dating. See Andreas N. Stratos, *Byzantium in the Seventh Century* (Amsterdam: 1975), III, 30, 269. I am indebted to my colleague John M. Barker for these references. Here and elsewhere, "Byzantine" translates *Rūm/Rūmī*—that is, "Roman," which is of course what the Byzantines called themselves—in Greek, *Rhomaioi*.

The Events of the Year 25

(October 28, 645–October 16, 646)

According to the account related to me by Aḥmād b. Thābit al-Rāzī—a traditionist (*muḥaddith*)—Isḥāq b. ʿĪsā—Abū Maʿshar: The conquest of Alexandria took place in the year 25.

According to al-Wāqidī: In this year, Alexandria repudiated its pact, and ʿAmr b. al-ʿĀṣ launched a bloody attack on them.[20] We [that is, al-Ṭabarī] have previously cited the report (of this event), mentioning also those who disagree with Abū Maʿshar and al-Wāqidī concerning the date.

[2810] Also according to al-Wāqidī: In this year, ʿAbdallāh b. Saʿd b. Abī Sarḥ sent cavalry forces against the Maghrib. (Al-Wāqidī) says: ʿAmr b. al-ʿĀṣ had previously sent an expedition to the Maghrib. They seized booty, and ʿAbdallāh sought and received permission from (ʿAmr) to raid Ifrīqiyah.[21]

---

20. *fa-ghazāhum ʿAmru b. al-ʿĀṣ wa-qatalahum.* Literally, "ʿAmr attacked and killed them."

21. Ifrīqiyah: the Roman-Byzantine province of Africa Proconsularis, essentially the northern half of modern Tunisia.

According to (al-Wāqidī): ʿUthmān led the pilgrimage in this year, appointing a deputy for Medina [during his absence].

Also according to him: In (this year) the fortresses [in Byzantine territory] were conquered, the commander being Muʿāwiyah b. Abī Sufyān.

Also according to him: In (this year) was born Yazīd b. Muʿāwiyah.[22]

Also according to him: In (this year) the first [attack on] Sābūr took place.[23]

---

22. The future Caliph (*regn.* 680–683), especially notorious as the tyrant responsible for the martyrdom of al-Ḥusayn at Karbalāʾ in 61/680. His troops were also accused of sacking Medina in 64/683 and of burning the Kaʿbah during the siege of Mecca (broken off at his death) later the same year. On his reign, see Wellhausen, *Arab Kingdom*, 145–68.

23. *kānat Sābūru'l-ūlā*. Following the emendation in Ibn al-Athīr, *Kāmil* (Beirut), III, 86, I have supplied the word *ghazwah* between *kānat* and *Sābūr*.

The Events of the Year 26

(October 17, 646–October 6, 647)

According to Abū Ma'shar and al-Wāqidī, the conquest of Sābūr took place during (this year). (This event) has previously been reported, in accordance with the account of authorities who contradict them on that (point).

Al-Wāqidī says: In (this year), 'Uthmān ordered the stones marking the limits of the sacred territory [around Mecca] to be
[2811] restored.[24]

He also says: In (this year), 'Uthmān added to and enlarged the Sacred Mosque.[25] He purchased [property] from one group of people, while others refused [to sell]. He then demolished [their

---

24. *amara 'Uthmānu bi-tajdīdi anṣābi al-ḥarami.* The whole of Mecca, and not merely the Ka'bah itself, was regarded as a *ḥaram*, an inviolable sanctuary under the protection of Allāh. Presumably 'Uthmān took this action because the precise boundaries of the sacred area were no longer clearly marked or were in dispute. Such delimited sacred territories were very common in ancient Arabia; any area generally recognized as protected by some deity was so regarded. In modern South Arabia, similar sanctuaries still existed down to the 1960s at least, under the name of *ḥawṭah*. See R. B. Serjeant, "Haram and Hawtah, the Sacred Enclave in Arabia," in *Mélanges Taha Husain*, ed. A. R. Badawi (Cairo: 1962), 41–58.

25. *al-masjid al-ḥarām*. This is the Ka'bah and the enclosed courtyard around it.

houses] in spite of them and put the prices [which he would have paid them] in the public treasury. When they shouted protests at ʿUthmān, he had them jailed, saying, "Do you know what has emboldened you against me? Only my forbearance! ʿUmar did the same thing to you, and you did not scream protests at him." Then ʿAbdallāh b. Khālid b. Asīd spoke with him on their behalf, and they were released.

(Al-Wāqidī) also says: ʿUthmān b. ʿAffān led the pilgrimage in this year.

According to al-Wāqidī: In this year, ʿUthmān removed Saʿd (b. Abī Waqqāṣ) from the governorship of Kūfah and appointed al-Walīd b. ʿUqbah.

According to Sayf: He removed him from (Kūfah) in the year 25 and made al-Walīd governor there. (Sayf) asserts that (ʿUthmān) had removed al-Mughīrah b. Shuʿbah from Kūfah when ʿUmar died, sending Saʿd there as governor (*ʿāmil*). He then governed in (Kūfah) on (ʿUthmān's) behalf for a year and some months.

The Reason Why ʿUthmān Removed Saʿd from Kūfah and Named al-Walīd His Governor There

It was transmitted to me in writing by al-Sarī—Shuʿayb—Sayf—ʿAmr—al-Shaʿbī: The first satanically inspired event among the inhabitants of Kūfah—which was the first garrison town in Islam where Satan instigated evil among (its people)—happened [in this way]. Saʿd b. Abī Waqqāṣ sought a loan from the public treasury from ʿAbdallāh b. Masʿūd,[26] and he issued it to him. But when (Ibn Masʿūd) demanded repayment, (Saʿd) was unable to do so. Words arose between the two of them, to the point that ʿAbdallāh sought

26. ʿAbdallāh b. Masʿūd was one of the earliest Companions of the Prophet and was regarded as one of the principal students and transmitters of the text of the Qur'ān. His personal origins are not entirely clear; he seems to have been a member (or perhaps only a protégé) of the Hudhayl tribe, but to have resided in Mecca as a client of one of the Quraysh clans. Though esteemed for his piety and learning, and present at such crucial battles as Badr (2/624), Uḥud (3/625), and Yarmūk (15/636), he was never assigned a major military or administrative office. He settled in Kūfah soon after its founding, and was made intendant of the public treasury there. With him are associated a number of persons who were prominent in the early pietist, pro-ʿAlid movement in Kūfah. See J. C. Vadet, "Ibn Masʿūd," *EI*², III, 873–75.

help from one part (*unās*) of the people in getting the money repaid, while Saʿd asked the assistance of another part in gaining a
[2812] deferral. Thus, (the people) split up into wrangling factions, with one group blaming Saʿd and the other ʿAbdallāh.

It was transmitted to me in writing by al-Sarī—Shuʿayb—Sayf—Ismāʿīl b. Abī Khālid—Qays b. Abī Ḥāzim: I was sitting in Saʿd's residence with his brother's son Hāshim b. ʿUtbah, when Ibn Masʿūd came to Saʿd and said, "Hand over the money that you owe!" Saʿd replied, "I think you are just heading for trouble. Are you anyone but the son of Masʿūd, a slave from the [tribe of] Hudhayl?"[27] Ibn Masʿūd said, "Indeed so. I am the son of Masʿūd, by God, while you are the son of Ḥumaynah." Hāshim said, "Yes indeed, and you are both Companions of the Messenger of God, and closely watched [by everyone]." Then Saʿd—a man with a violent temper—threw down a rod that he was holding, raised his hands, and said, "O God, Lord of the heavens and the earth!" ʿAbdallāh responded, "Woe to you! Speak with a blessing and do not curse." With that Saʿd said, "No, by God! But for the fear of God, I would call down on you a curse (*daʿwah*) that would not miss you." ʿAbdallāh hastily turned around and left.

It was transmitted to me in writing by al-Sarī—Shuʿayb—Sayf—al-Qāsim b. Walīd—al-Musayyab b. ʿAbd Khayr[28]—ʿAbdallāh b. ʿUkaym:[29] When the argument broke out between Ibn Masʿūd and Saʿd concerning the loan that ʿAbdallāh had extended to him and that Saʿd was unable to repay, ʿUthmān was angry at both of them. He snatched (Kūfah) away from Saʿd and fired him. He was angry at ʿAbdallāh but retained him in office. He then ap-

27. The Hudhayl tribe resided in the hills between Mecca and al-Ṭāʾif, and was closely linked genealogically to the Quraysh. They joined Quraysh in opposing Muḥammad, and were only brought over to Islam at the conquest of Mecca in 630. See G. Rentz, "Hudhayl," *EI²*, III, 540–41. I take "Ibn Masʿūd" here not as a name, but literally, "the son of Masʿūd." There seems no indication that ʿAbdallāh b. Masʿūd himself was ever a slave, but if he was the son of a man who had been one, that would explain the allusions to his client status as regards both Hudhayl and Quraysh. A further bit of evidence for his father's status: "Masʿūd" ("Fortunate") would have been a very uncommon name for a full member of a noble Arab tribe.

28. The printed text has Musayyab—ʿAbd Khayr, but de Goeje (*Introductio*, dcxxv) corrects this in accordance with Köprülü 1043.

29. Following the readings of de Goeje (*Introductio*, dcxxv) and Ibrāhīm, since the mss are uncertain on this name.

pointed as governor al-Walīd b. ʿUqbah, who had been ʿUmar's agent (*ʿāmil*) in charge of the Rabīʿah tribe in the Jazīrah. (Al-Walīd) arrived in Kūfah and did not mount a door on his residence down to the time when he departed from the city.

It was transmitted to me in writing by al-Sarī—Shuʿayb—Sayf—Muḥammad and Ṭalḥah: When ʿUthmān learned of what [2813] had been going on between ʿAbdallāh and Saʿd, he was angry and planned to take steps against both of them. Then he abandoned that [idea]. He recalled Saʿd and took [from him] what he owed, confirming ʿAbdallāh [in his office] and forwarding [the sum due] to him. To replace Saʿd he named as governor (*amīr*) al-Walīd b. ʿUqbah, who had been ʿUmar b. al-Khaṭṭāb's agent in charge of the Arabs of the Jazīrah. Al-Walīd arrived in the second year of ʿUthmān's caliphate, Saʿd having been governor there for one year and part of another. Once in Kūfah, (al-Walīd) was the most beloved of men among the people and the most courteous in dealing with them. Matters continued thus for five years; there was no door on his residence.

The Events of the Year 27

(October 7, 647–September 24, 648)

According to the account related to me by Aḥmad b. Thābit al-Rāzī—a traditionist—Isḥāq b. ʿĪsā—Abū Maʿshar: Among these was the conquest of Ifrīqiyah by ʿAbdallāh b. Saʿd b. Abī Sarḥ. This is the account of al-Wāqidī as well.

The Conquest [of Ifrīqiyah] and the Reason for the Appointment of ʿAbdallāh b. Saʿd b. Abī Sarḥ as Governor of Egypt and ʿUthmān's Removal of ʿAmr b. al-ʿĀṣ from (That Province)

It was transmitted to me in writing by al-Sarī—Shuʿayb—Sayf—Muḥammad and Ṭalḥah: At ʿUmar's death, ʿAmr b. al-ʿĀṣ governed Egypt, while the judgeship there was held by Khārijah b. Ḥudhāfah al-Sahmī. When ʿUthmān took office, he retained both of them for [the first] two years of his caliphate. Then he removed
[2814] ʿAmr from office and appointed ʿAbdallāh b. Saʿd b. Abī Sarḥ as governor.

It was transmitted to me in writing by al-Sarī—Shuʿayb—Sayf—Abū Ḥārithah and Abū ʿUthmān: When ʿUthmān took office, he confirmed ʿAmr b. al-ʿĀṣ in his governorship, for he did not depose anyone save on the basis of a complaint [against him] or an [official's] desire to step down apart from any complaint. ʿAbdallāh b. Saʿd belonged to the army (*jund*) of Egypt, and ʿUthmān put him in command of this army, reinforced him with [additional] men, and sent him off to Ifrīqiyah. With him he sent ʿAbdallāh b. Nāfiʿ b. ʿAbd al-Qays al-Fihrī and ʿAbdallāh b. Nāfiʿ b. al-Ḥuṣayn al-Fihrī. To ʿAbdallāh b. Saʿd he said: "If in the coming days God grants you victory in Ifrīqiyah, then from the spoils that God bestows on the Muslims, you will have as your personal share one-fifth out of the [Caliph's] fifth of the moveable booty."[30] He also assigned command over the [Egyptian] army to the two ʿAbdallāh al-Fihrī's, reinforced them with [additional] men, and sent them against Spain. He ordered the two of them and ʿAbdallāh b. Saʿd to combine forces against the Ajall.[31] Thereafter ʿAbdallāh b. Saʿd would remain in his province [namely, Ifrīqiyah] while the other two would continue toward their own province [namely, Spain].

They set forth, traversing Egypt. When they penetrated into the territory of Ifrīqiyah, they were intent on getting to the Ajall, who was accompanied by troops of various origins. The Ajall was killed in battle by ʿAbdallāh b. Saʿd, who conquered Ifrīqiyah, both the lowlands and mountains. Then (the inhabitants of Ifrīqiyah) agreed to accept Islam, and their submission [to the Caliphate] was sincere.

ʿAbdallāh divided up the booty that God had bestowed on them among the army, taking [for himself] one-fifth of the [Caliph's] fifth and sending the remaining four-fifths [of the Caliph's share]

30. The Qur'ān (8:42) had established that one-fifth of any battlefield spoils should go to the Prophet, to be used for the needs of himself and his family, as well as to assist orphans, the indigent, and travelers. (This was no innovation; the tribal chieftains of ancient Arabia followed a similar custom, though their traditional share was one-quarter). This privilege was retained of course by Muḥammad's successors.

31. The identity of this figure is obscure. Caetani, *Annali,* III, 196, identifies him merely as a Berber prince. His name in this text perhaps reflects some Byzantine title (*al-ajall* means "most noble," hence "nobilissimus"), but the military and administrative significance of this epithet is unclear. If Caetani is correct, the title might have been officially conferred on him as an ally or protégé of the Roman Empire, or it might have been self-bestowed.

back to ʿUthmān with Ibn Wathīmah al-Naṣrī. He established a
[2815] camp on the site of [the future city of] Qayrawān, and dispatched a delegation [to ʿUthmān].

When (his delegates) complained about ʿAbdallāh in regard to (the portion of the booty) that he had taken, (ʿUthmān) said to them, "I assigned that to him as his personal share. Things used to be done in this way, and I ordered him [to proceed] thus. Now it is up to you: if you are content, he will be permitted [to retain the booty]; and if you are displeased, it will be given back." They replied, "We are indeed displeased," and (ʿUthmān) said, "So, it will be given back." He wrote to ʿAbdallāh to give back (the disputed booty) and to try to reconcile them. But they said, "Remove him from us, for we do not wish him to hold command over us when such a thing has happened." So ʿUthmān wrote to him [as follows]: "Appoint as your successor in Ifrīqiyah a man who satisfies both you and (the army), and divide up [among them], for God's sake, the fifth that I had granted you as your share, for they are displeased about the booty." ʿAbdallāh b. Saʿd did [this] and returned to Egypt, having conquered Ifrīqiyah and killed the Ajall.

(The native allies and converts of Ifrīqiyah) remained among the most orderly and obedient of the provinces;[32] they were the most peace loving and loyal people (*ummah*), up to the time of Hishām b. ʿAbd al-Malik, when the Iraqis infiltrated among them. When the Iraqi agents[33] slipped in among them and incited them

32. A somewhat conjectural translation, since there is no clear antecedent for the subject of the verb in this sentence: *fa-mā zālū min asmaʿi ahli 'l-buldān wa-aṭwaʿihim. . . .* However, it is clear from the context that Sayf b. ʿUmar or his informants have conflated two separate stories here. Up to this point, the Muslims have been Arab garrison troops stationed in Egypt. But beginning with this sentence, he portrays a conflict between Arab garrison troops stationed in Ifrīqiyah (the governor's *jund*) and a body of second-class Muslim militia, who are never explicitly identified but must represent native Berber allies and converts to Islam. It was among these people that Kharijism was to have a special appeal in the mid-second/eighth century.

33. *duʿāt ahl al-ʿIrāq.* A *dāʿī* (pl. *duʿāt*) is a "missionary" working as a propagandist and organizer on behalf of some religio-political movement dedicated to the overthrow of the existing order and the restoration of the true community of Muslims. In this case, the Iraqi agents would not represent the Abbasid cause, as one might suppose from the date, but a variety of Kharijite sects. Religio-political dissidence in eighth- and ninth-century North Africa was almost always Kharijite in inspiration.

to rebel, they broke the staff [of unity] and divided themselves into sects even to the present day. The cause of their division is this. They rejected the heretics (*ahl al-ahwā'*), saying, "We shall not oppose the Imams [that is, the Caliphs] because of crimes committed by the governors; we do not hold them responsible for that." The (Iraqi agents) responded, "But (the governors) are only carrying out the orders of the (Imams)." (The people of Ifrīqiyah) said, "We shall not accept that until we have informed ourselves about them."

Thus, Maysarah set out with ten men or so to go to Hishām. They sought permission [to speak with him], but that proved hard to obtain. They came to al-Abrash[34] and said, "Inform the Com- [2816]
mander of the Faithful that our amīr [in Ifrīqiyah] takes both us and his regular troops (*jund*) on campaign. When he gains a victory, he assigns the spoils to them and excludes us, saying, 'They have a better right to it.' We would say, '(This booty) renders our *jihād* the more sincere, since we do not take any part of it. If (the booty) is ours, then they are free to have it. If it is not ours, we do not want it.'" (The delegates) continued: "When we besiege a city, he orders us to advance, but holds back his regular troops. Then we have responded, 'Advance, for this will strengthen the *jihād*; (men) like you support their brothers.' Now we have personally shielded them and supported them [in battle]. Then in addition, they set upon our livestock and began to cut them open to get the unborn lambs, seeking the white skins for the Commander of the Faithful, and killing a thousand sheep for a single skin. We said, 'How small a matter this is for the Commander of the Faithful.' We bore it patiently and permitted them [to do] that. Then in addition, they have deemed themselves so much above us that they take every pretty daughter of ours. We said, 'We do not find this in the Book of God nor in the practice of His Messenger, and we, too, are Muslims.'[35] We would like to know, then, whether the Commander of the Faithful approves of all this or not."

(Al-Abrash) replied, "We shall act [on this matter]." Now when

---

34. The chamberlain of Hishām.

35. Prym's text gives *lam najid hādhā fī kitābin wa-lā sunnatin*. I have followed the reading of Oxford Marsh 394.

they had waited a long time and their provisions were exhausted, they wrote their names on brief petitions (*riqaʿ*) and presented them to the ministers of state. They said, "These are our names and lineages. If the Commander of the Faithful asks you about us, inform him." Then, having returned to Ifrīqiyah, they revolted against Hishām's governor, killed him, and seized control of the country. When Hishām heard the news, he asked about the small band [of men who had petitioned him]. Their names were presented to him, and behold, they were the same band who were reported to be in revolt.

It was transmitted to me in writing by al-Sarī—Shuʿayb—
[2817] Sayf—Muḥammad and Ṭalḥah: Immediately after (their campaign in Ifrīqiyah), ʿUthmān sent ʿAbdallāh b. Nāfiʿ b. al-Ḥuṣayn and ʿAbdallāh b. Nāfiʿ b. ʿAbd al-Qays from Ifrīqiyah to Spain; they arrived there by way of the sea. ʿUthmān wrote [as follows] to those to whom he had delegated authority among the inhabitants of Spain: "To proceed: Only through Spain can Constantinople be conquered. If then you conquer (Spain), you will share the reward of those who conquer (Constantinople). Peace." Kaʿb al-Aḥbār[36] said, "Nations (*aqwām*) will cross the sea to Spain and they will conquer it. They will be known by their radiance on the Day of Resurrection."

It was transmitted to me in writing by al-Sarī—Shuʿayb—Sayf—Muḥammad and Ṭalḥah: They set out accompanied by the Berbers. They came (to Spain) by land and sea, and God bestowed it upon the Muslims and the Ifranjah.[37] They flourished under Muslim rule as did Ifrīqiyah. When ʿUthmān removed ʿAbdallāh b. Saʿd b. Abī Sarḥ, he sent to his province (*ilā ʿamalihi*) ʿAbdallāh b. Nāfiʿ b. ʿAbd al-Qays, and he ruled over it while ʿAbdallāh b.

36. Kaʿb al-Aḥbār was a Yemeni Jew who converted to Islam in the reign of ʿUmar b. al-Khaṭṭāb, and became a trusted counselor of both ʿUmar and ʿUthmān. He is so enmeshed in later legend that it is hard to say anything concrete about him. To him was attributed a vast knowledge of Jewish lore—he was indeed regarded as the main conduit through which this material was introduced into Islam—and he was also looked on as something of a seer. See M. Schmitz, "Kaʿb al-Aḥbār," *EI²*, IV, 316–17; G. Vajda, "Isrāʾīliyyāt," *EI²*, IV, 211–12.

37. The identity of the Ifranjah is not clear. Presumably the word (literally, "Franks") is here applied to another Germanic people, the Visigoths, who ruled Spain between the fifth century and the Muslim conquest. It may also refer to that part of the indigenous population that accepted and supported Islamic rule.

Sa'd returned to Egypt. The situation in Spain continued to be like that in Ifrīqiyah until the time of Hishām; the Berbers defended their land; those living in Spain kept their affairs in good order.

According to al-Wāqidī—Ibn Abī Sabrah—Muḥammad b. Abī Ḥarmalah—Kurayb: When 'Uthmān stripped 'Amr b. al-'Āṣ of Egypt, 'Amr was intensely angry and was filled with hatred for 'Uthmān. 'Uthmān now sent 'Abdallāh b. Sa'd with orders to proceed to Ifrīqiyah, and charged the people to undertake [the con- [2818]
quest] of that land. Thus 10,000 [troops] from Quraysh, the Helpers, and the Emigrants set forth.[38]

According to al-Wāqidī—Usāmah b. Zayd al-Laythī—Ibn Ka'b: When 'Uthmān sent 'Abdallāh b. Sa'd to Ifrīqiyah, the Patrician of Ifrīqiyah Gregory (*Jurjīr*)[39] made peace in return for [a tribute] of 2,520,000 dinars. The Byzantine Emperor dispatched a legate, ordering him to take from (the inhabitants of Ifrīqiyah) 300 *qinṭārs*[40] [of gold], just as 'Abdallāh b. Sa'd had done. So he gathered together the leading men (*ru'asā'*) of Ifrīqiyah and said, "The Emperor has commanded me to take from you 300 *qinṭārs* of gold, the same amount that 'Abdallāh b. Sa'd has taken from you." They answered, "We have no money to give. As for what we once possessed, we have used it to ransom ourselves. As to the Emperor, he is indeed our lord, so let him take the portion of our wealth that used to be lawfully his, on the same terms as we formerly paid him every year." When (the legate) heard this, he

38. The *Anṣār* ("Helpers") were the Medinese who had accepted Muḥammad's religion and political leadership at the time of the *hijrah*. The *Muhājirūn* ("Emigrants") were those Meccan followers who had gone into exile in Medina with Muḥammad. In this context, Quraysh must refer to those Meccans who had come over to Muḥammad only upon his occupation of the city in 630.

39. The Patrician Gregory was exarch (military governor) of Carthage, and had proclaimed himself emperor with the support of both local Byzantine troops and Berber tribes. (Ironically, the late Emperor Heraclius had also mounted his coup d'état in 610 from Carthage.) For that reason, the Arab invasion described here was something of a godsend to the Imperial government in Constantinople. See G. Ostrogorsky, *History of the Byzantine State*, 118. Cf. the account of Sayf b. 'Umar above, pp. 18–19 (text, I, 2814).

40. A *qinṭār* was equal to 100 *raṭls* ("pounds"), a unit of weight that varied wildly according to region and period, but most commonly approximated 400 grams. Since this story involves a Roman province and emperor, we might suppose that the Roman *librum* of 327.5 grams is the unit intended here. However, the legendary character of this narrative makes any effort at exactitude quite meaningless. See E. Ashtor, "Makāyīl and Mawāzin," *EI*², VI, 117–21.

ordered them to be imprisoned. They sent [for help] to a certain group among their associates (*aṣḥābihim*); they came against (the legate) and broke open the prison, so that the detainees escaped.

The terms on which ʿAbdallāh b. Saʿd made peace were 300 *qinṭārs* of gold, and ʿUthmān commanded it [to be turned over] to the family of al-Ḥakam.[41] I [that is, al-Wāqidī] said: "Or to Marwān?" He [that is, Usāmah b. Zayd] replied, "I don't know."

According to Ibn ʿUmar (al-Wāqidī)—Usāmah b. Zayd—Yazīd b. Abī Ḥabīb: ʿUthmān stripped ʿAmr b. al-ʿĀṣī of [control over]
[2819] the tax revenues (*kharāj*) of Egypt and made ʿAbdallāh b. Saʿd the chief fiscal officer. The two (men) were bitterly at odds. ʿAbdallāh wrote to ʿUthmān saying, "Verily ʿAmr has refused to turn over the tax revenues," while ʿAmr wrote, "Verily ʿAbdallāh has used the stratagems of war against me." ʿUthmān wrote ordering ʿAmr to depart, and gave ʿAbdallāh b. Saʿd authority over both the tax revenues and the army. ʿAmr arrived [in Medina] in a fury, and entered ʿUthmān's presence wearing a Yemeni cloak (*jubbah*) filled with cotton. ʿUthmān said to him, "What is the filling of your cloak?" He responded, "ʿAmr." ʿUthmān went on, "I knew that it was filled with ʿAmr. I didn't mean that. I was only asking whether it was cotton or something else."

According to al-Wāqidī—Usāmah b. Zayd—Yazīd b. Abī Ḥabīb: ʿAbdallāh b. Saʿd sent ʿUthmān a sum of money from Egypt that he had amassed. ʿAmr entered ʿUthmān's presence, and ʿUthmān said, "ʿAmr, do you know that those she-camels have given milk plentifully since you left?" And ʿAmr answered, "But their young have perished."

In this year, ʿUthmān b. ʿAffān led the pilgrimage.

According to al-Wāqidī: In this year occurred the second conquest of Iṣṭakhr, at the hand of ʿUthmān b. Abī al-ʿĀṣ.

Also according to him: In (this year), Muʿāwiyah attacked Qinnasrīn.

41. Al-Ḥakam b. Abī al-ʿĀṣ was a kinsman of ʿUthmān, but had been one of Muḥammad's bitterest opponents and was sent into exile after the occupation of Mecca. His restoration to respectability under ʿUthmān and the many benefactions showered upon him and his son Marwān were the basis for some of the most serious charges of corruption and nepotism levied against the Caliph. Marwān of course ultimately seized the Caliphate (64–65/684–85), and was the lineal ancestor of all the succeeding Umayyad caliphs in Damascus as well as the amirs of Córdoba after 756.

The Events of the Year 28

(September 25, 648–September 13, 649)

According to al-Wāqidī: Among these (events) is the conquest of Cyprus by Muʿāwiyah, who attacked it at the command of ʿUthmān. However, Abū Maʿshar says that [the conquest of] Cyprus took place in the year 33. This was related to me by Aḥmad b. Thābit—one who related it [to him]—Isḥāq b. ʿĪsā—(Abū Maʿshar).[42] [2820]

Some authorities say that [the conquest of] Cyprus took place in the year 27. According to their accounts, a body (*jamāʿah*) of the Companions of the Messenger of God attacked it—among them Abū Dharr, ʿUbādah b. al-Ṣāmit and his wife Umm Ḥarām, al-Miqdād, Abū al-Dardā', and Shaddād b. Aws.[43]

---

42. The text says simply "*ʿanhu.*" But Köprülü 1043 gives the name "Abū Maʿshar." Cf. the *isnād* of Aḥmad b. Thābit, above, p. 2.

43. On Abū Dharr, see below, pp. 64ff. and note 106; on Abū al-Dardā', see below, p. 65 and note 109.

Mu'āwiyah's Attack on Cyprus

It was transmitted to me in writing by al-Sarī—Shu'ayb—Sayf—al-Rabī' b. al-Nu'mān al-Naṣrī and Abū al-Mujālid Jarād b. 'Amr—Rajā' b. Ḥaywah; and [Sayf—] Abū Ḥārithah and Abū 'Uthmān—Rajā' and 'Ubādah and Khālid:[44] In the time of 'Umar b. al-Khaṭṭāb, Mu'āwiyah pleaded with him about naval campaigns (*ghazw al-baḥr*) and the closeness of the Byzantines to Ḥimṣ. He said, "In one of the villages of Ḥimṣ, the inhabitants hear the barking of (the Byzantines') dogs and the squawking of their chickens." [He pressed 'Umar] until he was on the verge of being won over. So 'Umar wrote to 'Amr b. al-'Āṣ, [saying,] "Describe the sea and the seafarer to me, for I am uneasy about it."

According to 'Ubādah and Khālid: When ('Umar) informed him
[2821] of the benefits for the Muslims and the damage to the Polytheists to be derived from (naval warfare), 'Amr wrote back to him [as follows]: "Verily I have seen a great creature [that is, the sea] ridden by a small one [that is, man]. If (the sea) is calm it rends the heart with anxiety, and if it is agitated it leads the mind into confusion. On it certainty shrinks and doubt increases. Those who are on it are like a worm on a twig; if it bends he is drowned, and if he is saved he is astounded." When 'Umar read (this letter), he wrote to Mu'awiyah [as follows]: "No, by Him who sent Muḥammad with the Truth, I shall never send any Muslim there."

It was transmitted to me in writing by al-Sarī—Shu'ayb—Sayf—Muḥammad b. Sa'īd—'Ubādah b. Nusayy—Junādah b. Abī Umayyah al-Azdī: Mu'āwiyah had written a letter to 'Umar to provoke his interest in naval campaigns, saying, "O Commander of the Faithful, in Syria there is a village whose inhabitants hear the barking of the Byzantines' dogs and the crowing of their roosters, for (the Byzantines) are directly opposite a certain stretch of the coast of [the district of] Ḥimṣ. Now 'Umar was doubtful about

44. This way of constructing the *isnād* is somewhat conjectural, since Abū Ḥārithah and Abū 'Uthmān could be read in conjunction with Rajā' b. Ḥaywah. However, two points suggest that Sayf is combining two separate chains of transmission here: (1) in other *isnād*s Abū Ḥārithah and Abū 'Uthmān are direct informants of Sayf; (2) the name Rajā' is repeated directly following Abū Ḥārithah and Abū 'Uthmān, this time along with two other informants.

this because (Muʿāwiyah) was the one who advised it. He therefore wrote to ʿAmr [as follows]: "Describe the sea for me and send me information about it." ʿAmr then wrote to him [as follows]: "O Commander of the Faithful, I have seen a mighty creature ridden by a small one. It is naught but sky and water, and (those who travel upon it) are only like a worm on a twig: if it bends he drowns, and if he is saved he is amazed."

It was transmitted to me in writing by al-Sarī—Shuʿayb—Sayf—Abū ʿUthmān and Abū Ḥārithah—ʿUbādah—Junādah b. [2822]
Abī Umayyah and Rabīʿ and Abū al-Mujālid: ʿUmar wrote to Muʿāwiyah [as follows]: "We have heard that the Mediterranean Sea (*baḥr al-Sha'm*) surpasses the longest thing upon the earth, seeking God's permission every day and every night to overflow the earth and submerge it. How then can I bring the troops to this troublesome and infidel being? By God, one Muslim is dearer to me than all that the Byzantines possess. Take care not to oppose me. I have given you a command; you know what al-ʿAlā' (b. al-Ḥaḍramī)[45] encountered at my hands, and I did not give him such categorical orders."

According to certain authorities (*qālū*): The Byzantine Emperor abandoned warfare and entered into correspondence with ʿUmar, establishing close relations with him. He asked him for a statement in which all knowledge (*ʿilm*) would be united, and ʿUmar wrote to him [as follows]: "Love for the people what you love for yourself, and hate for them what you hate for yourself. (This) will bring together all wisdom (*ḥikmah*) for you. And regard the people as your closest concern. (This) will combine for you all understanding (*maʿrifah*)."

The Byzantine Emperor wrote to him again, sending a long-necked bottle: "Fill this bottle for me with everything." So (ʿUmar) filled it with water and wrote, "Verily this is everything provided by this world." The Byzantine Emperor wrote to him [and asked], "What lies between truth and falsehood?" (ʿUmar) wrote back, "(There are) four fingers of truth in what the eyes see,

45. Al-ʿAlā' b. al-Ḥaḍramī was Abū Bakr's general in Baḥrayn during the Riddah wars, and later played a role in the Persian wars under ʿUmar, who did not really trust him. See Donner, *Early Islamic Conquests*, 86, 327; and E. Shoufani, *Al-Riddah and the Muslim Conquest of Arabia*, 131–34. See also the volumes in this series on Abū Bakr and ʿUmar.

while falsehood often lies in what has been heard about without being directly observed." Then the Emperor of the Byzantines wrote to ask him how far it is between the heavens and the earth
[2823] and between the East and the West. 'Umar wrote to him, "A journey of five hundred years, if it were a level road."

According to the narrator: Umm Kulthūm, the daughter of 'Alī b. Abī Ṭālib [and wife of 'Umar], sent to the Empress of the Byzantines perfume, drinking vessels, and cheap receptacles used for women's things. She inserted this into the official post (*al-barīd*), which conveyed it to her. (This material) having been taken from the post, the wife of Heraclius came and assembled her women, saying: "This is a gift from the wife of the King of the Arabs and the daughter [*sic*] of their prophet." She entered into correspondence with (Umm Kulthūm) and requited her in kind by sending her gifts, among them a superb necklace. Now when the official post brought (these gifts) to 'Umar, he ordered them to be seized and summoned [the people] together to pray. When they had assembled, he prayed two *rak'ah*s with them, and then said, "There is no good in any affair of mine that is decided without consultation. What about a gift that Umm Kulthūm sent to the wife of the Byzantine Emperor, who then sent a gift to her?" Some said, "It is (Umm Kulthūm's) along with what she [already] possesses. The Emperor's wife is neither under a pact of protection (*dhimmah*), so that she should try to conciliate [you] with (this gift), nor is she under your authority so that she should fear you." Others said, "We used to send garments as a gift in order to get something in return; we would send them to be sold and to obtain a [certain] price." Then 'Umar said, "But the envoy was the envoy of the Muslims, and the postal service was theirs. The Muslims are vexed [to see] (the necklace) on her breast." Thus, he ordered it to be returned to the public treasury, while he paid (Umm Kulthūm) the amount of her expenses.

It was transmitted to me in writing by al-Sarī—Shu'ayb—Sayf—Abū Ḥārithah—Khālid b. Ma'dān: The first to conduct naval warfare was Mu'āwiyah b. Abī Sufyān in the time of
[2824] 'Uthmān b. 'Affān. He had sought 'Umar's permission for this but did not obtain it. When 'Uthmān took office, Mu'āwiyah persisted until at last 'Uthmān decided to grant permission. He said, "Do not conscript the people or cast lots among them. Let them decide

for themselves, and whoever chooses [to go on] campaign in obedience [to your call], support and aid him." (Mu'āwiyah) did this, naming as his admiral (*wa'sta'mala 'alā al-baḥr*) 'Abdallāh b. Qays al-Jāsī, an ally (*ḥalīf*) of the Banū Fazārah.[46]

('Abdallāh) conducted fifty campaigns on the sea, in both winter and summer, and not one man was drowned or injured. He would call upon God to provide prosperity for his troops and to protect him and his soldiers against misfortune. So he went on, until the time when God decided to afflict him alone. He set out in advance [of his fleet] in a light boat (*qārib*). He reached the seaport in Byzantine territory; at that place beggars besought him for aid, and he gave them alms. A woman from among the beggars returned to her village and said to the men [there], "Do you want to find 'Abdallāh b. Qays?" "Where is he?" they said. "At the seaport," she answered. "O enemy of God," they said, "how do you know 'Abdallāh b. Qays?" She scolded them, saying, "You are too feeble for 'Abdallāh to hide from any one [of you]." Then they rose [2825]
up and attacked him. They did battle with one another, and ('Abdallāh) alone was struck down.

The sailor [of his boat] got away to ('Abdallāh's) comrades [in the main fleet]; they returned and landed under the command of Sufyān b. 'Awf al-Azdī. He advanced and did battle with (the Byzantines). In a state of anger, he began mocking and abusing his comrades. Then 'Abdallāh's slave girl said, "Alas, for 'Abdallāh! He did not speak like that when he was fighting." Sufyān responded, "So how did he speak?" She said, "A sea of troubles, and then it will vanish from us."[47] Thus, (Sufyān) stopped what he had been saying and stuck to "A sea of troubles, and then it will vanish from us." He was struck down among the Muslims on that day, and that ended the era of 'Abdallāh b. Qays al-Jāsī.[48] Afterwards, the woman [who had reported 'Abdallāh's presence] was

46. The text reads al-Ḥārithī, but de Goeje (*Introductio*, dcxxv) corrects to al-Jāsī. The Banū Jās were a clan of Fazārah, a powerful Najdī tribe that had rebelled during the Riddah wars, but was soon compelled to recognize the supremacy of the Caliphate, and then played an honorable part in the Persian campaign. See Donner, *Early Islamic Conquests*, 65, 85, 194, 262.

47. A proverb expressing confidence: see Freytag, *Arabum Proverbia*, II, 173.

48. In the text, "al-Ḥārithī." I have followed de Goeje's reading, *Introductio*, dcxxv.

asked, "How did you recognize him?" "By his alms," she answered. "He gave in the manner of kings, and was not grasping like the merchants."

It was transmitted to me in writing by al-Sarī—Shuʿayb—Sayf—Abū Ḥārithah and Abū ʿUthmān: The woman who had incited the Byzantines against ʿAbdallāh b. Qays was asked, "How did you recognize him?" She answered, "He looked like a merchant, but when I pleaded for alms, he gave to me like a king, and so I knew that he was ʿAbdallāh b. Qays."

(ʿUthmān) wrote to Muʿāwiyah and the [other] provincial officials: "To proceed: See to those matters concerning which you have departed from ʿUmar['s directives], and do not alter them. If you are in doubt about something, refer it to us; we shall convene
[2826] the Community (*ummah*) concerning it and then send (the proper course of action) back to you. Take care to alter nothing, for I shall accept from you only what ʿUmar would accept." That region (*nāḥiyah*) had been falling into disorder in (the period) between the peace treaty [established under] ʿUmar and the regime of ʿUthmān. He would thus send a certain man there and God would conquer it through him, and that [conquest] would be accounted as his. Regarding the conquests [in general], they were credited to the first man who was made governor over them.[49]

Abū Jaʿfar (al-Ṭabarī) says: When Muʿāwiyah attacked Cyprus, he agreed upon peace terms with its inhabitants, according to ʿAlī b. Sahl—al-Walīd b. Muslim—Sulaymān b. Abī Karīmah, al-Layth b. Saʿd, and other shaykhs of the coastal districts of Damascus: The peace terms for Cyprus (*ṣulḥ Qubrus*) consisted of a tribute (*jizyah*) of 7,000 dinars, to be paid to the Muslims every year. (The Cypriots) would also pay the same amount to the Byzantines, and the Muslims would not have the right to interfere in the payment of that tribute to the Byzantines.[50] In addition, (the Muslims) would neither raid (the Cypriots) nor fight

49. Presumably this paragraph deals with Syria, since Muʿāwiyah is the only person named and *tilka al-nāḥiyah* ("that region") seems to refer to a specific place. The new or restored conquests would then be the northern frontier zone in Cilicia and the Taurus mountains.

50. *Laysa li'l-muslimīna an yaḥūlū baynahum wa-bayna dhālika.* Literally, "It is not for the Muslims to intervene between them and that."

against anyone seeking their protection. (The Cypriots) were obliged to inform the Muslims of any expedition against them by their enemy the Byzantines; moreover, the Imam of the Muslims should appoint the Patrician over them from among themselves.

According to al-Wāqidī: Muʿāwiyah attacked Cyprus in the year 28. The troops in Egypt attacked it also, under the command of ʿAbdallāh b. Saʿd b. Abī Sarḥ, until they met up with Muʿāwiyah, who then wielded authority over [all] the Muslims [in this campaign].[51]

According to (al-Wāqidī)—al-Thawr b. Yazīd—Khālid b. Maʿdān—Jubayr b. Nufayr: When we took (the Cypriots) captive I saw Abū al-Dardā' weeping, and I said, "Why are you weeping on [2827] a day when God has exalted Islam and its adherents and abased infidelity and its partisans?" He struck my shoulder with his hand and said, "May your mother be bereft of you, Jubayr. How despicable mankind becomes to God when they abandon his commandments. Here was a mighty nation (*ummah*), which dominated (our) people and possessed royal power (*mulk*). Then they abandoned God's commandments; thus they fell into the condition that you see and God subjected them to captivity. If a people (*qawm*) is subjected to captivity, then God has no use for them."

According to al-Wāqidī—Abu Saʿīd: Muʿāwiyah b. Abī Sufyān established peace terms with the Cypriots in the reign of ʿUthmān, having been the first to attack the Byzantines [in Cyprus]. In the pact between (Muʿāwiyah) and (the Cypriots) was [the provision] that they would only contract marriages with our enemy the Byzantines with our permission.

According to al-Wāqidī: In this year, Ḥabīb b. Maslamah attacked Sūrīyah in Byzantine territory.

In this year, ʿUthmān married Nā'ilah bint al-Farāfiṣah.[52] She was a Christian, but converted to Islam before he consummated the marriage.

According to (al-Wāqidī): In (this year), ʿUthmān built his resi-

---

51. That is, over the combined Muslim forces from Syria and Egypt on Cyprus.
52. A woman of the tribe of Kalb.

dence [called] al-Zawrā' [that is, "bent," "slanting"] in Medina and brought it to completion.

According to (al-Wāqidī): In (this year), there took place the first conquest of Fārs and the definitive conquest of Iṣṭakhr, under the
[2828] command of Hishām b. 'Āmir.

According to (al-Wāqidī): In this year, 'Uthmān led the pilgrimage.

The Events of the Year 29

(September 14, 649–September 3, 650)

In (this year) ʿUthmān removed Abū Mūsā al-Ashʿarī from Baṣrah, after he had been his governor (*ʿāmil*) there for six years. As governor, he appointed ʿAbdallāh b. ʿĀmir b. Kurayz, who was then twenty-five years of age, and he proceeded (to Baṣrah). It is also said that Abū Mūsā was ʿUthmān's governor in Baṣrah only for three years.

According to ʿAlī b. Muḥammad (al-Madāʾinī)—Muḥārib—ʿAwf al-Aʿrābī: Ghaylān b. Kharashah al-Ḍabbī went up to ʿUthmān b. ʿAffān and said, "Indeed you[53] have a youngster whom you should treat as an adult and appoint as governor of Baṣrah. How long will this old man"—that is, Abū Mūsā—"govern Baṣrah?" Now he had been governor for six years since the death of ʿUmar.

(Al-Madāʾinī) goes on [as follows]: Thus, ʿUthmān deposed him and sent out ʿAbdallāh b. ʿĀmir b. Kurayz b. Rabīʿah b. Ḥabīb b.

53. Plural: *lakum ṣaghīr*. Presumably he is addressing the tribe of Quraysh, not ʿUthmān alone. See the more elaborate parallel versions below, pp. 35–37.

'Abd Shams. This man's mother was Dajjājah bt. Asmā' al-Sulamī, and he was the son of 'Uthmān b. 'Affān's maternal uncle.

According to Maslamah: He came to Baṣrah in the year 29, at the age of twenty-five.

The Reason for 'Uthmān's Removal of Abū Mūsā [al-Ash'arī] from Baṣrah

It was transmitted to me in writing by al-Sarī—Shu'ayb—Sayf—Muḥammad and Ṭalḥah: When 'Uthmān took office, he retained Abū Mūsā in Baṣrah for three years, deposing him in the fourth. He appointed 'Umayr b. 'Uthmān b. Sa'd as military commander of Khurāsān, and 'Abdallāh b. 'Umayr al-Laythī from [the tribe of]
[2829] Kinānah[54] as military commander in Sijistān. ('Abdallāh) fought relentlessly there as far as Kābul, while 'Umayr waged war in Khurāsān until he reached Farghānah, compelling every district (*kūrah*) this side of it to come to terms. ('Uthmān) sent 'Ubaydallāh b. Ma'mar al-Taymī to Makrān, and he battled unceasingly until he reached the river.[55] To Kirmān he sent 'Abd al-Raḥmān b. Ghubays, and a small band to Fārs and al-Ahwāz. He annexed the agricultural hinterland (*Sawād*) of Baṣrah to [the districts under] al-Ḥuṣayn b. Abī al-Ḥurr. Then ('Uthmān) removed 'Abdallah b. 'Umayr [from Sijistān] and put 'Abdallāh b. 'Āmir in charge, retaining him there for a year; in turn he deposed ('Abdallāh b. 'Āmir) and appointed 'Āṣim b. 'Amr. He also removed 'Abd al-Raḥmān b. Ghubays [from Kirmān] and sent back 'Adī b. Suhayl b. 'Adī.

During the third year [of 'Uthmān's reign], the inhabitants of Īdhaj[56] and the Kurds rebelled. Abū Mūsā called out the people, exhorting them and charging them [to repress the rebellion]. He

54. The text has Tha'labah; I have followed de Goeje's emendation, *Introductio*, dcxxv.

55. No certain identification is possible. Perhaps the Dasht is meant, which flows into the Indian Ocean near the present border between Iran and Pakistan. Conceivably the text refers to the far more prominent Helmand River, but this stream lies very far north for an army working its way along the Makrān coast.

56. Also known as Māl-Amīr. The chief town of southern Luristan, on the upper Kārūn River. It had originally been subjected to tribute in 17/638, and then had to be reconquered after the battle of Nihāwand (21/642). See C. E. Bosworth, "Īdhadj," *EI*², III, 1015–16; Le Strange, *Eastern Caliphate*, 245.

spoke of the merit in making the *jihād* on foot, so that a few men loaded up their animals and agreed to set forth as infantrymen. But others said, "No, by God! We will not hasten to act until we see what he does. If his actions are like his words, then we will do as our comrades have done." When the day came to set out, (Abū Mūsā) sent out his baggage from the governor's palace on forty mules. (The doubters) clung to his bridle and said, "Mount us on some of these extra (animals), and be as eager to go on foot as you asked us to be." He appeased these men until they let go of his animal; then he proceeded forward.

They came to ʿUthmān, however, and asked that he relieve them of (Abū Mūsā). They said, "We do not wish to say everything we know, but give us [someone else] in place of him." "Whom do you wish?" responded ʿUthmān. Then Ghaylān b. Kharashah said, "Anyone would be as good as this slave who has [2830] devoured our land and revived among us the way of the Time of Ignorance. Shall we not free ourselves from an Ashʿarī who regards his sovereignty (*mulk*) over the Ashʿarī tribesmen as a great thing and belittles sovereignty in Baṣrah? If you make a child or an old man our amir, he will be as good, and anyone of the people in between those two [extremes] will be better than (Abū Mūsā)." Thus, (ʿUthmān) summoned ʿAbdallāh b. ʿĀmir and made him governor (*ammarahu*) of Baṣrah.

(ʿUthmān) dispatched ʿUbaydallāh b. Maʿmar to Fārs, appointing ʿUmayr b. ʿUthmān b. Saʿd as governor over [ʿUbaydallāh's former] province. In the fourth year of his reign, he named Umayr[57] b. Aḥmar al-Yashkurī as governor of Khurāsān. In the same year, he assigned the governorship of Sijistān to ʿImrān b. al-Faṣīl al-Burjumī and the governorship of Kirmān to ʿĀṣim b. ʿAmr, who died there.

Fārs burst into rebellion during the regime of ʿUbaydallāh b. Maʿmar, and (the rebels) assembled against him in Iṣṭakhr. They clashed at the gate of Iṣṭakhr, and ʿUbaydallāh was killed and his army routed. When ʿAbdallāh b. ʿĀmir heard the news, he called the Baṣrans to arms, and the people marched forth with him, ʿUthmān b. Abī al-ʿĀṣ being in command of the vanguard. (The

57. Prym and Ibrāhīm read the name as Umayn, but Köprülü 1043, Ibn al-Athīr, and Balādhurī (*Futūḥ al-buldān*, 395) all give it as Umayr.

two armies) met at Iṣṭakhr, and he slaughtered many of (the reb-
[2831] els), as a result of which they remained submissive thereafter.

(ʿAbdallāh) wrote to ʿUthmān about this event, and the latter wrote back to him naming [the following men] as military commanders in the administrative districts (*kuwar*) of Fārs: Harim b. Ḥassān al-Yashkurī; Harim b. Ḥayyān al-ʿAbdī, of the [tribe of] ʿAbd al-Qays; al-Khirrīt b. Rāshid, of the [tribe of] Banū Sāmah; al-Minjāb b. Rāshid; and al-Tarjumān al-Hujaymī. He also divided Khurāsān among a group of six [men]: al-Aḥnaf [was put] in charge of the two Marws;[58] Ḥabīb b. Qurrah al-Yarbūʿī over Balkh, which was part of the territories conquered by the Kūfans; Khālid b. ʿAbdallāh b. Zuhayr over Herat; Umayr b. Aḥmar al-Yashkurī over Ṭūs; Qays b. al-Haytham[59] al-Sulamī over Nishapur—he was the first to set out [for his district]; and ʿAbdallāh b. Khāzim, who was his cousin (*ibn ʿammihi*). Then before his death ʿUthmān combined (all of Khurāsān) under (Qays b. al-Haytham), and when (ʿUthmān) died Qays [held authority] over Khurāsān. (ʿUthmān) appointed Umayr b. Aḥmar as governor in Sijistān, and then set over it ʿAbd al-Raḥmān b. Samurah, who belonged to the clan (*āl*) of Ḥabīb b. ʿAbd Shams. At the time of ʿUthmān's death, (ʿAbd al-Raḥmān b. Samurah) held authority in (Sijistān), ʿImrān in Kirmān, ʿUmayr b. ʿUthmān b. Saʿd in Fārs, and Ibn Kindīr al-Qushayrī in Makrān.[60]

According to ʿAlī b. Muḥammad (al-Madāʾinī)—ʿAlī b. Mujāhid—his shaykhs: Ghaylān b. Kharashah said to ʿUthmān b. ʿAffān, "Is there not among all of you some wretch for you to raise up? Is there no beggar for you to enrich? O men of Quraysh, how long will that aged Ashʿarī devour these lands?" The old man [that
[2832] is, ʿUthmān] grasped his point and named ʿAbdallāh b. ʿĀmir as governor [of Baṣrah].

According to ʿAlī b. Muḥammad (al-Madāʾinī)—Abū Bakr al-

---

58. Marw on the Murghāb River, the administrative center of Khurāsān in Umayyad and early Abbasid times; and Marw al-Rūdh.

59. Text: Hubayrah. De Goeje, *Introductio*, dcxxv, gives no authority for his emendation.

60. As the parentheses suggest, this paragraph is full of masculine singular pronouns with no clear antecedents. My reconstruction agrees with that of Caetani, *Annali*, VII, 292–93, who—here as elsewhere—puts little stock in the evidentiary value of Sayf's account.

Hudhalī: ʿUthmān named Ibn ʿĀmir as governor of Baṣrah. According to al-Ḥasan: Abū Mūsā said, "To you a youth of great shrewdness is coming. Through his grandmothers and his maternal and paternal aunts he is noble; under him the two armies will be combined."

According to (al-Madāʾinī)—al-Ḥasan: When Ibn ʿĀmir arrived, the army of Abū Mūsā and the army of ʿUthmān b. Abī al-ʿĀṣ al-Thaqafī were united under him. Now ʿUthmān b. Abī al-ʿĀṣ was one of those who had crossed over [to Khūzistān by ship] from ʿUmān and Baḥrayn.

It was transmitted to me in writing by al-Sarī—Shuʿayb—Sayf—Muḥammad and Ṭalḥah: In the time of ʿUthmān, Qays b. al-Haytham sent ʿAbdallāh b. Khāzim as his envoy to ʿAbdallāh b. ʿĀmir. ʿAbdallāh b. Khāzim was much esteemed by ʿAbdallāh b. ʿĀmir, and so he said to the latter, "Write a diploma (*ʿahd*) appointing me over Khurāsān should Qays b. al-Haytham leave (that province)." (Ibn ʿĀmir) did so and (ʿAbdallāh b. Khāzim) returned to Khurāsān. When the people heard the news of ʿUthmān's murder and the enemy grew turbulent, Qays said [to Ibn Khāzim], "What do you think, ʿAbdallāh?" "In my opinion," (ʿAbdallāh) responded, "you should leave me [here] as your deputy and not delay your departure, so that you can look into the situation." (Qays) did this, appointing (Ibn Khāzim) as his deputy. Then ʿAbdallāh (b. Khāzim) produced his diploma of appointment [from Ibn ʿĀmir], and he maintained authority over Khurāsān until the rise of ʿAlī. The mother of ʿAbdallāh (b. Khāzim) was ʿAjlā; [2833]
and Qays—in anger at how (Ibn Khāzim) had treated him—said, "I had a better right than ʿAbdallāh to be the son of ʿAjlā."

According to al-Wāqidī, and according to Aḥmad b. Thābit (al-Rāzī)—one who recounted it (to him)—Isḥāq b. ʿĪsā—Abū Maʿshar: In this year, ʿAbdallāh b. ʿĀmir conquered Fārs. As regards the account of Sayf, we have already given it.

In this year—that is, 29 (649–50)—ʿUthmān enlarged and widened the Mosque of the Messenger of God [in Medina].[61] He be-

61. On this incident, and the history of this structure in general, see the brilliant though conjectural account of Jean Sauvaget, *La mosquée omeyyade de Médine* (Paris: 1947). Sauvaget gives an exhaustive and very sophisticated account of the textual sources, among which Ṭabarī has only a modest place.

gan construction in Rabīʿ al-Awwal (November 12–December 11). Gypsum [to be used for stucco] was brought to ʿUthmān from Baṭn Nakhl. He built it with cut stone, making its pillars out of blocks of stone [held together] with lead [clamps] and constructing its roof from teakwood. He made it 160 cubits long and 150 cubits wide. He gave it six portals, as in the time of ʿUmar.

In this year, ʿUthmān led the pilgrimage. At Minā[62] he pitched a tent—this was the first tent that ʿUthmān pitched at Minā—and he completed the [rites of] prayer there and at ʿArafah.[63]

[ʿUthmān's Alterations to the Pilgrimage Rites]

According to al-Wāqidī—ʿUmar b. Ṣāliḥ b. Nāfiʿ—Ṣāliḥ, the client (*mawlā*) of al-Taw'amah—Ibn ʿAbbās: The people first began to talk openly about ʿUthmān [in the following circumstances]. During his reign, he had prayed two *rakʿah*s with the people at Minā, but in his sixth year he completed (the prayer rites) [with two additional *rakʿah*s]; more than one of the Prophet's Companions found that blameworthy. This was discussed among those who wished to make difficulties for him, until ʿAlī came to him with
[2834] certain others and said, "By God, there is no commandment new or old [concerning this]. You have observed your Prophet praying two *rakʿah*s, followed by Abū Bakr and ʿUmar and you yourself at the beginning of your reign. I do not know upon what this is based."[64] (ʿUthmān) replied, "It is a personal opinion that I hold."

According to al-Wāqidī—Dāwūd b. Khālid—ʿAbd al-Malik b. ʿAmr b. Abī Sufyān al-Thaqafī—his paternal uncle: ʿUthmān prayed four (*rakʿah*s) with the people at Minā. Then someone

---

62. One of the pilgrimage stations outside Mecca, the last place visited by the pilgrims. On 10 Dhū al-Ḥijjah, they throw stones at a construction called "Jamrat al-ʿAqabah," and later in the day carry out here the ritual sacrifice in commemoration of the sacrifice of Abraham. On the three days following the end of the *ḥajj* proper (*ayyām al-tashrīq*), Minā is visited again by the pilgrims for a new round of ritual stonings. See A. J. Wensinck and J. Jomier, "Ḥadjdj," *EI²*, III, 36–37.

63. Another of the pilgrimage stations, more commonly called "ʿArafāt," a valley some 25 kms. east of Mecca where the pilgrims congregate on 9 Dhū al-Ḥijjah after the circumambulation of the Kaʿbah and before proceeding to Minā for the ritual stoning and sacrifice. See Wensinck and Jomier, *ibid.*, 35–36; on the prayer rites observed during the Pilgrimage, see Wensinck, "Ṣalāt," *SEI*, 491–99, esp. p. 494.

64. Emending the text to read "*fa-mā adrī mā yarjaʿū ilayhi.*"

came to ʿAbd al-Raḥmān b. ʿAwf and said, "Do you know that your brother has prayed four *rakʿahs*) with the people?" ʿAbd al-Raḥmān prayed two *rakʿahs* with his companions and then set out to see ʿUthmān. He said to him, "Did you not pray two *rakʿahs* in this place with the Messenger of God?" (ʿUthmān) answered, "Indeed so." "And did you not pray two *rakʿahs* with Abū Bakr?" "Indeed so." "And did you not pray two *rakʿahs* with ʿUmar?" "Indeed so." "And did you not pray two *rakʿahs* at the beginning of your caliphate?" "Indeed so," said ʿUthmān. "But listen to me, Abū Muḥammad. I was informed that some of the Yemenis and ill-educated people who made the pilgrimage last year said, 'The ritual prayer consists of two *rakʿahs* for the permanent resident (*al-muqīm*); here is your imam ʿUthmān praying two *rakʿahs*.' In Mecca I am connected with a clan (*ahl*), and I have thought it best to pray four *rakʿahs* out of my fear for the people. In addition, I have taken a wife there, and in al-Ṭā'if I have property, which I sometimes supervise and reside in after the day of return from the Pilgrimage."[65]

ʿAbd al-Raḥmān b. ʿAwf said, "None of this gives you any excuse. You say that you are connected with a clan, but your wife is in Medina, going and coming as you wish, and living only where you do. You say that you have property in al-Ṭā'if, but between [2835] you and al-Ṭā'if is a three-day journey, and you are not one of the inhabitants of al-Ṭā'if. You say that the Yemenis and others who are making the pilgrimage are returning [home] and saying, 'Here is your imam ʿUthmān praying two *rakʿahs*, and he is a permanent resident.' But revelation would descend on the Messenger of God when Islam was rare among the people, [and yet he prayed two *rakʿahs*], and then Abū Bakr and ʿUmar did the same. Thus, Islam became established, and ʿUmar prayed two *rakʿahs* with them until he died." ʿUthmān replied, "It is my own personal opinion."

---

65. ʿUthmān's point is twofold. (1) Many ordinary Muslims were ignorant of the different number of ritual prostrations (*rakʿahs*) connected with the act of prayer at different times. Hence, they would assume that all prayers were to be performed with two *rakʿahs*, although in fact only those who were traveling or on pilgrimage were permitted to abbreviate the usual four *rakʿahs* in that manner. (2) ʿUthmān's property holdings and family ties made him a permanent resident in Mecca and al-Ṭā'if as well as Medina; hence, he felt obligated to observe the complete rite of four *rakʿahs* even during the Pilgrimage season. See note 271 below, and the discussion in Caetani, *Annali*, VII, 261–64.

According to al-Wāqidī: Then ʿAbd al-Raḥmān went out and met up with Ibn Masʿūd. (The latter said), "Abū Muḥammad, is it different from what we have heard?" "No," he replied. (Ibn Masʿūd) said, "So what shall I do?" (ʿAbd al-Raḥmān) said, "You should do what you know [to be right]." Then Ibn Masʿūd said, "Disagreement is an evil. I have heard that he has prayed four *rakʿah*s, and so I prayed four *rakʿah*s with my associates." ʿAbd al-Raḥmān b. ʿAwf replied, "I have heard that he has prayed four *rakʿah*s, and with my associates I prayed two. But now I shall do as you say; we shall, following him, pray four *rakʿah*s."

The Events of the Year 30

(September 4, 650–August 23, 651)

Among these was the campaign of Sa'īd b. al-'Āṣ in Ṭabaristān, according to the account related to me by Aḥmad b. Thābit—one who related it to him—Isḥāq b. 'Īsā—Abū Ma'shar. [2836]

[The same is said by] al-Wāqidī and by 'Alī b. Muḥammad al-Madā'inī, on whose authority 'Umar b. Shabbah related that to me.

As for Sayf b. 'Umar, he states that the *ispahbadh*[66] (of Ṭabaristān) had made peace with Suwayd b. Muqarrin based on the understanding that (Suwayd) would not attack (the region) in return for a certain tribute (*māl*) to be paid to him. The report concerning this has been given above, in the time of 'Umar.

It was related to me by 'Umar (b. Shabbah)—'Alī b. Muḥammad al-Madā'inī: No one attacked (Ṭabaristān) until 'Uthmān b. 'Affān came to power; then Sa'īd b. al-'Āṣ attacked it in the year 30 (650–51).

---

66. The *ispahbadh* was the military governnor of a major province in the late Sasanian Empire. Khusraw Anushirvan (531–579) had divided the empire into four quarters, each named after a cardinal point of the compass, and appointed an *ispahbadh* over each. For example, Iraq and Mesopotamia constituted the quarter

The Campaign of Sa'īd b. al-'Āṣ in Ṭabaristān

It was related to me by 'Umar b. Shabbah—'Alī b. Muḥammad (al-Madā'inī)—'Alī b. Mujāhid—Ḥanash b. Mālik: In the year 30 (650–51), Sa'īd b. al-'Āṣ set out on campaign from Kūfah, aiming at Khurāsān, accompanied by Ḥudhayfah b. al-Yamān and a group of the Companions of the Messenger of God. With him were al-Ḥasan, al-Ḥusayn, 'Abdallāh b. 'Abbās, 'Abdallāh b. 'Umar, 'Abdallāh b. 'Amr b. al-'Āṣ, and 'Abdallāh b. al-Zubayr. [At the same time] 'Abdallāh b. 'Āmir set out from Baṣrah for Khurāsān. He outstripped Sa'īd and laid siege to Abrashahr.[67] Sa'īd having learned of his siege of Abrashahr, he encamped at Qūmis, which was governed by a peace treaty that Ḥudhayfah had made with (its people) after Nihāwand.

Then Sa'īd came to Jurjān and concluded a treaty with it requiring [a tribute of] 200,000 [dirhams]. Then he came to Ṭamīsah,[68] which is situated between Ṭabaristān and Jurjān; it is a city on
[2837] the shore [of the Caspian] Sea, at the boundaries of Jurjān. Its inhabitants fought him until he performed the prayer of fear.[69] He had said to Ḥudhayfah, "How did the Messenger of God pray?" (Ḥudhayfah) told him, and Sa'īd performed there the prayer of fear while they were fighting.

On that day Sa'īd smote one of the polytheists on the sinews of his shoulder and his sword emerged below (the man's) elbow. He besieged them and they sought safe-conduct (*amān*). He granted it to them with the condition that he would not kill one man among them. Then they threw open the fortress and he put them all to death save one man.[70] He seized the contents of the fortress, and a man from [the tribe of] Banū Nahd came across a basket with a lock; he supposed it contained jewelry. Sa'īd learned of this

---

of the West. However, Sasanian provincial administration was extensively revamped under Khusraw Parviz (592–628), so that the scope of the authority of the official named here is not certain. See Morony, *Iraq after the Muslim Conquest*, 28, 38, 126, 148, 187.

67. Nishapur/Naysābūr. The name Abrashahr seems to have dropped out of use after the fourth/tenth century. See Le Strange, *Eastern Caliphate*, 383.

68. Also known as Ṭamīs; see Le Strange, *Eastern Caliphate*, 375.

69. The prayer of fear, *ṣalāt al-khawf*, is a shortened ritual performed in the near presence of an enemy. See Wensinck, "Ṣalāt," *SEI*, 496.

70. Thereby observing the letter of the peace terms.

and sent for the Nahdī tribesman. He brought the basket to him; they broke open its lock. Within it they found (another) basket. They opened it, and there was a black cloak rolled up. Spreading it out, they found a red cloak. They unfolded it, and there was a yellow cloak containing two penises, one maroon and one rose-colored. A poet said, ridiculing the Banū Nahd:

The noble-hearted have returned with captives as booty,
while the Banū Nahd have won two penises in a basket,
Maroon and rose-colored, both of ample size.
They thought them spoils; forbid yourself such an error!

Then Saʿīd b. al-ʿĀṣ conquered Nāmiyah, which is not a city but a desert.

It was related to me by ʿUmar b. Shabbah—ʿAlī b. Muḥammad (al-Madāʾinī)—ʿAlī b. Mujāhid—Ḥanash b. Mālik al-Taghlibī: In the year 30 (650–51), Saʿīd campaigned in Jurjān and Ṭabaristān. With him were ʿAbdallāh b. al-ʿAbbās, ʿAbdallāh b. ʿUmar, Ibn al-Zubayr, and ʿAbdallāh b. ʿAmr b. al-ʿĀṣ. A peasant (*ʿilj*) who used to serve them recounted the following to me [namely, Ḥanash]: "I used to bring them the serving tray, and when they had eaten, they ordered me to shake it off and hang it up. Then when evening came they gave me the leftover (food)." [2838]

According to (ʿUmar b. Shabbah): Muḥammad b. al-Ḥakam b. Abī ʿAqīl al-Thaqafī, the grandfather of Yūsuf b. ʿUmar,[71] perished [while on campaign] with Saʿīd b. al-ʿĀṣ. Yūsuf once said to Qaḥdham, "Qaḥdham, do you know where Muḥammad b. al-Ḥakam died?" He replied, "Yes, he found martyrdom in Ṭabaristān with Saʿīd b. al-ʿĀṣ." (Yūsuf) said, "No, he died there while he was [on campaign] with Saʿīd; then Saʿīd returned to Kūfah." Kaʿb b. Juʿayl lauded (Saʿīd), saying:

How excellent was the youth when dust swirled beneath him
and when they alighted from Dastabā—[72]

71. Yūsuf b. ʿUmar al-Thaqafī was one of the most prominent Umayyad governors of Iraq, noted particularly for his unrelenting harshness toward his rivals. He was appointed by the caliph Hishām in 738, and died during the Umayyad civil war in 744. On his career see Wellhausen, *Arab Kingdom*, 333–35, 357–59, 367–68, 376; Hawting, *First Dynasty of Islam*, 82–83, 93, 96–97.

72. Dastabā was "a large district (*kūrah*) divided between al-Rayy and Hamadhān. One section of it was named Dastabā al-Rāzī, and contained almost

then he was dazzling in his splendor.
Know, fortunate Sa'īd, that if my beast sits down,
I fear it is hamstrung.
[It is] as though you were a lion in a thicket
on the Day of the Cleft,
which left behind the lion in the wood
and went forth into the desert.
[2839] You command what no one before you has ever commanded—
eighty thousand men, [some] with armor and [some]
without.

It was related to me by 'Umar (b. Shabbah)—'Alī (b. Muḥammad al-Madā'inī)—Kulayb b. Khalaf and others: Sa'īd b. al-'Āṣ made peace with the inhabitants of Jurjān; then [later on] they became obdurate and manifested unbelief. No one came to Jurjān after Sa'īd, and they closed off that road, so that no one took the road to Khurāsān by way of Qūmis save in fear and dread before the Jurjānīs. The (usual) road to Khurāsān went from Fārs through Kirmān, and the first man to open up the road through Qūmis was Qutaybah b. Muslim when he became governor of Khurāsān.[73]

It was related to me by 'Umar (b. Shabbah)—'Alī (b. Muḥammad al-Madā'inī)—Kulayb b. Khalaf al-'Ammī—Ṭufayl b. Mirdās al-'Ammī and Idrīs b. Ḥanẓalah al-'Ammī: Sa'īd b. al-'Āṣ made peace with the inhabitants of Jurjān. At times the Jurjānīs would collect 100,000 [dirhams] and say, "This fulfills our peace treaty." At other times [the sum collected would be] 200,000 or 300,000. Sometimes they would pay this, sometimes not. Then they became obdurate and manifested unbelief, not paying any tribute

---

ninety villages. The other section was named Dastabā Hamadhān and was made up of numerous villages; at various times it was called 'Dastabā Qazwīn' because it was attached to the province ('*amal*) of Qazwīn." (Yāqūt, *Mu'jam al-buldān*, II, 573)

73. Qutaybah b. Muslim was named to this post in 705 by al-Walīd, and held it until his death in 715; he was the victim of a mutiny by his own troops when he tried to provoke a rebellion against the new Caliph Sulaymān b. 'Abd al-Malik. Qutaybah was the first Muslim general to achieve permanent conquests in Central Asia. On his career see Wellhausen, *Arab Kingdom*, 429–45 *et passim*; Barthold, *Turkestan down to the Mongol Invasion*, 185–86; Gibb, *The Arab Conquests in Central Asia*, 29–57; M. A. Shaban, *The 'Abbāsid Revolution*, 63–75 *et passim*.

(*kharāj*) until Yazīd b. al-Muhallab came against them.[74] When he arrived there no one could stand against him, and after he had made peace with Ṣūl and conquered al-Buḥayrah and Dihistān, he made peace with the inhabitants of Jurjān in accordance with the treaty of Saʿīd b. al-ʿĀṣ.

In this year—that is, the year 30 (650–51)—ʿUthmān removed al-Walīd b. ʿUqbah from Kūfah and made Saʿīd b. al-ʿĀṣ governor there, according to Sayf b. ʿUmar. [2840]

The Reason for ʿUthmān's Removal of al-Walīd and His Appointment of Saʿīd as Governor [in Kūfah]

It was transmitted to me in writing by al-Sarī—Shuʿayb—Sayf—Muḥammad and Ṭalḥah: When ʿUthmān learned of the conflict between ʿAbdallāh (b. Masʿūd) and Saʿd (b. Abī Waqqāṣ), he grew angry with both men and resolved [to deal with] them. Then he abandoned that [notion] and removed Saʿd [alone] from office, recovering [from him] what he owed [to the treasury in Kūfah]. He confirmed ʿAbdallāh in office and issued instructions to him. To replace Saʿd as governor he appointed al-Walīd b. ʿUqbah, who had been a fiscal officer (*ʿāmil*) over the bedouin (*al-ʿarab*) of the Jazīrah for ʿUmar b. al-Khaṭṭāb. So al-Walīd arrived (in Kūfah) in the second year of ʿUthmān's rule (*imārah*), after Saʿd had been governor there for one year and part of another.

Having arrived in Kūfah, (al-Walīd) was the most beloved among the people and the most courteous [in his dealings] with them. So it was for five years; there was no door on his residence. Then some of the young men of Kūfah put Ibn al-Ḥaysumān al-Khuzāʿī under surveillance, intending to overpower him. He was warned about them and went out against them sword in hand.

74. Yazīd b. Muhallab b. Abī Ṣufrah, of the tribe of Azd, was an Umayyad general and governor in the early eighth century. His father had achieved prominence by his bloody suppression of the Kharijite revolts in Iraq in the 690s and was named governor of Khurāsān in 698. Yazīd succeeded his father in that office in 702. He was soon deposed, but was reinstated in 715 to succeed Qutaybah b. Muslim. In 720 Yazīd led a revolt in Baṣrah (where the tribe of Azd was strong) against the new Caliph Yazīd II; at first this revolt ballooned dangerously, but it was quickly suppressed. See Wellhausen, *Arab Kingdom*, 250–51, 257–63, 312–18, 445–48; Hawting, *First Dynasty of Islam*, 69, 73–76.

When he saw their numbers, however, he shouted for help. They said, "Shut up! One blow, and we relieve you from the terror of this night." Abū Shurayḥ al-Khuzā'ī observed them when (Ibn al-Ḥaysumān) shouted at them; they struck and killed him. Then the people surrounded [the place] and seized them. Among others, [the youths] included Zuhayr b. Jundub al-Azdī, Muwarri' b. Abī
[2841] Muwarri' al-Asadī, and Shubayl b. Ubayy al-Azdī. Abū Shurayḥ and his son bore witness against them, [to the effect] that they had entered (Ibn al-Ḥaysumān's) house, some of them holding back others among the people, and then one of them had killed him. (Al-Walīd) wrote to 'Uthmān about (these young men), and he wrote back to put them to death. Thus, (al-Walīd) executed them at the gate of the Official Palace (*al-qaṣr*) in the square (*al-raḥabah*).

Concerning this (event) 'Amr b. 'Āṣim al-Tamīmī said:

Never feed on your neighbors immoderately,
O dissolute men, in the reign (*mulk*) of Ibn 'Affān.
For Ibn 'Affān, whom you have put to the test,
has cut off thieves by the well-established law
of [our] Salvation (*al-furqān*);
Without fail he acts in accordance with the Book,
keeping close watch over every neck
and fingertip among them.

It was transmitted to me in writing by al-Sarī—Shu'ayb—Sayf—'Abdallāh b. Sa'īd—Abu Sa'īd: Abū Shurayḥ al-Khuzā'ī was one of the Companions of the Messenger of God, and he had moved from Medina to Kūfah in order to be closer to the campaigns [against the infidel]. One night, while he was on his roof, his neighbor suddenly shouted for help. He looked over, and there he was with some Kūfan youths who had plotted against him. They began saying to [this neighbor], "Don't shout! It'll only take one blow for us to finish you off!" Then they killed him. So (Abū Shurayḥ) went to 'Uthmān, returning with his family to Medina. When this story gained wide currency, the collective oath
[2842] (*qasāmah*) was instituted for the first time, and thenceforth the statement of the murder victim's representative (*walī*) was accepted [as a valid accusation] against a [specified] group among

the people, so that the people [as a whole] would abstain from killing.[75]

It was transmitted to me in writing by al-Sarī—Shuʿayb—Sayf—Muḥammad b. Kurayb—Nāfiʿ b. Jubayr: ʿUthmān said, "The collective oath is the responsibility of the accused and his close associates (*awliyā'*). Fifty men among them will be made to swear an oath if there is no clear proof [of the guilt of the accused]. If their collective oath falls short [of the requisite number] or if one man abstains, then their oath is to be rejected and the plaintiffs shall be made responsible for swearing (the oath), and if fifty of them do so, their claim [for retaliation] shall be recognized."[76]

It was transmitted to me in writing by al-Sarī—Shuʿayb—Sayf—al-Ghuṣn b. al-Qāsim—ʿAwn b. ʿAbdallāh: Among ʿUthmān's innovations in Kūfah, in addition to the things reported above, is the following. He learned that a public crier, acting on behalf of Abū Sammāl al-Asadī and a small band of Kūfans, would call out when the purveyors came [to the city], "Whoever is here from [the tribe of] Kalb or the Banū Such-and-Such, their tribe (*qawm*) has no assigned residence (*manzil*) in (the city); Abū Sammāl[77] will be responsible for [giving him] a place to stay." So (ʿUthmān) took over the site of the house of ʿAqīl, the visitors' house, and the house of Ibn Habbār. The residence of ʿAbdallāh b. Masʿūd was located among the Hudhayl [tribe] in the place of al-Ramādah; he had lived in the place where his house was, but then turned his house over to be the

75. *walī al-dam*—According to tribal custom (sanctioned by the Qur'ān), the victim's closest male relative was charged with avenging the blood of his kinsman by finding and putting to death his assailant, or by obtaining a suitable blood price (*diyah*). In Ḥanafī law (originally based on the custom of Kūfah), the *qasāmah* is an oath of innocence sworn fifty times by the inhabitants of a locality that they were not involved in the murder of a person whose corpse was found in their midst. Faced with such an oath, the *walī al-dam* could not demand blood retaliation and would have to settle for the blood price. In Mālikī law (based on the custom of ancient West Arabia), the *qasāmah* is a collective oath (also sworn fifty times) by the kinsmen of the slain man, through which they formally accuse and demand vengeance against an alleged murderer. See J. Pedersen and Y. Linant de Bellefonds, "Ḳasām," *EI²*, IV, 689–90.

76. Hence ʿUthmān's ruling reflects—or rather (if we take this account at face value) underlies—both the Ḥanafī and Mālikī conception of the *qasāmah*.

77. Following Ibrāhīm's reading instead of the Leiden text.

guesthouse. Visitors resided in his house in the Hudhayl [quarter] when the area around the mosque became too restricted for them.

It was transmitted to me in writing by al-Sarī—Shu'ayb—Sayf—al-Mughīrah b. Muqsim—one who goes back to the time of the learned men of Kūfah: Abu Sammāl's public crier would call out in the marketplace and the Kunāsah,[78] "Whoever is here from the Banū Such-and-Such, and whoever has no assigned quarter (*khiṭṭah*) in (the city)—Abu Sammāl will be responsible for [giving him] a place to stay." So 'Uthmān took over certain residences [to provide] for visitors.

[2843] A similar account was transmitted to me in writing by al-Sarī—Shu'ayb—Sayf—a client (*mawlā*) of the clan of Ṭalḥah—Mūsā b. Ṭalḥah.

It was transmitted to me in writing by al-Sarī—Shu'ayb—Sayf—Muḥammad and Ṭalḥah: 'Umar b. al-Khaṭṭāb had named al-Walīd b. 'Uqbah as fiscal officer over the bedouin of the Jazīrah, and he resided among the Banū Taghlib.[79] Now both in the Time of Ignorance and in [the era of] Islam, Abū Zubayd lived among the Banū Taghlib until he converted to Islam. The Banū Taghlib were his relatives on his mother's side [literally, his maternal uncles]; these relatives wronged him in regard to a debt owed to him, so al-Walīd seized on his behalf what was owed him. (Abū Zubayd) was grateful to him for this; he became devoted to him and came to visit him in Medina. Now when al-Walīd became governor of Kūfah, (Abū Zubayd) came greeting and extolling him, just as he was accustomed to do in the Jazīrah and Medina. The last time Abū Zubayd came to pay court to al-Walīd, he resided in the visitors' house (*dār al-ḍīfān*); he would go seek out

78. The *Kunāsah* was originally a dumping ground outside the settled compound in Kūfah, but by Umayyad times it had become a caravan station and open-air market, like the *Mirbad* of Baṣrah. Either this locale had already obtained its new function by the time of 'Uthmān, or the story contains a serious anachronism (not uncommon in Sayf's narratives). See H. Djait, "al-Kūfa," *EI*², V, 347.

79. The Banū Taghlib were a Christian tribe who had long since established themselves along the middle Euphrates; they were pastoralists, but kept sheep and goats rather than camels. After an initial phase of resistance, they joined the Muslim Arab forces during the Conquest period and were given a privileged tax status, but were allowed to maintain their Christian religion until well into the Umayyad period. On them see Morony, *Iraq after the Muslim Conquest*, 218–20, 229–32, *et passim*; Donner, *Early Islamic Conquests*, 188, 251–53, *et passim*.

(the governor) and then return [to the visitors' house]. Before this time he was a Christian, but al-Walīd kept after him until, by the end of his governorship, he converted to Islam. His conversion was sincere and, when he became a Muslim, al-Walīd invited him to enter [his entourage], as he was a bedouin and poet at the time.

Now someone came to Abū Zaynab, Abū Muwarriʿ, and Jundub, who were full of bitterness against (al-Walīd) because he had executed their sons; they were keeping a close eye on him. (The informer) said to them, "Do you know that al-Walīd is drinking with Abū Zubayd?" They became excited about this, and Abū Zaynab, Abu Muwarriʿ, and Jundub said to a body of the leading men (*wujūh*) of Kūfah, "This man is your amir; Abū Zubayd is his chosen intimate, and they are both devotees of wine." Now al-Walīd's residence was in the central square (*al-raḥabah*) with [that of] ʿUmārah b. ʿUqbah, and had no door. Then (the Kūfan [2844] notables) arose with (the three accusers) and stormed in upon him from the mosque, for the entryway (of his house) opened into the mosque.[80] Al-Walīd was taken completely by surprise and shoved something under the dais (*al-sarīr*). Without seeking permission, one of (the intruders) reached in and pulled (the object) out. There was a platter of grape seeds and stems, which al-Walīd had pushed aside only out of embarrassment, for they would see his platter with nothing but these leavings. Then (the intruders) got up and went out to the people; some of them began blaming others. When the people heard these things, they began to revile and curse them. Some groups (*aqwām*) were saying, "May God be angry with (the intruder)." But others said, "The Book [of God] compelled him [to do this], and it called upon them to examine [al-Walīd's doings] thoroughly." Now al-Walīd forgave them for this, concealing it from ʿUthmān and taking no steps among the people in regard to it. He disliked arousing dissension among them, so he kept silent about it and bore it patiently.

It was transmitted to me in writing by al-Sarī—Shuʿayb—Sayf—al-Fayḍ b. Muḥammad, who says: I saw al-Shaʿbī sitting

80. In most of the early Islamic administrative centers, the governor's residence adjoined the mosque, usually on the *qiblah* side, thus permitting the governor to enter the mosque to lead the prayer without having to go outside. The arrangement is evidently both functional and symbolic.

with Muḥammad b. ʿAmr b. al-Walīd—namely, (Walīd) b. ʿUqbah—who was the deputy (*khalīfah*) of Muḥammad b. ʿAbd al-Malik. Muḥammad (b. ʿAmr) mentioned Maslamah's campaign,[81] and (al-Shaʿbī) said, "If you could only go back to the time of al-Walīd's campaigns and governorship! If he mounted a campaign against such-and-such [a place], he neither fell short [of his goal], nor did anyone mutiny against him, that is, up to the time he was removed from office. The chamberlain in those times was ʿAbd al-
[2845] Raḥmān b. Rabīʿah al-Bāhilī.[82] And indeed, among the increased benefits that ʿUthmān b. ʿAffān bestowed on the people through (al-Walīd) is that the surplus revenues were distributed to every slave (*mamlūk*) in Kūfah three [times] per month. By this means they were prospering, while their masters (*mawālī*) were not shortchanged of their rations (*arzāq*)."

It was transmitted to me in writing by al-Sarī—Shuʿayb—Sayf—al-Ghuṣn b. al-Qāsim—ʿAwn b. ʿAbdallāh:[83] Jundub and a band of men came to Ibn Masʿūd and said, "al-Walīd is addicted to wine." They spread this around until it was generally talked about among the people.[84] Ibn Masʿūd said, "If a man hides something from us, we do not pursue his flaws nor tear open his veil." Now (al-Walīd) sent for Ibn Masʿūd, who came to [see] him; he rebuked him for this (statement), saying: "Would it be acceptable

---

81. Muḥammad b. ʿAbd al-Malik, a son of the famous Caliph. He had a small role in the Umayyad civil war of 743–44 and died with the other Umayyads at al-Saffāḥ's bloody banquet. See Ibn al-Athīr *Kāmil* (Beirut), IV, 519; V, 295, 394, 430. Maslamah, a son of ʿAbd al-Malik by a slave mother, was commander of the unsuccessful siege of Constantinople in 715–17. A few years later, he suppressed the revolt of Yazīd b. al-Muhallab, and ultimately succeeded Muḥammad b. Marwān as governor of the Jazīrah and Armenia. His career is sketched in Wellhausen, *Arab Kingdom*, 317–19; Hawting, *First Dynasty of Islam*, 73, 76, 83. ʿĀmir b. Sharāḥīl al-Shaʿbī (d. ca. 721) was a famous traditionist and historian; he lived in Kūfah and is usually identified with a moderate pro-Alid tendency. On him see E. L. Petersen, *ʿAlī and Muʿāwiya in Early Arabic Tradition* (Copenhagen: 1964), 28–51, *et passim*; G. H. A. Juynboll, *Muslim Tradition* (Cambridge: 1983), 19–20, 59. These facts suggest that this anecdote should be placed in the 710s.

82. *wa-ʿalā ʾl-bābi yawmaʾidhin ʿAbdu ʾl-Raḥmān. . .* This clause appears to be parenthetical, and perhaps represents a marginal gloss incorporated by copyists into the text.

83. Text: ʿAmr b. ʿAbdallāh. I have followed de Goeje's emendation (*Introductio*, dcxxvi).

84. *ḥattā ṭuriḥa ʿalā alsuni ʾl-nāsi*: literally, "until it was thrown onto the tongues of the people."

for a man like you to respond to people who have suffered an unrequited injury as you have responded about me? What am I hiding? Such statements are only made about someone who is under suspicion." Then they heaped abuse on one another and separated in anger, but nothing else passed between them.

It was transmitted to me in writing by al-Sarī—Shuʿayb—Sayf—Muḥammad and Ṭalḥah: A sorcerer was brought to al-Walīd, and he sent to Ibn Masʿūd to inquire about the divinely ordained punishment[85] for him. (Ibn Masʿūd) asked, "How do you know he is a sorcerer?" (Al-Walīd) replied, "This band of men"—that is, the band of men who had brought (the accused man)—"allege that he is a sorcerer." Then he said (to the accusers), "And how do you know that he is a sorcerer?" They replied, "He himself says so." (Al-Walīd) said, "Are you a sorcerer?" "Yes," he answered. (Al-Walīd) said, "And you know what sorcery is?" "Yes," he said, and sprang toward an ass. He began to mount it from its tail, making it appear to them that he was emerging from its mouth and buttocks. "Kill him," Ibn Masʿūd said. Al-Walīd [2846] rushed off, and they cried out in the mosque that a man was playing with sorcery at al-Walīd's residence.

They approached, and Jundub seized (the opportunity) and stepped forward, saying, "Where is he? Where is he? Let me see him!" Then (Jundub) struck down (the sorcerer), and ʿAbdallāh (b. Masʿūd) and al-Walīd agreed to imprison (Jundub) until (al-Walīd) could write to ʿUthmān. ʿUthmān answered them as follows: "Obtain from (Jundub) an oath in God's name that he did not know your opinion (*ra'y*) regarding (the sorcerer), and that he is telling the truth when he states that he thought the divinely ordained penalty against him had been neglected. Reprimand him and let him go. Direct the people not to act on the basis of [their] personal suppositions nor to carry out the divinely ordained penalties without [authorization from] the government (*al-sulṭān*), for verily we restrain him who is in error and instruct him who does what is right." So (al-Walīd) did this with (Jundub); he

85. *ḥadd*; pl. *ḥudūd*. The punishments ordained in the Qur'ān for a limited number of offenses that "transgress God's limits." These are flogging for fornication, slander against virtuous women, and the drinking of intoxicants; severing of the hand for theft; and execution for highway robbery. See J. Schacht and B. Carra de Vaux, "Ḥadd," *EI²*, III, 20–21.

was left alone because he had carried out a divinely ordained penalty.[86]

Jundub's associates were angry on his account and went to Medina. Among them were Abū Khushshah al-Ghifārī and Jaththāmah b. Ṣa'b b. Jaththāmah, and Jundub [went along] with them. They sought al-Walīd's dismissal, but 'Uthmān said to them, "You are acting on the basis of personal supposition; you are in error about Islam, and you are coming here without permission, so go back." Thus he sent them home. When they returned to Kūfah, every man who nursed some grievance, without exception, came to see them. They [all] concurred on one opinion and expressed it publicly. Then they took advantage of al-Walīd's easy manner, for no curtain screened him off [from the public]. Thus, Abu Zaynab al-Azdī and Abu Muwarri' al-Asadī entered (his home) and snatched his signet ring; then they, along with a few individuals (*nafar*) known to be their supporters, went off to 'Uthmān and testified against him.

'Uthmān sent for (al-Walīd), and when he came, he put Sa'īd b. al-'Āṣ in charge of him. (Sa'īd) said, "O Commander of the
[2847] Faithful, I adjure you by God [not to act hastily], for by God these two are both aggrieved opponents [of al-Walīd]." ('Uthmān) responded, "That will bring you no harm; we are only acting in accordance with our information. If a man commits a wrong, God is responsible for taking vengeance against him; if a wrong is done to him, God is responsible for requiting him."

It was transmitted to me in writing by al-Sarī—Shu'ayb—Sayf—Abu Ghassān Sakan b. 'Abd al-Raḥmān b. Ḥubaysh: A band of Kūfans got together and endeavored to have al-Walīd deposed. Abū Zaynab b. 'Awf and Abū Muwarri' b. Fūlān[87] al-Asadī were deputed to testify against him. So (this group) called on al-Walīd and clung to him assiduously. One day, while they were with him

86. The story is not entirely clear here, even when one identifies the antecedents of all the pronouns. 'Uthmān's intervention is required because Jundub's blow has killed the sorcerer. This intervention demonstrates both 'Uthmān's clemency and his determination to retain authority in his own hands. The version of al-Ya'qūbī (*Ta'rīkh*, II, 190), more concise but clearer, has the sorcerer appearing to enter the animal's buttocks and then reemerge from its mouth.

87. Literally, "the son of so-and-so"; that is, the father's name is not known to the narrator.

in [his] house, al-Walīd fell asleep. Now he had two wives in the bedchamber, separated from the group (*qawm*) by a curtain; one of them was the daughter of Dhū al-Khimār, the other the daughter of Abū 'Aqīl. The group dispersed, but Abū Zaynab and Abū Muwarri' stayed put. One of them took his signet ring, and then both of them left. Al-Walīd awoke [and found] his two wives sitting by his head. Not seeing his signet ring, he asked them about it; however, he found that they knew nothing. Then he said, "Which of the group stayed behind?" "Two men whom we do not know," answered the women, "for they have only recently been coming to visit you." "Describe them," he said. "One of them had a coarse mantle (*khamīṣah*) while the other wore an embroidered cloak (*miṭraf*),[88] and the one with the embroidered cloak was farther away from you," they answered. "[Was he] the tall one?" he asked. "Yes," they answered, "and the one wearing the coarse mantle was closer to you." "[Was he] the short one?" he asked. They responded, "Yes, and we saw his hand touching yours." He said, "That one is Abū Zaynab, and the other is Abū [2848]
Muwarri'. They intend some dastardly deed; would that I knew what!" Then he sought for them but could not find them.

[Meantime] the two of them headed for Medina and approached 'Uthmān. With them was a small band made up of men whom 'Uthmān knew to be among those dismissed from [their] offices by al-Walīd. They all spoke to 'Uthmān, and he said, "Who testifies [against al-Walīd]?" "Abū Zaynab and Abū Muwarri'," they answered, "the others are too fearful." So 'Uthmān said, "How did you see [this]?"[89] "We were members of his entourage," they said. "We entered his presence and he was vomiting up wine." ('Uthmān) said, "Only a man who has been drinking wine vomits it up." Then he sent for (al-Walīd). When he entered 'Uthmān's presence, he saw (his two accusers) and recited [this verse]:

---

88. These two items of clothing are described in M. M. Ahsan, *Social Life under the Abbasids* (London and New York: 1979), 40–41: "The *miṭraf*, a garment made of silk and richly embroidered, was a large piece of cloth, sometimes so large as to enfold the whole body of the wearer. . . . It was generally worn by rich people and high dignitaries." The *khamīṣah* in contrast "was a long coarse stuff that could be used as a blanket," or "a black square blanket having two borders."

89. Text: *Kayfa ra'aytumā*. It might also mean, "What did he look like to you?"

I had no fear at all regarding a matter where I was alone,
so I did not fear thee prying into such things.

Then al-Walīd swore [his innocence] to ('Uthmān) and told him his story. 'Uthmān said, "We shall carry out the divinely ordained penalty [for wine drinking], and the false witness will bring hellfire upon himself. Suffer patiently, dear brother!" Then he gave the command to Sa'īd b. al-'Āṣ and he flogged (al-Walīd)—an act that has left a legacy of enmity between their two sons even to the present day. Al-Walīd was wearing a coarse mantle the day his flogging was ordered, and 'Alī b. Abī Ṭālib ripped it from him.

It was transmitted to me in writing by al-Sarī—Shu'ayb—Sayf—'Ubayd al-Ṭanāfisī—Abū 'Ubaydah al-Iyādī: Abū Zaynab and Abū Muwarri' set out and entered al-Walīd's presence at his house. Two women were there, the daughter of Dhū al-Khimār and the daughter of Abū 'Aqīl, and he was asleep. One of the two women said: "One (of these visitors) bent over him and took his signet ring." (Al-Walīd) asked the two women about it when he woke up, and they said, "We didn't take it." "Who was the last of the group (*qawm*) to remain behind?" asked (al-Walīd). The women responded, "Two men—a short one wearing a coarse mantle
[2849] and a tall one wearing an embroidered cloak—and we saw the one with the coarse mantle bending over you." "That was Abū Zaynab," he said; he set out to look for the two men. Just then they were heading away from a crowd of their associates, while al-Walīd did not understand what they meant to do. The two men came to 'Uthmān and told their story [namely, about al-Walīd's behavior] to him in the presence of the people. So ('Uthmān) sent for al-Walīd; he came, and lo and behold, there were (his two accusers). 'Uthmān summoned them and said, "How do you testify? Do you testify that you saw him drinking wine?" "No," they responded fearfully. 'Uthmān said, "How then [do you testify]?" "We wrung his beard," they said, "as he was vomiting up wine." So ('Uthmān) gave orders to Sa'īd b. al-'Āṣ. He flogged (al-Walīd). Thus a legacy of enmity has been left between their two families.

It was transmitted to me in writing by al-Sarī—Shu'ayb—Sayf—'Aṭīyyah—Abū al-'Arīf and Yazīd al-Faq'asī: In regard to al-Walīd, the people were divided into two factions, the ordinary folk (*'āmmah*) on his side, and the elite (*khāṣṣah*) against him. In regard to this (issue), they were diffident until [the battle of] Ṣiffīn.[90] Then Muʿāwiyah took power (*waliya*) and they began to say, "'Uthmān accused [al-Walīd] without cause." But ʿAlī said to them, "In your censure of ʿUthmān, you are really like the man who thrusts a lance through himself in order to kill the rider seated behind him. What was ʿUthmān's sin in regard to a man whom he struck because of his deeds[91] and dismissed from his office? And what was ʿUthmān's sin in what he did regarding us?"[92]

It was transmitted to me in writing by al-Sarī—Shuʿayb—Sayf—Muḥammad b. Kurayb—Nāfiʿ b. Jubayr: ʿUthmān said, "When someone is flogged [in accordance with] the divinely ordained penalty and then manifests his repentance, his testimony becomes legally acceptable." [2850]

It was transmitted to me in writing by al-Sarī—Shuʿayb—Sayf—Abū Kibrān—a female client (*mawlāt*) of theirs whom he commended highly: Al-Walīd had brought prosperity to the people, to such a degree that he began to distribute shares (*yuqsimu*) to serving girls and slaves.[93] Both free men and slaves were deeply

90. One of the most controversial events in Islamic history, Ṣiffīn was a battle in the summer of 37/657 between Iraqi (mostly Kūfan) forces loyal to ʿUthmān's successor ʿAlī b. Abī Ṭālib and Syrian forces led by the governor of Syria, Muʿāwiyah b. Abī Sufyān, who had challenged ʿAlī's right to the caliphate on the grounds that he had received his office from the rebels who had murdered ʿUthmān. The battle was inconclusive and led to an even more bitterly disputed arbitration issuing in the formal deposition of ʿAlī, though he continued the struggle against Muʿāwiyah until his own death at the hands of an assassin in 40/661. On Ṣiffīn see L. Veccia Vaglieri, "ʿAlī b. Abī Ṭālib," *EI²*, I, 383–84; E. L. Petersen, "ʿAlī and Muʿāwiyah: The Rise of the Umayyad Caliphate 656–61," *Acta Orientalia*, XXIII (1959), 181–96; M. Hinds, "The Siffin Arbitration Agreement," *JSS*, XVII (1972), 93–102; Hawting, *First Dynasty of Islam*, 28–30.

91. Reading *bi-fiʿlihi* instead of *bi-qawlihi*. See de Goeje, *Introductio*, dcxxvi.

92. Presumably the reference is to ʿUthmān's being chosen by the *shūrā* (electoral council) to succeed ʿUmar rather than ʿAlī. The point (in opposition to Shiʿite views) is that ʿAlī admits that ʿUthmān did nothing wrong to obtain the election.

93. Presumably this means that he began to pay stipends drawn from the taxes paid on the conquered lands not only to the Muslim Arab soldiers (*muqātilah*) but also to persons who, as chattels of these soldiers, could have had no claim to a share of revenues derived from conquest. It might also mean that he distributed actual land shares in the newly conquered territories; on this possibility see Donner, *Early Islamic Conquests*, 241–42. The story is probably a subtle piece of anti-Abbasid or anti-Shuʿūbī propaganda, intending to show that the Umayyads strove to do justice to all believers, whatever their personal status or ethnic origin.

distressed at (his deposition), and the serving girls, clad in mourning garments, were heard reciting:

Woe, al-Walīd has been deposed,
while Sa'īd has brought us hunger;
The measure [of rations] does not increase but shrinks,
and maidservants and slaves are made to starve.

It was transmitted to me in writing by al-Sarī—Shu'ayb—Sayf—al-Ghuṣn b. al-Qāsim: When al-Walīd was deposed and Sa'īd named governor, the people used to say:

Let not kingship be far off, since its traits have fled,
nor leadership, when scribes have become chiefs.

It was transmitted to me in writing by al-Sarī—Shu'ayb—Sayf—Muḥammad and Ṭalḥah, according to their [usual] chain of transmission: Sa'īd b. al-'Āṣ arrived [in Kūfah] in the seventh year of 'Uthmān's caliphate. Sa'īd b. al-'Āṣ was the best of [the lineage of] al-'Āṣ b. Umayyah, and his family (*ahl*) was numerous and unbroken from generation to generation. When God conquered Syria [for the Muslims], (Sa'īd) went there and resided with Mu'āwiyah, having been an orphan who had grown up under 'Uthmān's care. Now 'Umar was mindful of [the tribe of] Quraysh, and he asked after (Sa'īd) as part of his inquiry into the affairs of the people. He was told, "O Commander of the Faithful, (Sa'īd) is
[2851] in Damascus in the care of one who is looking after him attentively [namely, Mu'āwiyah], and he is mortally wounded.[94] So ('Umar) sent Mu'āwiyah [the following order]: "Dispatch Sa'īd b. al-'Āṣ to me in a litter." So (Mu'āwiyah) sent him to ('Umar), though he was desperately ill, and no sooner did he reach Medina than he recovered.

('Umar) said, "Nephew, I have heard of your courage and uprightness; grow [in these qualities] and God will cause you to grow in prosperity." ('Umar) said, "Do you have a wife?" "No," replied (Sa'īd). ('Umar) said, "Abū 'Amr [namely, 'Uthmān], what has kept you from finding a spouse for this young man?" "I did

94. *Huwa bi-Dimashqa 'ahdu 'l-'āhidi bihi wa-huwa ma'mūmun bi'l-mawt.*

offer [a bride] to him," said ('Uthmān), "but he refused." Then ('Umar) went out on a journey into the desert and at last came to a watering place. There he encountered four women. They stood up before him, and he said, "What are you doing, and who are you?" "[We are] the daughters of Sufyān b. 'Uwayf," they answered. Their mother was with them, and she said, "[I am] their mother. Our menfolk have perished, and if the men have perished, the women are lost. So find suitable marriage partners for (these girls)." Thus, ('Umar) married Sa'īd to one of them, 'Abd al-Raḥmān b. 'Awf to another, and al-Walīd b. 'Uqbah to the third. Then the daughters of Mas'ūd b. Nu'aym al-Nahshalī came to ('Umar) and said, "Our men have died and [only] the youths are left, so find suitable marriage partners for us." Thus, he married Sa'īd to one and Jubayr b. Muṭ'im to another, and Sa'īd participated in [marriages with] both of these (families). His uncles were men of long experience and early precedence in Islam, and had standing with the Messenger of God. Now 'Umar did not die before Sa'īd had become one of the leading men among the people.

Sa'īd came to Kūfah as governor during the caliphate of 'Uthmān. With him, from Mecca or Medina, set out al-Ashtar, [2852] Abū Khushshah al-Ghifārī, Jundub b. 'Abdallāh, and Abū Muṣ'ab b. Jaththāmah. These were among the men who had gone with al-Walīd to accuse him; now they were returning with (Sa'īd). [Upon arriving in Kūfah] Sa'īd mounted the pulpit. He praised and extolled God, and then said: "By God, I have been sent to you though I did not want to come. But, having been given an order, I found no way to evade carrying it out. Truly dissension (*fitnah*) has raised its snout and eyes, and by God I shall strike it in the face until I suppress it or it defeats me. Truly my soul is troubled today." Then he stepped down.

He inquired about the inhabitants of Kūfah and was preoccupied with their situation. He wrote to 'Uthmān about what he had learned [as follows]: "The affairs of the Kūfans are in turmoil. The nobles among them, the men of distinguished family (*buyūtāt*), and the veterans of the early campaigns (*ahl al-sābiqah wa'l-qudmah*) have been overwhelmed, and the dominant element in these lands are recent immigrants and bedouin who have attached themselves [to the regular forces. It has gotten] to the point that one does not see a man of noble lineage or experience among the settlers or youth (of this place)."[95] ʿUthmān wrote back [as follows]: "To proceed: Among those to whom God granted the conquest of these lands, give preference to the veterans of the early campaigns. Then let those who settled here because of (those veterans) be subordinate to them, unless the latter regard [their] obligations as a burden and fail to perform them, while (the newcomers) do strive to carry out their duties. Keep everyone in his proper rank, and give them all their due measure. For through knowledge about the people is justice attained."

Then Saʿīd sent to the leading men among the veterans of the
[2853] first battles in Iraq (*ahl al-ayyām*) and of al-Qādisiyyah, saying: "You are the 'faces' of those behind you, and the face speaks on behalf of the body. So convey to us the needs of those who are lacking and in want." Then he placed with them as many late joiners and recent immigrants as he could.[96] He secluded himself with Qur'ān reciters (*qurrā'*) and men devoted to prayer in his

95. A crucial passage for the early history of Kūfah. A major source of social and political tension in the city was the difference in status, pay, and privileges between Arab soldiers who participated in the earliest Iraqi campaigns and those who arrived there after the conquests. In this passage, the former class are termed *ahl al-sābiqah wa'l-qudmah*. *Sābiqah* refers to priority in conversion to Islam, and under ʿUmar's administrative system early converts typically enjoyed both higher status and a higher pay scale. A literal translation of the Arabic phrase would thus be "men of religious priority and precedence." The usual terms for the second class are *rawādif*, "those who follow behind, latecomers, recent immigrants"; and *lawāḥiq*, "those who join, attach themselves to others." Such latecomers began to flow into Kūfah (apparently in separate waves or blocs) in ʿUmar's last years, but do not seem to have posed an explosive problem until ʿUthmān's time. This issue has been extensively albeit inconclusively discussed in the recent literature; see Caetani, *Annali*, VII, 358–60; Donner, *Early Islamic Conquests*, 231–39; Hinds, "Kûfan Political Alignments and Their Background in the Mid-Seventh Century A.D.," *IJMES*, II (1971), 349, 352–56; Shaban, *Islamic History*, I, 44–55 (to be read critically); Morony, *Iraq after the Muslim Conquest*, 242, 256.

96. The point here is that these people would be officially recognized as *muqātilah* and as such would be paid stipends (albeit at a reduced rate) from the public treasury. However, they would not be registered as a separate group in their own right, but would be attached to the established tribal and section leaders (the *wujūh*), through whom their pay would be distributed to them. Thus, the newcomers were integrated into the existing administrative structure, but at the same time were locked into a visibly inferior status.

evening gatherings. It was as if Kūfah were dry tinder engulfed by a fire; people kept entirely to their own class, and gossip and rumor were everywhere.

Sa'īd wrote to 'Uthmān about this, and 'Uthmān's herald called out, "The [next] prayer will be performed with the congregation." (The Medinese) assembled, and ('Uthmān) informed them of what he had written to Sa'īd, and what (the latter) had written to him concerning (the Kūfans). He also told them of the gossip and rumor that he had heard. "You have done the right thing," (his hearers) said, "Do not humor (the Kūfans) in this, and do not let them aspire after something for which they are not fit. For if someone undertakes matters in which he is incompetent, he cannot manage them and [instead] corrupts them." Then 'Uthmān said, "People of Medina, prepare yourselves and hold fast, for dissensions (*fitan*) have crept in among you." Then he stepped down [from the pulpit] and repaired to his dwelling. And he quoted [these verses] as a proverb about himself and the kind [of people] who had begun quarreling:

Banū 'Ubayd, have your partisans heard
what you say, and the poet's verse about you?
If you have heard these things, gird yourselves;
for javelins have eyes for the unarmored man.

It was transmitted to me in writing by al-Sarī—Shu'ayb—Sayf—Hishām b. 'Urwah: 'Uthmān had the people learn to recite [2854] one line [of the poem], then two lines, and [finally] lines three to five.

It was transmitted to me in writing by al-Sarī—Shu'ayb—Sayf—Sa'īd b. 'Abdallāh al-Jumaḥī—'Ubaydallāh b. 'Umar, who says, I heard him [*sic*] say to my father: 'Uthmān assembled the Medinese and said, "Men of Medina, the people are tossing and turning in dissension. By God, I will surely recover your (property) for you so that I may transfer it to you, if you think that is right. Is it your opinion that those who shared with the settlers in Iraq (*ahl al-'Irāq*) in the conquests should go and reside there with them in their lands?" Then ('Uthmān's listeners) rose up and said, "O Commander of the Faithful, how will you transfer to us those lands [in Iraq] that God has given us as booty?" He responded,

"We shall sell it to anyone who wishes in exchange for his [present] holdings in the Ḥijāz."[97]

They were delighted, and God thereby opened up for them an opportunity (*amr*) that they had not counted on. So they dispersed, and by (this means) God gave them deliverance from (dissension). All the lots (*suhmān*) in Khaybar, in addition to his other holdings, were combined together by Ṭalḥah b. 'Ubaydallāh. Thus, in exchange for his properties in Khaybar and other places, Ṭalḥah purchased al-Nashāstaj, which was part of the assigned share (*naṣīb*) [of conquered land in Iraq] that belonged to those Medinese who had fought at al-Qādisiyyah and Ctesiphon, but had remained [in Medina] without emigrating to Iraq to settle. (Ṭalḥah) also purchased, in exchange for the Well of Arīs, a property (*shay'*) of 'Uthmān's in Iraq. Marwān b. al-Ḥakam purchased the River of Marwān, which at that time was a swampy canebrake, from ('Uthmān) in exchange for a property of his that
[2855] 'Uthmān had given to him. Certain men from the tribes in Iraq who were drawn from the inhabitants of Medina, Mecca, al-Ṭā'if, Yemen, and Ḥaḍramawt, purchased (land in Iraq) in exchange for properties that they had in the Arabian Peninsula.[98] Among that which al-Ash'ath purchased from ('Uthmān), in exchange for a property of his in Ḥaḍramawt, was a holding in Tīzanābādh.

'Uthmān wrote to the inhabitants of the frontier provinces (*ahl al-āfāq*) about this (exchange), about the number of *jarībs* [99]of

---

97. This and the following paragraphs report a property exchange devised by 'Uthmān to turn public lands in Iraq over to Medinese and Iraqi notables, while obtaining control of some of the wealthiest estates in the Ḥijāz for the caliphate. This policy ensured that the Caliph would have greater revenues under his direct control, while rewarding and presumably reinforcing the loyalty of the leading class in the Muslim community. The ordinary tribesmen in Iraq were of course disadvantaged by this—another cause of the tensions that would ultimately lead to revolt against 'Uthmān. On this exchange see Caetani, *Annali*, VII, 360–62; and M. Hinds, "Kûfan Political Alignments," 359–60. I have been unable to identify the place names given here. As Caetani notes, this account is "singolarmente oscura."

98. *Wa'shtarā minhu rijālun min 'l-qabā'ili bi'l-'Irāqi bi-amwālin kānat lahum fī Jazīrati 'l-'Arabi min ahli 'l-Madīnati wa-Makkata wa'l-Ṭā'ifi wa'l-Yamani wa-Ḥaḍramawta.*

99. The *jarīb* was the standard unit of land in Iraq; in the Sawād (alluvial plain) it was equivalent to sixty square cubits—roughly .16 hectares or .4 acres. See Morony, *Iraq after the Muslim Conquest*, 100–4, 531.

conquered land (*fay'*), and about the conquered land that the inhabitants of the garrison towns had claimed for themselves. (The conquered land) had belonged to the kings, such as Chosroes and Caesar, and to the inhabitants of their dominions who had succeeded them. They had then been abandoned by them. Thus, something was carried out for (the people) that they knew to be good. ('Uthmān) took the [conquered lands] in proportion to the number of the Medinese who had participated in (the conquests in Iraq) and in proportion to their assigned share [of the conquered land]; he then assigned (these lands) to them. They purchased (the newly assigned lands) in exchange for nearby properties in the Ḥijāz, Mecca, the Yemen, and Ḥaḍramawt. (Conquered land in Iraq) was transferred to the inhabitants (of these districts) who were Medinese and who had participated in the conquests.[100]

A similar account was transmitted to me in writing by al-Sarī—Shu'ayb—Sayf—Muḥammad and Ṭalḥah, except as follows: Men from every tribe who had property there [that is, in Iraq] purchased this category [of land], for they wished to take it in exchange for their nearby holdings [in Arabia]. Thus, they took possession [of the conquered lands]; this was lawful for them since it was based on mutual agreement with them and with the people [as a whole] and on a confirmation of [their] rightful claims. However, those who were not veterans of the early campaigns[101] did not obtain as much as those who enjoyed priority [in conversion to Islam], precedence in the councils, leadership, and prestige. Then (the men of lower status) censured [such] preferential treatment, regarding it as an act of harshness and contempt. They concealed [their true feelings] concerning this matter, barely letting them become known, since they had no documentary proof (*ḥujjah*) [to support their claims]; the people were against them. [2856]
Now if some late joiner, whether youth, bedouin, or freedman, attached himself to (these malcontents), he would approve of their speech. Thus, (the malcontents) were on the increase and

100. A somewhat conjectural reading of this passage: *wa-akhadha bi-qadri 'iddati man shahadahā min ahli 'l-Madīnati wa-bi-qadri naṣībihim wa-ḍamma dhālika ilayhim fa-bā'ūhu bi-mā yalīhim min 'l-amwāli bi'l-Ḥijāzi wa-Makkata wa'l-Yamani wa-Ḥaḍramawta yuraddu 'alā ahlihā 'lladhīna shahadū 'l-futūḥa min bayni ahli 'l-Madīnati.*

101. *alladhīna lā sābiqita lahum wa-la qudmata.* See above, note 91.

the people were decreasing [in proportion]. As a result, evil prevailed.

It was transmitted to me in writing by al-Sarī—Shuʿayb—Sayf—Muḥammad and Ṭalḥah: Ḥudhayfah was transferred from the Rayy campaign to the campaign against al-Bāb[102] in order to reinforce ʿAbd al-Raḥmān b. Rabīʿah, and Saʿīd b. al-ʿĀṣ accompanied him as far as Ādharbayjān. Thus, they lent support to the people. (Saʿīd) remained [there] until Ḥudhayfah came back, and then they both returned [to Kūfah].

In this year—that is, the year 30 (650–51)—the signet ring of the Messenger of God fell from ʿUthmān's hand into the Well of Arīs, which lay some two miles [103]from Medina. It was one of the poorest wells in [yield of] water, but its bottom has not been plumbed until this very hour.

How the Signet Ring Fell from ʿUthmān's Hand into the Well of Arīs

It was related to me by Muḥammad b. Mūsā al-Ḥarashī—Abū Khalaf ʿAbdallāh b. ʿĪsā al-Khazzāz, the associate (*sharīk*) of Yūnis b. ʿUbayd—Dāwūd b. Abī Hind—ʿIkrimah—Ibn ʿAbbās: The Messenger of God decided to write letters to the non-Arabs (*aʿājim*), summoning them to Almighty God. A certain man said to him, "O Messenger of God, they will not accept a letter unless it is sealed." So the Messenger of God ordered a signet ring to be
[2857] fashioned out of iron for him, and he placed it on his finger. Then Gabriel came to him and said, "Take it from thy finger." The Messenger of God did so and ordered another signet ring to be made for him. A new signet ring was thus fashioned for him out of copper, and he placed it on his finger. Then Gabriel said to him, "Take it from thy finger." The Messenger of God did so and ordered a signet ring of silver. A signet ring of silver was fashioned for him, and he placed it on his finger. [This time] Gabriel con-

---

102. Bāb al-Abwāb, the Caspian seaport of Darband, which stood astride the main corridor through the Caucasus; it marked the northern limits of the early Arab conquests in this region. See D. M. Dunlop, "Bāb al-Abwāb," *EI²*, I, 835–36; Le Strange, *Eastern Caliphate*, 180.

103. The Arabic mile (*mīl*) is equal to one-third of a *farsakh*—that is, about two km. See W. Hinz, *Islamische Masse und Gewichte*, 63. See also below, note 119.

sented to it, and commanded that "Muḥammad, the Messenger of God" be engraved upon it. Then (Muḥammad) began sealing [his correspondence] with it and writing to those non-Arabs to whom he had decided to write. The inscription on the signet was in three lines.

He wrote a letter to Kisrā b. Hurmuz[104] and sent it with ʿUmar b. al-Khaṭṭāb. ʿUmar brought it to Kisrā and it was recited aloud, but he paid no heed to (the Prophet's) letter. ʿUmar said, "O Messenger of God, may God make me thy ransom! You sit upon a couch woven out of palm fibers, while Kisrā b. Hurmuz sits upon a throne of gold covered with brocade." The Messenger of God replied, "Are you not content for them to have this world while we have the next?" "May God make me thy ransom," said ʿUmar, "I am content." (The Prophet) wrote a second letter and sent it with Diḥyah b. Khalīfah al-Kalbī to Heraclius, Emperor of the Byzantines, summoning him to Islam. (Heraclius) recited it aloud, pressed it to himself, and placed it nearby.

Thus, the Messenger of God wore the signet ring on his finger until Almighty God took him. Then Abū Bakr became caliph and wore it until Almighty God took him. Afterwards ʿUmar b. al-Khaṭṭāb ruled, and he began wearing it until God took him. Then [2858]
after him ʿUthmān b. ʿAffān ruled and wore it for six years. He dug a well in Medina to supply water for the Muslims. He was sitting on the edge of the well and began fiddling with the ring and twisting it around his finger. The ring slipped off and fell into the well. They searched for it and [even] drained the well of its water, but without success. (ʿUthmān) established a magnificent reward for anyone who could bring it [to him] and became deeply depressed on account of (the lost ring). When he despaired of [finding] the signet ring, he ordered another one like it in form and appearance and made of silver to be fashioned for him.[105] On it was engraved "Muḥammad, the Messenger of God." Then (ʿUthmān) placed it on his finger until he perished. When he was

104. Khusraw Parviz or Chosroes II, *regn.* 592–628, not only a symbol of imperial grandeur but also of overweening pride, which brought down not only himself but his kingdom.

105. A somewhat conjectural reading: *amara fa-ṣuniʿa lahu khātamun ahkaru mithlahu ḥalaqahu/khilquhu min fiḍḍatin ʿalā mithālihi wa-shibhihi.*

murdered the ring disappeared from his hand, and no one knew who had taken it.

The Reports Concerning Abū Dharr [al-Ghifārī][106]

In this year—that is, the year 30 (650–51)—occurred (the events) that have been recorded about the affair of Abū Dharr and Muʿāwiyah, and about Muʿāwiyah's exiling him from Syria to Medina. Many things have been recorded as to why he sent him into exile, most of which I am loathe to mention. As for those who excuse Muʿāwiyah in this (affair), they have told a story (*qiṣṣah*) about it [which runs as follows]:

It was transmitted to me in writing by al-Sarī, stating that Shuʿayb had personally recited [it] to him (*ḥaddathahu*) on the authority of Sayf—ʿAṭiyyah—Yazīd al-Faqʿasī: When Ibn al-Sawdā'[107] came to Syria he met Abū Dharr and said, "Abū Dharr, are you not astonished at Muʿāwiyah for saying, 'The public mon-
[2859] eys are God's property.'[108] Verily, everything belongs to God. [It is] as if he intends to seize it [for himself] to the exclusion of the Muslims and to efface the Muslims' names [from the fiscal registers]." Abū Dharr came to (Muʿāwiyah) and said, "What leads you to use the term 'God's property' for the public moneys of the Muslims?" "God be merciful to you, Abū Dharr," responded Muʿāwiyah. "Are we not God's slaves, the public moneys His

106. The matter of Abū Dharr is discussed at length in Caetani, *Annali*, VII, 365—79, with references to the other principal accounts, especially the pro-Shiʿite versions of Yaʿqūbī and Masʿūdī. To these add Balādhurī, *Ansāb*, V, pp. 52–56, whose account mainly follows the tradition of al-Wāqidī and Abū Mikhnaf. Abū Dharr has always been regarded by Shiʿites as a voice protesting the corruption of ʿUthmān's regime and calling for a restoration of the ascetic piety and social equality of the original community. It is not surprising that Abū Dharr has become a potent figure in the ideology of contemporary Islamic radicals. On his life and significance, see Cameron, *Abu Dharr*.

107. Literally, "son of the black woman." A name for the sinister ʿAbdallāh b. Sabā', a legendary (and perhaps fictitious) figure whom a certain strand of tradition identified as the principal source of political dissension as well as extremist Shiʿite ideas in early Islam. He is supposed to have been a converted Yemeni Jew. This report marks his first appearance in Ṭabarī's chronicle; here and later, Sayf b. ʿUmar is the main authority for his activities. On him see M. G. S. Hodgson, "ʿAbd Allāh b. Sabā'," *EI*², I, 51.

108. *al-mālu mālu 'llāh*.

property, the created world His creation, and public authority (*al-amr*) His authority?" (Abū Dharr) said, "Do not use this expression." He continued, "Indeed, I do not say that (the public moneys) do not belong to God, but I shall call them 'the property of the Muslims.'"

(The narrator) continues: Ibn al-Sawdā' came to Abū al-Dardā',[109] who said to him, "Who are you? By God, I think you are a Jew!" Then he came to 'Ubādah b. al-Ṣāmit and attached himself to him. ('Ubādah) brought him to Mu'āwiyah and said, "By God, this is the man who provoked Abū Dharr against you." Now Abū Dharr rose up in Syria and began saying, "O men of wealth, show charity to the poor. To 'those who treasure up gold and silver and do not expend them in the way of God,' declare [that there will be] branding irons from a fire, 'and therewith their foreheads and their sides and their backs shall be branded.'"[110] He persisted in such (statements) until the poor were set aflame and compelled the rich to do this, and until the rich complained about (the behavior) that they were encountering from the people.

Mu'āwiyah wrote [as follows] to 'Uthmān: "Abū Dharr has become a problem for me, and his case has involved such-and-such matters." 'Uthmān wrote him [in response]: "Verily dissension has protruded its snout and eyes and is poised to jump. Do not scrape the scab, but rather dispatch Abū Dharr to me. Send a guide along with him, give him adequate provisions, and treat him gently. Restrain the people and yourself as far as you can, for you will keep control [of affairs] only so long as you keep control of yourself."

So (Mu'āwiyah) sent Abū Dharr away accompanied by a guide. [2860]
When (Abū Dharr) reached Medina and saw the homes (*majālis*) at the foot of Sal',[111] he said, "Declare to the Medinese [that they will suffer] a devastating attack and a terrible war." Then he

109. Abū al-Dardā' al-Anṣārī al-Khazrajī, a Medinese Companion revered for his ascetic piety and his knowledge of the Qur'ān. We are told that he was sent to Damascus to serve as a qāḍī there: in any event, he died and was buried there in 32 (652). See A. Jeffery, "Abū 'l-Dardā'," *EI*², I, 113–14.

110. Qur'ān 9:34–35.

111. Sal' is a hill on the outskirts of Medina, about a kilometer northwest of the Prophet's Mosque.

entered ʿUthmān's presence, and (ʿUthmān) said, "Abū Dharr, why are the Syrians complaining about the wounds inflicted by you?" (Abū Dharr) informed him that it was improper to say, "God's property," nor was it proper for the rich to grasp after wealth. (ʿUthmān) responded, "Abū Dharr, I must carry out my own obligations and take what is owed by the subjects (*raʿiyyah*). I cannot compel them to be ascetics; rather, I am required to summon them to heed God's commandments and to follow the path of moderation." (Abū Dharr) said, "Then permit me to leave, for Medina is no home for me." (ʿUthmān) replied, "And will you replace it save with [someplace] worse?" (Abū Dharr) said, "The Messenger of God commanded me to leave (Medina) when the built-up area (*al-binā'*) reached Salʿ." "Well, do as he commanded you," said ʿUthmān.

(The narrator) continues: So (Abū Dharr) set out until he settled in al-Rabadhah, and there he traced out a mosque.[112] ʿUthmān allocated to him a small herd of camels and gave him two slaves (*mamlūkayn*). He also instructed him [as follows]: "Bind yourself to Medina by compact, lest you revert to being a bedouin." (Abū Dharr) did so.[113]

It was transmitted to me in writing by al-Sarī—Shuʿayb—Sayf—Muḥammad b. ʿAwn—ʿIkrimah—Ibn ʿAbbās: Fearing [that he might revert to] the bedouin way of life, Abū Dharr traveled repeatedly from al-Rabadhah to Medina, though he loved isolation and seclusion. [Once] he entered ʿUthmān's presence, and there with him was Kaʿb al-Aḥbār. (Abū Dharr) said to ʿUthmān, "Be not content that the people refrain from wrongdoing until they strive for the good. One who fulfills the alms tax (*zakāt*) should not confine himself to that until he treats neighbors and

---

112. *wa-khaṭṭa bihā masjidan.* A mosque need not be a building, but can be any patch of ground, properly oriented toward Mecca, which has been marked off and set aside for the ritual prayer. The earliest mosques in the great garrison towns of Iraq appear to have been just such open spaces. See J. Pedersen, "Masdjid," *SEI*, 331.

113. Since Abū Dharr was living outside any settled community of Muslims, it was necessary for him to demonstrate his adherence to Islam and his acceptance of the political and religious authority of the Caliph through a formal pact of submission, precisely as Muḥammad had required the bedouin tribes to do during his lifetime. See Donner, *Early Islamic Conquests*, 263–67, for ʿUmar's attitudes toward the bedouin.

brothers generously and brings [benefit to his] kinsmen." Ka'b said, "He who fulfills the divine commandment (*farīḍah*) has fully met his obligations." Then Abū Dharr raised his staff and struck him, cracking open [his head]. 'Uthmān asked (Abū Dharr) for (the staff) and he turned it over to him. ('Uthmān) said, "Abū Dharr, fear God and restrain thy hand and tongue." For (the latter) had said to (Ka'b), "Son of the Jewess, what are you doing here? By God, you will learn from me, or I shall do violence to you." [2861]

It was transmitted to me in writing by al-Sarī—Shu'ayb—Sayf—al-Ash'ath b. Siwār—Muḥammad b. Sīrīn: Abū Dharr went away to al-Rabadhah on his own account when he saw that 'Uthmān did not incline to him, and Mu'āwiyah expelled his household after him. They set forth to [join] him, taking with them a sack almost too heavy to carry.[114] (Mu'āwiyah) said, "Look at the possessions of this man who proclaims the renunciation of this world!" But (Abū Dharr's) wife responded, "No, by God, it contains neither gold nor silver coins, but only copper ones, so that if his official salary (*'aṭā'*) runs out, he can take some small coins from it for our necessities."

When Abū Dharr settled in al-Rabadhah, the ritual prayer was performed under the leadership of a man who was in charge of the alms tax (*al-ṣadaqah*).[115] He said, "Come forward [to lead the prayer], Abū Dharr." He replied, "No, you go forward, for the Messenger of God said to me, 'Listen and obey, even if a crop-nosed slave be set over you.' You are a slave, though not crop-nosed." This man, a black named Mujāshi', was one of the slaves acquired through the alms tax (*raqīq al-ṣadaqah*).

It was transmitted to me in writing by al-Sarī—Shu'ayb—Sayf—Mubashshir b. al-Fuḍayl—Jābir: Every day 'Uthmān be-

---

114. *wa-ma'ahum jirābun yuthqilu yada 'l-rajuli.*

115. The word used in the preceding paragraph for alms tax is *zakāt*, while here it is *ṣadaqah*. Both words occur in the Qur'ān as financial obligations owed by the believers as acts of purity and sincerity. The Qur'ānic distinction, if any, between them is not clearly defined. In later times *zakāt* came to refer to the compulsory alms tax levied upon Muslims, while *ṣadaqah* had more the sense of voluntary alms, though it often continued to be an exact synonym for *zakāt*. See T. H. Weir, "Ṣadaḳa," *SEI*, 483–84; and J. Schacht, "Zakāt," *SEI*, 654–56. Donner, *Early Islamic Conquests*, 252, 265, argues that there was a systematic distinction during the Conquest period at least: *ṣadaqah* would refer to the tax on animals levied against Muslim nomads, while *zakāt* meant the tax paid by settled Muslims.

stowed the leg of a slaughtered camel on Abū Dharr and the same on Rāfiʿ b. Khadīj. Both of them had withdrawn from Medina because something they had heard was not explained to them. They tried to understand [this statement] but were bested [in discussion about it].

It was transmitted to me in writing by al-Sarī—Shuʿayb—
[2862] Sayf—Muḥammad b. Sūqah—ʿĀṣim b. Kulayb—Salamah b. Nabātah: We set out to perform the Lesser Pilgrimage[116] and came to al-Rabadhah. We looked for Abū Dharr in his house but did not find him. (The people there) said, "He has gone to the watering place." We withdrew and made camp near his house. Then he passed by with a camel's leg, which a servant boy was helping him to carry. He greeted us and then went on to his house. He stayed [there] only briefly before returning. Sitting down before us, he said, "The Messenger of God said to me, 'Listen and obey, even if a crop-nosed Abyssinian be set over you.' I settled at this oasis, and some of the slaves acquired by the Public Treasury (*raqīq māl Allāh*) were in authority over it, and over them was set an Abyssinian, albeit not crop-nosed. I did not know him, but I commend him highly. Every day they have a slaughter camel, and from it I get a leg that I and my household eat." I [namely, the narrator Salamah b. Nabātah] said, "What do you get from the Treasury?" "A small herd of sheep and a troop of camels," he answered. "My servant boy takes care of one, my serving girl the other, and my servant boy will be free at the New Year." (Ibn Nabātah) continues: I said, "Indeed your companions in our presence here are the wealthiest of the people." (Abū Dharr) answered, "Certainly they have no claim on the Public Treasury that I do not equally have."

As for the other (narrators of these events), they recount many things concerning them, repugnant matters that I am loath to repeat.

In this year, according to one (authority), Yazdagird b. Shahriyār fled from Fārs to Khurāsān.

---

116. On this ritual see R. Paret, "'Umra," *SEI*, 604–6. The *ʿumrah*, in contrast to the *ḥajj* proper, may be performed at any time of year; the rites are those of the earlier stages of the *ḥajj* (circumambulation of the Kaʿbah, running between al-Ṣafā and al-Marwah), but there is no visitation of the sacred places outside Mecca and no sacrifice at the conclusion of the ceremonies.

[The Flight of Yazdagird from Fārs to Khurāsān]

According to ʿAlī b. Muḥammad (al-Madāʾinī)—Maslamah—Dāwūd: Ibn ʿĀmir arrived in Baṣrah; then he set out for Fārs and [2863] conquered it. Yazdagird fled from Jūr—which is [the chief town of the district of] Ardashīr-Khurrah[117]—in the year 30 (650–51). Ibn ʿĀmir sent Mujāshiʿ b. Masʿūd al-Sulamī in pursuit, and he followed (Yazdagird) to Kirmān. Mujāshiʿ made camp with the army at al-Sīrajān,[118] while Yazdagird fled to Khurāsān. According to (al-Madāʾinī), [the tribe of] ʿAbd al-Qays states that Ibn ʿĀmir sent Harim b. Ḥayyān al-ʿAbdī [in pursuit of Yazdagird], while [the tribe of] Bakr b. Wāʾil says that he dispatched Ibn Ḥassān al-Yashkurī. (Al-Madāʾinī) says: The soundest (identification) in our opinion is Mujāshiʿ.

According to ʿAlī (b. Muḥammad al-Madāʾinī)—Salamah b. ʿUthmān, who was an accomplished man—a scholar (*shaykh*) among the inhabitants of Kirmān, and al-Faḍl al-Kirmānī—his father: Al-Mujāshiʿ set out from al-Sīrajān and followed Yazdagird. While he was at the castle in Bīmand, the one [now] called Qaṣr Mujāshiʿ, they were struck by blizzards. Snow fell and the cold became intense; the snow reached the height of a lance. The army perished, but Mujāshiʿ and a man with a slave girl were saved. He slit open the stomach of a pack camel, put (the girl) in it and fled. The next day he came back, found her alive, and carried her away. That castle was named Qaṣr Mujāshiʿ because his army perished in it while he was five or six *farsakh*s[119] from al-Sīrajān.

According to ʿAlī (b. Muḥammad al-Madāʾinī)—Abū al-Miqdām—one of his teachers: Mujāshiʿ left Tustar[120] in com- [2864]

117. Jūr, renamed Fīrūzābād in Būyid times, is located about sixty miles due south of Shīrāz. Founded by the first Sasanian king Ardashīr (226–241), it was one of the largest towns of Fārs under that dynasty, and a major link on the road from Iṣṭakhr to the port of Ṣīrāf. See Le Strange, *Eastern Caliphate,* 255–56.

118. Sīrjān was the Sasanian and early Islamic capital of the province of Kirmān down to Būyid times, when the capital was transferred to its modern site. It remained a large and prosperous town until its conquest in 796 (1394) by Tīmur, who left it in ruins as a punishment for its obstinate resistance to his armies. Sīrjān is located about 100 km. southwest of modern Kirmān. See Le Strange, *Eastern Caliphate,* 300–2.

119. A *farsakh* is the most common unit of distance in medieval Islamic texts, equal approximately to six km. See W. Hinz, "Farsakh," *EI²*, II, 812–13.

120. Tustar (or Shushtar) was the second city of the province of Khūzistān,

mand of the Baṣran force. Among them was al-Aḥnaf; he captured, in one sweep during a single morning, 50,000 [horses]. He got to [the one named] al-Ṣafrāʾ bt. al-Gharrāʾ bt. al-Ghabrāʾ first, but ʿUmar took her from him when his agents divided up the booty.

ʿAlī (b. Muḥammad al-Madāʾinī) states: I said to Naḍr b. Isḥāq, "Abū al-Miqdām has recounted this story." He said, "He has told the truth; I have heard it from several of the [tribesmen of] al-Ḥayy and others." His mare was al-Ṣafrāʾ bt. al-Gharrāʾ bt. al-Ghabrāʾ, and he is Mujāshiʿ b. Masʿūd b. Thaʿlabah b. ʿĀʾidh b. Wahb b. Rabīʿah b. Yarbūʿ b. Sammāl b. ʿAwf b. Imruʾul-Qays b. Buhthah b. Sulaym, and his *kunyah* is Abū Sulaymān.

(Al-Madāʾinī) says: In this year, ʿUthmān added the third call to [the Friday prayer and had it proclaimed from] al-Zawrāʾ; he prayed four (*rakʿah*s) at Minā.[121]

In this year, ʿUthmān led the Pilgrimage.

---

located some sixty miles due north of the capital Ahwāz, along the Kārūn River. See Le Strange, *Eastern Caliphate*, 233–36.

121. Al-Zawrāʾ was ʿUthmān's residence in Medina; see above, pp. 31–32/2827, *sub anno* 28; on his innovations in the prayer at the pilgrimage station in Minā, see above, pp. 38–40/2833–2836, *sub anno* 29.

The Events of the Year [2865]

31

(August 24, 651–August 11, 652)

Among these, according to al-Wāqidī, was the expedition of the Muslims against the Byzantines that is called the Battle of the Masts.

It was related to me by Aḥmad b. Thābit al-Rāzī—someone who mentioned it—Isḥāq b. ʿĪsā—Abū Maʿshar: The Battle of the Masts took place in the year 34 (654–55). (Abū Maʿshar) says: In the year 31 (651–52) took place [the expedition] by sea against the blacks[122] and the events that befell Kisrā [that is, the King of Iran, Yazdagird III].

Al-Wāqidī says: The Battle of the Masts and the expedition against the blacks both took place in the year 31 (651–52).

---

122. This is a disastrous naval expedition against Abyssinia (*ghazwat al-asāwidah*) led by ʿAlqamah b. Mujazziz al-Mudlifī, which other authorities date to the year 20 (641). See Caetani, *Annali*, VI, 366–67, VIII, 94. See also Ṭabarī, I, 2595.

The Account of the Battles [of the Masts and against the Blacks]

According to al-Wāqidī—Muḥammad b. Ṣāliḥ—ʿĀṣim b. ʿUmar b. Qatādah:[123] The Syrians set out under the command of Muʿāwiyah b. Abī Sufyān, all Syria having been unified under him.

The Reason Why (Syria) was Unified under [Muʿāwiyah]

It was transmitted to me in writing by al-Sarī—Shuʿayb—Sayf—ʿAbd al-Malik, al-Rabīʿ, Abū Mujālid, Abū ʿUthmān, and Abū Ḥārithah: When Abū ʿUbaydah died, he named ʿIyāḍ b. Ghanm to succeed him in his governorship (*ʿamal*). ʿIyāḍ was [both] his maternal uncle and the son of his father's brother. (ʿIyāḍ) had been governor (*waliya ʿamalan*) in the Jazīrah, but ʿUmar b. al-Khaṭṭāb
[2866] had deposed him. So he attached himself to Abū ʿUbaydah in Syria and remained with him. (ʿIyāḍ) was generous and famed for his liberality, stinting nothing and refusing no one. ʿUmar was told about that, and the people said to him, "You deposed Khālid (b. al-Walīd)[124] and reproved him for being openhanded. Now ʿIyāḍ is the most generous and openhanded of the Arabs, refusing nothing that is asked of him." ʿUmar replied, "How long has ʿIyāḍ faced such demands on his own wealth that he should make use of ours? Even so, I have not altered any decision (*amr*) which Abū ʿUbaydah has laid down."

ʿIyāḍ b. Ghanm died after Abū ʿUbaydah, and ʿUmar named Saʿīd b. Ḥidhyam al-Jumaḥi as military governor of his province (*ammara ʿalā ʿamalihi*). Afterwards Saʿīd died, and to replace him ʿUmar appointed ʿUmayr b. Saʿd al-Anṣārī as military governor. ʿUmar died while Muʿāwiyah held authority over [the provinces

---

123. Reading ʿUmar for ʿUmayr, in accordance with de Goeje, *Introductio*, dcxxvi.

124. Perhaps the most famous and brilliant Arab general of the Riddah wars and the early Conquests; see P. Crone, "Khālid b. al-Walīd," *EI*², IV, 928–29 (reflects a radical critique of the sources); Donner, *Early Islamic Conquests*, 119–32, 135–42, 173–90, *et passim*.

of] Damascus and Jordan and 'Umayr b. Sa'd over [the provinces of] Ḥimṣ and Qinnasrīn. However, Mu'āwiyah b. Abī Sufyān made Qinnasrīn a garrison center for those among the inhabitants of the two Iraqs[125] who came to join him.

When Yazīd b. Abī Sufyān[126] had died, 'Umar named Mu'āwiyah to replace him and announced his death to [his father,] Abū Sufyān. (The latter) said, "Whom have you set over his province ('*amal*), Commander of the Faithful?" "Mu'āwiyah," replied ('Umar). Then (Abū Sufyān) said, "You have treated kinsmen generously." Thus, Jordan and Damascus were combined under Mu'āwiyah. When 'Umar died, Mu'āwiyah held authority over Damascus and Jordan, 'Umayr b. Sa'd over Ḥimṣ and Qinnasrīn, 'Alqamah b. Mujazziz over Palestine, and 'Amr b. al-'Āṣ over Egypt.

It was transmitted to me in writing by al-Sarī—Shu'ayb—Sayf—Mubashshir—Sālim: The first governor ('*āmil*) appointed by 'Uthmān b. 'Affān was Sa'd b. Abī Waqqāṣ, in accordance with the testament of 'Umar. Then 'Umayr b. Sa'd was stricken by plague. He was severely weakened by this and sought leave from 'Uthmān to step down and return to his kinsmen. He granted his [2867]
request and attached Ḥimṣ and Qinnasrīn to Mu'āwiyah's [sphere of authority].

It was transmitted to me in writing by al-Sarī—Shu'ayb—Sayf—Abū Ḥārithah and Abū 'Uthmān—Khālid b. Ma'dān: When 'Uthmān took office, he confirmed 'Umar's governors in Syria.

125. In later centuries, at least, "the two Iraqs" would refer to Iraq 'Arabī—that is, the lower Tigris-Euphrates Valley—and Iraq 'Ajamī (also called al-Jibāl), the Zagros highlands to the east that included the great cities of Hamadhān, Iṣfahān, Rayy, and Kermānshāh. Since the only Arab garrison town (not a very important one) in the latter region was Qum, however, Baṣrah and Kūfah are clearly meant here.

126. Yazīd was Mu'āwiyah's elder brother, and Abū 'Ubaydah's successor as governor of Syria. He commanded one of the four principal expeditionary forces sent in 13/634 to undertake the conquest of Syria, and initially was responsible for Transjordan. When Abu 'Ubaydah and several other senior Companions died in the devastating Plague of 'Amwās in 18/639, the supreme command fell to Yazīd. But Yazīd himself died later in 18/639 during the same epidemic. See Donner, *Early Islamic Conquests*, 151–53; and Lawrence Conrad, "The Plague in the Early Medieval Near East," Ph.D. diss., Princeton University, 1981, 201–15, 225–31.

When ʿAbd al-Raḥmān b. ʿAlqamah al-Kinānī, who had authority over Palestine, died, (ʿUthmān) attached his province to Muʿāwiyah. ʿUmayr b. Saʿd fell victim to a long-drawn-out illness during ʿUthmān's caliphate and sought his permission to step down. (ʿUthmān) granted his request and attached his province to Muʿāwiyah's [sphere of authority]. Thus, [all] Syria was unified under Muʿāwiyah during [the first] two years of ʿUthmān's caliphate. ʿAmr b. al-ʿĀṣ held authority in Egypt in the time of ʿUmar. It was unified under him, and ʿUthmān confirmed him in office at the outset of his caliphate.

Return to al-Wāqidī's Account of the Two Battles Mentioned Above

The Syrians set out under Muʿāwiyah b. Abī Sufyān, while ʿAbdallāh b. Saʿd b. Abī Sarḥ was in command of the men from the maritime districts (*ahl al-baḥr*).[127]

According to (al-Wāqidī): In that same year, Constantine the son of Heraclius[128] set forth, because of what the Muslims had done to them [that is, the Byzantines] in Africa, in a fleet (*jamʿ*) whose like had not been assembled by the Byzantines since the coming of Islam. They set out in five hundred ships and encountered (the Muslims) under ʿAbdallāh b. Saʿd. Some of them provided protection for others, until they yoked together the spars of the Muslims' and Polytheists' ships.

According to Ibn ʿUmar (al-Wāqidī)—ʿĪsā b. ʿAlqamah—ʿAbdal-
[2868] lāh b. Abī Sufyān—his father—Mālik b. Aws b. al-Ḥadathān: I was with them. We met [the enemy] at sea; we had never seen such ships. The wind was against us, so we rode at anchor for an

127. ʿAbdallāh b. Saʿd b. Abī Sarḥ had replaced ʿAmr b. al-ʿĀṣ as governor of Egypt in 25 (645–646), and the naval forces on this expedition were based in Egypt. The sailors were Egyptian Christians, while the warriors on shipboard were Muslim Arabs garrisoned in Egypt.

128. Heraclius' grandson Constans II Pogonatus (641–668), whose official throne name was Constantine. In spite of numerous military disasters, his reign did see much stiffer and more systematic resistance to the Muslim advance than had heretofore been the case. In ways that we do not as yet fully grasp, his efforts must have laid the foundation for the later consolidation of Byzantine control in Anatolia and the Aegean. On his troubled reign see Ostrogorsky, *History of the Byzantine State*, 110–23.

hour; they, too, were anchored nearby. Then the wind abated and we said, "[Let there be] safe passage between you and us." "You and we must all decide on that," they replied.[129] Then we said, "If you like [we shall fight] on the shore, until whoever is the shorter-lived—whether you or us—shall die; but, if you prefer, the sea." (Al-Wāqidī) continues: They gave a snort and said, "The water." We drew up to them and bound the ships fast to one another, until we were striking at one another on both their ships and ours. We fought most bitterly; men fell upon one another, striking with swords and thrusting with daggers upon the ships, until the blood was washed up on shore by the pounding waves. The breakers threw up men's corpses in heaps.

According to Ibn ʿUmar (al-Wāqidī)—Hishām b. Saʿd—Zayd b. Aslam—his father—one who was present on that day: I saw the beach where the wind was driving the waves; upon it was what looked like a great hill of human corpses, and there was more blood than water. A great many Muslims were killed on that day; however, of the unbelievers the number was beyond counting. On that day, the Muslims endured what they had never endured anywhere; then God sent down His aid upon the people of Islam, and [2869]
Constantine turned tail and fled. He was routed due only to the killing and injuries that befell him, for on that day he suffered injuries and lay wounded for some time.

According to Ibn ʿUmar (al-Wāqidī)—Sālim, the client of Umm Muḥammad—Khālid b. Abī ʿImrān—Ḥanash b. ʿAbdallāh al-Ṣanʿānī: The first thing heard from Muḥammad b. Abī Ḥudhayfah[130] occurred while the people were at sea in the year 31 (651–52). When ʿAbdallāh b. Saʿd b. Abī Sarḥ led the people in the afternoon prayer, Muḥammad b. Abī Ḥudhayfah proclaimed "God is most great!". He raised his voice until the imam ʿAbdallāh b. Saʿd b. Abī Sarḥ had finished. Upon leaving, (ʿAbdallāh b. Saʿd) asked, "What is this?" He was told, "That is Muḥammad b. Abī Ḥudhayfah proclaiming God's greatness." So ʿAbdallāh b. Saʿd summoned him and said, "What is this innovation and novelty?" (Muḥammad) replied, "This is no innovation or novelty, for there is no

---

129. *Qālū dhālika lakum wa-lanā minkum.*

130. One of the chief conspirators against ʿUthmān; on his controversial role see below, *sub annis* 34 and 35.

harm in proclaiming the greatness of God." ('Abdallāh) said, "You are not to do it again."

(Al-Wāqidī) continues: Thus Muḥammad b. Abī Ḥudhayfah was silenced. But when 'Abdallāh b. Sa'd led the prayer at sunset, Muḥammad b. Abī Ḥudhayfah proclaimed God's greatness even more loudly than before. ('Abdallāh) sent to him [as follows]: "You are a foolish boy. Indeed, by God, were I not uncertain that the Commander of the Faithful would agree, I would drag you away in fetters." Muḥammad b. Abī Ḥudhayfah replied, "By God, you have no way to do that. If you were determined to do so you could not." ('Abdallāh) said, "Leave off! [It will be] better for you. By God, you are not sailing with us." (Muḥammad) responded, "Shall I sail with the Muslims [at all]?" ('Abdallāh b. Sa'd) said,
[2870] "Go wherever you want."

(Al-Wāqidī) continues: So (Muḥammad b. Abī Ḥudhayfah) sailed by himself, in a ship with no one but the Copts,[131] until they reached [the site of] the Battle of the Masts. [There] they encountered the Byzantine forces, with 500 or 600 ships and with Constantine the son of Heraclius present among them. (Constantine) said, "Give me your counsel." (His officers) said, "We will observe [the situation] tonight." They passed the night striking their wooden clappers[132] while the Muslims spent the night praying and calling on God.

Then the morning came. Constantine had resolved to do battle, and (the Byzantines) drew their ships into tight formation. The Muslims likewise drew [their ships] up in tight formation and lashed them together. 'Abdallāh b. Sa'd formed the Muslims in ranks along the sides of the ships and began ordering them to recite the Qur'ān aloud and to stand fast. The Byzantines jumped into the Muslims' ships and assailed their ranks until they broke them up; they were fighting in disorder.

(Al-Wāqidī) continues: So they fought bitterly. At length God aided the Believers, and they made a great slaughter among the Byzantines, among whom only those who fled made it to safety.

(Al-Wāqidī) continues: 'Abdallāh remained at [the site of] the

131. That is, the sailors *per se.*

132. The Eastern churches traditionally used wooden clappers to summon people to worship, rather than bells or the human voice.

Battle of the Masts for some days after the enemy (*qawm*) had fled, then turned about to come back. Muḥammad b. Abī Ḥudhayfah began saying to the army, "Yes, by God, in reality we have left the *jihād* behind us." His listener would ask, "What *jihād*?" Then (Muḥammad b. Abī Ḥudhayfah) would say, "'Uthmān b. 'Affān has done this and done that." He continued until he had corrupted the people. By the time they approached their own country he had corrupted them, for they were openly saying things that they had not [previously] uttered.

According to Muḥammad b. 'Umar (al-Wāqidī)—Ma'mar b. Rāshid—al-Zuhrī: Muḥammad b. Abī Ḥudhayfah and Muḥammad b. Abī Bakr set out when 'Abdallāh b. Sa'd did. They publicly [2871] proclaimed the shameful deeds of 'Uthmān and how he had altered and contradicted [the policies] of Abū Bakr and 'Umar, and [they declared] that 'Uthmān's blood was lawful. They would say, "('Uthmān) named 'Abdallāh b. Sa'd as governor—a man whose blood the Messenger of God declared to be lawful, and one whose unbelief was revealed in the Qur'ān. The Messenger of God exiled a certain clan (*qawm*) and ('Uthmān) permitted them to return. ('Uthmān) has removed from office the Companions of the Messenger of God and appointed Sa'īd b. al-'Āṣ and 'Abdallāh b. 'Āmir."[133] Word of this got to 'Abdallāh b. Sa'd b. Abī Sarḥ, and he said, "You two will not sail with us." Thus, they sailed on a ship upon which there was not a single Muslim.

The Muslims had met the enemy, while these two were the feeblest[134] in battle of [all] the Muslims. People spoke to them about this, but they replied, "How shall we fight alongside a man whose authority it is not right to accept? 'Abdallāh b. Sa'd was appointed by 'Uthmān, and 'Uthmān has done thus and so." Thus, they corrupted the participants in this battle, having censured 'Uthmān in the severest terms. 'Abdallāh b. Sa'd sent to them, absolutely forbidding them [to act in this manner]. He said, "By God, were I not uncertain that the Commander of the Faithful would agree, I would punish and imprison you both."

According to al-Wāqidī: In this year, Abū Sufyān b. Ḥarb passed away, at the age of eighty-eight.

133. The governors of Kūfah and Baṣrah respectively.
134. Reading *akall* rather than *ankal*. See de Goeje, *Introductio*, dcxxvi.

According to al-Wāqidī: In this year—that is, the year 31 (651–52)—Armenia was conquered by Ḥabīb b. Maslamah al-Fihrī.
[2872] In this year, Yazdagird, the king of Persia (*Fārs*), was killed.

The Cause of [Yazdagird's] Murder

There is a difference of opinion regarding the cause of his murder and how it came about.

According to ʿAlī b. Muḥammad (al-Madāʾinī)—Ghiyāth b. Ibrāhīm—Ibn Isḥāq: Yazdagird fled with a tiny escort from Kirmān to Marw. He sought money from its marzubān,[135] but (the latter) refused him. Then (the people of Marw) were afraid for themselves and sent to the Turks, seeking their support against (Yazdagird). (The Turks) came and sprang a nighttime attack against him; they killed his companions, and Yazdagird fled until he came to the home of a millstone cutter on the banks of the Murghāb.[136] (Yazdagird) took shelter with him overnight, and as he slept (the millstone cutter) killed him.

According to ʿAlī (b. Muḥammad al-Madāʾinī)—al-Hudhalī: Yazdagird came to Marw in flight from Kirmān, and sought money from its marzubān and populace. But they refused him, and in fear of him they sprang a nighttime attack against him. [In spite of what certain authorities allege,] they did not ask the Turks to mobilize an army against him. They killed his companions, while he fled on foot, carrying his belt, his sword, and his crown, until at last he came to the home of a stonecutter on the banks of the Murghāb. When Yazdagird became careless, the stonecutter killed him, took his belongings, and flung his corpse into the Murghāb. In the morning, the people of Marw followed (Yazdagird's) footsteps until they lost track of them at the stonecutter's dwelling. They seized (the stonecutter); he confirmed

135. The *marzubān* or *marzbān* was the military governor of a frontier district under the Sasanian Empire. After the provincial reform of Khusraw Anushirvan, he was theoretically under the authority of the *ispahbadh* in whose quarter his district lay. By the date of this story, obviously, a *marzubān* was usually quite autonomous. See Morony, *Iraq after the Muslim Conquest*, 28, 131, *et passim*.

136. The Murghāb is the river flowing by Marw; shortly east of the city it flows into a shallow desert basin where it is swallowed up. The river was dammed shortly upstream from Marw, and the resultant lake fed the city's complex of canals. See Le Strange, *Eastern Caliphate*, 397–400.

that he had murdered (the king) and brought out his belongings. Then they killed the stonecutter along with the members of his household, and seized his belongings along with those of Yazdagird. Taking (the king's body) out of the Murghāb, they placed it in a wooden coffin.

According to (al-Madā'inī): One of (my authorities) alleges that they bore (Yazdagird's body) to Iṣṭakhr[137] and that he was buried there at the beginning of the year 31 (651–52). Marw was named "The Lord's Enemy" (*Khudhāh Dushman*). Yazdagird had had [2873] intercourse with a woman there, and she bore him a boy deformed on one side. This (birth) took place after Yazdagird had been murdered, (the boy) being named al-Mukhdaj [that is, "the Deformed."] [A number of] children were born to the latter in Khurāsān, and when Qutaybah (b. Muslim) conquered al-Ṣughd[138]or some other place he found two servant girls. He was told that they were among the children of al-Mukhdaj, so he sent them, or one of them, to al-Ḥajjāj b. Yūsuf. He [in turn] sent her to al-Walīd b. ʿAbd al-Malik, and to al-Walīd she bore Yazīd b. al-Walīd al-Nāqiṣ [that is, "the Lacking"].[139]

According to ʿAlī (b. Muḥammad al-Madā'inī)—Rawḥ b. ʿAbdallāh—Khurdādhbih al-Rāzī: Yazdagird came to Khurāsān with Khurrazādh-Mihr, the brother of Rustam. (Khurrazādh-Mihr) said to Māhawayh, the marzubān of Marw, "I have entrusted the king to you." He then left for Iraq. Yazdagird remained in Marw and resolved to depose Māhawayh. Thus, Māhawayh wrote to the Turks, informing them of Yazdagird's flight and his coming to him. He made a compact with (the Turks) to support (the people of Marw) against (Yazdagird), giving them free entry [into Khurāsān].

According to (al-Madā'inī): The Turks reached Marw, and

---

137. That is, to the Sasanian dynasty's city of origin in southwestern Iran.

138. Al-Ṣughd, ancient Sogdiana, can be broadly defined as the region between the middle Oxus and Jaxartes Rivers dominated by Bukhārā and Samarqand. More narrowly, it seems to refer to the district of Samarqand. See Le Strange, *Eastern Caliphate*, 460.

139. The future Yazīd III, a would-be reformer whose caliphate lasted a bare six months in 744. If one wishes to accept this story, Yazīd would have been the great-grandson of Yazdagird, albeit through a lineage of minimal prestige. His nickname comes from his having reduced the pay of his soldiers. See Wellhausen, *Arab Kingdom*, 362–69.

Yazdagird went out to meet them with the companions who were with him. He fought them, supported by Māhawayh with the heavy cavalry (*al-asāwirah*) of Marw.[140] Yazdagird made a great slaughter among the Turks, and Māhawayh feared they would flee. Thus, he went over to them with the heavy cavalry of Marw. Yazdagird's troops fled and were killed, while his horse was
[2874] wounded in the course of the evening. He fled on foot until at last he reached a house with a mill on the banks of the Murghāb, staying there two nights while Māhawayh searched in vain for him. Then on the morning of the second day, the millowner entered his house. Seeing the form of Yazdagird, he said, "What are you, human or demon?" (Yazdagird) responded, "Human. Do you have any food?" "Yes," he said, and brought it to him.

Then (Yazdagird) said, "I am a Magian, so bring me what I need to perform my rites!"[141] So the miller went to one of the cavalrymen and sought from him what he needed to perform Magian rites. (The soldier) asked, "What are you going to do with it?" "I have in my house a man whose like I have never seen, and he has sought this from me." (The cavalryman) brought (the miller) before Māhawayh, who said, "This is Yazdagird. Go and bring me his head." The Magian priest (*mawbādh*) said to him, "That is not yours to do. You know that religion and kingship are twins; one of them cannot stand without the other. If you do [this deed], you will defile all that is most sacred."

The people spoke up, looking upon this as a grave enormity. But Māhawayh cursed them and said to the heavy cavalry, "Whoever speaks up, kill him." Then he commanded a number [of men] to go with the miller and kill Yazdagird. They rushed off, but when they saw him they found killing him hateful and refused to do it. They said to the miller, "You go in and kill him." So he entered (Yazdagird's) presence while he slept; he crushed his head with a stone. Then he severed his head, handed it over to

140. The *asāwirah* (Middle Persian *usvārān*) were the heavy mailed cavalry who constituted the core of the Sasanian army and were its most distinctive element. They carried lances and swords but were most noted as archers, able to launch clouds of arrows against an opponent. Given the cost of their equipment and training, they were inevitably drawn from at least the petty aristocracy. See Morony, *Iraq after the Muslim Conquest*, 198, 207–8, 528.

141. *Innī muzamzimun fa'tinī bimā azamzimu bihi.*

them, and threw his corpse into the Murghāb. A party (*qawm*) of Marwazīs went out, slew the miller, and razed his mill. The bishop of Marw went and removed the body of Yazdagird from the Murghāb and placed it in a coffin. He bore it to Iṣṭakhr and laid it [2875] in a tomb (*nāwūs*).[142]

According to other authorities—Hishām b. Muḥammad (b. Sā'ib al-Kalbī)—his sources: Yazdagird fled after the battle of Nihāvand, this being the last of (the Arabs') battles [against him], until he happened upon the territory of Iṣfahān. In this place there was a man named Maṭyār; he was one of the dihqāns,[143] who was the one charged with fighting the Arabs when the Persians retreated from (that city). He called (the people of Iṣfahān) before him and said, "If I take charge of your affairs and lead you out against (the Arabs), what will you do for me?" They answered, "We shall acknowledge to you your merit." So he led them out and gained some slight victory over the Arabs, by which he won the esteem of (the Iṣfahānīs) and obtained the highest rank among them. When Yazdagird saw the situation in Iṣfahān and halted there, Maṭyār came to visit him that very day. (Yazdagird's) gatekeeper placed (the king) in seclusion and said to (Maṭyār), "Stay here until I gain permission for you to enter his presence."

---

142. *Nāwūs* is derived from Greek *naos*, meaning the inner chamber of a temple where the god's image is placed. Some lexicographers believe that *nāwūs* refers to a Christian burial place; others use it for a sarcophagus. Presumably here it refers to some kind of permanent tomb chamber, either a mausoleum or one cut into the rock.

143. *Dihqān*/pl. *dahāqīn:* literally, "village lord." In Sasanian and early Islamic times, this term referred to the landowners who resided in the villages of Iraq and Iran, and who were the monarch's local fiscal administrators. In Iraq and western Iran, where the monarchy was relatively strong, the dihqans represented the lower levels of the aristocracy. In Khurāsān, however, the situation was more complex. While some dihqans were simply small freeholders and village notables, others were powerful and wealthy figures who governed entire districts. A long text below refers to the *dihqān Marw*—not a petty rural aristocrat in this case, obviously, but the powerful (and presumably autonomous) lord of a major city and oasis. (See above, p. 78 and note 135, where the same figure carries the more precise and prestigious title of *marzubān*). In view of this range of meanings, the best translation might be the comprehensive term "landed aristocracy." In Iraq and western Iran their status began to fall rapidly from the ninth century on, as fiscal rights on the land were increasingly assigned directly to state officials. In modern Persian, *dihqān* simply means "peasant." See Morony, *Iraq after the Muslim Conquest*, 187–89, 199–208; A. K. S. Lambton, "Dihḳān," *EI*², II, 253–54.

But (Maṭyār) jumped on him, smashing open his head in pride and fury, because he had blocked access to (Yazdagird).

The gatekeeper, all bloody, entered Yazdagird's presence. When Yazdagird looked at him, he was terrified. Within the hour he rode out of Iṣfahān. Since the Arabs were distracted from him by their own concerns, he was advised to go to the uttermost part of his kingdom and remain there for a time. So he betook himself to the district (*nāḥiyah*) of Rayy, and when he approached it the overlord (*ṣāḥib*) of Ṭabaristān went forth to meet him. He described his lands to (Yazdagird) and informed him of their impregnability, saying to him, "If you do not respond favorably to me this very day and then come to me, I shall not receive you or give you refuge." Yazdagird refused, but wrote for him [an appointment to] the office of *iṣpahbadh*, for he had previously held a humbler rank than this.

According to one of (the authorities): Immediately thereupon
[2876] Yazdagird proceeded to Sijistān, and then went from there to Marw accompanied by a thousand men from the heavy cavalry.

According to one of (the authorities): Yazdagird entered the territory of Fārs and dwelt there four years; then he came to the territory of Kirmān and remained there two or three years. Now the dihqān of Kirmān pleaded with him to remain with him. However, (Yazdagird) did not do [that], and asked the dihqān to leave a hostage with him [so as to ensure his personal safety]. The dihqān of Kirmān would give him nothing, and so (the king) would not accede to his request. Then (the dihqān of Kirmān) seized him by the leg, dragged him out, and expelled him from his lands. (Yazdagird) moved on from (Kirmān) to Sijistān, remaining there for some five years. Then he decided to settle in Khurāsān, so that he might reassemble his forces and lead them against those who had robbed him of his kingdom. He went with his escort to Marw, accompanied by hostages taken from among the sons of the dihqāns. With him, among the leading members (of this group), was Farrukhzād. When (Yazdagird) reached Marw, he appealed[144] to the kings for aid and reinforcements. [He wrote in

144. Reading *fīhā* with Köprülü 1043, rather than *minhum* as given in Prym's text.

the same vein] to the Lord (*ṣāḥib*) of China, the King of Farghānah, the King of Kābul, and the King of the Khazars.

At that time the dihqān in Marw was Māhawayh b. Māfanāh b. Fayd, the father of Barāz. Māhawayh put his son Barāz in charge of the city proper (*madīnah*) of Marw, and it was under the latter's authority. Yazdagird decided to enter the city in order to inspect it and its citadel (*quhandiz*), but Māhawayh, fearing his deceitful cunning and treachery, had directed his son not to open (the city) to him if he desired entrance. Yazdagird rode out on the day on [2877]
which he intended to enter the city, and made a circuit of the walls. When at last he reached a certain gate and attempted to enter there, Barāz's father shouted to Barāz, "Open!" [But he said this] while he was tightening his belt and signaling [to his son] not to do so. One of Yazdagird's companions spotted this and informed him of it; he sought his permission to behead Māhawayh, saying, "If you do this, affairs in this district will clear up completely for you." But (Yazdagird) refused.

According to one of (the authorities): [It did not happen that way.] Rather, Yazdagird had named Farrukhzād as governor of Marw and ordered Barāz to turn the citadel and the city over to him. However, the city's inhabitants refused [to do] that, because Barāz's father Māhawayh had directed them not to. (Māhawayh) had said to them, "This man [that is, Yazdagird] is no king for you, for he has come to you beaten and wounded, and Marw should not suffer what other districts (*kuwar*) are suffering. Now when I come before you tomorrow [with Yazdagird], do not open the gate." So when he came before them, they did as he had said.

Farrukhzād went and knelt down before Yazdagird, saying, "Marw has proved an intractable problem for you, and these Arabs have caught up with you." (Yazdagird) said, "What is [your] opinion?" (Farrukhzād) replied, "[My] advice is that we get to the country of the Turks and remain there until the situation of the Arabs has become clear to us, for (the Arabs) do not leave a town until they have entered it [as conquerors]." (Yazdagird) said, "I will not do [this], but instead will go back and begin again." Thus, he opposed (Farrukhzād) and did not accept his advice. Yazdagird set out and came to Barāz, the dihqān of Marw, having decided to transfer the dihqānate to Sanjān, the son of his brother.

[2878] Māhawayh, the father of Barāz, learned of that and undertook to destroy Yazdagird. He wrote to Nīzak Ṭarkhān, informing him that Yazdagird had come to him a defeated man. He invited (Nīzak) to come to him in order that they might join hands to seize (Yazdagird), and to make a compact either to kill (Yazdagird) or to enter into a treaty with the Arabs against him. If (Nīzak) would relieve him of (Yazdagird), (Māhawayh) offered to pay him a thousand dirhams per day. He asked (Nīzak) to use a letter to deceive Yazdagird in order to separate him from the main body of his soldiers, thereby leaving him with a weak and powerless segment of his army and personal retinue (*khawāṣṣ*).[145] (Māhawayh) said, "In your letter you should inform him of the sincere counsel and aid against his Arab enemies that you have resolved upon, so that he may overcome them. And you should petition him, in a letter sealed with gold, to confer upon you one of the titles belonging to the men of rank. You should also inform him that you will not come to meet him until Farrukhzād parts from him."

Nīzak wrote to Yazdagird in this manner, and, when his letter reached him, he sent to the magnates of Marw and sought their advice. Sanjān said to him, "I do not think it wise to dismiss your army and Farrukhzād for any reason." Abū Barāz [that is, Māhawayh] responded, "On the contrary, I believe that you should
[2879] join Nīzak and accede to his request." (Yazdagird) accepted his advice, dispersed his troops, and ordered Farrukhzād to go to the reedbeds of Sarakhs.[146] Farrukhzād cried out and rent the neckhole [of his garment]. He took a post in his hands, intending to smite Abū Barāz with it. "You murderers of kings," he said, "you have killed two kings [already], and I believe you will be the murderers of this one!" Farrukhzād did not set out until Yazdagird had written a letter to him in his own hand, [as follows]: "This is a letter to Farrukhzād. Verily you have turned Yazdagird, his household, his children, his retinue, and his pos-

145. *wa-yaḥṣula fī ṭā'ifatin min 'askarihi wa-khawāṣṣihi fa-yakūnu aḍ'afa li-ruknihi wa-ahwana li-shawkatihi*: literally, "so that he would be among a section of his army and his personal retinue, but it would be too weak to be his pillar and too pliant to be his sharp thorn."

146. The marshlands north of the city of Sarakhs; they are formed by the Tajand River as it empties into a shallow basin in the desert. See Le Strange, *Eastern Caliphate*, 395–96.

sessions over safe and secure to Māhawayh, the dihqān of Marw. And hereby I bear witness to this."

Nīzak approached a locality between the two Marws called Ḥulsidān,[147] and, when Yazdagird decided to go out to meet him, Abū Barāz advised him not to meet (Nīzak) bearing arms, lest he suspect his intentions and flee. On the contrary, (Yazdagird) should encounter him with reed pipes and musical instruments. He did so, going out with the escort which Māhawayh had suggested and [even] designated for him. Abū Barāz held back from (Yazdagird), while Nīzak formed his companions into squadrons. When the two men drew near to each other, Nīzak went on foot to receive Yazdagird, while the latter remained on horseback. He commanded that one of his spare horses [be provided] for Nīzak, who mounted it. When (Yazdagird) was in the midst of (Nīzak's) army, the two men halted, and Nīzak said to him, among other things, "Give me one of your daughters in marriage, that I may give you loyal counsel and fight alongside you against your enemy." Yazdagird answered, "You are being insolent with me, you dog!" Then Nīzak was on him with his whip. Yazdagird shouted, "The traitor has betrayed [us]." He fled headlong, while Nīzak's companions laid about with their swords among (Yazdagird's escort), killing many of them.

Yazdagird's flight ended up at a place in the territory of Marw. Dismounting from his horse, he entered the house of a miller and [2880] remained there for three days. Then the miller said to him, "Unhappy man, come out and eat something, for you have fasted for three days now." (Yazdagird) said, "I will only do that in accordance with Magian rites."[148] A man who was one of the Magians (*zamāzimah*) of Marw had brought some wheat for the miller to grind, and the latter spoke to him about performing the Magian rites in his house so that (his guest) might eat. (The man) did so;

---

147. "The two Marws"—Marw and Marw al-Rūdh (or Marw-i Kūchik, "Little Marw"). The latter is a city some 260 km. to the southeast of Marw, also on the Murghāb River and about halfway on the road to Herat. See Le Strange, *Eastern Caliphate*, 397, 404–5. The reading "Ḥulsidān" is supplied by Ibrāhīm, but the mss are unclear. Balādhurī, *Futūḥ al-Buldān*, 316, gives "Junābadh," but this place is located far to the southwest, about 200 km. south of Nishapur—much too far away to fit the context here.

148. *Lastu aṣilu ilā dhālika illā bi-zamzamatin.*

then, when he had gone back, he heard Abū Barāz mentioning Yazdagird. He asked (Abū Barāz's entourage) about (Yazdagird's) jewelry. They described it for him, and he informed them that he had seen (Yazdagird) in a miller's house—a curly-haired man with joined eyebrows[149] and fine teeth, adorned with earrings and bracelets.

Thereupon (Māhawayh) sent one of the heavy cavalry to take (Yazdagird). If he got hold of him, he had orders to strangle him with a bowstring and then to throw him into the river of Marw. They encountered the miller and beat him so that he would point out (Yazdagird), but he would not do so. He denied to them that he knew where (Yazdagird) had gone. But when they decided to leave him, one man among them said to (his companions), "I detect the odor of musk." He discerned the edge of a silk brocade garment in the water, pulled it toward him, and there was Yazdagird.[150] (Yazdagird) implored (the soldier) not to kill him and not to identify him; [in return] he would give him his signet ring, his bracelets, and his belt. The other said, "Give me four dirhams and I will let you go." Yazdagird responded, "Alas, my signet ring is yours, and its price is beyond counting." But he refused, and Yazdagird said, "I had been told that I would be in need of four dirhams and would be reduced to eating cat food, and I have seen this turn out to be the truth."[151] Then (Yazdagird) took one of his earrings and gave it to the miller as his reward for having concealed him.

[2881] (The miller) drew close to (the soldier) as if to speak to him about something, then described (Yazdagird's) hiding place to him.[152] The man notified his companions and they came to (Yazdagird). Then Yazdagird pleaded with them not to kill him, saying, "Woe to you. Verily we find in our books that he who dares to kill kings will be chastised by God with fire in the nether

149. *rajulun jaʿdun maqrūnun:* possibly meaning "a compact and well-made man."

150. There is clearly a minor gap in the narrative at this point; as things stand, Yazdagird's sudden appearance here is quite unexplained.

151. *fa-qad ʿāyantu wa-jāʾanī bi-ḥaqīqatihi.* The last sentence is not really clear and seems to be missing a word or phrase; see de Goeje, *Introductio,* dcxxvi.

152. Again the narrative is confused. This paragraph seems to repeat some of the action, though not the words, of the one preceding. See Prym's note in the apparatus.

world (*al-dunyā*) for his audacity. So do not kill me; take me to the dihqān [of Marw] or send me off to the Arabs, for they will spare the life of a king like me."

But they took the jewelry he was wearing, put him in a sack and sealed it, and then strangled him with a bowstring and threw him in the river of Marw. The water carried him away until he reached the opening of the Razīq [canal],[153] where he was caught and held by a branch. The bishop of Marw came to him and bore him away. He wrapped him in a musk-scented cloak (*ṭaylasān*), placed him in a coffin, and brought him to Bā'y Bābān below Mājān.[154] Having laid (Yazdagird) in a vaulted chamber (*'aqd*), which had previously served as the bishop's audience hall, he walled it up. Abū Barāz asked about one of the two earrings when he noticed it missing; he seized the person who was pointed out to him and beat him to death. He sent what had been obtained (of Yazdagird's jewelry) to the reigning caliph, and the caliph required the dihqān to reimburse the value of the lost earring.

According to others: [It did not happen that way.] Rather, Yazdagird left Kirmān before the Arabs got there, taking the road through al-Ṭabasayn and Quhistān[155]until he approached Marw with some 4000 men. [His intention] was to recruit troops from the Khurāsānīs and to turn back on the Arabs and fight them. He

153. South of Marw (that is, upstream) the Murghāb is dammed up and the water is channeled into four canals, which form the district's great oasis. The Razīq is one of these canals, and flows through the walled city. There is a possibility of confusion, since the name Razīq was sometimes given to the river itself. See Le Strange, *Eastern Caliphate,* 398–401.

154. Bā'y (or Bāb) Bābān: presumably a village near Marw, unidentified. Mājān: the principal western suburb of Marw. See Le Strange, *Eastern Caliphate,* 399, 403.

155. Quhistān is a mountainous province in eastern Iran, lying between the Dasht-i Kavīr (Great Desert) on the west and Khurāsān to the north and east. Al-Ṭabasayn is a dual form referring to the two towns in this province named Ṭabas. (1) Ṭabas Gīlakī or Ṭabas al-Tamr (Tabas of the Dates) lies on the western edge of the province, just on the edge of the desert. As its name implies, it was a date-palm oasis. (2) Ṭabas Masīnān or Ṭabas al-'Unnāb (Tabas of the Jujube Tree) lies some eighty km. due east of Birjand in the southeastern part of the province. It was a substantial town but far less important than Ṭabas al-Tamr. Al-Ṭabasayn sometimes refers to a single one of the two towns; in this case Ṭabas al-Tamr must be meant, since it lay on one of the principal roads from Kirmān and was called by Balādhurī the Gate of Khurāsān. See Le Strange, *Eastern Caliphate,* 359–61, 362–63.

was met by two military chiefs (*qā'idān*) in Marw, each filled with hatred and envy towards the other, one named Barāz and the other Sanjān. Both having pledged obedience to him, he took up residence in Marw.

[2882] He made Barāz his special favorite, and Sanjān envied him on that account. Barāz began seeking the ruin of Sanjān and arousing Yazdagird's fury against him. He so defamed and discredited Sanjān that (Yazdagird) resolved to kill him. He divulged his purpose to a woman of his with whom Barāz was in collusion, and she sent to Barāz a woman who declared that Yazdagird had decided to kill Sanjān. What Yazdagird had resolved to do became general knowledge. Sanjān having been warned, he took precautions and gathered around himself a force like Barāz's companions and the soldiers who accompanied Yazdagird. Then (Sanjān) went to the palace where Yazdagird was residing. Barāz learned of this and stayed clear of Sanjān due to the number of his troops. Sanjān's force so dismayed and frightened Yazdagird that he left his palace in disguise and fled on foot in order to save himself.

He walked some two *farsakh*s (twelve km.) until he came to a certain mill. He entered the millhouse and sat down in fatigue and exhaustion. The millowner saw him with his fine bearing, knotted scarf (*ṭurrah*),[156] and noble attire. He spread [a carpet] for him and he sat down; then he brought him food and he ate. (Yazdagird) stayed with him a day and a night. The millowner having requested some compensation from him,[157] he offered him a jewel-studded belt that he was wearing. This the millowner refused to accept and said, "Instead of this belt, I would really be content with four dirhams with which I might eat and drink." But (Yazdagird) informed him that he had no silver currency (*waraq*) with him. So the millowner flattered him until, when he dozed off, he went up to him with an ax, struck his head with it, and killed him. Then he cut off his head, took the garments and belt

156. *Ṭurrah* usually means "fringe," that is, a fringe of hair or the fringe on a piece of cloth. Here it seems to refer to the long scarf knotted onto the headpiece or crown of Sasanian kings. This scarf was one of the insignia of royalty, and symbolized the divine *farr* or effulgence that marked a king as enjoying the favor of Ahura-Mazda.

157. *Fa-sa'alahu ṣāḥibu 'l-raḥā an ya'mura lahu bi-shay'in.* Literally: "The millowner asked him to command something for him."

that he was wearing, and threw his corpse into the river whose water turned his mill. He slit open his belly and in it inserted some tamarisk roots that were growing in that river in order to [2883] keep (Yazdagird's) body where he had thrown it, lest it should be recognized as it floated downstream. For the murderer feared he would be sought along with the spoils that he had taken. Then he fled in haste.

A man from Ahwāz named Iliyā', who was the archbishop (*muṭrān*) of Marw, learned of the murder. He assembled the Christians who were under his authority and said to them, "The King of the Persians has been murdered, the son of Shahriyār son of Kisrā. Now Shahriyār is the child of Shīrīn the Believer[158], whose just conduct and beneficence toward her coreligionists you must know. This king [that is, Yazdagird] had a Christian lineage.[159] [We should note as well] the honor that the Christians obtained during the reign of his grandfather Kisrā, and the good previously received by them during the regime of certain kings among his ancestors. He even built some churches for them and settled [the debts] of some of their coreligionists. It is therefore fitting for us to bewail the murder of this king because of his generosity, [which was] commensurate with the beneficence of his ancestors and his grandmother Shīrīn toward the Christians. Now I think it right that I build a tomb (*nāwūs*) for him and bear his body in honor in order to inter it there."

The Christians answered, "O archbishop, we submit to your command and concur with you in this opinion of yours." Thus, the archbishop ordered a tomb to be built within the Garden of the Archbishops in Marw. He himself, accompanied by the Christians of Marw, went out and took the corpse of Yazdagird from the river, wrapped it, and placed it in a coffin. Then the Christians who were with him bore it on their shoulders until they brought it to the tomb that he had commanded to be built, interred it [2884] therein, and walled up the doorway.

---

158. Shīrīn, a princess of Armenian birth, became the queen of Khusraw Parviz (592–628). Her love and fidelity for him became one of the great romantic subjects of New Persian literature, first stated in the final chapters of the *Shāh-nāmeh*, but most fully and movingly elaborated in Niẓāmī's *Khusraw va-Shīrīn*, one of the poems in his *Khamseh*.

159. *Wa-li-hādhā 'l-maliki 'unṣurun fī 'l-Naṣrāniyyah.*

The reign of Yazdagird lasted twenty years, among them four years in peace and quiet and sixteen in fatigue due to the ruthless warfare of the Arabs against him. He was the last king of the lineage of Ardashīr son of Bābak to reign, and after him kingship passed to the Arabs.

In this year—that is, the year 31 (651–52)—ʿAbdallāh b. ʿĀmir set out for Khurāsān. He conquered Abrashahr, Ṭūs, Abīward, and Nasā, reaching as far as Sarakhs. In (the same year) he made a peace treaty with the inhabitants of Marw.

[ʿAbdallāh b. ʿĀmir's Campaign in Khurāsān]

It is recounted that when Ibn ʿĀmir had conquered Fārs, Aws al-Tamīmī went before him and said, "May God uphold the amir! Verily this land lies within your grasp, and you have conquered but little of it. Go forward, then, for God is your helper." (Ibn ʿĀmir) replied, "Have we not ordered [the expedition] to set forth?" He disliked showing that he had taken (Aws's) advice.

According to ʿAlī b. Muḥammad (al-Madā'inī)—Maslamah b. Muḥārib—al-Sakan b. Qatādah al-ʿUraynī: Having conquered Fārs, Ibn ʿĀmir returned to Baṣrah. As his deputy in Iṣṭakhr he
2885] appointed Sharīk b. al-Aʿwar al-Ḥārithī, who built the mosque of Iṣṭakhr. A man of the Banū Tamīm entered Ibn ʿĀmir's presence. According to (al-ʿUraynī): We used to say that (this man) was al-Aḥnaf. It is also said [that he was] Aws b. Jābir al-Jushamī—that is, [the clan of] Jusham in [the tribe of] Tamīm.

(The man) said to (Ibn ʿĀmir), "Verily your enemy flees in terror before you and the lands are vast. Set forth, for God is your helper and will glorify His religion." Ibn ʿĀmir mobilized [his forces], ordering the people to outfit themselves for the campaign. He left Ziyād in Baṣrah as his deputy. Proceeding to Kirmān, he led [his troops] to Khurāsān. However, there is a body of authorities (*qawm*) who say that he took the road to Iṣfahān and then went on to Khurāsān.

According to ʿAlī (b. Muḥammad al-Madā'inī)—al-Mufaḍḍal al-Kirmānī—his father: The scholars (*ashyākh*) of Kirmān used to recount that Ibn ʿĀmir made camp with the army at al-Sīrajān, then proceeded to Khurāsān. As his deputy in Kirmān, he appointed Mujāshiʿ b. Masʿūd al-Sulamī. Ibn ʿĀmir traveled by way of the

Desert of Rāvar, which is [a distance of] eighty *farsakhs*.[160] Then he went to al-Ṭabasayn, aiming at Abrashahr, which is the [present] city of Nīshāpūr. Al-Aḥnaf b. Qays was in command of his vanguard. (Al-Aḥnaf) led [his forces] to Quhistān and set out for Abrashahr. The Hephthalites, who were the inhabitants of Herāt, came out against him, but al-Aḥnaf routed them in battle.[161] Then Ibn ʿĀmir came to Nīshāpūr.

According to ʿAlī (b. Muḥammad al-Madāʾinī)—Abū Mikhnaf—Numayr b. Waʿlah—al-Shaʿbī: Ibn ʿĀmir went by way of the Desert of Khabīṣ, then through Khwāst. It is also said that he went by way of Yazd, then through Quhistān.[162] He placed al-Aḥnaf in the vanguard. (The latter) was met by the Hephthalites, but he routed them in battle and came to Abrashahr, and Ibn ʿĀmir laid siege to it. Saʿīd b. al-ʿĀṣ came to Jurjān with the Kūfan army, intending [to proceed to] Khurāsān. But when he learned that Ibn ʿĀmir was besieging Abrashahr he returned to Kūfah. [2886]

According to ʿAlī (b. Muḥammad al-Madāʾinī)—ʿAlī b. Mujāhid: Ibn ʿĀmir laid siege to Abrashahr, conquering one-half of it by assault. The other half was held by Kanārā, together with half of Nasā and Ṭūs. Ibn ʿĀmir, having failed to get through to Marw, negotiated a peace with Kanārā. (The latter) turned over to him his son Abū al-Ṣalt b. Kanārā and his brother's son Salīm as hostages. (Ibn ʿĀmir) sent ʿAbdallāh b. Khāzim to Herāt and Ḥātim b.

---

160. Rāvar (in the Arabic text, Rābar) is a town on the western edge of the Dasht-i Kavīr, some 80 miles north of Kirmān. It is not really clear whether "eighty *farsakhs*" refers to the distance from Kirmān or the distance across the desert to al-Ṭabasayn. See Le Strange, *Eastern Caliphate*, 305. The place names and persons mentioned here recapitulate those given above, p. 87 (text, I, 2881), at the beginning of the account of the death of Yazdagird, but here the fugitive Sasanian king is completely absent.

161. *al-Hayāṭilah*. The Hephthalites or "White Huns" were a nomadic people from central Asia, presumably related to the European Huns of Attila. Their ethnic-linguistic background is unclear, but they seem to have been Turkic. In any case, the Hephthalites appeared on the northeastern frontiers of the Sasanian Empire in A.D. the fifth century and proved an extraordinarily dangerous and persistent foe. In the seventh century, Hephthalite elements were permanent settlers in the region of Herāt. See A. D. H. Bivar, "Hayāṭila," *EI²*, III, 303–4.

162. This passage indicates as clearly as anything can the uncertainties surrounding Ibn ʿĀmir's route. Khabīṣ, like Rāvar, lies on the western edge of the desert but is 160 km southeast of Rāvar, while Khwāst is roughly the same distance from Ṭabas Gīlakī (al-Ṭabasayn) on the desert's eastern margin. Yazd is 320 km. northwest of Kirmān, 240 km. from Rāvar.

al-Nu'mān to Marw. Ibn 'Amir seized the two sons [*sic*] of Kanārā; they came into the possession of al-Nu'mān b. al-Afqam al-Naṣrī,
[2887] and he manumitted them.

According to 'Alī (b. Muḥammad al-Madā'inī)—Abū Ḥafṣ al-Azdī—Idrīs b. Ḥanẓalah al-'Ammī: Ibn 'Āmir captured the inner city (*madīnah*) of Abrashahr by assault and conquered the places around it—Ṭūs, Abīward, Nasā, and Ḥumrān. This took place in the year 31 (651–52).

According to 'Alī (b. Muḥammad al-Madā'inī)—Abū al-Sarī al-Marwazī—his father: I heard Mūsā b. 'Abdallāh b. Khāzim say: My father negotiated a peace with the inhabitants of Sarakhs. 'Abdallāh b. 'Āmir had dispatched him against them from Abrashahr, while he himself established a peace treaty with the inhabitants of Abrashahr. (The latter) gave (Ibn 'Āmir) two serving girls of the lineage of Kisrā—Bābūnaj and Tahmīj, or Tamhīj—and he brought them along with him. He dispatched Umayr b. Aḥmar al-Yashkurī, and he conquered the places around Abrashahr—Ṭūs, Abīward, Nasā, and Ḥumrān—until he ended up at Sarakhs.

According to 'Alī (b. Muḥammad al-Madā'inī)—al-Ṣalt b. Dīnār—Ibn Sīrīn: Ibn 'Āmir sent 'Abdallāh b. Khāzim to Sarakhs, and he conquered it. Ibn 'Āmir acquired two serving girls of the lineage of Kisrā; he gave one of them to al-Nūshajān,[163] while Bābūnaj died.

According to 'Alī (b. Muḥammad al-Madā'inī)—Abū al-Dhayyāl Zuhayr b. Hunayd al-'Adawī—certain Khurāsānī scholars (*ashyākh*): Ibn 'Āmir dispatched al-Aswad b. Kulthūm al-'Adawī—[that is, from the tribe of] 'Adī belonging to the confederation of Ḍabbah[164]—to Bayhaq, which was part of Abra-
[2888] shahr, being separated from the city proper by sixteen *farsakhs*. Al-Aswad b. Kulthūm conquered it but was killed.

According to (al-Madā'inī): He was a man of distinction in his religion. He was one of the companions of 'Āmir b. 'Abdallāh al-'Anbarī, and 'Āmir used to say, after he had been expelled from Baṣrah, "I grieve for nothing in Iraq except thirsting in the noon-

163. A figure unknown to me, who appears nowhere else in Ṭabarī.

164. *'Adī al-ribāb.* According to Lane's authorities, *al-ribāb* was a name for five confederate tribes who shared a common ancestor in one Ḍabbah. The tribes are variously identified in different sources, but all agree on 'Adī and Taym. E. W. Lane, *Arabic-English Lexicon,* III, 1005, col. 1.

day heat,[165] the sonorous harmony of the muezzins, and brethren like al-Aswad b. Kulthūm."

According to ʿAlī (b. Muḥammad al-Madāʾinī)—Zuhayr b. Hunayd—one of his paternal uncles: Ibn ʿĀmir conquered Nīshāpūr and proceeded toward Sarakhs. The inhabitants of Marw sued for peace, and Ibn ʿĀmir sent them Ḥātim b. al-Nuʿmān al-Bāhilī. He made peace with Abraz [*sic*], the marzubān of Marw, in return for [a tribute of] 2,200,000 [dirhams].

According to (ʿAlī b. Muḥammad al-Madāʾinī)—Muṣʿab b. Ḥayyān—his brother Muqātil b. Ḥayyān: He made peace with them in return for [a tribute of] 6,200,000 [dirhams].

In this year, ʿUthmān led the people on the Pilgrimage.

---

165. *Zimāʾ al-hawājir.* Presumably he is referring to the pious discipline imposed by the midday prayer.

The Events of the Year

32

(August 12, 652–August 1, 653)

Among these was the expedition of Muʿāwiyah b. Abī Sufyān to
[2889] the Bosphorus—that is, the straits of Constantinople. He was accompanied by his wife ʿĀtikah bt. Qurṭah b. ʿAbd ʿAmr b. Nawfal b. ʿAbd Manāf. [Her name] is also said to be Fākhitah. This was related to me by Aḥmad b. Thābit (al-Rāzī)—someone who mentioned it—Isḥāq (b. ʿĪsā)—Abū Maʿshar. It is [also] the account of al-Wāqidī.

According to Sayf, in this year Saʿīd b. al-ʿĀṣ named Salmān b. Rabīʿah as his deputy on the frontier (*farj*) at Balanjar,[166] and sent the Syrians to reinforce the army encamped there with Ḥudhayfah. (The Syrians) were commanded by Ḥabīb b. Maslamah al-Fihrī. During (this year) dissension over the command arose between Salmān and Ḥabīb, and the Syrians and Kūfans quarreled with one another about this.

166. Balanjar was in this period the chief political center of the Khazar confederation. Its precise location is uncertain, but it probably lay some 175 km. to the northwest of Bāb al-Abwāb (Darband). After the disastrous campaign recounted below, it was ultimately captured by Umayyad forces ca. 750. See D. M.

[The Disaster at Balanjar]

It was transmitted to me in writing by al-Sarī—Shuʿayb—Sayf—Muḥammad and Ṭalḥah: ʿUthmān wrote to Saʿīd ordering Salmān to attack al-Bāb. (ʿUthmān) wrote also to ʿAbd al-Raḥmān b. Rabīʿah, who was in command at al-Bāb: "Verily greed and arrogance have made many of the subjects (*raʿiyyah*) reckless. Curtail [your campaign] and do not plunge ahead with the Muslims so boldly, for I fear they may face severe trials." But this [letter] did not restrain ʿAbd al-Raḥmān from his goal and he would not stop short of Balanjar. In the ninth year of ʿUthmān's caliphate, he mounted an expedition, and when he reached Balanjar, (his forces) besieged it, setting up mangonels (*majānīq*) and ballistas (*ʿarrādāt*) against it. However, no one could begin to approach (the city) [2890] without being captured or killed. (The defenders) dashed out against the people, and during those days Miʿḍad was killed.

Then the Turks[167] agreed [with the inhabitants of Balanjar] on a day [for a combined attack]. The men of Balanjar sallied forth, the Turks came to their support, and they joined battle. ʿAbd al-Raḥmān b. Rabīʿah—known as Dhū al-Nūr[168]—was struck down, and the Muslims scattered in flight. Those who took the road to Salmān b. Rabīʿah were given sanctuary by him until they left al-Bāb. Those who followed the road to the Khazars and their lands went by way of Jīlān and Jurjān; among these were Salmān

---

Dunlop, "Balandjar," *EI*², I, 985. The following account continues the account of the Armenian-Caucasian wars given above, pp. 8–9 (text, I, 2805–2806, *sub anno* 24) on the authority of Abū Mikhnaf through Hishām b. Muḥammad b. Sāʾib al-Kalbī. However, Ṭabarī has here dropped Abū Mikhnaf's narrative in favor of the one constructed by Sayf b. ʿUmar, perhaps because of the overt pietism of Sayf's version of events.

167. Presumably he is referring to the Turkish elite among the Khazars. These were a confederation of steppe peoples that emerged in the northern Caucasus and lower Volga basin in the mid-sixth century, under the leadership of a Turkish *khagan* and aristocracy. After the Arab invasion in the mid-eighth century, their political center was transferred to Atil, near the mouth of the Volga. Allies of the Byzantines during the bitter war against the Sasanians of the early seventh century, they were among the most formidable opponents faced by the Caliphate in the first three Islamic centuries. See C. E. Bosworth, "Ḳabḳ," *EI*², IV, 343–45; W. Barthold and P. B. Golden, "Khazar," *EI*², IV, 1172–75.

168. Both manuscripts as well as Ibn al-Athīr and Ibn Kathīr read "Dhū al-Nūn."

al-Fārisī and Abū Hurayrah.[169] This people (*qawm*, i.e., the Khazars) took the body of ʿAbd al-Raḥmān and placed it in a casket. It has remained among them, and to this day they ask for rain through him and seek his aid [in battle].

It was transmitted to me in writing by al-Sarī—Shuʿayb—Sayf—Dāwūd b. Yazīd—al-Shaʿbī: By God, Salmān b. Rabīʿah knew more about the vulnerable spots on the body than does a butcher about the joints of a slaughter camel.

It was transmitted to me in writing by al-Sarī—Shuʿayb—Sayf—al-Ghuṣn b. al-Qāsim—a man of the Banū Kinānah: When the expeditions against the Khazars were taking place one after another, they complained and reproached themselves [in the following words]: "We used to be a nation (*ummah*) that no one would approach until this little nation (*ummah*) came along, and we have not been able to stand up to them." They said to one another, "These [men] do not die, for if they were subject to death they would not hurtle themselves against us." Now no one [among the Muslims] was injured in the expeditions against (the
[2891] Khazars) until the very end of ʿAbd al-Raḥmān's campaign. (The Khazars) said [to their soldiers], "Will you not try [to oppose them]?" Thus, they hid themselves in the thickets, and men from the [Muslim] army who were passing by ran into the ambush. They shot at them from (the thickets), killed them, and cut off their heads. Then they summoned one another to war against (the Muslims) and agreed on a day [to attack]. They joined battle, and ʿAbd al-Raḥmān was killed. This [news] spread quickly among the people and they split into two groups. One group [went] toward al-Bāb, where Salmān (b. Rabīʿah) gave them sanctuary before sending them on, while another group proceeded toward the Khazars, coming to Jīlān and Jurjān. Among them were Salmān al-Fārisī and Abū Hurayrah.

It was transmitted to me in writing by al-Sarī—Shuʿayb—Sayf—al-Mustanīr b. Yazīd—his brother Qays—his father: Yazīd b. Muʿāwiyah, ʿAlqamah b. Qays, Miʿḍad al-Shaybānī, and Abū

169. Two of the most famous Companions and transmitters of the Prophet's sayings. The geography in this and the following anecdote seems rather confused, since Jīlān and Jurjān lie on the southern shores of the Caspian—a very indirect route at best to the lands of the Khazars.

Mufazzir al-Tamīmī were in one tent, while ʿAmr b. ʿUtbah, Khālid b. Rabīʿah, al-Ḥalḥāl b. Dhurrī, and al-Qarthaʿ were in another. They were all neighbors of one another in the camp at Balanjar. Al-Qarthaʿ used to say, "How beautiful the sheen of blood on one's garments!" And ʿAmr b. ʿUtbah used to say, addressing a white coat (*qabāʾ*)[170] that he was wearing, "How beautiful the redness of blood upon your whiteness!" The Kufans attacked Balanjar for years during ʿUthmān's caliphate, and during this time no woman [of theirs] was widowed nor was any youth orphaned through violence[171] until the ninth year [of his reign]. [2892]

But in that year, two days before the battle, Yazīd b. Muʿāwiyah saw a gazelle brought to his tent, and he never saw one more beautiful until he was shrouded [for burial] in his blanket. Then he was brought to a grave, at which four persons [were standing], and never did he see a finer and more perfectly level grave until he was interred within it. Now when the people assembled early in the morning [for battle] against the Turks, Yazīd was struck by a stone that smashed his head, and it was as though his clothing was adorned rather than soiled by the blood. Thus, he himself was that gazelle which he had seen, and by that blood upon his coat he became [a figure] of beauty.

One day before the battle, [the Muslims] assembled [for battle] early in the morning, and Miʿḍad said to ʿAlqamah, "Lend me your mantle (*burd*) and I'll tie it around my head." He did this and came to the tower (*burj*) where Yazīd had been struck down. He shot at them, killing [a number] of them. Then (Miʿḍad) was struck by a ballista stone that crushed his skull. His companions dragged him away, burying him beside Yazīd. ʿAmr b. ʿUtbah was wounded; he saw his coat as he had longed [to see it], and was killed.

On the day of the battle, al-Qarthaʿ fought until he had been perforated by lance thrusts, and it was as if his coat were a gar-

170. Ahsan defines the *qabāʾ* as "a kind of sleeved, close-fitting coat resembling the *qafṭān*, generally reaching the middle of the calf, divided down the front and made to overlap the chest." It seems to have been part of the official attire of viziers in the Abbasid period. Ahsan, *Social Life under the Abbasids*, 41–42.

171. Reading *min qatlin* rather than *min qablu*, as given in Prym's text. See de Goeje, *Introductio*, dcxxvi.

ment with a white ground and red ornamentation. The people had remained steadfast until he was wounded, but upon his death they fled.

It was transmitted to me in writing by al-Sarī—Shuʿayb—Sayf—Dāwūd b. Yazīd: On the Day of Balanjar, Yazīd b. Muʿāwiyah al-Nakhaʿī, ʿAmr b. ʿUtbah, and Miʿḍad were struck
[2893] down. As for Miʿḍad, he was wearing a mantle of ʿAlqamah's. He was hit by a sliver from a mangonel stone that pierced his head. Thinking it a minor matter, he placed his hand upon it and died. ʿAlqamah washed (Miʿḍad's) blood but it would not rinse out, and he would wear (the bloody mantle) to the Friday prayer. He said, "Miʿḍad's blood upon it makes it all the more precious to me." As to ʿAmr, he wore a white coat and said, "How beautiful blood would be on this!" Then a stone hit and killed him, soaking (the coat) in blood. As for Yazīd, something was dropped on him and killed him. They had dug out and prepared a grave. Upon examining it, Yazīd said, "How fine it is!" It was revealed in a dream[172] that a gazelle, the most beautiful ever seen, was brought to be buried in (the grave), and he was that gazelle. Yazīd was a gentle and handsome man. When ʿUthmān learned of all this, he said, "Verily, we are God's and to Him we return. The people of Kūfah have been betrayed. O God, forgive them and accept them."

It was transmitted to me in writing by al-Sarī—Shuʿayb—Sayf—Muḥammad and Ṭalḥah: Saʿīd (b. al-ʿĀs) named Salmān b. Rabīʿah as his deputy on that frontier and put Ḥudhayfah b. al-Yamān in command of the campaign with the men of Kūfah. Before this, ʿAbd al-Raḥmān b. Rabīʿah was in charge on that frontier. In the tenth year [of his caliphate], ʿUthmān reinforced (the Kūfans) with Syrian forces under the command of Ḥabīb b. Maslamah al-Qurashī. Salmān claimed to be his superior officer, but Ḥabīb rejected this. The Syrians even said, "We are determined to strike down Salmān." At that point the people (*al-nās*) said, "Then by God we shall smite Ḥabīb and put him in prison. And if you refuse [to recognize Salmān] there will be many slain among both you and ourselves.

Concerning this Aws b. Maghrā' said:

172. *Wa-uriya fīmā yarā 'l-nā'imu anna ghazālan . . . jī'a bihi.* See above, p. 97 (text, I, 2892).

If you smite Salmān we shall smite
your beloved one (*ḥabībakum*),
If you make a journey to Ibn ʿAffān so shall we.
If you act rightly, the frontier is our amir's; [2894]
This (man) is an amir advancing with the squadrons.
We were charged to be the frontier's guardians,
Shooting [arrows] and repelling [assaults]
during the nighttime on every frontier.

Ḥabīb decided to assert his authority over the ruler (*ṣāḥib*) of al-Bāb, as the commander of the army used to do when he came from Kūfah.

When Ḥudhayfah perceived [this situation], he agreed [to accept the command], and [the other Muslims] acknowledged [his status]. Ḥudhayfah b. al-Yamān launched three expeditions against (the Khazars),[173] and during the third campaign ʿUthmān was killed. When they learned of his death, (Ḥudhayfah) said, "O God, curse the murderers of ʿUthmān and those who attacked and reviled him. O God, indeed we used to reprove him, and he would reprove us, whenever those who were with him reproved us and we them. But they have taken that as a ladder to rebellion. O God, do not let them die save by the sword!"

In this year ʿAbd al-Raḥmān b. ʿAwf died. According to al-Wāqidī—ʿAbdallāh b. Jaʿfar—Yaʿqūb b. ʿUtbah: At his death he was seventy-five years old.

According to (al-Wāqidī): In (this year) al-ʿAbbās b. ʿAbd al-Muṭṭalib died at the age of eighty-eight. He was three years older than the Messenger of God.

According to (al-Wāqidī): In (this year) died ʿAbdallāh b. Zayd b. ʿAbd Rabbih, to whom [the use of the voice for] the call to prayer was revealed [in a dream].

According to (al-Wāqidī): In (this year) ʿAbdallāh b. Masʿūd passed away in Medina. He was buried in al-Buqayʿ. One (authori-

173. A very elliptical and difficult passage. The original reads: *fa-lammā aḥassa Ḥudhayfatu aqarra wa-aqarrū fa-ghazāhā Ḥudhayfatu 'bnu 'l-Yamān thalātha ghazawātin.* In the last clause, the pronominal suffix of *ghazāhā* might also refer to Balanjar. Ibn al-Athīr, obviously uncertain of the precise sense of the passage, contents himself with a loose paraphrase: *Kāmil* (Beirut), III, 133.

ty) says that ʿAmmār (b. Yāsir) led the funeral prayer for him, while another states that the prayer was led by ʿUthmān.

[2895] According to (al-Wāqidī): In (this year) Abū Ṭalḥah died.

According to Sayf: In (this year) Abū Dharr died.

The Account of the Death of [Abū Dharr al-Ghifārī]

It was transmitted to me in writing by al-Sarī—Shuʿayb—Sayf—ʿAṭiyyah—Yazīd al-Faqʿasī: When the time for Abū Dharr's death arrived, in Dhū al-Ḥijjah of the eighth year of ʿUthmān's caliphate, (the Angel of Death)[174] came down to Abū Dharr. When (Abū Dharr) perceived him he said to his daughter, "Be watchful, my daughter. Look, do you see anyone?" "No," she replied. "My hour is not yet come," he said. Then he ordered her to slaughter and roast a sheep. Then he said, "When those who are to bury me come to you, say to them: 'Abū Dharr adjures you not to ride off until you have eaten.'" Now when her pot had cooked thoroughly, he said to her, "Look, do you see anyone?" "Yes," she answered, "there are riders approaching." He said, "Put me facing the Kaʿbah." She did so. He went on, "In the name of God, and by God, and [blessings] on the community (*millah*) of the Messenger of God—may God bless him and give him peace."

Then his daughter went out to meet them, saying, "God have mercy on you. Behold Abū Dharr." "Where is he?" they said. She pointed him out to them—he had already died—saying, "Bury him." They said, "We shall indeed. What a true blessing. By this God has honored us." Now these riders were Kūfans, among them Ibn Masʿūd. They turned to him, and Ibn Masʿūd was saying as he wept, "The Messenger of God spoke truly: 'He will die alone and be resurrected alone.'" Then they washed (Abū Dharr's body), wrapped him for burial, performed the prayer for him, and buried him. When they washed to leave, (his daugher) said to them, "Verily Abū Dharr greets you in peace, and he has adjured you not to ride off before you have eaten." So they did this, and carried [his family with them] until they brought them to Mecca. They

174. The text reads *nazala* only, without an explicit subject; I have followed the editor's suggestion (*angelus mortis*). Cf. the account in Balādhurī, *Ansāb*, V, 52–56.

announced his death to 'Uthmān, and he attached (Abū Dharr's) daughter to his own household, saying, "God will be merciful to Abū Dharr, and forgive Rāfi' b. Khadīj for his remaining at home."[175] [2896]

It was transmitted to me in writing by al-Sarī—Shu'ayb—Sayf—al-Qa'qā' b. al-Ṣalt—a certain man—Kulayb b. al-Ḥalḥāl—al-Ḥalḥāl b. Dhurrī: We set out with Ibn Mas'ūd in the year 31 (651–52), numbering fourteen riders, and ultimately came to al-Rabadhah. There was a woman who met us and said, "Behold Abū Dharr." Now we were completely uninformed about his situation, so we said, "Where is Abū Dharr?" She pointed to a tent, and we said, "What's going on with him?" She said, "He left Medina due to a certain matter that he heard about there, so he went away." Ibd Mas'ud said, "What induced him to [live among] the bedouin?" She said, "Indeed the Commander of the Faithful disliked that, but (Abū Dharr) used to say, '(Medina) is corrupt and abased.'"[176] Then Ibn Mas'ūd turned toward him in tears. We washed (his body) and wrapped him. Now his tent was permeated with musk, and we said to the woman, "What is this?" "It was a bit of musk," she replied. "When he was brought [here], he said: 'Witnesses will come to the dead man and find the stench [of death] and will not eat. So dissolve that musk in water and sprinkle the tent with it. Receive them hospitably with its scent and cook this meat, for a group of pious men will see me and take charge of my burial, so receive them hospitably.'"

When we had buried him, she summoned us to eat. After eating, we decided to take her with us. Ibn Mas'ūd said, "The Commander of the Faithful is nearby; we will seek his instructions." We came to Mecca and informed him of the news. He said, "God will be merciful to Abū Dharr and forgive him for settling in al-Rabadhah." When he left [Mecca after the end of the Pilgrimage], he took the road to al-Rabadhah and attached (Abū Dharr's) family to his own household. Then he headed for Medina while we went on to Iraq. Our number included Ibn Mas'ūd, Abū Mufazzir al-Tamīmī, Bakr b. 'Abdallāh al-Tamīmī, al-Aswad b. Yazīd al-

175. Rāfi' b. Khadīj: I have been unable to identify this figure.

176. The sentence is a pun: *hiya ba'adun wa-hiya madīnatun. Ba'ad* is literally "distant, remote." *Madīnah* is a feminine adjective, *madīn*, "burdened by debt."

[2897] Nakhaʿī, ʿAlqamah b. Qays al-Nakhaʿī, al-Ḥalḥāl b. Dhurrī al-Ḍabbī, al-Ḥārith b. Suwayd al-Taymī, ʿAmr b. ʿUtbah b. Farqad al-Sulamī, Ibn Rabīʿah al-Sulamī, Abū Rāfiʿ al-Muzanī, Suwayd b. Mathʿabah al-Tamīmī, Ziyād b. Muʿāwiyah, the brother of al-Qarthaʿ al-Ḍabbī, and the brother of Miʿḍad al-Shaybānī.

In the year 32 (652–53), Ibn ʿĀmir conquered Marwarūdh, al-Ṭāliqān, al-Fāryāb, al-Jūzajān, and Ṭukhāristān.

[ʿAbdallāh b. ʿĀmir's Conquests in Northeastern Iran]

According to ʿAlī (b. Muḥammad al-Madāʾinī)—Salamah b. ʿUthmān and others—Ismāʿil b. Muslim—Ibn Sīrīn: Ibn ʿĀmir dispatched al-Aḥnaf b. Qays to Marwarūdh, and he besieged its inhabitants. They came out and fought, but the Muslims routed them and forced them back into their fortresses. Then (the inhabitants of Marwarūdh) looked out upon them and said, "You Arabs are not what we expected. Had we known what you were like, matters between you and us would be different than they are. Grant us a respite and we will consider now [what we should do]. Go back to your camp (*ʿaskar*)." Thus, al-Aḥnaf returned, going out to them the next morning [to learn of their decision]. They had made ready for war, and one of the Persians emerged from the city with a letter (*kitāb*) and announced, "I am an ambassador; give me safe-conduct." [Al-Aḥnaf] did so. Now he was an envoy from the marzubān of Marwarūdh,[177] [and was also] his nephew and interpreter, and the letter from the marzubān was [addressed]
[2898] to al-Aḥnaf. He read out the letter, which said: "To the commander of the army: We praise God, in whose hand are the turns of fortune, who transfers kingship as He pleases, who lifts up whomever He wishes after abasement and brings down whomever He wishes after exaltation. Verily He has called upon me to arrange peace terms with you on the [same] lines as my grandfather's submission and with the marks of honor and rank that your master (*ṣāḥibkum*) thinks appropriate. So welcome to you, and rejoice. I summon you to peace between you and us, based on [the following conditions]: (1) that I render you a tribute

177. The text has *marzubān Marw,* but presumably Marwarūdh is intended.

(*kharāj*) of 60,000 dirhams; (2) that you confirm me in the possession of what Kisrā, King of Kings, conceded (*aqṭaʿa*) to my great-grandfather, when he killed the serpent that was feeding on the people and cutting the roads that connected the lands and villages along with their inhabitants; (3) that you take no tribute whatever from any member of my house; (4) that the office of marzubān not be taken from my house and given to any other. If you do all this for me, I will come forth to you. I have sent you my nephew Māhak to seek a pact with you concerning my requests."

According to (al-Madā'inī): Al-Aḥnaf wrote back to him [as follows]: "In the name of God, the Merciful, the Compassionate. From Ṣakhr b. Qays, commander of the army, to Bādhān, marzubān of Marwarūdh, and the heavy cavalry (*asāwirah*) and the Persians who are with him. Peace be upon him who follows the Divine guidance, believes truly, and fears God. To proceed: Your nephew Māhak has come before me, striving sincerely on your behalf and informing [me] about you. I have presented (your proposals) to the Muslims who are with me. I and they agree as to what is incumbent upon you. We consent to what you have [2899]
sought and laid before me. To wit: you will pay 60,000 dirhams from your plowmen, peasants, and cropland to me and to any commander of the Muslims who is governor (*wālī*) after me. Excepted are those lands that you have mentioned, where Kisrā—the man who wronged himself—conceded them to your great-grandfather, because he had killed the serpent that had done evil in the earth and cut the roads, 'for the earth belongs to God and His Messenger, and he bequeaths [it] to whomever He pleases among His servants.'[178] You, together with the heavy cavalry who are with you, are likewise obliged to aid the Muslims and fight their enemies, if the Muslims so wish and decide. In return you are owed the aid of the Muslims against anyone who fights against those members of your community (*millah*) who follow you. Concerning all this there will be a letter from me, which you will possess after me. And no tribute whatever [will be levied] against you [personally] nor against any relatives from your household. If you become a Muslim and follow the Messenger, you and your brother will have from the Muslims [the same]

178. Qur'ān 7:125.

salary, status, and rations [which the Muslims receive].[179] For this you have my covenant (*dhimmah*), the covenant of my father, and the covenants of the Muslims and their ancestors. The contents of this document have been duly witnessed by Jaz' b. Muʿāwiyah—or, Muʿāwiyah b. Jaz'—al-Saʿdī; Ḥamzah b. al-Hir-
[2900] mās and Ḥumayd b. Khiyār, both men of [the tribe of] al-Māzin; and ʿIyāḍ b. Warqa' al-Usaydī. It was written by Kaysān, protegé (*mawlā*) of the Banū Thaʿlabah, on Sunday in the Month of God, al-Muḥarram." It was sealed by the commander of the army, al-Aḥnaf b. Qays, and the inscription on al-Aḥnaf's seal reads, "We serve God."

According to ʿAlī (b. Muḥammad al-Madā'inī)—Muṣʿab b. Ḥayyān—his brother Muqātil b. Ḥayyān: Ibn ʿĀmir made peace with the inhabitants of Marw, and sent al-Aḥnaf with 4,000 [troops] to Ṭukhāristān. He advanced until he made camp at the [present-day] location of the Castle of al-Aḥnaf [in the district of] Marwarūdh.[180] Against him assembled the inhabitants of Ṭukhāristān, al-Jūzajān, al-Ṭāliqān, and al-Fāryāb, constituting three armies of 30,000 (men). News about them and the forces that they had gathered having reached al-Aḥnaf, he sought counsel from the people. They differed among themselves: one person said, "We should return to Marw"; another said, "We should go back to Abrashahr"; another said, "We should remain here and call for reinforcements"; another said, "We should confront them in battle."

According to (al-Madā'inī): That evening, al-Aḥnaf went out for a walk in the camp and listened to the people's conversation. He was passing by the people in one tent, where a man was kindling a fire under a stew or kneading dough. They were all talking about the enemy. One of them said, "The right choice for the commander [namely, al-Aḥnaf] is to set out in the morning and to meet this nation (*qawm*) in battle, wherever that may happen, for (this) will be more alarming to them." The man with the stew or dough responded, "If he does that, he and all of you will commit a
[2901] blunder. Will you order him to confront the elite forces of the

179. The bracketed words are from Ibn Ḥubaysh, *Kitāb al-Ghazawāt.*
180. On Qaṣr al-Aḥnaf, on the Murghāb a day's march from Marwarūdh, see Le Strange, *Eastern Caliphate,* 405.

enemy by advancing into their territory? [In that case] he would face a great number with but a few men. If they have room to maneuver, they will annihilate us. Instead, the right thing is for him to establish his camp between the Murghāb and the mountain, putting the Murghāb on his right and the mountain on his left. Then the enemy, though they may be many, will only confront him with a number equal to that of his own comrades." Then al-Aḥnaf returned [to his own tent] convinced by what the latter had said. He fixed his camp where he was. Now the people of Marw sent to him, proposing to fight alongside him, but he responded, "I dislike having to seek the aid of Polytheists. Adhere to the terms that we agreed upon with you. For if we are victorious, we shall stand on what we promised you. And if they are victorious over us and fight you, then fight on your own behalf."

According to (al-Madā'inī): Now the Muslims were performing the afternoon prayer when the Polytheists suddenly fell upon them. But the Muslims fought back staunchly, and the two sides held their ground until the evening as al-Aḥnaf recited the verse of Ibn Ju'ayyah al-Aʿrajī:

He who most rightly hates not fatal destiny
    is a strong youth who has no children.

According to ʿAlī (b. Muḥammad al-Madā'inī)—Abū al-Ashhab al-Saʿdī—his father: At night al-Aḥnaf and the Muslims encountered the inhabitants of Marwarūdh, al-Ṭāliqān, al-Fāryāb, and al-Jūzajān, fighting with them the whole night through. Then God routed (the enemy), and the Muslims slew them until at last they [2902]
came to Raskan,[181] which is some twelve *farsakhs* from the Castle of al-Aḥnaf. The marzubān of Marwarūdh had delayed bringing the (tribute) in return for which (the Muslims) had made peace with him in order to see how things would turn out for them.

According to (al-Madā'inī): When al-Aḥnaf gained the victory, he sent two men to the marzubān with orders not to speak to him until they had arrested him. They did [that], and knowing that they would not treat him thus unless they had been victorious, he fulfilled his obligations.

According to ʿAlī (b. Muḥammad al-Madā'inī)—al-Mufaḍḍal al-

181. Not identified.

Ḍabbī—his father: Al-Aqraʿ b. Ḥābis went to al-Jūzajān, al-Aḥnaf having sent him with a detachment (*jarīdah*) of cavalry to pursue remnants of the [enemy] forces routed by al-Aḥnaf. (Al-Aqraʿ) fought them and the Muslims ranged far and wide. Some of the [Muslim] cavalrymen were killed, but then God bestowed victory over them upon the Muslims and they routed and killed them. Ibn Kuthayyir al-Nahshalī said, in a long poem:

The rain clouds poured when the struggles
of valiant youths began at al-Jūzajān,
As far as the two castles in the district (*rustāq*) of Khūṭ;
the two bald men (*al-aqraʿān*) commanded them there.

In this year occurred the peace between al-Aḥnaf and the inhabitants of Balkh.

[2903]

[The Peace between al-Aḥnaf and the People of Balkh]

According to ʿAlī (b. Muḥammad al-Madāʾinī)—Zuhayr b. Hunayd—Iyās b. al-Muhallab: Al-Aḥnaf advanced from Marwarūdh to Balkh and besieged its inhabitants. They made peace with him in return for [a tribute of] 400,000 [dirhams]. He was satisfied with that, appointing his nephew, Asīd b. al-Mutashammis, as his deputy to collect from them the amount agreed to in the peace treaty. Then he marched on to Khwārazm and remained there until winter assailed him. He asked the opinion of his comrades, and Ḥuṣayn [b. al-Mundhir][182] said to him: ʿAmr b. Maʿdīkarib has said to you:

If you cannot do a thing, put it aside;
pass it by to get to what you can do.

According to (al-Madāʾinī): So al-Aḥnaf ordered [his forces] to move on, then departed for Balkh. His nephew took charge of the (tribute) agreed to in the peace treaty, and while he was levying [it] from them the festival of Mihrgān[183] came around. They gave

182. The bracketed words are from Ibn al-Athīr, *Kāmil* (Beirut), III, 127, *sub anno* 31.

183. Mihrgān is the autumn festival (16 Mihr/26 October), one of the two chief

him gifts—gold and silver vessels, dīnārs and dirhams, furniture, and garments. Al-Aḥnaf's nephew said, "This is the (tribute) in return for which we made peace with you." "No," they responded, "this is rather something that we do on this day for our ruler in order to conciliate him." (Al-Aḥnaf's nephew) said. "What is this day?" They answered, "Mihrgān." "I do not know what that is," he said. "I hate to refuse (such gifts), for perhaps they are rightfully mine. But I will take them and set them aside until I can look into (the matter)." Thus, he took possession of [2904] them. When al-Aḥnaf arrived, he informed him [about the matter], and (al-Aḥnaf) asked (the Balkhīs) about it. They told him what they had told his nephew. (Al-Aḥnaf) said, "I will bring (these gifts) to the commander." Thus, he took them to Ibn ʿĀmir and informed him about them. (Ibn ʿĀmir) said, "Keep them, Abū Baḥr, they are yours." "I have no need of them," replied (al-Aḥnaf). Then Ibn ʿĀmir said, "Take them for yourself, Mismār."

According to (al-Madā'inī)—al-Ḥasan: So al-Qurashī seized them greedily.

According to ʿAlī (b. Muḥammad al-Madā'inī)—ʿAmr b. Muḥammad al-Murrī—certain shaykhs of the Banū Murrah: As his deputy in Balkh al-Aḥnaf appointed Bishr b. Mutashammis.

According to ʿAli (b. Muḥammad al-Madā'inī)—Ṣadaqah b. Ḥumayd—his father: When Ibn ʿĀmir made peace with the inhabitants of Marw and al-Aḥnaf did the same with the inhabitants of Balkh, Ibn ʿĀmir dispatched Khulayd b. ʿAbdallāh al-Ḥanafī to Herat and Bādghīs,[184] which he conquered. Then later they rebelled (*kafarū*) and sided with Qārin.

According to ʿAlī (b. Muḥammad al-Madā'inī)—Maslamah—Dāwūd: When al-Aḥnaf returned to Ibn ʿĀmir, the people said to the latter, "No one has been granted such conquests as you—Fārs, Kirmān, Sijistān, and all Khurāsān." Ibn ʿĀmir responded, "I

---

festivals of ancient Iran, Nawrūz (New Year in the spring) being the other. See Morony, *Iraq after the Muslim Conquest*, 73, 201–2.

184. Bādghīs is the fertile district in northwestern Afghanistan lying between the Herāt river (Harī Rūd) and the Murghāb river. It is crossed by several tributaries of the Murghāb, but the main source of water appears to be wells and the rainfall inspired by the Paropamisus mountains on the east. Through it pass the roads connecting Herāt to Marwarūdh. See Le Strange, *Eastern Caliphate*, 412–15; Barthold, *Historical Geography*, 47–49.

shall most assuredly manifest my gratitude to God for that by setting forth in a state of consecration from this place in order to perform the Lesser Pilgrimage (*ʿumrah*). Thus, he performed the rites of consecration in Nishapur for a Lesser Pilgrimage. When he came to ʿUthmān, the latter rebuked him for having consecrated himself in Khurāsān, saying, "You should observe this (rite) strictly at the time when the people consecrate themselves."[185]

According to ʿAlī (b. Muḥammad al-Madāʾinī)—Maslamah—al-
[2905] Sakan b. Qatādah al-ʿUraynī: As his deputy in Khurāsān, Ibn ʿĀmir appointed Qays b. al-Haytham, and Ibn ʿĀmir departed from (that province) in the year 32 (652–53).

According to (al-Madāʾinī): Qārin assembled a great host from the district (*nāḥiyah*) of al-Ṭabasayn and from the inhabitants of Bādghīs, Herāt, and Quhistān, and advanced with 40,000 [men]. [Qays b. al-Haytham][186] said to ʿAbdallāh b. Khāzim, "What is your opinion?" (Ibn Khāzim) said, "I think you should leave the country, for I am its governor (*amīr*). I possess a diploma of appointment (*ʿahd*) from Ibn ʿĀmir: if war breaks out in Khurāsān, I will be its governor." And he produced a document that he had deliberately fabricated.[187] Qays, disgusted by his seditious conduct, left him and the country and came to Ibn ʿĀmir. Ibn ʿĀmir rebuked him, saying, "You have come to me having abandoned [those] lands in wartime." (Qays) answered, "ʿAbdallāh (b. Khāzim) came to me with a diploma of appointment from you." Then (Ibn ʿĀmir's) mother said to him, "I forbade you to leave

185. On the *ʿumrah* see above, note 116. On the rites of consecration for pilgrimage to Mecca, see A. J. Wensinck and J. Jomier, "Iḥrām," *EI*², III, 1052–53. The rites includes a formal statement of intention, a major ablution, shaving and cutting the hair, and the donning of a distinctive white garment, as well as abstinence from shaving, intercourse, etc. while performing the pilgrimage. The point of ʿUthmān's rebuke is that pilgrims are supposed to assume a state of *iḥrām* only at certain specified places, variously 50 to 200 km. from Mecca. Ibn ʿĀmir's piety here is an excessive act that deviates from the established practice of the Muslims.

186. Supplied from a marginal note in Ibn Ḥubaysh, *Kitāb al-Ghazawāt*. See editor's note.

187. Cf. the account of this event given above, p. 37 (text, I, 2832, *sub anno* 29) on the authority of Sayf b. ʿUmar. Note that Sayf connects Ibn Khāzim's usurpation not with the revolt of Qārin but with the turbulence following the murder of ʿUthmān.

both of them in one place, precisely because (Ibn Khāzim) would make trouble for (Qays)."

According to (al-Madā'inī): Ibn Khāzim went out against Qārin with 4000 [troops], commanding the people to take grease [with them]. When he drew near (Qārin's) camp, he gave orders to the people, saying, "Let every man of you tie any rag or cotton or wool he has with him around the head of his spear, then soak it with grease—ghee, oil, pitch, or melted fat." Then he moved on until, when evening had come, he sent ahead his vanguard of 600 [men]. He then followed behind them; upon his orders the people set their spear heads ablaze, with some of them taking the flame from others.

According to (al-Madā'inī): His vanguard reached Qārin's camp, coming upon them in the middle of the night. They had sentinels, and (the Muslim vanguard) skirmished with them, sowing utter confusion among them by the night attack while they themselves were secure. Ibn Khāzim approached (the enemy), who saw fires right and left, moving forward and backward, sinking and rising, [2906] but without being able to perceive anyone. They were terrified by this, even as Ibn Khāzim's vanguard was fighting them. Then Ibn Khāzim led the Muslims down upon them. Qārin was slain and the enemy fled, while the Muslims followed them, killing them at will and capturing many prisoners. A shaykh of the Banū Tamīm claims that the mother of al-Ṣalt b. Ḥurayth was one of the captives taken from Qārin['s followers], as were the mothers of Ziyād b. al-Rabī' and 'Awn Abū 'Abdallāh b. 'Awn the jurist.

According to 'Alī (b. Muḥammad al-Madā'inī)—Maslamah: Ibn Khāzim seized Qārin's camp and its contents, and wrote to Ibn 'Āmir of the victory. The latter was pleased and confirmed (Ibn Khāzim) in authority over Khurāsān. He continued in power there until after the Battle of the Camel, when he came to Baṣrah. He was present at the uprising (*waq'ah*) of Ibn al-Ḥaḍramī, with whom he was staying in the house of Sunbīl.[188]

---

188. Ibn al-Ḥaḍramī was one of Mu'āwiyah's agents during the first civil war. In 38 (658) he was dispatched to Baṣrah to incite the Tamīm to revolt against 'Alī. The revolt was quashed by 'Alid loyalists from the tribe of Azd, however, and Ibn al-Ḥaḍramī was killed in the fray. Wellhausen, *Arab Kingdom*, 100, citing Ṭabarī, I, 3414ff., on the authority of al-Madā'inī.

According to ʿAlī (b. Muḥammad al-Madāʾinī)—al-Ḥasan b. Rashīd—Sulaymān b. Kathīr al-Khuzāʿī:[189] Qārin assembled a great host against the Muslims, and the Muslims became anxious about their situation. Al-Qays b. al-Haytham said to ʿAbdallāh b. Khāzim, "What is your opinion?" He responded, "My opinion is that you cannot handle the great number of those who confront us. Betake yourself to Ibn ʿĀmir and inform him about the vast forces who have assembled against us. As for us, we shall remain in these strongholds and hold them off until you reach us with your reinforcements."

According to (al-Madāʾinī): So Qays b. al-Haytham departed, for as he pondered [this advice], Ibn Khāzim showed [him] a diploma of appointment, saying, "Ibn ʿĀmir has made me governor of Khurāsān." Then (Ibn Khāzim) advanced against Qārin, gaining the victory over him. He wrote of the victory to Ibn ʿĀmir, and the latter confirmed him in authority over Khurāsān. The Baṣrans continued to attack those Khurasānīs who had not negotiated peace terms [with them]; and when they came back [to Baṣrah], they left behind 4000 men to complete the task.[190] (These latter) kept on with this until the civil war (*fitnah*) broke out.

189. Not the famous Abbasid *naqīb* in Khurāsān. See de Goeje, *Introductio*, dcxxvii.

190. *Fa-idhā rajaʿū khallafū arbaʿata ālāfin li'l-ʿaqabati.*

The Events of the Year 33 [2907]

(August 2, 653–July 21, 654)

In (this year), according to al-Wāqidī, took place Muʿāwiyah's attack on the Castle of the Woman (Ḥiṣn al-Mar'ah) in the Malaṭyah district of the land of the Byzantines.

In (this year) took place ʿAbdallāh b. Saʿd b. Abī Sarḥ's second campaign in Ifrīqiyah when its inhabitants repudiated [their] pact (*ʿahd*).

In (this year), according to al-Wāqidī, ʿAbdallāh b. ʿĀmir sent al-Aḥnaf b. Qays to Khurāsān, for its inhabitants had rebelled. (Al-Aḥnaf) conquered both [of the cities named] Marw—Marw Shāhjān[191] by a negotiated peace (*ṣulḥan*), and Marw al-Rūd after a bitter struggle. ʿAbdallāh b. ʿĀmir followed him out; he laid siege to Abrashahr and occupied it through a negotiated peace.

According to the account related to me by Aḥmad b. Thābit al-Rāzī—someone who related it [to him]—Isḥāq b. ʿĪsā—Abū Maʿshar: [The conquest of] Cyprus took place in the year 33 (653–

191. On this epithet see Le Strange, *Eastern Caliphate*, 398.

54). But in the report on Cyprus we have already given the statement of those who contradict (Abū Ma'shar) concerning this.[192]

In (this year) 'Uthmān b. 'Affān sent certain Iraqis into exile in Syria.

The Exile of the Kūfans Whom ['Uthmān] Sent [to Syria][193]

The authorities (*ahl al-siyar*) disagree on this matter.

Sayf's account was transmitted to me in writing by al-Sarī—Shu'ayb—(Sayf)—Muḥammad and Ṭalḥah: Sa'īd b. al-'Āṣ used to receive visits only from those long settled in Kūfah, the leading men among the veterans of the earliest battles in Iraq (*wujūh ahl al-ayyām*) and of al-Qādisiyyah, the Qur'ān reciters (*qurrā'*)[194]
[2908] among the Baṣrans, and the pious-minded. These were his confidants when he retired [to his private quarters]. Now when he held audience for the people, then everyone might enter his presence. One day he held such an audience and the people came in. While they were seated conversing with one another, Ḥubaysh al-Asadī—whose father's name is unknown[195]—said, "How gener-

---

192. See above, pp. 25–31 (text, I, 2819–2827, *sub anno* 28). Ṭabarī follows the date given by Wāqidī, while the principal authority for his narrative is Sayf b. 'Umar.

193. Another version of the story, based largely on the tradition of Wāqidī and more sympathetic to the dissidents, is given in Balādhurī, *Ansāb*, V, 39–47. Ṭabarī also gives a version derived from Wāqidī, pp. 120–25 (text, I, 2915–2921).

194. *Qurrā'* is a mysterious word. It was long interpreted in both Islamic and Orientalist tradition as "Qur'ān-reciters"—that is, men of piety and religious learning who had memorized the Qur'ān. At first such men provided the ideological cadres for the Muslim forces, but later on they became the nucleus of the irreconcilable Kharijite opposition to "worldly power." But this concept was challenged by M. A. Shaban, *Islamic History*, I, pp. 50–55, where he argues that they are the early settlers in Iraq, *ahl al-qurā*, literally, "men of the towns." Shaban's suggestion remains controversial, but has been further explored by Martin Hinds and G. Juynboll. Hinds ("Kûfan Political Alighnments," pp. 357–61) identifies them as those early comers to Iraq who had the fewest followers, and hence possessed the lowest status and received the most meager rewards; however, he still connects them with the term *qāri'*, "Qur'ān-reciter." The literature is accurately but inconclusively reviewed in T. Nagel, "Ḳurrā'," *EI*², V, 499—500. In the present context the traditional interpretation seems to fit reasonably well, as also above, p. 58 (text, I, 2853). Cf. the "respectable classes" here with those mentioned above, pp. 57–58 (text, I, 2852–2853, *sub anno* 30).

195. *Ḥubaysh b. Fulān al-Asadī.* Prym has restored the name as "Khunays,"

ous is Ṭalḥah b. ʿUbaydallāh!" Saʿīd b. al-ʿĀṣ replied, "If a man possesses a place like al-Nashāstaj,[196] it is only right that he be generous. By God, if I possessed anything like it, God would provide you all with a life of ease."

Then ʿAbd al-Raḥmān b. Ḥubaysh, who was a young man, said, "By God, I wish that this al-Milṭāṭ[197] were yours"—that is, the Sasanian crown lands alongside the Euphrates adjacent to Kūfah. (The others present) said, "May God seal your mouth! By God, we have something in mind for you!" Then Ḥubaysh said, "[He's only] a boy, don't argue with him."[198] "He desires part of our Sawād for himself," they said. (Ḥubaysh) answered, "And for you he desires many times as much." "He should desire nothing either for us or for himself," they said. "What's wrong with you," said (Ḥubaysh). "By God, you ordered him to do this," they responded. Then (a group of them) rose up in fury against (ʿAbd al-Raḥmān b. Ḥubaysh) and seized him—al-Ashtar, Ibn Dhī al-Ḥabakah, Jundub, Ṣaʿṣaʿah, Ibn al-Kawwāʾ, Kumayl, and ʿUmayr b. Ḍābiʾ.[199] His father [that is, Ḥubaysh al-Asadī] went to his de-

but "Ḥubaysh" seems much better attested. See 2908, note b, and de Goeje, *Introductio,* dcxxvii. In favor of Prym's reading, however, see Balādhurī, *Ansāb,* V, 40: ʿAbd al-Raḥmān b. Khunays al-Asadī, *ṣāḥib shuraṭihi.*

196. On Ṭalḥah's acquisition of al-Nashāstaj, see above, p. 60 (text I, 2854, *sub anno* 30).

197. Al-Milṭāṭ is the land bordering the Euphrates in the vicinity of Kūfah; al-Muthannā camped there with his army on the eve of the battle of Buwayb. See Yāqūt, *Muʿjam al-buldān,* IV, 633; other references in Ṭabarī: I, 2185, 2255, 2485.

198. Reading *lā tujāruhu* instead of *lā tujāzuhu.* See de Goeje, *Introductio,* dcxxvii. The subject of the sentence is somewhat ambiguous; it reads, "*Qāla Ḥubayshun ghulāmun fa-lā tujāruhu.*" Caetani (*Annali,* VIII, 32) takes Saʿīd b. al-ʿĀṣ as the implicit subject and translates as follows: "Disse Saʿīd: 'Khunays é un ragazzo. . . .'" This alters the dialogue's dramatic development, obviously, since Saʿīd becomes the boy's chief defender, but it does not change the general import of the passage—namely, that Ḥubaysh and his son were attacked with little provocation by inveterate malcontents. In any case, I believe that Caetani is in error here: (1) Ḥubaysh (that is, Khunays) is clearly a mature man in the text, not "un ragazzo"; (2) Ibn al-Athīr, *Kāmil* (Beirut), III, 138, paraphrases the sentence to read, *Qāla abūhu ghulāmun fa-lā tujāzuhu,* and "*abūhu*" can only be the subject of "*qāla.*"

199. Maqrīzī, *al-Muqaffā,* gives fuller versions of two of these names: Kaʿb b. Dhī al-Ḥabakah al-Nahdī, and Kumayl b. Ziyād. See de Goeje, *Introductio,* dcxxvii. Note also that, according to Sayf's account, several of the dissidents here were involved in the conspiracy against Saʿīd's predecessor as governor of Kūfah, al-Walīd b. ʿUqbah. Ṭabarī's list should be compared with the one given in Balādhurī, *Ansāb,* V, 40–41.

fense, but they beat both of them unconscious. Saʿīd (b. al-ʿĀṣ) began pleading with them [to stop], but they refused scornfully until they had worked their will upon (their two victims).

The Banū Asad [that is, the tribe of Ḥubaysh and his son] having heard of this, came—Ṭulayḥah among them—and surrounded the [governor's] palace. The tribes (*al-qabā'il*) mounted [their horses] and took refuge [from the Banū Asad] with Saʿīd, saying, "Get us to safety." So Saʿīd went out to the people and said, "O people, a band of men (*qawm*) have quarreled and fought with one another, but now God has bestowed forgiveness [on
[2909] them]." Then (the Banū Asad) backed off and returned [home], continuing their discussions. Saʿīd censured (the assailants of Ḥubaysh and ʿAbd al-Raḥmān)[200] and sent them away. When the two men recovered consciousness, he said, "Are you alive?" "Your associates (*ghāshiyah*) have killed us," they replied. "They will not come to call on me again, by God," he said, "now hold your tongues and do not embolden the people against me."[201] And they did [as he said].

When the hopes of those individuals were frustrated, they sat in their homes and busied themselves with spreading rumors until the Kūfans blamed (Saʿīd) for their situation. He [al-Ashtar?] said, "This (man) is your governor (*amīr*), and he has prevented me from stirring anything up. Whoever among you intends to get things moving, let him act." Then the notables and upright men of Kūfah (*ashrāf ahl al-Kūfah wa-ṣulaḥā'hum*) wrote to ʿUthmān to have (the dissidents) expelled. He wrote, "If your council of notables (*mala'*) is agreed on that, then put them in Muʿāwiyah's charge." So they expelled them, and they were led away in humiliation until they reached him, some ten in number.

(The Kūfan notables) having written about this to ʿUthmān, he wrote to Muʿāwiyah [as follows]: "The Kūfans have expelled and sent to you certain innately rebellious individuals. Therefore hasten them along[202] and keep close watch on them. If you observe right conduct in them, then receive them hospitably. But if

200. Reading *fa-sā'ahum* instead of *fa-sa'alahum*. See 2909, note a, and de Goeje, *Introductio*, dcxxvii.

201. Reading *wa-lā tujarri'a 'alayya 'l-nāsa*. See de Goeje, *Introductio*, dcxxvii.

202. Reading *fa-zaʿhum* instead of *fa-ruʿhum*. See de Goeje, *Introductio*, cclxxxi, dcxxvii.

they are burdensome to you, then send them back to (the Kūfans)." When (the exiles) came to Muʿāwiyah, he welcomed them, housing them in a church named after Mary. In accordance with ʿUthmān's orders, he had them treated as they had been in Iraq, and he began taking the noon and evening meals with them constantly.

One day he said to them, "You are a group of Arabs who possess maturity and eloquence.[203] Through Islam you have attained nobility, conquered the nations (*umam*), and taken possession of their official ranks and their estates. I have learned that you are [2910] embittered against Quraysh. But were it not for Quraysh you would again be abject and despised, just as you used to be. Down to the present day your imāms have been your armor, so do not be without[204] your armor. Today your imāms are patient for your sake in the face of wrongdoing, and they bear the burden of providing for you. By God, you must end [your dissidence] or God will most assuredly put you to the test with (rulers) who impose heavy demands on you and then do not praise you for enduring [them]. Then you will be their accomplices in (the evils) that you have brought upon the subjects (*raʿiyyah*) both during your lifetime and after your death."

Then a man belonging to the band [of exiles][205] said, "As for what you said about Quraysh—in the Time of Ignorance, they were certainly not the most numerous or formidable of the Arabs so that they can frighten us [now]. As for what you said about armor—when the armor is pierced matters will be in our hands."[206]

Muʿāwiyah responded, "Now I recognize you [pl.]. I know that it is simplemindedness which has seduced you into this. You [that is, Ṣaʿṣaʿah] are the spokesman for this band, and I see no intelligence in you. To you I extol the cause (*amr*) of Islam and remind you of it, while to me you recall the Time of Ignorance. I

203. *Innakum qawmun min 'l-ʿarabi la-kum asnānun wa-alsinatun.*
204. Reading *tashidhdhū* rather than *tasdū*. See de Goeje, *Introductio*, dcxxvii.
205. Identified as Ṣaʿṣaʿah in Ibn al-Athīr, *Kāmil* (Beirut), III, 139.
206. *Fa-inna 'l-junnata idhā ukhturiqat khuliṣa ilaynā.* A conjectural translation; I have followed Caetani's version, which seems to reflect the situation accurately (*Annali*, VIII, 33): "Quanto poi allo scudo, quando sará lacerato, tutto torner á in mano nostra."

have given you godly admonishment, while you claim that what shields you will be pierced. But what can be pierced has no connection with armor. May God put to shame any band of men (*aqwām*) that glorifies your [pl.] conduct and lauds [it] before your caliph. You must understand—as I doubt you do—that Quraysh was given power and prestige, both in the Time of Ignorance and under Islam, only by Almighty God. (Quraysh) were neither the most numerous nor the most warlike of the Arabs, but among them they were the noblest in public esteem, the purest in lineage, the mightiest in face of danger, the most perfect in manly
[2911] qualities. In the Time of Ignorance, while the people were devouring one another, they abstained [therefrom] only through God. Those whom He has exalted are not scorned, and those whom He has raised up are not thrown down, for He has reserved for them "a sanctuary secure, while all around them the people are snatched away."[207] Do you know of Arabs or non-Arabs, Black or Red, whom fate (*dahr*) has not struck down in their own country and sanctuary by some turn of fortune (*dawlah*), save only Quraysh. For whenever anyone laid a plot against (Quraysh) God abased him,[208] until God willed that whoever honors and follows His religion should be saved from disgrace in this world and an evil return in the next. Therefore He approved the best of His creatures [that is, Muḥammad], and for him He approved companions, the best of whom were [from] Quraysh. Then upon (Quraysh) He erected this royal power (*mulk*), and among them He fixed this caliphal authority (*khilāfah*), and all this is appropriate for no one save them. For God guarded (Quraysh) in the Time of Ignorance while they were yet unbelievers. Do you imagine that He will not protect them now when they have accepted His religion, and when He sheltered them in the Time of Ignorance from the [foreign] kings who used to subjugate you?

I would feel disgust for you [sing.] and your associates even if someone besides you had spoken, but you began. As for you, Ṣaʿṣaʿah, your town (*qaryah*) is surely the worst of Arab towns—the one whose vegetation is most malodorous, whose riverbed is

207. Qur'ān 29:67.

208. *illā jaʿala Allāhu khaddahu 'l-asfala.* Lit., "except that God put his cheek lowest."

deepest, whose evildoing is most notorious, and whose protégés (*jīrān*) are vilest.[209] No one of noble or humble birth has ever dwelt there without being insulted on that account and without (that fact) being a defect in him. Moreover, they had the ugliest nicknames among the Arabs, the basest marriage ties, and were [2912] the outcasts of the nations. You [yourselves] were protégés in al-Khaṭṭ[210] and lackeys of Persia until the Prophet's call befell you. His summons touched you [sing.] while you were an outcast isolated in 'Umān rather than a resident of Baḥrayn, so that you might share with them in the Prophet's call. You are the worst of your people, to such a degree that when Islam has brought you out [of isolation], mingled you with the people, and lifted you up over the nations that heretofore had dominated you, you begin desiring crookedness in God's religion and inclining towards wickedness and baseness. But that does not derogate from Quraysh; it will neither harm them nor prevent them from fulfilling their obligations. Verily Satan is not heedless of you [pl.]. He has recognized you by the evildoing within your community (*ummah*). Thus, he has aroused the people against you while he casts you down. He knows that he cannot oppose through you any judgment that God has decreed nor any command that God has willed. [He knows also] that you can never cause evil in any affair unless God has disgraced [you] by imbuing you with evil from him."

Then (Mu'āwiyah) got up and left him. They quarreled among themselves and felt humiliated. Some time later, (Mu'āwiyah) came to them and said, "I give you leave [to depart], so go where you will. No, by God, God will certainly neither benefit nor harm anyone through you. You are not men [capable] of benefit or injury, but rather men [full] of blame and hostility. If you desire

209. *Jār*, pl. *jīrān*—a person who has left his own tribe to seek residence with and the protection of another. Such a "protected neighbor" remains a free man, but obviously enjoys a distinctly lower status than the full members of his adoptive tribe. *Jīrān* here presumably refers to those persons, non-Arabs for the most part, who had come to Kūfah to seek affiliation with one or another of the tribes settled there.

210. Al-Khaṭṭ is the strip of coast along the Persian Gulf running between Baḥrayn and 'Umān. E. Grohman, "al-Khaṭṭ," *EI²*, IV, 1130–31. The text alludes to the fact that the Arab tribes of this region were inevitably tributaries if not full subjects of the Sasanian kings.

salvation, adhere to your community (*jamāʿah*). Let what has sufficed the masses be sufficient for you; let not the bestowing of benefits (upon you) make you arrogant, for the good are not afflicted by arrogance. Go where you will, for I am writing to the Commander of the Faithful about you."

When they had gone, (Muʿāwiyah) called them back and said, "I
[2913] reiterate to you that the Messenger of God was protected (from sin), and he bestowed authority upon me and brought me into his affairs. Then Abū Bakr was named his successor, and he bestowed authority upon me. ʿUmar and ʿUthmān did the same upon their succession. I have not acted on behalf of any of them, nor did any of them put me in authority, without his being satisfied with me. The Messenger of God sought for office only men fully capable of acting on behalf of the Muslims. For (these posts) he did not want men strained beyond their powers, ignorant in (such matters), and too weak for them.[211] Verily God attacks and exacts retribution, deceiving those who have deceived Him. Do not embark upon a matter when you know that your true character is different from your public behavior, for God will not leave you without examining you and revealing your secrets to the people. Almighty God has said, 'Alif, Lām, Mīm. Do the people reckon that they will be left to say, "We believe," and will not be tried?' "[212]

Muʿāwiyah wrote to ʿUthmān (as follows): "Bands of men (*aqwām*), who possess neither reason nor religion, have come before me. Islam is burdensome to them and justice vexes them. In nothing are they mindful of God, nor do they speak on a basis of proof (*ḥujjah*). Their only aim is dissidence (*fitnah*) and the wealth of the non-Muslim subjects. God will be the one to test and examine them, then expose and humilate them. They are not (men) who can injure anyone unless they are allied with others. Therefore keep Saʿīd (b. al-ʿĀṣ) and his followers (*man qibalahu*) away from them, for they are no more than troublemakers and slanderous gossipers."[213]

211. *Wa-innamā ṭalaba rasūlu'allāhi ṣl'm li'l-aʿmāli ahla 'l-jazā'i ʿan 'l-muslimīna wa'l-ghanā'i wa-lam yaṭlub lahā ahla 'l-ijtihādi wa'l-jahli bihā wa'l-ḍuʿfi ʿanhā.* The meaning of *ijtihād* adopted here is not attested in Lane, but fits the context as well as many senses of the root *JHD.*

212. Qur'ān 29:1.

213. Reading *takthīr* rather than *nakīr,* though either word will do. See 2912, note o, and de Goeje, *Introductio,* dcxxvii.

Then the band [of dissidents] left Damascus. [Some among them] said, "Do not go back to Kūfah, for they will gloat over your problems. Have done with Iraq and Syria, and follow our preference for the Jazīrah." Thus, they sought refuge in the Jazīrah. ʿAbd al-Rahṃān b. Khālid b. al-Walīd heard of them. Muʿāwiyah had made him governor of Ḥimṣ, while the governor [2914] of the Jazīrah had authority over Ḥarrān and al-Raqqah. (ʿAbd al-Raḥmān) summoned them and said, "O instruments of Satan, you are not welcome here. Satan has come back exhausted, while you are still full of energy. I do not know whether you people are Arabs or non-Arabs. But may God ruin ʿAbd al-Raḥmān if he does not chastise you until he wears you out, lest you speak to me as I heard you have spoken to Muʿāwiyah. I am the son of Khālid b. al-Walīd—the son of a man tested by long experience, and of the man who gouged out the eye of the Secession (*al-riddah*).[214] By God, O Ṣaʿṣaʿah, son of shame, if I learn that anyone among my followers has smashed your nose and then called you a filthy sucker, I will send you off on a very long flight."[215]

He forced them to remain for some months. Whenever (ʿAbd al-Raḥmān) went out to ride, he had them go on foot. When he passed by (Ṣaʿṣaʿah), he said, "O son of a base-born man, do you know that one who is not reformed by good will be reformed by evil? Why are you not speaking as I have heard that you would speak to Saʿīd and Muʿāwiyah?" (Ṣaʿṣaʿah) and (his associates) would say, "We turn to God in repentence. You abrogate our [offense] and God will abrogate yours." They did not cease doing this until (ʿAbd al-Raḥmān) said, "God has turned to you in forgiveness," and granted al-Ashtar leave [to go] to ʿUthmān. (ʿAbd al-Raḥmān) said to them, "As you wish. You are free to go or to remain." Al-Ashtar left and came to ʿUthmān in repentance and regret, renouncing [the previous conduct of] himself and his associates. (ʿUthmān) said, "May God preserve you." Saʿīd b. al-ʿĀṣ having come [to Medina], ʿUthmān said to al-Ashtar, "Take up residence where you wish." (Al-Ashtar) replied, "With ʿAbd al-

---

214. On Khālid's role in the Riddah wars, see the present translation, vol. X; P. Crone, "Khālid b. al-Walīd," *EI*², IV, 928–29; Elias Shoufani, *Al-Riddah and the Muslim Conquest of Arabia*.

215. The point is presumably that Ṣaʿṣaʿah would have instigated a quarrel. The translation "filthy sucker" is slightly euphemistic.

Raḥmān b. Khālid." He mentioned (ʿAbd al-Raḥmān's) beneficence. "That is up to you," said (ʿUthmān). Thus, al-Ashtar returned to ʿAbd al-Raḥmān.

[2915] According to Muḥammad b. ʿUmar (al-Wāqidī)—Abū Bakr b. Ismāʿīl—his father—ʿĀmir b. Saʿd: ʿUthmān sent Saʿīd b. al-ʿĀṣ to Kūfah to serve as governor (*amīr*) there when witnesses formally charged al-Walīd b. ʿUqbah with wine drinking, and he ordered (Saʿīd) to dispatch al-Walīd b. ʿUqbah to him.

According to (al-Wāqidī): Saʿīd b. al-ʿĀṣ arrived in Kūfah and sent to al-Walīd [as follows]: "The Commander of the Faithful orders you to come before him."

According to (al-Wāqidī): (Saʿīd) procrastinated for some days, and then said to (al-Walīd), "Hasten to your brother, for he has ordered me to send you to him."

According to (al-Wāqidī): Saʿīd did not mount the pulpit in Kūfah until he had commanded it to be cleansed [of al-Walīd's vomit]. Certain men of Quraysh, members of the Banū Umayyah, who had gone out to Kūfah with him, pleaded with him and said, "This is disgraceful. By God, if someone besides you had intended to do this, it would be right for you to prevent [him] from it; the shame of this [act] would cling to him forever."

According to (al-Wāqidī): However, (Saʿīd) insisted on doing it and washed the pulpit. He sent to al-Walīd to vacate the governor's palace (*dār al-imārah*). (Al-Walīd) did so, taking up residence in the house of ʿUmārah b. ʿUqbah. Then al-Walīd came before ʿUthmān. Having assembled (al-Walīd) and his opponents, (ʿUthmān) decided to flog him and inflicted the penalty fixed by God (*al-ḥadd*).

According to Muḥammad b. ʿUmar (al-Wāqidī)—Shaybān—Mujālid—al-Shaʿbī: When Saʿīd b. al-ʿĀṣ arrived in Kūfah, he began to choose the leading men (*wujūh al-nās*) to enter his presence and pass evenings in discussion. One night, the leading men
[2916] of Kūfah were holding conversation in his residence. Among them were Mālik b. Kaʿb al-Arḥabī, al-Aswad b. Yazīd and ʿAlqamah b. Qays—both of the clan of al-Nakhaʿ—and al-Mālik al-Ashtar with [a number of] men. Saʿīd said, "This Sawād is but a garden for Quraysh." Al-Ashtar replied, "Do you claim that the Sawād, which God made booty for us by our swords, is a garden for you and your tribe (*qawm*)? God gives no additional share in it

even to the most deserving of you; on the contrary, he should be like one of us." And the whole group (*qawm*) spoke in his support.[216]

According to (al-Wāqidī): ʿAbd al-Raḥmān al-Asadī, who was in command of Saʿīd's guard (*shurṭah*), said, "Do you dispute the governor's statement?" He berated them harshly. Then al-Ashtar said, "Everyone here, this man must not get away from you." They jumped on him and trampled him severely until he passed out. Then he was dragged by the leg, tossed out, and showered with water. When he came to, Saʿīd said to him, "Are you alive? He answered, "Those whom you have chosen for their Islam—so you claim—have killed me." Then (Saʿīd) said, "By God, not one of them will ever attend evening sessions with me again."

(The dissidents) began sitting in their meeting places (*majālis*) and houses, vilifying ʿUthmān and Saʿīd. The people assembled together around them until those who were frequenting them had become numerous. Saʿīd wrote to ʿUthmān informing him about all this, as follows: "There is a gang among the Kūfans"—[here] he gave him ten names—"who are inciting them and banding [2917] together to disgrace you and me and to impugn [the sincerity of] our religion. If their movement gets firmly established, I fear they will become numerous." Thus, ʿUthmān wrote to Saʿīd, [directing him] to send them in exile to Muʿāwiyah, who at that time held authority over Syria, and (Saʿīd) did so. They numbered nine persons, among them Mālik al-Ashtar, Thābit b. Qays b. Munqaʿ, Kumayl b. Ziyād al-Nakhaʿī, and Ṣaʿṣaʿah b. Ṣūḥān.

From this point (al-Wāqidī's) account approximates the narrative of al-Sarī—Shuʿayb—Sayf (b. ʿUmar), except as follows: Ṣaʿṣaʿah said, "If the armor is pierced, will not matters be in our hands?" Muʿāwiyah replied, "The armor will not be pierced, so think about Quraysh in the most favorable manner."[217]

---

216. As always, *qawm* is troublesome; it might simply refer to the group of Kūfans assembled here and opposing Saʿīd, or—since those named (including al-Ashtar) mostly belonged to the lineage of al-Nakhaʿ—it might mean "tribe" or "clan." This incident is discussed in Donner, *Early Islamic Conquests*, 241–42, with references to other versions of the story. See also Caetani, *Annali*, VIII, 38–41.

217. A very close parallel to Sayf's version of this exchange, except for Muʿāwiyah's riposte; see above, pp. 115–16 (text, I, 2910). The Arabic text of the

Concerning this, (al-Wāqidī) adds that when Muʿāwiyah returned to them the following year [that is, 34/654–55] and reminded them [of their situation], he spoke as follows: "By God, I do not order you to do anything unless I myself, my household, and my personal retinue (*khāṣṣatī*) have started [doing] it. The Quraysh recognized that Abū Sufyān was the noblest among them and the son of the noblest, save for what God did for His prophet, the prophet of mercy. For indeed God elected him and showed him honor. God did not create upright qualities in anyone
[2918] without singling out (the prophet) for the noblest and finest of them. Nor did He create evil qualities in anyone without ennobling him beyond (such things) and keeping him utterly free of them. Now in fact I believe that if the people were sons of Abū Sufyān, they would all be prudent and resolute men."[218]

Ṣaʿṣaʿah replied, "You lie! They are sons to a better man than Abū Sufyān—one whom God created by His own hand, 'into whom He breathed His spirit,'[219] before whom He commanded the angels to bow down. Among (the people) are the pious and the sinner, the stupid and the clever."

That night (Muʿāwiyah) departed from them. Then he came to them the following night and spoke at length among them. He said, "O band of men (*qawm*), answer me properly or be still. Reflect and consider what will bring benefit to you, your households, your tribes, and the whole community (*jamāʿah*) of Muslims. If you seek this, you will prosper and we shall prosper with you." Ṣaʿṣaʿah replied, "You are not worthy of that, nor is your noble rank such that you should be obeyed in defiance of God." (Muʿāwiyah) said, "Did I not begin by commanding you to fear God and obey Him and His prophet, to 'hold fast to His bond, together, and do not scatter.'"[220] "On the contrary," they an-

---

last clause is as follows: *fa-ḍaʿ amra Qurayshin ʿalā aḥsani mā yaḥḍuruka*. Lit., "so place the matter of Quraysh on the best of what is present in your mind."

218. *Wa-innī la-aẓunnu anna Abā Sufyāna law walada 'l-nāsa lam yalid illā ḥāziman*. See de Goeje, *Introductio*, dlxvi, "*walada*."

219. Qur'ān 32:8.

220. Qur'ān 3:98. The context of this line is highly significant; 3:98, 100–1 reads as follows: "And hold you fast to God's bond, together, and do not scatter; remember God's blessing upon you when you were enemies, and He brought your hearts together, so that by His blessing you became brothers. . . . Let there be one nation of you, calling to good, and bidding to honor, and forbidding dishonor;

swered, "you have commanded schism and opposition to what the Prophet has brought."

(Mu'āwiyah) said, "Well, then, I command you now. If I have done [what you say], I turn to God and His prophet, and I command you to fear Him and obey Him and His prophet, to adhere to the community and to abhor schism, to revere your imams and to direct them so far as you are able to every good thing, and to admonish them gently and graciously concerning anything that comes from them." [2919]

Ṣa'ṣa'ah replied, "And we then command you to resign your office (*'amal*), for among the Muslims there is one who has a better right to it than you." (Mu'āwiyah) asked, "Who is that?" (Ṣa'ṣa'ah) answered, "Someone whose father had a higher standing in Islam than did yours, and who himself has a higher standing than you."[221] (Mu'āwiyah) said, "By God, I have some standing in Islam. There were others whose standing surpassed mine, but in my time there is no one better able to do my job than I. 'Umar b. al-Khaṭṭāb was of this opinion, and had there been a man more capable than I, 'Umar would not have been indulgent in regard to me or anyone else. Nor have I instituted any innovation that would require me to resign my office. Had the Commander of the Faithful and of the Community of Muslims thought so, he would have written to me by his own hand and I would have stepped down from office. Should God decree that he do this, I hope that he would not decide on someone for this (position) unless (that person) were better. Go easy, or Satan will find what he hopes for and commands in this (situation) and others like it. By my life, if affairs were decided according to your opinion and wishes, things

---

those are the prosperers. Be not as those who scattered and fell into variance after the clear signs came to them; those there awaits a mighty chastisement."

221. *Qāla: man kāna abūhu aḥsana qadaman min abīka wa-huwa bi-nafsihi aḥsanu qadaman minka fī 'l-islāmi.* Caetani (*Annali*, VIII, 40) translates *qadam* by "precedenza," but this rendering seems a bit too restrictive. Other words derived from QDM (e.g., *qidam*) do refer to seniority or length of time. *Qadam* (lit., "foot") can have the general meaning of "merit"—cf. Biberstein Kazimirski, II, 690. Obviously early conversion or seniority in the faith was an important element in one's religious merit, but it was not the only thing that conferred standing on a person. In the present case, Mu'āwiyah's opponents, who seem generally to belong to the tribes of Yemen (especially the Nakha' clan of Madhḥij), hardly converted to Islam earlier than he.

would not go well for the people of Islam either day or night. But (affairs) are determined and directed by God, and 'He attains His purpose.'[222] So come back to what is good and speak of that."

They responded, "You are not fit for that." He said, "By God, in truth it belongs to God to attack and take vengeance. Indeed I fear for you, lest you become so entangled in submission to Satan that submission to Satan and rebellion against the Merciful One will cause you to reside in the abode of humiliation from God's vengeance in the present and (in the abode of) everlasting abasement
[2920] in the future."

Then they jumped on him and seized his head and beard. He said, "Hey, this is not the province of Kūfah! By God, if the Syrians saw what you have done to me, their imām, I could not restrain them from killing you. By my life, you always act the same way." Then he arose from among them and said, "By God, I shall never enter your presence again as long as I live." Then he wrote to 'Uthmān [as follows]: "In the name of God, the Merciful, the Compassionate. To the servant of God, 'Uthmān, Commander of the Faithful, from Mu'āwiyah b. Abī Sufyān. To proceed: O Commander of the Faithful, you sent to me certain bands of men speaking with the tongue of devils, saying things which (these latter) were dictating to them. They come to the people, so they allege, for the sake of the Qur'ān, but they render [it] obscure and ambiguous. Not all of the people understand what they mean to do, for they only desire schism and they bring discord (*fitnah*) nearer. Islam has been a burden to them and has vexed them. The spells of Satan have become fixed in their hearts, and they corrupted many of the people among the Kūfans who were around them. If they remain in the midst of the Syrians, I worry that they may delude them with their sorcery and depravity. Send them back to their garrison town [that is, Kūfah] and let them reside there, where their dissembling first appeared. Peace."

'Uthmān wrote and commanded him to send them back to Sa'īd b. al-'Āṣ in Kūfah, and (Mu'āwiyah) did so. But when they re-
[2921] turned they were even more inflammatory [than before]. Sa'īd wrote to 'Uthmān complaining intensely about them, and

---

222. Qur'ān 65:3.

ʿUthmān wrote back to him to send them away to ʿAbd al-Raḥmān b. Khālid b. al-Walīd, who was governor (*amīr*) in Ḥimṣ. (ʿUthmān) wrote to al-Ashtar and his associates [as follows]: "To proceed: I am exiling you to Ḥimṣ. When this letter of mine reaches you, go there, for you do not desist from evil against Islam and its adherents. Peace."

When al-Ashtar read the letter, he said, "O God, (ʿUthmān) is the worst of us in his concern for the subjects (*raʿiyyah*) and the one who does most to arouse rebellion among them, so hasten [your] vengeance against him!" Saʿīd wrote to ʿUthmān about that, and al-Ashtar and his associates traveled to Ḥimṣ. ʿAbd al-Raḥmān b. Khālid b. al-Walīd settled them in the coastal districts (*al-Sāḥil*) and had rations provided for them.

According to Muḥammad b. ʿUmar (al-Wāqidī)—ʿĪsā b. ʿAbd al-Raḥman—Abū Isḥāq al-Hamdānī: A few individuals from among the nobles of Iraq (*ashrāf ahl al-ʿIrāq*) gathered in Kūfah to defame ʿUthmān: Mālik b. al-Ḥārith al-Ashtar, Thābit b. Qays al-Nakhaʿī, Kumayl b. Ziyād al-Nakhaʿī, Zayd b. Ṣūḥān al-ʿAbdī, [his brother Ṣaʿṣaʿah b. Ṣūḥān],[223] Jundub b. Zuhayr al-Ghāmidī, Jundub b. Kaʿb al-Azdī, ʿUrwah b. al-Jaʿd, ʿAmr b. al-Ḥamiq al-Khuzāʿī, [and Ibn al-Kawwāʾ].[224] Saʿīd b. al-ʿĀṣ wrote to ʿUthmān to inform him about their activities. (ʿUthmān) wrote back, ordering him to exile them to Syria and to make them stay in the mountain passes [in Cilicia].[225]

ʿUthmān's Exile of Certain Baṣrans to Syria [2922]

It was transmitted to me in writing by al-Sarī—Shuʿayb—Sayf—ʿAṭiyyah—Yazīd al-Faqʿasī: When Ibn ʿĀmir had been governor for three years, he learned that there was a man in [the residential quarter of the tribe of] ʿAbd al-Qays who was staying with

223. The name in brackets is supplied by Maqrīzī, *al-Muqaffā;* see de Goeje, *Introductio,* dcxxvii. With the names supplied here and in note 219, the list totals ten—that is, the number of troublemakers mentioned in Saʿīd's first letter to ʿUthmān above, p. 121 (text, I, 2916).

224. Ibid. *Kawwāʾ* means "one who cauterizes, brands," but by extension "slanderer." Perhaps Ibn al-Kawwāʾ should be taken as a pejorative nickname here.

225. *Wa-alzimhum ʾl-durūba.* For the translation, see Caetani, *Annali,* VIII, 41. The point of course was to put the dissidents in a place remote from the main political centers.

Ḥukaym b. Jabalah. Now Ḥukaym b. Jabalah was a robber. When the armies would return [from campaign], he would slip away from them and hurry off to Fārs to raid the protected non-Muslims (*ahl al-dhimmah*), treat them wrongfully, sow corruption in the land, and do whatever he desired; then he would come back. The protected non-Muslims and the Muslims both complained about him to ʿUthmān, and he wrote to ʿAbdallāh b. ʿĀmir: "Arrest (Ḥukaym) and anyone like him; he is not to leave Baṣrah until you see him acting uprightly." (Ibn ʿĀmir) arrested him and he was unable to leave (the city).

Now when Ibn al-Sawdāʾ came, he resided with (Ḥukaym). A few individuals gathered around him, and Ibn al-Sawdāʾ presented [legal and theological problems] to them without explaining them fully. However, they accepted [what he said] and believed him to be a man of importance. Ibn ʿĀmir sent to him and asked, "What are you?" (Ibn al-Sawdāʾ) informed him that he was a man from among the People of the Book who desired [to convert to] Islam and to live under (Ibn ʿĀmir's) protection. But (Ibn ʿĀmir) said, "That is not what I hear. Get away from me." So he left and came to Kūfah. Then he was expelled from there and established himself in Egypt. He and (his sympathizers in Iraq) began to corre-
[2923] spond with one another, and men were traveling back and forth in great numbers.

It was transmitted to me in writing by al-Sarī—Shuʿayb—Sayf—Muḥammad and Ṭalḥah: Ḥumrān b. Abān had married a woman during her period of waiting, and ʿUthmān punished him severely and compelled them to separate.[226] He exiled (Ḥumrān) to Baṣrah, where he joined the entourage of Ibn ʿĀmir. One day they all discussed going out to ride and calling on ʿĀmir b. ʿAbd Qays, who lived in seclusion from the people. Ḥumrān said, "I'll go ahead of you all and inform him [that you are coming]." He set off and entered ʿĀmir's presence while he was reading from the Qurʾān (*muṣḥaf*). (Ḥumrān) said, "The governor (*amīr*) has decided to call on you, and I wished to inform you [of this]." But ʿĀmir

226. On the *ʿiddah*, the period (usually three months) that must elapse between a woman's divorce or widowhood and her remarriage, see Y. Linant de Bellefonds, "Idda," *EI*,[2], III, 1010–13. A marriage contracted during the *ʿiddah* is null and void and the couple must be separated.

would not break off his reading and pay any attention to him, so (Ḥumrān) rose to go. When he had gotten to the door, he encountered Ibn ʿĀmir and said, "I come to you from a man who does not regard even the lineage of Abraham as superior to himself."

Ibn ʿĀmir then asked to come in; he entered (ʿĀmir's) presence and sat down before him. Then ʿĀmir closed the Qur'ān and spoke with him for an hour. "Surely you will come to visit us," said Ibn ʿĀmir. (ʿĀmir) replied, "Saʿīd b. Abī al-ʿArjā' would enjoy the honor [of such invitations]." Then (Ibn ʿĀmir) said, "Indeed we shall appoint you to office." "Ḥuṣayn b. Abī al-Ḥurr would like government office (*ʿamal*)," said (ʿĀmir). "Then we shall arrange a marriage for you," said (Ibn ʿĀmir). He said, "Women are pleasing to Rabīʿah b. ʿIsl." (Ibn ʿĀmir) said, "This man [that is, Ḥumrān] claims that you do not regard the lineage of Abraham as superior to yourself." Then (ʿĀmir) leafed through the Qur'ān and the first passage he came upon was [this one]: "God chose Adam and [2924]
Noah and the House of Abraham and the House of ʿImrān above all beings."[227] When Ḥumrān was sent back [to Medina], he strove assiduously to discredit (ʿĀmir) in this matter, and [a number of] groups (*aqwām*) testified in support of (Ḥumrān). (ʿUthmān) thus sent (ʿĀmir) into exile in Syria. When (the Syrians) found out the truth about him, they gave him permission [to return to Baṣrah], but he refused and remained in Syria.

It was transmitted to me in writing by al-Sarī—Shuʿayb—Sayf—Muḥammad and Ṭalḥah: ʿUthmān exiled Ḥumrān b. Abān for having married a woman during her period of waiting; he compelled them to separate, flogged him, and sent him off to Baṣrah. When (Ḥumrān) had served some time in exile and (ʿUthmān) received a satisfactory report about him,[228] he gave him permission [to return]. (Ḥumrān) came before (the caliph) in Medina, accompanied by a band of men (*qawm*) who calumnied ʿĀmir b. ʿAbd Qays, [saying] that he did not approve of marriage, nor did he eat meat or attend the Friday prayer. Now ʿĀmir was a man who lived in seclusion, and everything he did was done in

227. Qur'ān 3:30.

228. *Fa-lammā atā ʿalayhi ma shā'a 'llāhu wa-atāhu ʿanhu 'lladhī yuḥibbu. . . .* Sayf's taste for difficult constructions and pronouns without clear antecedents is evident here again.

secret. ('Uthmān) wrote to 'Abdallāh b. 'Āmir about this matter, and he placed ('Āmir) under Mu'āwiyah's authority.

When Mu'āwiyah came to him he found him agreeable. ('Āmir) had a portion of bread prepared with broth and meat, and ate unfamiliar food. Then (Mu'āwiyah) knew that lies had been told about this man and said, "Do you know why you were expelled [from Baṣrah]?" "No," replied ('Āmir). (Mu'āwiyah) said, "The caliph was informed that you would not eat meat, but I have seen you do so and know that people have lied about you. [He was also told] that you do not approve of marriage or attend the Friday prayer." ('Āmir) said, "As to the Friday prayer, I attend it in the rear of the mosque; then I am among the first of the people to go back home. As for marriage, I have gone out [to find a bride] and I am [now] betrothed. As for meat, you have seen for yourself, but I
[2925] was a man who would not eat animals killed by butchers ever since I saw a butcher dragging a sheep to be slaughtered. Then he placed a knife on its throat and repeated over and over, 'For sale, for sale,' until it dropped dead." (Mu'āwiyah) said, "Go back [to Baṣrah]." "I shall not go back to a place whose people have felt it permissible to behave toward me as they have," ('Āmir) said. "I shall instead remain in this place that God has chosen for me." He used to reside in the coastal districts and would encounter Mu'āwiyah [there]. Mu'āwiyah would frequently ask, "[What] do you need?" And ('Āmir) would reply, "I need nothing." When (Mu'āwiyah) pressed him, he said, "If you gave me back some of Baṣrah's heat, perhaps fasting would be something difficult for me, for in your country it is easy."

It was transmitted to me in writing by al-Sarī—Shu'ayb—Sayf—Abū Ḥārithah and Abū 'Uthmān: When the exiles from Kūfah came to Mu'āwiyah, he settled them in a house and then went to see them alone. He and they each spoke, and when they had finished he said, "You were brought here only because of [your own] folly. By God, I perceive neither any relevant speech, clear excuse nor wise forbearance nor forcefulness—and you, Ṣa'ṣa'ah, are the most stupid among them. Do and say what you will so long as you do not neglect anything that God has commanded. Indeed everything can be tolerated from you save rebellion against Him. As for what passes between you and us, you are in command of yourselves."

Then (Mu'āwiyah) saw them later when they were attending the prayer and standing alongside the congregation's preacher (*qāṣṣ al-jamā'ah*).[229] One day he entered their presence as some of them were teaching others how to recite [the Qur'ān], and he said, "In this there is indeed a change from the yearning for the Time of Ignorance that you had when you came to me. Go where you [2926]
wish, and know that if you adhere to your community (*jamā'ah*) you will thereby be happier than they, while if you do not adhere to it, you will thereby be more wretched than they. Do no injury to anyone." Then they blessed him [for these words] and extolled him.

Then (Mu'āwiyah) said, "Ibn al-Kawwā', what kind of man am I?" He answered, "[A man of] vast wealth and numerous flocks, possessing sound intuition and profound judgment. A man dominated by forbearance, one of the pillars of Islam. By you a dreaded breach has been closed up." (Mu'āwiyah) said, "Then inform me about the partisans of innovation (*ahl al-iḥdāth*) among the inhabitants of the camp cities [of Iraq], for you are the most intelligent of your associates." (Ibn al-Kawwā') responded, "I have corresponded with them and they with me; they pretend not to know me, but I am acquainted with them. As for the innovators among the Medinese, they are the members of the community (*al-ummah*) most intent on evil and least capable of doing it. As for the innovators among the Kūfans, they are those among the people most likely to discern small shortcomings and most given to the commission of great sins. As to the innovators among the Baṣrans, they arrive united and leave in discord. As for the innovators among the Egyptians, they are the ones among the people who actually do the greatest evil and who most quickly repent. As for the innovators among the Syrians, they are the most obedient of the people to one who guides them aright, and the most rebellious against one who leads them astray."

---

229. *Qāṣṣ* is a difficult word. In archaic usage, it can simply refer to the man who recites the bidding prayer (*khuṭbah*) on Friday, and it might mean that here, though this service is identified simply as *ṣalāt*, not specifically as *jum'ah*. More generally, it refers to one who tells edifying sermons and stories or who expounds scripture. After he became caliph, Mu'āwiyah is supposed to have established an official *qāṣṣ* to explicate the Qur'ān, and this might be simply an anachronistic reference to that institution. See Ch. Pellat, "Ḳāṣṣ," *EI*², IV, 733–35.

In this year, ʿUthmān led the people on the Pilgrimage.

Abū Maʿshar claims that the conquest of Cyprus took place in this year, but I have already mentioned those who contradict him in this regard.[230]

230. See above, pp. 25 (text I, 2820) and 111–12 (I, 2907).

The Events of the Year 34 [2927]

(July 22, 654—July 10, 655)

In (this year) took place the Battle of the Masts, according to the account related to me by Aḥmad (b. Thābit al-Rāzī)—one who related [it] to him—Isḥāq (b. ʿĪsā)— Abū Maʿshar. We have already given the account of this battle and mentioned those who contradict Abū Maʿshar's chronology.[231]

In (this year), the Kūfans drove Saʿīd b. al-ʿĀṣ out of the city.

In (this year), those who were alienated from ʿUthmān b. ʿAffān wrote to one another, planning to gather together in order to confront him with (those matters) concerning which they were angry at him.

The Character of the Meeting [to Confront ʿUthmān] and [the Day of] al-Jaraʿah[232]

It was transmitted to me in writing by al-Sarī—Shuʿayb—Sayf—al-Mustanīr b. Yazīd—Qays b. Yazīd al-Nakhaʿī: When Muʿāwi-

---

231. See above, p. 71 (text, I, 2865).

232. Bracketed words from Ibn al-Athīr, *Kāmil* (Beirut), III, 147.

yah sent the exiles away, they said, "Iraq and Syria are no home for us; you [*sic*] must choose the Jazīrah." They came there freely, and ʿAbd al-Raḥmān b. Khālid went out to meet them. He dealt severely with them, and they humbled themselves before him and submitted to his authority. (ʿAbd al-Raḥmān) sent al-Ashtar to ʿUthmān, who received him, saying, "Go wherever you wish." (Al-Ashtar) answered, "I shall return to ʿAbd al-Raḥmān," and he did that.

In the eleventh year of ʿUthmān's caliphate, Saʿīd b. al-ʿĀṣ came to confer with ʿUthmān. A year and more before Saʿīd's departure from Kūfah, he had sent out [a number of deputies to the provinces under his authority, as follows]: al-Ashʿath b. Qays over Ādharbayjān; Saʿīd b. Qays over al-Rayy—Saʿīd had held authority
[2928] in Hamadhān but was removed and replaced by al-Nusayr al-ʿIjlī; al-Sā'ib b. al-Aqraʿ over Iṣfahān; Mālik b. Ḥabīb al-Yarbūʿī over Māh;[233] Ḥukaym b. Salāmah al-Ḥizāmī over Mosul; Jarīr b. ʿAbdallāh over Qarqīsiyā';[234] Salmān b. Rabīʿah over al-Bāb; al-Qaʿqāʿ b. ʿAmr as military commandant [in Kūfah];[235] and ʿUtaybah b. al-Nahhās over Ḥulwān.[236]

Thus, Kūfah was emptied of leaders (*ru'asā'*), save for those who had been stripped of office or afflicted with the spirit of dissension.[237] Then Yazīd b. Qays set out with the intention of deposing ʿUthmān. He entered the mosque and sat down. Those

---

233. Māh is an abbreviation for Māh al-Kūfah, a district in the western Jibāl (ancient Media, modern Iranian Kurdistan) subject to the governor of Kūfah. Its boundaries and administrative status fluctuated considerably in the first decades of Islamic rule. See Morony, *Iraq after the Muslim Conquest*, 141–42.

234. Qarqīsiyā' (ancient Circesium) is a modest but strategically situated town, at the confluence of the Khābūr and Euphrates Rivers. It is located about 525 km. northwest of Kūfah. See Le Strange, *Eastern Caliphate*, 105; M. Streck, "Ḳarḳīsiyā," *EI²*, 654–55.

235. *Wa-ʿalā 'l-ḥarbi 'l-Qaʿqāʿa 'bna ʿAmrin.* One would expect a place name here, but no "Ḥarb" is noted in any geographical reference. Al-Qaʿqāʿ had been one of Saʿd b. Abī Waqqāṣ' most effective generals in the conquest of Iraq. On him see the numerous references in Donner, *Early Islamic Conquests*, esp. 390–91.

236. Ḥulwān is a strategic city on the frontier between Iraq and the Iranian highlands, located on the main road between lower Iraq and Hamadhān. See Le Strange, *Eastern Caliphate*, 191; Morony, *Iraq after the Muslim Conquest*, 141 et passim.

237. *Maftūn*: lit., "tried by fire." It can also mean "stricken by insanity." In the present context, however, "affected by *fitnah*" seems best suited to the context. See Lane, *Lexicon*, VI, 2334–36.

with whom Ibn al-Sawdā' had been corresponding there gathered around (Yazīd). Al-Qa'qā' fell upon Yazīd b. Qays and seized him, but he said, "We are only seeking Sa'īd's resignation." (Al-Qa'qā') replied, "That is something that you will not get. Do not sit [here] to discuss this, and (these malcontents) must not come and meet with you. Seek what you really need, and by my life it will be given to you." Then (Yazīd) returned to his house and hired a man, giving him a sum of dirhams and some mules, on condition that he should go to the exiles [in the Jazīrah]. (Yazīd) wrote to them [as follows]: "Do not let my letter out of your hands until you come, for the inhabitants of the garrison town [namely, Kūfah] have joined our cause."

The man (hired by Yazīd) slipped away and came to (the exiles), [to whom] al-Ashtar had already returned. He presented (Yazīd's) letter to them, and they asked, "What is your name?" "Bughthur," he replied. "What is your tribe?" they asked. "Kalb," he said. "A vile predator that disgusts (*yubaghthir*) the soul. We have no need of you," they said.[238] But al-Ashtar disagreed with them, and returned in rebellion [to Kūfah]. When he had gone, his associates said, "God has exiled both us and him. We shall find no escape from what he has done. If 'Abd al-Raḥmān learns about us, he will not believe us and he will not take this lightly." So they followed after (al-Ashtar) but did not join up with him. 'Abd al-Raḥmān learned that they had departed and searched for them in [2929] the Sawād. Al-Ashtar made the journey in seven [days], the other exiles (*al-qawm*) in ten.

Now one Friday the people unexpectedly found al-Ashtar at the mosque portal, saying, "O people, I have come to you from the Commander of the Faithful 'Uthmān. When I left Sa'īd he was trying to get (the caliph) to cut [the state pension of] your women to a hundred dirhams, and to reduce [the salary] of the long-term veterans (*ahl al-balā'*) among you to 2000.[239] (Sa'īd) was saying,

---

238. Kalb was a tribe belonging to the Quḍā'ah confederation in southern Syria. There is a pun here, of course, since *kalb* means "dog," not a highly esteemed animal in the Islamic world. On the tribe, see Donner, *Early Islamic Conquests*, 106–7 et passim; J. W. Fück and A. A. Dixon, "Kalb b. Wabara," *EI*², IV, 492–94. On the animal, F. Viré, "Kalb," *EI*², IV, 489–92.

239. The stipend for the veterans of the first Iraqi campaigns (that is, those that took place before the battle of al-Qādisiyyah) had originally been set at 3000

'How important are the noble women (*ashrāf al-nisā'*)? This is just an extra burden on top of the others.'[240] He claims that your conquered lands (*fay'*) are the private garden of Quraysh. I traveled with him a day's march, and he was constantly reciting doggerel about (these matters) up to the time I separated from him:

Woe to the noble women from me—
as strong and violent as though I were a demon (*jinn*).

He has disparaged the people. Men of intelligence have begun to denounce him, and among them he is not needed."

There was a sudden commotion, and Yazīd went out and ordered a public herald to call out, "Whoever wishes to join Yazīd b. Qays in driving out Sa'īd and seeking a new governor, let him act!" The far-sighted, the nobles, and the leading men among the people remained in the mosque, but the others went out. At that time, 'Amr b. Ḥurayth was (Sa'īd's) vicegerent (*khalīfah*), and he mounted the pulpit. Having praised and extolled God, he said, "'Remember God's blessing upon you when you were enemies, and He brought your hearts together so that by His blessing you became brothers. You were upon the brink of a pit of Fire, and He delivered you from it.'[241] Do not revert to an evil from which Almighty God has delivered you. After Islam and its guidance and its practice (*sunnah*), will you not recognize truth and aim straight for its gate?"

Then al-Qa'qā' b. 'Amr said, "Will you turn the flood aside from
[2930] its course? Then divert the Euphrates from its channel. How foolish! No, by God, only Mashrafī swords[242] will silence the mob, and they are on the point of being drawn. Then (these people) will bawl like goats and long for their present situation. God

---

dirhams per year. See Donner, *Early Islamic Conquests*, 231; Hinds, "Kûfan Political Alignments," 349.

240. *Wa-yaqūlu: mā bālu ashrāfi 'l-nisā'i wa-hādhihi 'l-'ilāwatu bayna hādhayni 'l-idlayni*. The *'ilāwah* is an extra load placed between the two evenly balanced loads (*'idl*) carried on each side of a camel.

241. Qur'ān 3:98–99.

242. *al-mashrafiyyah*. The origin of this term is somewhat obscure, but it seems to refer to the locale—either in the Yemen or close to Syria—in which these swords were made. Lane, *Lexicon*, IV, 1539.

will never restore (Saʿīd's) authority over them, so endure patiently." "I will endure patiently," (ʿAmr) said, and went to his house.

Yazīd b. Qays, accompanied by al-Ashtar, went out and established camp at al-Jaraʿah.[243] Saʿīd had halted on the road, and then came upon them as they were encamped waiting for him. They said, "We want nothing to do with you." He replied, "What are you quarreling about now? It would have sufficed for you to send one man to the Commander of the Faithful and to put another man in my place. Do a thousand rational men set out against one man?" Then he left them, and they noticed a freedman (*mawlā*) of his on a camel that was worn out [from the journey]. (The freedman) said, "By God, it does not behoove Saʿīd to go back [to Medina]." And al-Ashtar struck off his head.

Saʿīd proceeded until he reached ʿUthmān, whom he informed of the news. (ʿUthmān) said, "What do they want? Have they withdrawn their hand from obedience?" (Saʿīd) responded, "They proclaim that they want a change [of governors]." "Whom do they want?" asked (ʿUthmān). "Abū Mūsā (al-Ashʿarī)," replied (Saʿīd). (ʿUthmān) said, "Then we have set Abū Mūsā over them. By God, we shall create no excuse for anyone, nor will we leave them any proof [against us]. We shall endure patiently, as we have been commanded to do, until we attain what they desire."

Those who held sub-governorships (*ʿamal*) near Kūfah returned [to Medina], as did Jarīr from Qarqīsiyā' and ʿUtaybah from Ḥul- [2931]
wān. In Kūfah, Abū Mūsā arose to speak, saying, "O people, do not hasten into such an affair, and do not do such a thing again. Adhere to your community (*jamāʿah*) and cling to obedience. Beware of acting precipitously. Endure patiently, just as if you had a governor (*amīr*)." They responded, "Lead us in prayer." He said, "I will not, unless you heed and obey ʿUthmān b. ʿAffān." They replied, "We will heed and obey ʿUthmān."

It was related to me by Jaʿfar b. ʿAbdallāh al-Muḥammadī—ʿAmr b. Ḥammād b. Ṭalḥah and ʿAlī b. Ḥusayn b. ʿĪsā—Ḥusayn b. ʿĪsā—his father—Hārūn b. Saʿd—al-ʿAlā' b. ʿAbdallāh b. Zayd al-ʿAnbarī: A body of Muslims gathered together to review the deeds and conduct of ʿUthmān. They concurred in a decision to

243. A place near al-Qādisiyyah; see below, p. 139 (text, I, 2934).

dispatch a man to speak to him and inform him of his blameworthy innovations (*aḥdāth*). To him they sent ʿĀmir b. ʿAbdallāh al-Tamīmī al-ʿAnbarī, who is the one known as ʿĀmir b. ʿAbd Qays. (ʿĀmir) came and entered (ʿUthmān's) presence, saying, "A body of Muslims have met together and examined your actions, and they find that you have committed grave misdeeds. So fear Almighty God; turn to Him in repentance and refrain from (such acts)."

ʿUthmān said to him, "Look at this man! The people assert that he is a man learned in the Qur'ān (*qārī'*), and then he comes to speak to me about utterly trivial things. By God, he does not know where God is." ʿĀmir responded, "So I do not know where God is?" "Yes, by God," said (ʿUthmān), "you do not know where God is." ʿĀmir said, "Yes, indeed, by God! I know that God is
[2932] lying in watch for you."[244]

Then ʿUthmān sent to Muʿāwiyah b. Abī Sufyān, to ʿAbdallāh b. Saʿd b. Abī Sarḥ, to Saʿīd b. al-ʿĀṣ, to ʿAmr b. al-ʿAṣ b. Wā'il al-Sahmī, and to ʿAbdallāh b. ʿĀmir. He brought them together in order to consult with them about his situation, about what had been demanded of him, and about what he had learned from them. When they had assembled at his residence, he said to them, "Every man has ministers (*wuzarā'*) and counselors. Now you are my ministers, my counselors, and my trusted men. The people have acted as you see, demanding that I depose my governors (*ʿummāl*), and that I turn away from that which they hate toward that which they love. So decide what you think is right and advise me."

ʿAbdallāh b. ʿĀmir said to him, "My advice to you, Commander of the Faithful, is that you command them to undertake a *jihād* that will divert their attention from you, and that you keep them on campaign until they act humbly before you. In this way every one of them will be concerned only about himself, about the saddle sores of his pack animal, and about the lice on his scalp."

---

244. Probably an allusion to Qur'ān 89:5–13. "Hast thou not seen how thy Lord did with ʿAd, Iram of the pillars, the like of which was never created in the land, and Thamud, who hollowed the rocks in the valley, and Pharaoh, he of the tent pegs, who all were insolent in the land and worked much corruption therein? Thy Lord unloosed on them a scourge of chastisement; surely thy Lord is ever on the watch."

Then ʿUthmān came to Saʿīd b. al-ʿĀṣ and asked him for his opinion. He said, "O Commander of the Faithful, if you desire our opinion, cure yourself of the disease and amputate from yourself what you fear. Follow my advice, and you will attain your goal." "What is it?" said (ʿUthmān). (Saʿid) answered, "Every group has leaders. When these are eliminated, they will disperse and will be unable to agree on anything." ʿUthmān said, "This would indeed be the right opinion, were it not for what it involves!"

He approached Muʿāwiyah and said, "What is your view?" He answered, "O Commander of the Faithful, I think it best for you to send your governors back, on condition that they administer their provinces with care, and I will be the guarantor for you of my province."[245]

Then (ʿUthmān) came to ʿAbdallāh b. Saʿd and said, "What do you think?" He answered, "O Commander of the Faithful, in my opinion the people are greedy. Bestow upon them some of this wealth and their hearts will incline to you."

Then (ʿUthmān) approached ʿAmr b. al-ʿĀṣ and sought his opinion. He said, "I think that you have perpetrated things against the [2933]
people that they detest, so resolve to do justice. If you reject [this course], then make up your mind to abdicate. If you reject [that], then be firm in your resolve and continue straight ahead." ʿUthmān replied, "What is wrong with you? May your scalp crawl with lice! Are you serious about this?" ʿAmr refused to answer him for some time, until [the rest of] the assembly (*qawm*) had dispersed. Then ʿAmr said, "No, O Commander of the Faithful, you are dearer to me than that, but I knew that the people would hear about the statements of every man among us. I wanted them to learn what I said so that they would trust me, and thereby I would bring you good and ward off evil."

It was related to me by Jaʿfar—ʿAmr b. Ḥammād and ʿAlī b. Ḥusayn—Ḥusayn—his father—ʿAmr b. Abī al-Miqdām—ʿAbd al-Malik b. ʿUmayr al-Zuhrī: ʿUthmān assembled the commanders of the armies (*umarāʾ al-ajnād*)—Muʿāwiyah b. Abī Sufyān, Saʿīd b. al-ʿĀṣ, ʿAbdallāh b. ʿĀmir, ʿAbdallāh b. Saʿd b. Abī Sarḥ, and

---

245. *an tarudda ʿummālaka ʿalā ʾl-kifāyati limā qibalahum wa-anā ḍāminun laka [mā] qibalī.* See de Goeje, *Introductio,* cdlv, sub verbo *kafā.*

ʿAmr b. al-ʿĀṣ. He said, "Give me your advice, for the people have become as threatening to me as leopards."

Muʿāwiyah said to him, "I advise you to order the commanders of your armies that every one of them should administer his province carefully on your behalf, and I will administer the people of Syria carefully on your behalf." ʿAbdallāh b. ʿĀmir said, "In my opinion you should keep them tied up in these campaigns until every one of them is concerned about the saddle sores of his pack animal. Thus, you will keep them too preoccupied to spread calumnies about you." ʿAbdallāh b. Saʿd said, "I advise you to look into what has angered them and give them satisfaction; then you should distribute to them this wealth and divide [it] among them."

Then ʿAmr b. al-ʿĀṣ rose up and said: "O ʿUthmān, you have afflicted the people with men like the Banū Umayyah.[246] You and they have both spoken [in anger], and you and they have both gone astray. So do justice or abdicate. But if you reject [this counsel], be firm in your resolve and continue straight ahead." Then
[2934] ʿUthmān replied, "What is wrong with you? May your scalp crawl with lice! Are you serious about this?" ʿAmr remained silent until (the others) had dispersed; then he said, "No, Commander of the Faithful, you are dearer to me than that, but I knew that at the portal there was a band of men (*qawm*). These knew that you had assembled us to obtain our advice, and I wanted them to hear about my statement, so that I might bring you good or ward off evil from you."

Then ʿUthmān sent his governors (*ʿummāl*) back to their provinces, commanding them to maintain stringent control of those under their authority and to keep the people tied up on campaigns. He decided also to deny them their stipends, so that they would submit to him and be in need of him. He sent Saʿīd b. al-ʿĀṣ back as governor (*amīr*) of Kūfah, but the Kūfans came forth in arms against him, confronted him, and made him return [to

246. The Umayyad clan of Quraysh, under the leadership of Abū Sufyān b. Ḥarb, had of course been the heart and soul of Meccan opposition to Muḥammad. One of the most persistent and damaging charges against ʿUthmān (at least as represented in our texts) was his favoritism toward these old enemies of the Prophet, who were also his own kinsmen.

Medina]. They said, "No, by God, he will not rule over us while we still bear our swords."

It was related to me by Ja'far—'Amr and 'Alī b. Ḥusayn[247]—his father—Hārūn b. Sa'd—Abū Yaḥyā 'Umayr b. Sa'd al-Nakha'ī: In my mind I can still see al-Ashtar Mālik b. al-Ḥārith al-Nakha'ī. His face was covered with dust, and he was girt with a sword and saying, "By God, he—that is, Sa'īd—will not enter (our city) against us while we still bear our swords." That was the Day of al-Jara'ah. Al-Jara'ah is a high place near al-Qādisiyyah, and there the Kūfans met (Sa'īd).

It was related to me by Ja'far—'Amr and 'Alī—Ḥusayn—his father—Hārūn b. Sa'd—'Amr b. Murrah al-Jamalī—Abū al-Bakhtarī al-Ṭā'ī—Abū Thawr al-Ḥadā'i, Ḥadā' being a section of [the tribe of] Murād: I came to Ḥudhayfah b. al-Yamān and Abū Mas'ūd 'Uqbah b. 'Amr al-Anṣārī while they were in the mosque of Kūfah on the Day of al-Jara'ah, where the people dealt with [2935]
Sa'īd b. al-'Āṣ as they did. Abū Mas'ūd was treating this as a serious matter and saying, "I do not think [the affair] will be brought to an end without blood being spilled."[248] Ḥudhayfah replied, "By God, it will surely come to an end without producing even a cupping glass of blood. I do not know anything about it today that I did not know when Muḥammad was alive. Verily a man is a follower of Islām in the morning; then in the evening he has nothing to do with it. Then on the morrow he fights the Muslims (*ahl al-qiblah*) and God kills him, so that his heart recoils and he doubles up in fear."[249]

Then I [that is, Abū al-Bakhtarī al-Ṭā'ī] said to Abū Thawr, "Perhaps it was [that way]." He replied, "No, by God, it was not."

[According to al-Ṭabarī:] When Sa'īd b. al-'Āṣ returned to 'Uthmān, having been expelled [from Kūfah], he sent Abū Mūsā to

---

247. Prym proposes two possible emendations in the *isnād*, both of which seem reasonable in view of the other *isnād*s attached to Ja'far b. 'Abdallāh al-Muḥammadī: either (a) 'Amr and 'Alī—Ḥusayn—his father; or (b) 'Amr and 'Alī b. Ḥusayn—Ḥusayn b. 'Īsā—his father.

248. *Mā arā an turadda 'alā 'aqibayhā ḥattā yakūna fīhā dimā'un.*

249. *fa-ta'luwahu istuhu.* Literally: "so that his buttocks rise above him." This entire passage seems quite obscure.

be governor (*amīr*) in Kūfah, and (the Kūfans) confirmed him in authority over it.

It was transmitted to me in writing by al-Sarī—Shu'ayb—Sayf—Yaḥyā b. Muslim—Wāqid b. 'Abdallāh—'Abdallāh b. 'Umayr al-Ashja'ī: (Abū Mūsā) rose up in the mosque during the troubles (*fitnah*) and said, "O people, be still. For I heard the Messenger of God say, 'He who departs [from the Community] when there is an imām over the people'—and by God, he did not say a just imām—'in order to shatter their staff and to break up their community, kill him whoever he may be.'"

It was transmitted to me in writing by al-Sarī—Shu'ayb—Sayf—Muḥammad and Ṭalḥah: When Yazīd b. Qays caused the people to howl at Sa'īd b. al-'Āṣ, word of this came to 'Uthmān.
[2936] Then al-Qa'qā' b. 'Amr approached (Yazīd) and seized him. (Yazīd) said, "What do you want? Do you have any reason to prevent us from seeking (Sa'īd's) resignation?" (Al-Qa'qā') replied, "No. [Are you trying to do anything] beside that?" "No," said (Yazīd). "Then seek his resignation," said (al-Qa'qā'). Yazīd summoned his associates from where they were staying, and they drove Sa'īd back [to Medina] and demanded Abū Mūsā [as his successor].

Then 'Uthmān wrote to them [as follows]: "In the name of God, the Merciful, the Compassionate. To proceed: I have named as your governor the one whom you have chosen, and I have relieved you of Sa'īd. By God, I will surely expose my honor to your abuse, and wear out my patience, and use every effort to seek reconciliation with you. So do not fail to ask for whatever you desire, so long as it does not involve rebellion against God. Nor should you fail to demand relief from whatever you hate, so long as it does not involve rebellion against God. Thus, I will comply with whatever you desire until you have no argument (*ḥujjah*) against me."

('Uthmān) wrote in this vein to the [other] garrison towns. Thus came about the governorship of Abū Mūsā and the expedition of Ḥudhayfah. Abū Mūsā became governor, the governors (*'ummāl*) returned to their provinces, and Ḥudhayfah proceeded to al-Bāb.

According to al-Wāqidī—'Abdallāh b. Muḥammad—his father: In the year 34 (654–55) certain of the Companions of the Messenger of God wrote to others [as follows]: "Come, for if you desire the *jihād*, then the *jihād* is here with us." The people maligned[250] 'Uthmān and censured him in the harshest language ever used against anyone, while the Companions of the Messenger of God were giving their opinions and listening, and among them no one forbade or prevented this save a few individuals: Zayd b. Thābit, Abū Usayd al-Sā'idī, Ka'b b. Mālik, and Ḥassān b. Thābit.

The people assembled and spoke to 'Alī b. Abī Ṭālib, and he entered 'Uthmān's presence and said, "The people stand behind me, and they have spoken to me about you. By God, I do not know what to say to you. I know nothing of which you are ignorant, nor can I point out to you any affair with which you are not well acquainted. Indeed you know what we know. We have not perceived something before you have, so that we must inform you of it. Nor have we gained sole knowledge of anything so that we must bring it to your attention. In no affair have we been assigned greater distinction than you. You have seen and heard the Mes- [2937]
senger of God; you were one of his Companions and became a son-in-law to him. (Abū Bakr) b. Abī Quḥāfah was not better suited than you to act rightly, nor did ('Umar) b. al-Khaṭṭāb enjoy greater merit in any way, and indeed you had a closer blood-relationship to the Messenger of God [than either of them]. You obtained a marriage tie to the Messenger of God such as they never did, nor did they have any precedence over you.[251] Remember God! You are not being given your sight after you were blind, by God, nor are you being instructed after you were in ignorance. Verily the path is manifest and clear, and the signposts of true religion are standing upright.

---

250. Reading *kaththara* instead of *kathura*. See de Goeje, *Introductio*, dcxxvii; and *WKAS*, sub verbo *kaththara*, p. 61, col. 2.

251. 'Uthmān, like Muḥammad, belonged to the Qurashi lineage of 'Abd Shams—that is, the two men had a common great-great-grandfather in the paternal line. 'Umar b. al-Khaṭṭāb and Abū Bakr were both members of the tribe of Quraysh, but their clans (Makhzūm and Taym respectively) were only remotely connected with Muḥammad. In addition, 'Uthmān's mother, Arwā bt. Kurayz, was the granddaughter of 'Abd al-Muṭṭalib on her mother's side; that is, she and Muḥammad were first cousins. As to marriage ties between the first three caliphs and the Prophet: Abū Bakr's daughter 'Ā'ishah became Muḥammad's favorite wife; 'Uthmān married the Prophet's daughter Ruqayyah, who predeceased her husband; 'Umar had no such links, since Muḥammad thought him too harsh for any of his daughers.

"Know, ʿUthmān, that the best of God's servants in His eyes is a just imām, one who has been guided aright and who himself gives right guidance, for he upholds accepted prescriptions (*sunnah maʿlūmah*) and destroys rejected innovations (*bidʿah matrūkah*). By God, everything is clear. Sound prescriptions stand clearly marked, as do blameworthy innovations. The worst of men in God's sight is a tyrannical imām, one who has gone astray himself and by whom others are led astray, for he destroys an
[2938] accepted prescription and revives a rejected innovation. Verily, I heard the Messenger of God say, 'The Day of Resurrection will be brought by the tyrannical imām; he will have no helper and no advocate, so that he will be cast into Hell, turning about in Hell as the mill turns, and then he will plunge into the fiery flood of Hell.' I tell you to beware of God and His sudden assault and His vengeance, for His punishment is harsh and painful indeed. I tell you to beware lest you be the murdered imām of this Community. Indeed it is said that an imām will be killed in this Community, and that bloody strife will be loosed upon it until the Day of Resurrection, and its affairs will become hopelessly entangled. (God) will leave them as sects (*shiyaʿ*), and they will not see the truth due to the great height of falsehood. They will toss therein like waves and wander in confusion."

Then ʿUthmān replied, "By God, I knew that (people) would be saying what you have said. But by God, if you were in my place I would not have berated you nor left you in the lurch nor shamed you nor behaved foully. If I have favored kinsmen, filled a need, sheltered an impoverished wretch, and appointed as governors men like those whom ʿUmar used to appoint, [then what have I done wrong?] I adjure you by God, O ʿAlī, do you know that al-Mughīrah b. Shuʿbah is not there?" "Yes," he answered. (ʿUthmān) said, "Do you know that ʿUmar made him a governor?"[252] "Yes," he answered. Then (ʿUthmān) said, "So why do you blame me for having appointed Ibn ʿĀmir, simply because of his close kinship [with me]?"

ʿAlī said, "I will tell you that everyone appointed by ʿUmar b. al-

252. Of Baṣrah, after the resignation of ʿUtbah b. Ghazwān, probably in 14/635–636. See Donner, *Early Islamic Conquests*, 217, 264. I admit to finding this reference to al-Mughīrah somewhat puzzling.

Khaṭṭāb was kept under close scrutiny by him.[253] If ('Umar) heard a single word concerning him he would flog him, then punish him with the utmost severity. But you do not do [that]. You have been weak and easygoing with your relatives." "They are your relatives as well," answered 'Uthmān. 'Alī said, "By my life, they are closely related to me indeed, but merit is found in others." 'Uthmān said, "Do you know that 'Umar kept Mu'āwiyah in office throughout his entire caliphate, and I have only done the same." 'Alī answered, "I adjure you by God, do you know that Mu'āwiyah was more afraid of 'Umar than was 'Umar's own slave Yarfa'?" "Yes," said ('Uthmān). 'Alī went on, "In fact Mu'āwiyah makes decisions on issues without [consulting] you, and you know it. Thus, he says to the people. 'This is 'Uthmān's command.' You hear of this, but do not censure him."[254] Then 'Alī left him, and 'Uthmān went out on his heels. [2939]

Then ('Uthmān) took his seat upon the pulpit and said, "To proceed: For everything there is some bane and in every situation there is some defect. The bane of this Community (*ummah*) and the defect in this [divinely bestowed] beneficence are the maligners and slanderers who let you see what is pleasing to you and conceal what is hateful to you. They talk and talk to you. Men who resemble ostriches follow the first one to make a noise. Their favorite watering place is the one far away; they fail to quench their thirst and they get only the sediment. No leader arises, affairs have worn them out, and they possess no means of gain."

"By God, you have surely blamed me for things like those which you accepted from Ibn al-Khaṭṭāb. But he trampled you underfoot, smote you with his hand, and subdued you by his tongue, and so you submitted to him whether you liked it or not. I [2940] have been lenient with you. I let you tread on my shoulders while I restrained my hand and tongue, and therefore you have been insolent toward me. By God, I am stronger [than he] in kinsmen, I have allies closer at hand, I possess more supporters. It is more

253. *fa-innamā yaṭa'u 'alā ṣimākhihi*: literally, "indeed he would trample on his ear." See de Goeje, *Introductio*, dlix.

254. Reading *tu'ayyiru* instead of *tughayyiru*, in accordance with de Goeje's suggestion. See de Goeje, *Introductio*, ccclxxxiii, sub verbo *'ayyara*, dcxxvii.

fitting for me [than for him] to say 'Come!' and have [men] come to me. I have appointed over you your peers.[255] I have cheerfully lavished benefits upon you. But you have attributed to me a nature that I do not possess and statements that I have not uttered. Restrain your tongues and your slandering and maligning of your rulers (*wulāt*), for I have kept from you a man who would satisfy you with less than these words of mine were he the one [now] speaking to you. Nay, but which of your rights are you deprived of? By God, I have achieved no less than did my predecessors or those about whose [standing in the Community] you have not disagreed. There is a surplus of wealth, so why should I not do as I wish with the surplus? Why otherwise did I become imām?"

Then Marwān b. al-Ḥakam stood up and said [to the assembly], "If you wish, by God, we will cause the sword to judge between us and you—ourselves and you, by God! As the poet has said,

We have exposed our honor to your abuse;
unfit for you are
the overnight encampments which you erect
in the dung lying on the ground.

[2941] 'Uthmān said, "Be still now. Leave to me and my associates anything you have to say concerning this matter. Did I not command you not to speak?" Marwān fell silent and 'Uthmān descended [from the pulpit].

In this year, Abū 'Abs b. Jābir, a veteran of Badr, died in Medina. Two other veterans of Badr also died: Misṭaḥ b. Uthāthah, and 'Āqil b. Abī al-Bukayr, of [the clan of] Banū Sa'd b. Layth, an ally (*ḥalīf*) of the Banu 'Adī.

In this year, the Pilgrimage was led by 'Uthmān b. 'Affān.

255. *Wa-laqad a'dadtu lakum aqrānakum.* See de Goeje, *Introductio,* cdxxii, who offers the following interpretation: "*Pares vobis apposui, non quod mihi licuit, numero et auctoritate praepollentes.*"

The Events of the Year 35

(July 11, 655–June 29, 656)

Among these was the encampment of the Egyptians at Dhū Khushub.

Concerning that event, it was related to me by Aḥmad b. Thābit—someone who related it [to him]—Isḥāq b. ʿĪsā—Abū Maʿshar: Dhū Khushub took place in the year 35 (655–56). Al-Wāqidī concurs in this.

An Account of the Egyptians Who Went to Dhū Khushub, and the Reason Why Certain Iraqis Went to Dhū al-Marwah

It was transmitted to me in writing by al-Sarī—Shuʿayb—Sayf—ʿAṭiyyah—Yazīd al-Faqʿasī: ʿAbdallāh b. Sabāʾ was a Jew from [2942]
Ṣanʿāʾ, and his mother was a black woman. He converted to Islam in the time of ʿUthmān, then roamed about the lands of the Muslims attempting to lead them into error. He began in the Ḥijāz, and then [worked] successively in Baṣrah, Kūfah, and Syria. He was unable to work his will upon a single one of the Syrians; they drove him out and he came to Egypt. He settled among the Egyp-

tians, saying to them, among other things, "How strange it is that some people claim that Jesus will return [to the earth], while denying that Muḥammad will return. Now Almighty God has said, 'He who has ordained the Qur'ān for thee shall surely restore thee to a place of return.'[256] Now Muḥammad is more worthy than Jesus to return."

(Yazīd al-Faqʿasī) says: This gained the approval [of his listeners], and so he fabricated for them [the notion of] the Return (*rajʿah*), and they discussed it among themselves.[257] Later on, (Ibn Sabā') said to them, "Verily there have been a thousand prophets (*nabī*); every prophet has an executor (*waṣī*) and ʿAlī was the executor of Muḥammad."[258] He continued, "Muḥammad is the seal of the prophets, and ʿAlī is the seal of the executors." Then after that he said, "Who commits a greater wrong than a man who has not carried out the testament of the Messenger of God, who has attacked the executor of the Messenger of God, and who has usurped power over the Community?" Then he told them, "Verily ʿUthmān has taken it without right, while this one [that is, ʿAlī] is the executor of the Messenger of God. Therefore champion this cause and set it going. Begin by censuring your governors (*umarā'*). Proclaim publicly the commanding of good and the forbidding of evil,[259] and you will win over the people. Summon them to this cause."

Then he dispersed his agents (*duʿāt*) and wrote to those whom he had corrupted in the garrison towns. They returned his corre-

256. Qur'ān 28:85. I have slightly altered Arberry's rendering to fit the meaning proposed by Ibn Sabā'.

257. The doctrine of the Return or Second Coming—here applied to Muḥammad, but more characteristically to ʿAlī or the seventh or twelfth imam—is one of the characteristic doctrines of the *ghulāt* (Shiʿite extremists) in the late seventh and eighth centuries. In spite of the dubious origins of this idea, it was ultimately applied by mainstream Shiʿism to the Twelfth Imam, who remains in a state of occultation until his coming again to usher in the last age. See A. A. Sachedina, *Messianism in Twelver Shiism* (Albany, N.Y.: 1981); Wadad al-Qadi, "The Development of the Term *'Ghulāt'* in Muslim Literature with Special Reference to the Kaysāniyya," *Akten VII Kongr. f. Arabistik u. Islamwissenschaft* (Göttingen: 1976), pp. 295–319.

258. Another characteristic Shiʿi doctrine. See W. Madelung, "Imāma," *EI*², III, 1166—67.

259. The fundamental public duty of every adult Muslim; one may not be in position to compel the rulers to obey God's commandments, but one always has the obligation to warn and rebuke wherever sin is observed.

spondence and secretly preached their notions [to others]. In public they proclaimed the commanding of good and the forbidding of [2943
evil. They began sending letters to the garrison towns, filling them with censure of their rulers, while their brethren would write back to them in similar terms. Among [these dissidents] the inhabitants of each garrison town would write about their activities to another garrison town. Those involved would read this aloud in their various garrison towns, until finally they extended this [agitation] to Medina and spread his message throughout the earth. Their real aim was different from the one that they proclaimed in public, and what they kept secret was different from that which they presented openly. Thus, the inhabitants of every garrison town were saying, "We are secure from the trials facing everyone except the Medinese." As the latter became aware of [the agitation] in all the garrison towns, they said, "We are secure from the situation facing the people."

At this point [the narrator] is joined by Muḥammad and Ṭalḥah: [The Medinese] came to ʿUthmān and said, "O Commander of the Faithful, have you heard what we hear concerning the people?" He answered, "No, by God. I have only heard about order and security." They continued, "[Certain things] have come to our attention," and they told him what had been communicated to them. Then [ʿUthmān] said, "You are my associates (*shurakā'*) and the men of probity (*shuhūd*)[260] among the Believers, so advise me." They responded, "We advise you to send men whom you trust to the garrison towns so that they may bring back their reports to you."

Then he summoned Muḥammad b. Maslamah and dispatched him to Kūfah; he also sent Usāmah b. Zayd to Baṣrah, ʿAmmār b. Yāsir to Egypt, and ʿAbdallāh b. ʿUmar to Syria. In addition to these, he sent men to various other places. They all returned before ʿAmmār and said, "O people, we did not disapprove of anything [which we found during our tours of inspection], nor did the notables (*aʿlām*) or commoners (*ʿawāmm*) among the Muslims." They said also, "The affairs of the Muslims are in good

260. In Islamic law, *shuhūd* are witnesses whose testimony is admissible in court. They must be persons of recognized religious and moral probity, and that seems to be what is at issue here.

order if only their governors (*umarā'*) act equitably among them and keep watch over them."[261] The people waited so long for ʿAmmār that they imagined he had been murdered. Then unexpectedly they got a letter from ʿAbdallāh b. Saʿd b. Abī Sarḥ, in-
[2944] forming them that a band of men (*qawm*) in Egypt had focused all their efforts on ʿAmmār and won him to their cause. Among these were ʿAbdallāh b. al-Sawdā' [that is, Ibn Sabā'], Khālid b. Muljam, Sūdān b. Ḥumrān, and Kinānah b. Bishr.

It was transmitted to me in writing from al-Sarī—Shuʿayb—Sayf—Muḥammad and Ṭalḥah and ʿAṭiyyah: ʿUthmān wrote to the inhabitants of the garrison towns [as follows]: "To proceed: I require the governors (*ʿummāl*) to appear before me during the Pilgrimage season every year, and I have enjoined the Community (*ummah*) to command the good and forbid the evil ever since I took office. Nothing has been demanded from me or from any of my governors that I have not granted. Neither I nor my household claims any priority in rights over the subjects (*raʿiyyah*) save (the rights) bequeathed to them.[262] Now the Medinese have represented to me that some groups are being vilified and others beaten. If then anyone alleges that he has suffered clandestine beatings or verbal abuse, let him come [before me] during the Pilgrimage season and obtain his due, whether it be from me or from my governors. Beyond that, 'be charitable, for God recompenses the charitable.' "[263]

When (this letter) was read out in the garrison towns, it caused the people to weep, and they invoked blessings upon ʿUthmān, saying, "Verily the Community is groaning in labor with evil." ʿUthmān sent to the governors (*ʿummāl*) of the garrison towns and

261. A somewhat conjectural reading: *al-amru amru 'l-muslimīna illā anna umarā'ahum yuqsiṭūna baynahum wa-yaqūmūna ʿalayhim.* Caetani's paraphrase (*Annali*, VIII, 111) seems to distort the meaning: "essi riferirono di non aver trovato nulla di anormale o di riprovevole, se non che i governatori erano trattati e giudicati ingiustamente dai loro dipendenti." A parallel to the first clause can be found below (text, I, 2947, l. 16): *kāna 'l-amru amrahum wa'l-nasū tabaʿun lahum.*

262. *Wa-laysa lī wa-li-ʿiyālī ḥaqqun qabla 'l-raʿiyyati illā matrūkun lahum.* The problem phrase here is *matrūk lahum.* Presumably it refers to the property and income rights that the Caliph held as head of the Community; these were rooted in the one-fifth share of booty and conquests claimed by the Prophet and his successors. See Qur'ān 9:42; Donner, *Early Islamic Conquests*, 241–43.

263. Qur'ān 12:88.

they came to him: ʿAbdallāh b. ʿĀmir, Muʿāwiyah, and ʿAbdallāh b. Saʿd. He also sought the counsel of Saʿīd (b. al-ʿĀṣ) and ʿAmr (b. al-ʿĀṣ). Then he said, "Woe to you! What is this complaining and protest? By God, I fear that you are rightly accused and that I alone will be reproached for (your misdeeds)." They answered him, "Did you not send [to us], and did we not inform you about the faction [of malcontents]?[264] (Your envoys) returned, did they not, without having heard anything untoward from anyone? No, by God, (these complainers) have not told the truth or been sincere, and we know of no valid basis for this situation. You are not a man who should allow someone to get you upset about things.[265] All this is mere allegation that should not be taken seriously or inquired into." [2945]

(ʿUthmān) said, "Give me your advice, then." Saʿīd b. al-ʿĀṣ said, "This is a contrived affair, fabricated in secret so that it can be conveyed to some unknowing person. Then he will pass it on, and in this way it will be discussed in their assemblies (*majālis*)." (ʿUthmān) said, "What is the remedy for that?" (Saʿīd) replied, "First, seek out these dissidents (*hā'ulā' al-qawm*); then kill those among whom this movement emerges."

ʿAbdallāh b. Saʿd said, "Take from the people what they owe if you have given them what is theirs, for that is better than neglecting them."[266]

Muʿāwiyah said, "You have made me a governor, and I rule a group of men (*qawm*) about whom you hear nothing but good. Now these two men [that is, Saʿīd b. al-ʿĀṣ of Kūfah and ʿAbdallāh b. Saʿd of Egypt] know best about their own districts." (ʿUthmān) said, "What do you advocate?" (Muʿāwiyah) replied, "Excellent discipline."

(ʿUthmān) asked, "What do you think, ʿAmr?" (ʿAmr) replied, "In my opinion you are too lenient; you have been lax in dealing

---

264. *Alam narjaʿ ilayka 'l-khabara ʿan 'l-qawmi.* Ibn al-Athīr, *Kāmil* (Beirut), III, 155, gives a slightly different wording: *alam yarjaʿ ilayka l-khabaru ʿan 'l-ʿawāmmi. ʿAwāmm* ("the masses, the common people, the populace") seems to fit better here than *qawm,* which in this portion of Ṭabarī most often refers to a band of men united by a common objective—namely, hostility to ʿUthmān—though in principle it could mean "the Muslim people."

265. *Wa-mā kunta li-ta'khudha aḥadan fa-yuqīmaka ʿalā shay'in.*

266. The final clause is a conjectural translation: *fa-innahu khayrun min an tadaʿahum.*

with them. You have increased [their stipends] beyond the levels set by 'Umar. I believe that you must follow the path of your two predecessors, showing severity or leniency according to the situation. Severity is the right policy for the man who constantly does evil to the people, while leniency is appropriate for one who deals with the people in good faith. However, you have shown leniency to both without distinction."

Then 'Uthmān arose. Praising and extolling God, he said, "I have heard everything that you have advised me to do. Every affair has an exit door. The present affair has emerged, and on account of it one fears for this Community. The door (out of this affair) is bolted shut, and thus leniency, generous treatment, and the gratification [of desires] will be shown only in conformity
[2946] with the commandments (*ḥudūd*) of Almighty God; for in none of these may one manifest any shortcoming. If something blocks (this door) kindness and generosity [will open it]. By God, (the door out of this affair) will surely be opened. Against me no man has any valid proof, and God knows that I have not neglected any good for the people or for myself. By God, the mill of revolt (*fitnah*) is turning; blessed will 'Uthmān be if he dies without having set it in motion. Restrain the people, bestow their rights upon them, and forgive them. But where God's rights are concerned, do not be lax in regard to those."[267]

When 'Uthmān terminated [the council], he dispatched Mu'āwiyah and 'Abdallāh b. Sa'd to Medina, while Ibn 'Āmir returned [to Iraq] along with Sa'īd. When 'Uthmān was left alone, the caravan leader sang (these verses):

The lean camels knew,
    and the she-camels bent like a bow,
That the amir after him would be 'Alī;
    in al-Zubayr there is a worthy successor,
And the fiery Ṭalḥah is an heir thereto.[268]

---

267. This speech is very difficult to construe. Ibn al-Athīr, *Kāmil* (Beirut), III, 156, offers only an abridged paraphrase, thus implying that he did not really understand it either.

268. In accordance with the editor of Ibn al-Athīr, *Kāmil* (Beirut), III, 156, and Ibrāhīm, I read *lahā* instead of *lamā* in the following verse: *wa-ṭalḥatu 'l-ḥāmī lahā waliyyu.*

Ka'b (al-Aḥbār) said as he traveled behind 'Uthmān, "By God, the amir after him will be the master of the she-mule," and he pointed to Mu'āwiyah.

It was transmitted to me in writing by al-Sarī—Shu'ayb—Sayf—Badr b. al-Khalīl b. 'Uthmān b. Quṭbah al-Asadī—a man from the Banū Asad: Mu'āwiyah did not cease to hope for (the caliphate) after he came to 'Uthmān, at the time when (the latter) called his governors together to meet with him during the Pilgrimage season. Then (Mu'āwiyah) departed and the poet chanted:

Verily the amir after him will be 'Alī, [2947]
and in al-Zubayr there is a worthy successor.

Ka'b (al-Aḥbār) said, "You lie; after him will come the master of the gray (she-mule)"—that is, Mu'āwiyah. Mu'āwiyah was informed [of this] and asked (Ka'b) about what he had heard. (Ka'b) said, "Yes, you are to be the amir after him, but you will not obtain (this office) until you deny this statement of mine." This made a profound impression on Mu'āwiyah.

At this point (the authorities previously mentioned) are joined by Abū Ḥārithah and Abū 'Uthmān—Rajā' b. Ḥaywah and others: When 'Uthmān arrived in Medina [after the conclusion of the Pilgrimage], he had the governors return to their provinces. All of them proceeded on, but Sa'īd stayed behind. When Mu'āwiyah bade farewell to 'Uthmān, he left (the latter's) residence attired for the journey, wearing his sword and with his bow on his shoulder. Then (Mu'āwiyah) happened to meet a few of the Emigrants, among them Ṭalḥah, al-Zubayr, and 'Alī.

He rose and greeted them; then he leaned on his bow and said, "You know that this situation has come about because the people are struggling among themselves to achieve supremacy for certain men. There is not one among you but that some member of his clan used to claim leadership over him, dominate him, and decide matters without him, seeking neither testimony nor advice from him. Then at last Almighty God sent His Prophet, through him ennobling those who heeded him. When (the Muslims) turned the leadership over to his successors, they did so through consultation among themselves, assigning superiority on the basis of priority [of conversion], precedence [in religion], and legal judgment (*ijtihād*). If (the Community's leaders) act on that

basis, then they will keep control of matters and the people will submit to them. But if they pay heed to the things of this world and seek them in a struggle for supremacy with one another, they will be deprived of (power) and God will give it back to those who used to lead them. Otherwise, let them beware of the vicissitudes of fortune, for God has the power to alter [His decree], and He can dispose as He wishes of the kingship and authority that are His. I have left among you an old man, so display good will toward him
[2948] and protect him. Thereby you will be more fortunate than he."

Then (Muʿāwiyah) bade them farewell and went on his way. ʿAlī said, "I see no good in this (man)." Al-Zubayr said, "No, by God, there was never anything more distressing to you or us than he was this morning."

It was related to me by ʿAbdallāh b. Aḥmad b. Shabbawayh—his father—ʿAbdallāh—Isḥāq b. Yaḥyā—Mūsā b. Ṭalḥah: ʿUthmān sent for Ṭalḥah, and I accompanied him. When he entered ʿUthmān's presence, there were ʿAlī, Saʿd (b. Abī Waqqāṣ), al-Zubayr, ʿUthmān, and Muʿāwiyah. Muʿāwiyah praised God and extolled Him as He merits, and then he said, "You are the Companions of the Messenger of God, the best [of His followers] on earth, and those charged with the affairs of this Community. No one other than you can hope for that. You have chosen your companion [as caliph] without compulsion or personal ambition. He has grown old and his life has passed by. If you had waited for decrepitude [to afflict] him, that would be near at hand. However, I hope that he has revered God so that He will allow him to reach that stage of life. Talk has spread, and I fear it for your sakes, for you have not denounced it in any way. You have my aid (in this matter). Do not inspire the people to long for your government, for by God, if they desire that, you will never see them do anything but turn tail and flee."

ʿAlī replied, "What is that to you, and what do you know about it? You have no mother!" (Muʿāwiyah) said, "Leave my mother her place [in the Community]. She is not the worst of your mothers. She accepted Islam and swore fidelity to the Prophet.[269] Now answer me in regard to what I am saying to you."

269. Muʿāwiyah's mother Hind bt. ʿUtbah had accompanied Meccan forces to the battle of Uḥud in 3/625, as the women of a tribe often did in ancient Arabia.

Then ʿUthmān said, "The son of my brother has spoken the truth. I will tell you in regard to myself and my conduct in office that my two predecessors wronged both themselves and those who followed in their path. Indeed the Messenger of God used to [2949] bestow [public funds] upon his relatives, while my near kinsmen were impoverished and possessed few of life's necessities. Thus, I laid my hands on some of that wealth because of my concern for them. It was my opinion that (this wealth) was mine. Now if you regard that as an error, return (the money); my authority will be subject to yours."

They replied, "You are right and have done well." They continued, "You gave [public funds] to ʿAbdallāh b. Khālid b. Asīd and to Marwān," alleging that he had given Marwān 15,000 [dirhams] and Ibn Asīd 50,000, and they took (these sums) back from those two. They were satisfied with this and departed content.

Here the narrative reverts to the account of Sayf and his authorities: On the morning that Muʿāwiyah bade farewell to ʿUthmān and departed, he said to him, "O Commander of the Faithful, come with me to Syria before you are attacked by men against whom you cannot defend yourself, for the Syrians are steadfastly loyal." (ʿUthmān) answered, "I will not exchange my proximity to the Messenger of God for anything, even if my throat is slashed because of that." (Muʿāwiyah) said, "I will send you an army from (Syria), which will remain among the Medinese to confront any ill fortune that may befall Medina or you." (ʿUthmān) replied, "With an army quartered among them, I will stint the rations allocated to the neighbors of the Messenger of God, and I will create scarcity for the inhabitants of the Abode of Refuge and Support (*Dār al-Hijrah wa'l-Naṣrah*)." (Muʿāwiyah) said, "By God, O Commander of the Faithful, you will surely be assassinated or attacked." (ʿUthmān) responded, "God suffices for me, and what an excellent guardian is He!"[270] Then Muʿāwiyah said, "Little slaughter camels! Where are the slaughter camels?"

When the prophet's uncle Ḥamzah was killed in the fighting she cut open his breast and bit off a piece of his liver—again a traditional gesture of revenge. See Ibn Isḥāq, *Sīrah*, 581; Guillaume transl., 385.

270. Qur'ān 3:264.

He set out until he came upon the band [of Companions mentioned above], and then he proceeded on.

Now the Egyptians had corresponded with their fellow partisans in Kūfah and Baṣrah, and with all those who had agreed
[2950] with them to rebel against their governors. They fixed a day when their governors would be away, but save for the Kūfans, none of them carried (the scheme) out properly and rose in revolt. In (Kūfah) Yazīd b. Qays al-Arḥabī rebelled and his comrades gathered around him. The military commandant was al-Qaʿqāʿ b. ʿAmr. He came to (Yazīd), and the people surrounded (Yazīd's followers) and implored them [to break off their revolt].

Then Yazīd said to al-Qaʿqāʿ, "What recourse do you have against me and these men? By God, I submit to authority, and I adhere to my Community (*jamāʿah*) and to them. However, I and those whom you observe are calling for the termination of Saʿīd's governorship. (Al-Qaʿqāʿ) answered, "The elite (*khāṣṣah*) seeks to end a state of affairs with which the masses (*ʿāmmah*) are content." He continued, "That is a matter for the Commander of the Faithful." Then he left them and [their] call for [Saʿīd's] resignation, while they could proclaim nothing else. They encountered Saʿīd and drove him back from al-Jaraʿah. The people concurred in Abū Mūsā [as their next governor] and ʿUthmān confirmed him in office.

When the governors returned [from their meeting in Mecca], the sect of Ibn Sabā' (*al-Sabā'iyyah*) had no way to get to the garrison towns. They wrote their adherents in the garrison towns that they should assemble in Medina in order to decide what they meant to do. They pretended that they were simply "commanding the good" and interrogating ʿUthmān about certain issues. Their aim was for these to circulate among the people and become verified against him.

Thus, they assembled in Medina, and as his envoys ʿUthmān sent two men, one from the clan of Makhzūm and the other from the clan of Zuhr. He said, "Find out what they mean to do and learn all about them." These two men were among those who had won ʿUthmān's respect by their refined behavior (*adab*); they patiently sought the truth and harbored no malevolence. When (the dissidents) saw them, they revealed their secrets to them and informed them of their aims. (ʿUthmān's two envoys) said, "Who

among the Medinese supports you against this man [namely, ʿUthmān]?" "Three persons," they answered. The two men said, "Is there anyone else?" "No," they said. The two (envoys) went on, "So what do you intend to do?" They replied, "We want to mention to (ʿUthmān) certain misdeeds that we have planted in the hearts of the people. Afterwards we shall go back to them and claim that we compelled him to confess these things, but that he did not abandon them or repent. Then we will set out in the guise of pilgrims until we reach [Medina]. We will surround him and [2951]
depose him, and if he refuses we will kill him." And so it happened.

The two (envoys) returned to ʿUthmān with the news, and he laughed, saying, "O God, preserve these (enemies of mine), for if You do not preserve them, they will be wretched indeed. As for ʿAmmār (b. Yāsir), he violently assaulted ʿAbbās b. ʿUtbah b. Abī Lahab. As for Muḥammad b. Abī Bakr, he was highly regarded until he supposed that he was not bound by rights and obligations (*ḥuqūq*). As for Ibn Sahlah, he faces trial and tribulation."

Then (ʿUthmān) sent to the Kūfans and Baṣrans, and summoned them to pray in congregation. They assembled before him at the base of the pulpit, and the Companions of the Messenger of God came and surrounded them. Then (ʿUthmān) praised and extolled God, and told them the news of this band [of dissidents]. Then the two (former envoys) arose, and all (those present) said, "Kill (the dissidents)! Verily the Messenger of God has said, 'God's curse is on any man who has summoned [others] to join him or anyone else while there is an imām over the people, so put him to death.' And ʿUmar b. al-Khaṭṭāb said, 'I permit you only to kill (such a man), and I am your partner [in that deed].' "

Then ʿUthmān responded, "Nay, but we do our utmost to pardon and accept and enlighten them, and we oppose no one until he violates a divine commandment (*ḥadd*) or manifests unbelief. Now these (dissidents) have mentioned various matters, concerning which you and they are equally well informed. However, they allege that they are bringing (these matters) to my attention in order to compel me [to respond] to them in the presence of those who remain uninformed."

"They say, 'He has performed the complete prayer rite while [2952]
traveling [by performing four *rakʿah*s instead of two], when for-

merly this was not done."[271] But in fact I came to a town [namely, Mecca] where my household was residing, [while I had property in al-Ṭā'if], and on account of these two things I carried out the full rite.[272] Is this the case?" (The assembled people) said, "O God, it is so."

"They say, 'You prohibited public use of a grazing reserve.'[273] But by God, (the pasture land) whose use I restricted had already been reserved before me. By God, they [namely, 'Uthmān's predecessors] did not forbid grazing rights to anyone. They only reserved (grazing land) that the inhabitants of Medina had usurped, and they prevented no one from pasturing [his animals]. They used it only for the alms taxes[274] due from the Muslims, guarding them lest there be a dispute between anyone and the official in charge of (the alms tax). But they neither barred nor ejected anyone from it, save those who offered a dirham.[275] I possess no camels save two riding animals; I have no other livestock at all. When I became caliph, I had more camels and sheep than any of the Arabs, and today I have neither sheep nor camels, except for two camels to use for the Pilgrimage. Is this the case?" (The people) said, "O God, it is so."

"(The dissidents) say, 'The Qur'ān used to be [preserved in a number of different] written versions (*kutub*), and you have abandoned all but one.' But verily the Qur'ān is one, and came through one [man]. In this matter I have only followed these.[276] Is this the case?" "Yes," they replied. They sought to have him kill (the dissidents).

"(The dissidents) say that I brought al-Ḥakam back after the

---

271. A reference to 'Uthmān's additions to the rites of prayer at Minā during the Pilgrimage; see above, pp. 38–40 (text, I, 2833–2835, *sub anno* 29), and note 65.

272. The phrase in brackets is supplied in accordance with Prym's suggestion; see note a.

273. There is a somewhat fuller parallel account of this dispute in Balādhurī, *Ansāb*, V, 38.

274. That is, these taxes (*ṣadaqāt*) had been paid in animals—presumably camels—rather than cash.

275. That is, rich men who tried to gain privileged access to the grazing reserve by bribery. See de Goeje, *Introductio*, cccii.

276. The reference of course is to 'Uthmān's decision to establish a single definitive recension of the Qur'ān, and to destroy the existing versions with their many discrepancies. "These" presumably refers to the board of editors (headed by Zayd b. Thābit) whom he appointed to carry out the task.

Messenger of God had exiled him. Now al-Ḥakam was a Meccan; the Messenger of God exiled him from Mecca to al-Ṭā'if, and then he brought him back. Thus, the Messenger of God both sent him into exile and had him return. Is that the case?" They said, "O God, it is so."

"(The dissidents) say, 'You have appointed youths as governors.' But I only appointed a man who was capable and commanded broad support [namely, 'Abdallāh b. 'Āmir in Baṣrah]. These (dissidents) are inhabitants of his province, so pay them no heed regarding him.[277] My predecessors appointed younger men than these to office, and people spoke more harshly to the Messenger of God than they have to me in connection with his appointment of Usāmah.[278] Is that the case?" They responded, "O God, it is so. (These dissidents) denounce to the people things that they leave unexplained."

"(The dissidents) say that I gave to Ibn Abī Sarḥ the booty that God bestowed upon him [during the campaign in Ifrīqiyah].[279] But in fact out of the booty that God gave, I only turned over to him one-fifth out of the one-fifth [legally allocated to the caliph]. The amount was 100,000 [dirhams], and Abū Bakr and 'Umar did the same thing. The army claimed to find this reprehensible, and so I have restored to them [the 100,000 dirhams], though it was not really theirs. Is that the case?" They said, "Yes."

"(The dissidents) say that I love my kinsmen and that I make [2953] gifts to them [from the public treasury]. As to my love, it has not been turned into wrongdoing for their benefit; on the contrary, it is the weightiest of [my] obligations to them. As to [my] gifts to them, what I give them is drawn from my own property; I do not regard the wealth of the Muslims as lawful for myself or for anyone else among the people. I used to give large and much-coveted gifts from my personal property in the time of the Messenger of God, Abū Bakr, and 'Umar, and at that time I was ava-

277. I have emended the text in accordance with Prym's suggestion, note 1.

278. In 11/632, shortly before his death, Muḥammad put the young Usāmah b. Zayd b. Ḥārithah in command of a raid into the Balqā' (the district around Karak east of the Dead Sea) and al-Dārūm (a fortress just south of Gaza). See Ibn Isḥāq, *Sīrah*, 776, 970, 999; Guillaume transl., 523, 652, 678. Al-Dārūm: Le Strange, *Palestine under the Moslems*, 412, 437.

279. On this incident see above, pp. 19–20 (text, I, 2814–2815, *sub anno* 27).

ricious and greedy. Now when I have attained the usual life-span of my family, when my life has reached its end and I have distributed my property among my relatives, do the heretics (*mulḥid*) say such things? Indeed, by God, no one can rightfully say that I have had any garrison town surrender [its] surplus revenues, for I have returned (the surpluses) to them.[280] I have received only the twenty percent [legally allocated to the caliph], and from this I have allowed nothing for myself. The Muslims have taken charge of registering (these revenues) for the proper recipients with no involvement from me, and not a penny of God's wealth has been diverted. Now what is beyond that and what I use to sustain myself I consume only from my own property."

"(The dissidents) say, 'You have given the land to certain men.' As regards these lands, when they were conquered, the Emigrants and Helpers shared in them with (these men). If a man remained any place within these conquered territories, his family followed his lead. If a man has returned to his family [from the conquered lands], that does not negate [his claim to lands] that God has acquired for him. I determined what should be distributed to them out of (the conquests) that God had bestowed upon them. Then, at their request, I purchased (property of equivalent value) for them from [other] men who owned land in Arabia. Then I transferred their share [of the conquered territories] to (these latter), and it is now in their hands."[281]

[2954] ʿUthmān had divided his wealth and lands among the Banū Umayyah, treating his own children as he did the other recipients. He began with the Banū Abī al-ʿĀṣ, giving the men in the lineage of al-Ḥakam (b. Abī al-ʿĀṣ) 10,000 [dirhams] each; they

---

280. *Wa-innī wa-'llāhi mā ḥamaltu ʿalā miṣrin min 'l-amṣāri faḍlan fa-yajūza dhālika liman qālahu wa-laqad radadtuhu ʿalayhim.* See de Goeje, *Introductio,* cdiv, sub verbo *faḍl.*

281. This passage refers to ʿUthmān's grants of estates and villages within the conquered territories (Iraq in particular) to powerful individuals. ʿUmar had done the same thing, but ʿUthmān was thought to be overly generous in this regard. See Donner, *Early Islamic Conquests,* 241–45. There have been numerous allusions above to this and to the resentment inspired by it. For example, see pp. 58, 59–61, 112–13, 120–21 (text, I, 2852, 2854–2855, 2908, 2916). The last sentence is difficult: *Fa-biʿtuhu lahum bi-amrihim min rijālin ahli ʿaqārin bi-bilādi 'l-ʿArabi fa-naqaltu ilayhim naṣībahum fa-huwa fī aydihim dūnī.* See Caetani, *Annali,* VIII, 203.

took 100,000 dirhams [altogether]. To his own sons he gave a like amount. (The remainder) was divided among the Banū al-ʿĀṣ, the Banū al-ʿĪṣ, and the Banū Ḥarb.[282]

ʿUthmān's retinue (*ḥāshiyah*) had dealt leniently with those bands [of dissidents]. The Muslims demanded nothing short of putting them to death, while (ʿUthmān) insisted on letting them go. Thus, (the dissidents) departed and returned to their own provinces, having agreed to attack him[283] [when they came back] in the guise of pilgrims in the company of [genuine] pilgrims. They corresponded with one another, saying, "Rendezvous in Shawwāl at the outskirts of Medina." Thus, in Shawwal of the year 12 [of ʿUthmān's reign; April 656] they erected tents in the manner of pilgrims and made camp near Medina.

It was transmitted to me in writing by al-Sarī—Shuʿayb—Sayf—Muḥammad and Ṭalḥah and Abū Ḥārithah and Abū ʿUthmān: In Shawwāl of the year 35 (April 656), the Egyptians set out in four companies under the leadership of four commanders. The lowest number cited is six hundred, while the highest is one thousand. Leading the companies were ʿAbd al-Raḥmān b. ʿUdays al-Balawī, Kinānah b. Bishr al-Tujībī,[284] Sūdān b. Ḥumrān al-Sakūnī, and Qutayrah b. Fulān al-Sakūnī. In command of the whole body of men (*qawm*) was al-Ghāfiqī b. Ḥarb al-ʿAkkī. They dared not inform the people that they were setting off to war and went instead in the guise of pilgrims. Accompanying them was Ibn al-Sawdāʾ [that is, ʿAbdallāh b. Sabāʾ].

The Kūfans [likewise] set out in four companies, led by Zayd b. Ṣūḥān al-ʿAbdī, al-Ashtar al-Nakhaʿī, Ziyād b. al-Naḍr al-Ḥārithī, and ʿAbdallāh b. al-Aṣamm, a member of the tribe of ʿĀmir b. Ṣaʿṣaʿah. Their numbers were the same as those of the Egyptians, and ʿAmr b. al-Aṣamm was in overall command. [2955]

The Baṣrans set out in four companies, led by Ḥukaym b. Ja-

282. The lineage of the Umayyad clan—or more strictly, the descendants of ʿAbd Shams b. ʿAbd Manāf—is given in Appendix I, adapted from the tables in Gernot Rotter, *Die Umayyaden und der zweite Bürgerkrieg (680–692)* (Wiesbaden 1982), 253–57.

283. Reading *yaghzuwahu* rather than *yaghzuwahum*. See de Goeje, *Introductio*, dcxxviii.

284. Reading "al-Tujībī" instead of "al-Laythī." See de Goeje, *Introductio*, dcxxviii.

balah al-ʿAbdī, Dhurayḥ b. ʿAbbād al-ʿAbdī, Bishr b. Shurayḥ al-Ḥuṭam b. Ḍubayʿah al-Qaysī, and Ibn al-Muḥarrish b. ʿAbd ʿAmr al-Ḥanafī. Their number was the same as that of the Egyptians, and Ḥurqūṣ b. Zubayr al-Saʿdī was in command over them all, save for those among the people who followed after them.

As for the Egyptians, they yearned for ʿAlī [as caliph], while the Baṣrans desired Ṭalḥah and the Kūfans al-Zubayr. They all set out simultaneously. The people had disparate [aims], and every faction (*firqah*) was certain that it would obtain complete success to the exclusion of the other two. Thus, they proceeded until, three days from Medina, a group of men from among the Baṣrans went forward and made camp at Dhū Khushub. A section of the Kūfans made camp at al-Aʿwaṣ, and a group of Egyptians came to join them, having left the main body of (their compatriots) behind at Dhū al-Marwah.[285]

[2956] Ziyād b. al-Naḍr and ʿAbdallāh b. al-Aṣamm traveled back and forth between the Egyptians and Baṣrans saying, "Do not be overhasty or force us to rush, so that we can enter Medina and explore the situation for you. We have in fact heard that (the Medinese) have mobilized their troops against us. By God, if the Medinese fear us and deem it lawful to fight us when they have no solid knowledge about us, they will be even more hostile when they do obtain this, and our movement will fail. On the other hand, if they do not deem it lawful to fight us and we find that what we have heard is false, then we will bring that news back to you." (The Baṣrans and Egyptians) said, "Go ahead."

Thus, the two men entered Medina and met with the wives of the Prophet and with ʿAlī, Ṭalḥah, and al-Zubayr. They said, "We have only come here[286] to seek from this ruler [that is, ʿUthmān] the removal of certain of our governors. We have come only for

285. Dhū Khushub: "A valley lying a night's journey from Medina, often mentioned in hadith and accounts of the Prophet's campaigns" (Yāqūt, *Muʿjam al-Buldān*, II, 444—45. Al-Aʿwaṣ: "A locale in the vicinity of Medina, mentioned in accounts of the Prophet's campaigns . . . lying a very few miles from Medina" (*Ibid.*, I, 317). Dhū al-Marwah: "A town in the Wādī al-Qurā; it is also said to lie between Khushub and the Wādī al-Qurā" (*ibid.*, IV, 513). Yāqūt's data are laconic, but they do place all three locales immediately to the north of Medina; al-Aʿwaṣ appears to be closest to the city, Dhū al-Marwah the most distant.

286. *Qāla: innamā naʾtammu hādhā ʾl-bayta wa-nastaʿfī hādhā ʾl-wāliya min baʿḍi ʿummālinā.*

that." The two men sought their permission for the people to enter Medina, but every one of them utterly refused, saying, "Surely an egg will hatch!"[287] Then (Ziyād and ʿAbdallāh) returned to (their camp).

Then some Egyptians banded together and came to ʿAlī, while a party of Baṣrans came to Ṭalḥah and a few Kūfans to al-Zubayr. Each of these groups said, "If (the loyalists in Medina) render the oath of allegiance to our companion, [well and good].[288] Otherwise, we shall plot against them, shatter their unity and cohesion (*jamāʿah*), and then turn round and take them by surprise."

The Egyptians reached ʿAlī while he was with an army at Aḥjār al-Zayt. He was wearing a white-striped cloak and a turban wound from a strip of red Yemeni cloth; he was girt with a sword [2957] but did not have on a shirt. He had dispatched al-Ḥasan to ʿUthmān along with those who had joined him [in his camp]. Thus, al-Ḥasan was staying with ʿUthmān while ʿAlī was at Aḥjār al-Zayt. The Egyptians greeted him and presented [their aims] to him. He shouted at them and drove them away, saying, "The upright know that the armies at Dhū al-Marwah and Dhū Khushub have been cursed by the tongue of Muḥammad. Go back, and may God be no friend to you!" They said, "So be it," and thereupon departed from him.

The Baṣrans came to Ṭalḥah while he was with another group of men [encamped] adjacent to ʿAlī. He had sent his two sons to [support] ʿUthmān. The Baṣrans greeted him and presented [their aims] to him. He shouted at them and drove them away, saying, "The Believers know that the armies at Dhū al-Marwah and Dhū Khushub and al-Aʿwaṣ have been cursed by the tongue of Muḥammad."

The Kūfans came to al-Zubayr while he was with yet another body of men. He had sent his son ʿAbdallāh to [support] ʿUthmān. They greeted him and presented [their aims] to him, and he shouted at them and drove them away, saying, "The Muslims

287. *Bayḍun mā yufrikhanna.* That is, some evil will occur. See de Goeje, *Introductio*, cccxcix.

288. The Arabic text is elliptical, but the point is clear. Each of the three factions attacking ʿUthmān hopes to gain support for its own candidate for the caliphate: ʿAlī, Ṭalḥah, or al-Zubayr respectively.

know that the armies at Dhū al-Marwah, Dhū Khushub, and al-Aʿwaṣ have been cursed by the tongue of Muḥammad."

Then the dissidents (*al-qawm*) departed and made a show of going back [to their homes]. They withdrew from Dhū Khushub and al-Aʿwaṣ until they reached their encampments, situated three days away; they intended for the Medinese to disperse, and then they would turn around and come back. At their departure the Medinese did in fact disperse. When the dissidents reached their encampments, they wheeled around to attack (the Medinese). They took the Medinese by surprise, and all at once the cry "God is most great!" was heard throughout the city. (The dissidents) occupied the sites of the encampments [previously established by ʿAlī, Ṭalḥah, and al-Zubayr] and surrounded ʿUthmān. "Whoever restrains his hand [and does not resist us]," they announced, "will be secure."

[2958] ʿUthmān led the people in prayer for some days, but the people stayed in their houses. (The dissidents) prevented no one from discussing [the situation], and so the people, ʿAlī among them, came and talked with them. (ʿAlī) said, "What brought you back after you had changed your minds and gone?" They responded, "We seized a letter [ordering] us to be killed from an official courier."[289] Then Ṭalḥah came and the Baṣrans said the same thing, as did the Kūfans with al-Zubayr. The Kūfans and Baṣrans said, "We are united in supporting and aiding our brothers, as they were promised." Then ʿAlī said to them, "How, O men of Kūfah and Baṣrah, did you know what had befallen the Egyptians, for you traveled a certain number of days and then turned back toward us? By God, this is a conspiracy (*amr*) woven [while you were] in Medina." "Explain it however you wish," they said. "We reject this man [namely, ʿUthmān]. Let him be removed from us! He still leads (the people) in prayer, and they perform the prayer behind him. Anyone who wishes comes to visit [him]. In his eyes (the people) are less than dirt." (The dissidents) had not been

289. *Barīd,* the official postal and information service, inherited from Roman and Sasanian usage. The system reached its fullest elaboration under the early Abbasids. The term "*barīd*" normally refers to the institution, but here it clearly indicates an individual courier. See D. Sourdel, "Barīd," *EI*², I, 1045–46.

preventing anyone from discussing [the situation], but they were forming bands in Medina that barred the people from assembling.

'Uthmān wrote to the inhabitants of the garrison towns to seek their aid: "In the name of God, the Merciful, the Compassionate. To proceed: Verily Almighty God sent Muḥammad 'with the truth, both good news and warning,'[290] and he conveyed from God what He had commanded him [to say]. Then he departed, having fulfilled the duties laid upon him, and left among us His book, wherein is found what He permits and forbids and a clear statement of the matters that He has foreordained. Thus, he accomplished (these things), both those that God's servants desired and those that they hated.

"Abū Bakr and 'Umar succeeded him, and then I was included in the consultation [on the succession to 'Umar],[291] without any [2959]
knowledge [on my part of what would happen] or any dispute as regards the Community's considered opinion. Then the electoral council agreed on me,[292] in accordance with the judgment of its members and the people, without my having sought or desired anything. I have acted toward them in a manner that they fully approve, neither have I submitted to any self-appointed leader, adhered to any innovator, or followed the example of any hypocrite. When affairs came to their conclusion and evil had been betrayed by its own partisans, then malevolence and selfish desires appeared, though no crime or wrongful violence had been committed [by me], but only the carrying out of the Book of God.[293] Lacking any valid proof or excuse, (the malcontents) have in reality sought one goal while publicly proclaiming another. They have blamed me for things that were previously acceptable to them, and for clearly upright conduct (*ashyā'*) consonant with the considered opinion of the Medinese. For years I have forced

290. Qur'ān 2:113; 35:22.

291. On the electoral process (*shūrā*, "consultation") through which 'Uthmān was named caliph, see Ṭabari, I, 2776–2797.

292. See de Goeje, *Introductio*, dcxxviii.

293. *Fa-lammā intahat 'l-umūru wa'ntakatha 'l-sharru bi-ahlihi badat ḍaghā'inu wa-ahwā'u 'alā ghayri ijrāmin wa-lā tiratin fīmā maḍā illā imḍā'a 'l-kitābi.*

myself to be patient with them, and have restrained myself while seeing and hearing [all this].

"Now their insolence toward Almighty God has so increased that they have attacked us in the very precincts of the Messenger of God, in His sanctuary,[294] and in the territory of the Hijrah. Now the Bedouin have returned to them, and (these dissidents) are like the hostile confederates during their battles [against us],[295] or like those who attacked us at Uḥud, save in regard to their public statements. He who can join our cause, let him do so."

The letter reached the inhabitants of the garrison towns, and they set out on camels both stubborn and docile. Muʿāwiyah dispatched Ḥabīb b. Maslamah al-Fihrī. ʿAbdallāh b. Saʿd sent Muʿāwiyah b. Ḥudayj al-Sakūnī. From among the Kūfans, al-Qaʿqāʿ b. ʿAmr set forth. In Kūfah those who urged support for the
[2960] Medinese included ʿUqbah b. ʿAmr, ʿAbdallāh b. Abī Awfā, and Ḥanẓalah b. al-Rabīʿ al-Tamīmī, along with others like them from among the Prophet's Companions. The Successors[296] in Kūfah who urged [support for ʿUthmān] included the disciples (*aṣḥāb*) of ʿAbdallāh (b. Masʿūd)—namely, Masrūq b. al-Ajdaʿ, al-Aswad b. Yazīd, Shurayḥ b. al-Ḥārith, and ʿAbdallāh b. ʿUkaym, along with others like them. They would go about (the city) and make the circuit of tribal councils (*majālis*), saying, "O people, today is the time to talk, not tomorrow. Today it is good to examine [the crisis], while tomorrow it will be hateful. Today fighting is law-

294. Yathrib had been declared a sanctuary (*ḥarām*)—that is, a sacred place where blood feuds were forbidden and whose guardians were inviolate—in a clause of the Constitution of Medina, perhaps around 6/628. See R. B. Serjeant, "The *Sunnah Jāmiʿah,* Pacts with the Yathrib Jews, and the *Taḥrīm* of Yathrib," *BSOAS,* XLI (1978), 34–35, 38–40.

295. *Fa-hum ka'l-aḥzābi ayyāma 'l-aḥzābi.* These were the Meccans and their bedouin allies who besieged Medina in the Battle of the Trench in 5/627. ʿUthmān compares his opponents to these implacable enemies of God and His prophet. See Qur'ān 33:20–27.

296. The Successors (*tābiʿun*) are the second generation of Muslims—those who never knew Muḥammad directly and were converted by his Companions, or the children of the Companions. The Successors represent a sort of apostolic succession; as immediate heirs to the faith and doctrine of the Companions, they came to be almost as highly revered as these latter as teachers and exemplars for later generations of Muslims. This passage seems to represent one of the earliest mentions of this group. See V. Carra de Vaux, "Tābiʿ," *SEI,* 557.

ful, while tomorrow it will be forbidden. Rise up, defend your caliph and your affairs."

In Baṣrah, ʿImrān b. Ḥuṣayn, Anas b. Mālik, and Hishām b. ʿĀmir arose along with other Companions of the Prophet like them and made similar statements. Among the Successors [in Baṣrah], Kaʿb b. Sūr, Harim b. Ḥayyān al-ʿAbdī, and others like them were also saying such things.

In Syria, ʿUbādah b. al-Ṣāmit, Abū al-Dardāʾ, and Abū Umāmah rose up with other like-minded Companions of the Prophet to make statements of this kind. Among the Successors Sharīk b. Khubāshah al-Numayrī, Abū Muslim al-Khawlānī, and ʿAbd al-Raḥmān b. Ghanm spoke in the same vein. In Egypt Khārijah and others like him arose [to make their voices heard].

Now some of those urging [aid for ʿUthmān] had witnessed the coming (of the dissidents). When they perceived the state of affairs among these latter, they departed for their own garrison towns with that [information] and rose up there [to speak about it].

When it was the hour of the Friday prayer in the mosque of the Messenger of God, which fell immediately after the Egyptians had set up camp, ʿUthmān came forth to lead the people in prayer. Then he stood up on the pulpit and said, "O you enemies! Fear God, fear God! By God, the Medinese know that you have been [2961] cursed by the tongue of Muḥammad, so wipe out your errors by doing what is right. For verily Almighty God only eradicates evil through what is good."

Muḥammad b. Maslamah arose and said, "I bear witness to that." Then Ḥukaym b. Jabalah seized him and forced him to sit down. Zayd b. Thābit stood up and said, "Get the letter [from ʿUthmān to the governor of Egypt] for me." From another side Muḥammad b. Abī Qutayrah stood up beside him and with harsh words made him sit down. Then the dissidents (*al-qawm*) all rose up together and threw stones at the people until they had driven them from the mosque. They threw stones at ʿUthmān until he fell unconscious from the pulpit. He was carried off and brought into his house. Now the Egyptians expected support from only three men among the Medinese, for these had been in correspondence with them: Muḥammad b. Abī Bakr, Muḥammad b. Abī Ḥudhayfah, and ʿAmmār b. Yāsir. A certain group among the people prepared themselves to face death; among these were Sa'd b. Mālik, Abū Hurayrah, Zayd b. Thābit, and al-Ḥasan b. 'Alī. 'Uthmān firmly instructed them to leave [his house], and they did so. 'Alī came back and entered 'Uthmān's presence after he had fallen [from the pulpit], as did Ṭalḥah and al-Zubayr, and [all three] expressed their sorrow. Then they returned to their own homes.

[2962] It was transmitted to me in writing by al-Sarī—Shu'ayb—Sayf—Abū 'Amr—al-Ḥasan: I [namely, Abū 'Amr] said to him, "Did you witness the siege of 'Uthmān?" (Al-Ḥasan) responded, "Yes. At that time I was a youth [and was] in the mosque with associates of mine. When the clamor grew intense, I rose to my knees or stood up. Then the dissidents came and ensconced themselves in the mosque and its environs. A certain group among the Medinese gathered around them, saying that what they had done was distressing, while the dissidents approached the Medinese with threats. As they were thus clamoring around the gate, 'Uthmān arose, and it was as if a fire had been extinguished. He went over to the pulpit and mounted it. He praised God and extolled Him. One man got to his feet and another made him sit down, then yet another arose and someone else forced him to sit down. Then the dissidents rose up and threw stones at 'Uthmān until he fell unconscious. He was carried away and brought to [his house]. For twenty days he led them in prayer, and then they barred him from attending the prayer.

It was transmitted to me in writing by al-Sarī—Shu'ayb—Sayf—Muḥammad and Ṭalḥah and Abū Ḥārithah and Abū 'Uthmān: 'Uthmān led the people in prayer for thirty days after (the dissidents) had ensconced themselves in the mosque. Then they barred him from the prayer, and their chief al-Ghāfiqī led the people in prayer. The Egyptians, Kūfans, and Baṣrans submitted to him, while the Medinese dispersed to their walled compounds and stayed in their houses. None of them would venture out or attend any council unless he was wearing a sword whereby he could defend himself from the tyranny of the dissidents. The siege lasted forty days, and during this period the [caliph's] murder took place. (The dissidents) used arms against anyone who resisted them, though heretofore they had refrained [from violence] for thirty days.

As to (authorities) other than Sayf, some of them say that the dissidents' dispute with ʿUthmān and the reasons why they besieged him are correctly described in the account related to me by Yaʿqūb b. Ibrāhīm—Muʿtamir b. Sulaymān al-Taymī—his father—Abū Naḍrah—Abū Saʿīd, the client of Abū Usayd al-Anṣārī:[297] ʿUthmān learned of the approach of the Egyptian delegation, and he received them while he was in a village of his outside Medina. He states: When (the Egyptians) heard about him, they approached him at the place where he then was. He says: ʿUthmān did not want them to come to him in Medina—or words to that effect. [2963]

So they came to him and said, "Send for the Qur'ān (*muṣḥaf*)," and he did so. Then they said, "Open to the ninth (chapter)." Now they used to call the Chapter of Jonah the ninth.[298] Then (ʿUthmān) recited it until he came to this verse: "Say: Have you considered the provision God has sent down for you, and you have made some of it unlawful, and some lawful? Say: Has God given you leave, or do you forge against God?"[299] They told ʿUthmān to stop and then said to him, "Have you considered the pasture rights that you set aside? Has God given you leave, or do you forge against God?" He replied, "Enough! (This verse) was revealed in connection with such-and-such a matter." He continued, "And as to the reserved pasture, before my time ʿUmar set aside pasture for the camels that had been paid as alms tax. When I became caliph, the alms-tax camels had increased in number, and so I increased the reserved pasture in accordance with that fact. Enough." Then they began berating him with the verse, and he would say, "Enough! It was revealed in connection with such-and-such a matter."

The man responsible for transmitting ʿUthmān's words was the same age at that time as you are now—Abū Naḍrah says, "Abū

297. The following narrative is persistently interrupted by the word *qāla*—that is, "(the narrator) states." I have for the most part omitted these editorial interjections, unless they seem to mark a significant shift in the narrative. However, the new paragraphs in this passage normally begin with such an editorial *qāla*.

298. The text reads *al-sābiʿah*, "the seventh." Cf. de Goeje, *Introductio*, dcxxviii. In the modern numeration the Surah of Jonah is number ten; presumably the Fātiḥah (number one) was not counted in the earliest times.

299. Qur'ān 10:60.

[2964] Sa'īd would say that to me." Abū Naḍrah said [to Abū Sa'īd], "I am the same age [now] as you were then." (Abū Naḍrah) continued, "At that time my beard had not yet started to grow." I don't know, and perhaps he said on another occasion, "At that time I was thirty years old."[300]

Then they took ('Uthmān) to task for things from which he could find no escape. Recognizing these, he said, "I seek God's forgiveness and turn to Him in repentance." Then he said to them, "What do you want?" They made a compact (*mīthāq*) with him, and he said, "I regard this as valid." They wrote out conditions to be imposed on him. Then ('Uthmān) obligated them to break no rod [namely, of loyalty and obedience] nor to withdraw from unity (*jamā'ah*) so long as he fulfilled their conditions or acted in accordance with what they required of him.

('Uthmān) said to them, "What do you want?" They replied, "We want the Medinese to take no stipend [from the Public Treasury], for this money belongs to those who fight and to those venerable men (*shuyūkh*) who are Companions of the Messenger of God." They were content with this and accompanied him to Medina satisfied [as to their demands]. ('Uthmān) rose and gave the Friday sermon, saying, "By God, I have seen no delegation on earth that is better for my misdeeds than this delegation that has come to me." Another time he said, "I am afraid of this delegation from Egypt. Verily let him who possesses a field go out to his field, and let him who possesses milk animals milk them. You shall have no Treasury payments from us.[301] This money belongs only to those who fight and to those venerable men who are Companions of the Messenger of God." Then the people were angry and said, "This is a trick by the Banū Umayyah."

Then the Egyptian delegation went back satisfied, and while they were on the road [back to Egypt], suddenly they noticed a rider coming up beside them and then leaving them behind. Then he came back toward them and again left them behind, scrutiniz-

---

300. This paragraph represents one of Ṭabarī's rare explicit editorial interventions. The point of this somewhat muddled interchange is to demonstrate that the ultimate authority for this story, Abū Sa'īd, was mature enough (between his late teens and thirty) to have given a reliable account of 'Uthmān's statements.

301. *A-lā innahu lā māla lakum 'indanā.*

ing them carefully.[302] They said to him, "What are you doing? Certainly you are engaged on some matter. What is your business?" (The rider) responded, "I am the envoy of the Commander of the Faithful to his governor in Egypt." So they searched him, and there was a letter framed in ʿUthmān's words, with his seal upon it, to his governor in Egypt. [It stated] that he should crucify them or slaughter them or have their hands and feet alternately cut off.[303] Then (the Egyptians) set out and came to Medina. [2965]

They came to ʿAlī and said, "Did you not see that the enemy of God [namely, ʿUthmān] wrote such-and-such concerning us? Verily God has made his blood lawful! Rise up against him with us." (ʿAlī) said, "By God, I shall not rise up with you," until they said, "So why did you write us?" Then he said, "By God, I never wrote anything to you at all." Then they looked at one another, some saying to others, "Is it for this man that you are fighting, or on his account that you are angered?" So ʿAlī departed and left Medina for a certain village.

They departed and entered ʿUthmān's presence, saying, "You wrote such-and-such concerning us." (ʿUthmān) answered, "There are but two (alternatives). Either you must produce two men from among the Muslims to bear witness against me, or [you must accept] my oath in the name of God, other than Whom there is no god, that I neither wrote nor dictated nor knew [of this letter]." He continued, "Perhaps you know that the letter is [falsely] ascribed to this man [that is, ʿUthmān himself], and it may be that the seal [on the letter] was forged."[304] They responded, "By God, God has made your blood lawful, and you have violated the pact and covenant [which you made with us]." And so they laid siege to him.

---

302. Cf. de Goeje, *Introductio*, cccxviii, dcxxviii.

303. An allusion to the Qur'ān 5:37: "This is the recompense of those who fight against God and His Messenger, and hasten about the earth to do corruption there: they shall be slaughtered, or crucified, or their hands and feet shall alternately be struck off, or they shall be banished from the land. That is a degradation for them in this world; and in the world to come awaits them a mighty chastisement."

304. The text of this somewhat puzzling statement reads as follows: *wa-qad taʿlamūna anna 'l-kitāba yuktabu ʿalā lisāni 'l-rajuli wa-qad yunqashu 'l-khātamu ʿalā 'l-khātami.* Caetani (*Annali*, VIII, 144) settles for a loose paraphrase.

As for al-Wāqidī, he has recounted many things concerning the reasons why the Egyptians went to ʿUthmān and made camp at Dhū Khushub. Among these are things that I have already mentioned, and there are others that I have refused to mention because I find them offensive. Among his various accounts, (al-
[2966] Wāqidī) mentions that it was related to him by ʿAbdallāh b. Jaʿfar—Abū ʿAwn, the client of al-Miswar:[305] ʿAmr b. al-ʿĀṣ had been ʿUthmān's governor (*ʿāmil*) in Egypt. Then he stripped him of authority over the tax revenues (*kharāj*) and put him in charge of the public prayers.[306] (ʿUthmān) assigned authority over the tax revenues to ʿAbdallāh b. Saʿd, and then combined both offices under ʿAbdallāh. When ʿAmr b. al-ʿĀṣ arrived in Medina, he launched vitriolic attacks upon ʿUthmān.

One day ʿUthmān sent for him and met with him alone. He said, "Ibn al-Nābighah, how quickly the neckhole of your gown has become louse-ridden! You faithfully carried out your duties as governor for a year previous [to this]. Do you attack me, bearing one countenance in my presence and another in my absence? By God, were it not for a morsel of food [proffered you by my enemies], you would not do that."[307] ʿAmr replied, "Indeed much of what the people say and communicate to their rulers is falsehood. So fear God, O Commander of the Faithful, in regard to your subjects." ʿUthmān said, "By God, I appointed you as governor in spite of your faults and all the talk about you." ʿAmr responded, "I was governor on behalf of ʿUmar b. al-Khaṭṭāb, and at the time of his passing he was well satisfied with me."

ʿUthmān said, "If I had controlled you as stringently as ʿUmar did, by God, you would act rightly. But I have been lenient with you and so you have been insolent with me. By God, I possess greater glory than you through my next of kin in the Time of Ignorance and before I acquired my present authority." ʿAmr replied, "Stop this! Praise be to God, who honored and guided us by

---

305. As in the preceding account, this one contains numerous editorial *qālas*, omitted in this translation.

306. That is, he left ʿAmr as titular head of the Muslim community in Egypt; presumably he also continued to be commander-in-chief of the garrison stationed there.

307. *Lawlā akālatun mā faʿalta dhālika.* For the sense of this idiom see Lane, I, sub verbo *akl.*

Muḥammad. I saw [my father] al-ʿĀṣī b. Wā'il and I saw your father ʿAffān, and by God al-ʿĀṣ was nobler than your father!" ʿUthmān was caught short and said, "Why should we be referring to the Time of Ignorance?"

ʿAmr departed, and Marwān entered and said, "O Commander of the Faithful, you have come to a state of things where ʿAmr b. al-ʿĀṣ can talk about your father!" ʿUthmān replied, "Leave off! If [2967] a man mentions [other] men's fathers, they will mention his father."

Thus, ʿAmr departed from ʿUthmān filled with hatred for him. At one point he came to ʿAlī to incite him against ʿUthmān. Then he approached al-Zubayr and Ṭalḥah in succession to incite them. He confronted the Pilgrimage caravan to inform them of ʿUthmān's wrongful innovations. When ʿUthmān was besieged for the first time, (ʿAmr) went from Medina until he reached a property that he owned in Palestine called al-Sabʿ, and took up residence in a castle of his named al-ʿAjlān.[308] He would say, "It is wonderful what we hear about Ibn ʿAffān."

While he was seated in that castle of his, with Salāmah b. Rawḥ al-Judhāmī and his two sons Muḥammad and ʿAbdallāh, a rider passed by them. ʿAmr called out to him. "Where have you come from?" "From Medina," he answered. (ʿAmr) said, "What has that man done?"—that is, ʿUthmān. (The rider) said, "I left him tightly besieged." ʿAmr said, "I am Abū ʿAbdallāh. Perhaps the jackass is breaking wind and the flatiron is in the fire."[309]

(ʿAmr) had not left his seat before a second rider passed by. ʿAmr called out to him, "What has that man done?"—that is, ʿUthmān. "He has been killed," he replied. (ʿAmr) said, "I am Abū ʿAbdallāh. When I rub a scab, I scrape it off.[310] I have been inciting [people] against him, even the shepherd on the mountaintop with

308. According to Yāqūt (*Muʿjam al-Buldān*, II, 19), al-ʿAjlān was an estate belonging to ʿAmr b. al-ʿĀṣ and located in Bayt Jibrīn, a town situated about two-thirds of the way between Jerusalem and Gaza (i.e., 25 km. from the latter). Yāqūt says that this estate was named after a client of ʿAmr's, but the name is probably an Arabization of Biblical Eglon, whose location fits his data very neatly.

309. A rather crude way of saying that the crisis is imminent and that ʿUthmān is too weak and frightened to oppose it effectively. See Lane, V, 1786, sub verbo *ḍaraṭa*, and Freytag, *Arabum Proverbia*, II, 248.

310. Freytag, *Arabum Proverbia*, I, 43, and Lane, II, 614, sub verbo *ḥakka*. The meaning is "When I desire an object I attain it."

his flock." Then Salāmah b. Rawḥ said to him, "O leaders of Quraysh, verily there was a strong gate between you and the Arabs and you have broken it down. Whatever led you to do
[2968] that?" ('Amr) said, "We wanted to draw the truth out of the pit of falsehood and to have the people be on an equal footing as regards the truth."

'Uthmān's half-sister on his mother's side, Umm Kulthūm bt. 'Uqbah b. Abī Mu'ayṭ, used to dwell with 'Amr; then he separated from her when ('Uthmān) deposed him.

According to Muḥammad b. 'Umar (al-Wāqidī)—'Abdallāh b. Muḥammad—his father: Muḥammad b. Abī Bakr and Muḥammad b. Abī Ḥudhayfah were in Egypt inciting [people] against 'Uthmān. Muḥammad b. Abī Bakr came [to Medina], while Muḥammad b. Abī Ḥudhayfah remained in Egypt. When the Egyptians set out [for Medina], 'Abd al-Raḥmān b. 'Udays al-Balawī took 500 (men) with him. Claiming that they intended to perform the Lesser Pilgrimage, they set out in Rajab (January 656). 'Abdallāh b. Sa'd [the governor of Egypt] dispatched a messenger who journeyed eleven nights to inform 'Uthmān that Ibn 'Udays and his comrades were heading toward him, and that Muḥammad b. Abī Ḥudhayfah had accompanied them as far as 'Ajrūd[311] and then turned back.

In public Muḥammad stated, "This band of men (*qawm*) has set out to perform the Lesser Pilgrimage." But in secret he said, "This band of men has set out to confront their imām. If he abdicates, [well and good], but otherwise they will kill him."

The dissidents (*al-qawm*) proceeded along the way stations [on the road to Medina], bypassing none of them until they established camp at Dhū Khushub. 'Abdallāh b. Sa'd's messenger having reached him before they arrived, 'Uthmān said, "This is a band of Egyptians who claim to be performing the Lesser Pilgrimage. By God, I do not believe that is their intention. On the contrary, the people have been taken in by them, and they hasten toward rebellion (*fitnah*). They feel that my life has lasted too long. But by God, if I depart from them, they will wish that every
[2969] day of my life had lasted a year, on account of the bloodshed, the

311. 'Ajrūd: a locale that I have been unable to find.

ancient hatreds, the blatant selfishness, and the overturned commandments that they will witness."

When the dissidents established their camp at Dhū Khushub, the news spread that they intended to kill 'Uthmān if he did not abdicate. At night their envoy came to 'Alī, Ṭalḥah, and 'Ammār b. Yāsir successively. Muḥammad b. Abī Ḥudhayfah had joined them in writing a letter to 'Alī; they brought this to 'Alī, but he did not examine its contents. When 'Uthmān perceived all this, he came to 'Alī. He entered his house and said, "O cousin, nothing owed to me can be neglected; my kinship [with you] is close, and I have a strong claim upon your support. You see the trouble caused by this band of dissidents when they came to me today.[312] I know that you enjoy prestige among the people and that they will listen to you. I want you to ride out to them and send them away from me. I do not wish them to come before me, for that would be an insolent act toward me on their part. Let others hear of this as well."

'Alī said, "On what grounds shall I send them away?" ('Uthmān) replied, "On the grounds that I shall carry out what you have counseled me to do and thought right, and that I will not deviate from your direction." Then 'Alī said, "In fact I have spoken to you time after time, and you and I have discussed such matters at length.[313] All this is the doing of Marwān b. al-Ḥakam, Sa'īd b. al-'Āṣ, Ibn 'Āmir, and Mu'āwiyah. You have heeded them and defied me." 'Uthmān said, "Then I shall defy them and heed you."

('Alī) thus issued orders to the people, and both Emigrants and Helpers rode forth with him [to meet with the dissidents].

'Uthmān sent to 'Ammār b. Yāsir, telling him to set forth with 'Alī, but he refused. Then 'Uthmān sent to Sa'd b. Abī Waqqāṣ and told him that he should go to 'Ammār and direct him to ride out with 'Alī. Sa'd set out and entered 'Ammār's presence. He said, "O [2970]
Abū al-Yaqẓān, will you not go forth with the others, all the more

312. *Wa-qad jā'a mā tarā min hā'ulā'i 'l-qawmi wa-hum muṣabbiḥiyya.*

313. A paraphrase, since the original seems to defeat an exact rendering: *Fa-qāla 'Aliyyun innī qad kuntu kallamtuka marratan ba'da marratin fa-kulla dhālika nakhruju fa-tukallamu wa-naqūlu wa-taqūlu.*

as ʿAlī is going? Set out with him, then, and drive these dissidents away from your imām, for I reckon that you will take no ride more beneficial to you than this one."

ʿUthmān sent to Kathīr b. al-Ṣalt al-Kindī, who was one of his loyal supporters (*aʿwān*), and said, "Follow close behind Saʿd and listen to what he and ʿAmmār say to each other; then come right back to me." Kathīr set out and found Saʿd meeting privately with ʿAmmār in the latter's home. He put his eye up to the keyhole in the door. Without knowing who was there, ʿAmmār came over to him with a staff in his hand and inserted it into the keyhole where Kathīr had placed his eye. Kathīr jerked his eye away from the hole, turned tail, and fled, covering his face. Then ʿAmmār came out, recognized his footprints, and shouted, "You runt, son of a runt's mother, were you spying on me and listening to my conversation? By God, had I known it was you, I would have poked out your eye with this staff, for the Messenger of God permitted that." Then ʿAmmār returned to Saʿd, and Saʿd spoke with him and began trying by every means to turn him away [from his previous opinions]. But the end result of this was that ʿAmmār said, "By God, I shall never drive (the dissidents) away from (ʿUthmān)." Then Saʿd returned to ʿUthmān and informed him of what ʿAmmār had said. ʿUthmān suspected that Saʿd was not giving him sincere advice; Saʿd therefore swore an oath to him in God's name that (ʿAmmār) had tried to incite [him against the caliph], and ʿUthmān accepted [this] from him.

ʿAlī rode out to the Egyptians and sent them away from (ʿUthmān); and they departed and headed back [toward Egypt].

According to Muḥammad b. ʿUmar (al-Wāqidī)—Muḥammad b.
[2971] Ṣāliḥ—ʿĀṣim b. ʿUmar—Maḥmūd b. Labīd: When (the Egyptians) established their camp at Dhū Khushub, ʿUthmān told ʿAlī and the Companions of the Messenger of God to send them away from him. So ʿAlī rode out with a few of the Emigrants, among them Saʿīd b. Zayd, Abū Jahm al-ʿAdawī, Jubayr b. Muṭʿim, Ḥakīm b. Ḥizām, Marwān b. al-Ḥakam (*sic!*), Saʿīd b. al-ʿĀṣ, and ʿAbd al-Raḥmān b. ʿAttāb b. Asīd. The Helpers who set out included Abū Usayd al-Sāʿidī, Abū Ḥumayd al-Sāʿidī, Zayd b. Thābit, Ḥassān b. Thābit, and Kaʿb b. Mālik; they were accompanied by Niyār b. Mikraz from among the Bedouin. Beside these there were thirty other men. ʿAlī and Muḥammad b. Maslamah, in their position as

leaders [of the Medinan delegation], spoke to (the dissidents), and these listened to their statement and turned back.

According to Maḥmūd (b. Labīd)—Muḥammad b. Maslamah:[314] We did not leave Dhū Khushub until they had set out on their journey back to Egypt. They began to say their farewells to me, and I [namely, Muḥammad b. Maslamah] shall not forget the statement of ʿAbd al-Raḥmān b. ʿUdays: "O Abū ʿAbd al-Raḥmān, do you enjoin anything upon us?" I responded, "You should fear God alone, Who has no partner,[315] and you should send those around you away from their imām, for he has promised us that he will return [to what is good] and desist [from what is evil]." Ibn ʿUdays said, "I shall, God willing." Thus, the delegation (*qawm*) returned to Medina.

According to Muḥammad b. ʿUmar (al-Wāqidī)—ʿAbdallāh b. Muḥammad—his father: When ʿAlī returned to ʿUthmān, he informed him that they had gone and said to him some things which were on his mind. He said to him, "Know that I am saying [2972] more about you than I have said previously." Then he went home.

ʿUthmān remained at home that day, until Marwān came to him the next day and said, "Speak and inform the people that the Egyptians have gone back, and that what they had heard about their imām was false. Your sermon (*khuṭbah*) will spread throughout the lands before the people can gather against you from their garrison towns [in such numbers] that you are unable to fend them off." ʿUthmān refused to go out, but Marwān kept after him until he went forth and took his seat upon the pulpit. (ʿUthmān) praised and extolled God, and then said: "To proceed: As to this band of Egyptians, a certain matter concerning their imām had come to their attention. But when they were certain that what they had heard about was false they returned to their own land." Then from one side of the mosque ʿAmr b. al-ʿĀṣ called out to him: "Fear God, O ʿUthmān, for you have borne great dangers, as we have done along with you. Turn to God, and we shall turn to Him!" ʿUthmān shouted back, "So you are over there, Ibn al-Nābighah. By God, your robe has become louse-

---

314. In the following report numerous editorial *qāla*s have been omitted.
315. Qur'ān 6:163.

ridden since I removed you from office." From another direction someone else shouted, "Turn to God and show repentance. Then the people will restrain themselves from you." ʿUthmān stretched out his hands and turned to face the *qiblah*, saying, "O God, verily I am the first to repent." Then he went back to his house, while ʿAmr b. al-ʿĀṣ proceeded to his residence in Palestine. (ʿAmr) used to say, "By God, if I were to run across a shepherd I would incite him against (ʿUthmān)."

According to Muḥammad b. ʿUmar (al-Wāqidī)—ʿAlī b. ʿUmar—his father: ʿAlī came to ʿUthmān after the Egyptians had gone and said to him: "Make a statement which the people will testify that
[2973] they have heard from you, and God will be witness as to whether or not you desire to repent in your heart.[316] The provinces are in turmoil against you, and I fear another company of riders may come from Kūfah. You will say, 'ʿAlī, ride out to meet them,' but I cannot go out and get [them] to listen to any excuse. Still other riders will come from Baṣrah, and you will say, 'O ʿAlī, ride out to meet them.' If I do not do that, you will think I have betrayed our bonds of kinship and belittled your claims [on me]."

Thus, ʿUthmān went out and preached the sermon in which he laid before the people his heartfelt desire to repent. He arose, praising and extolling God as He merits, and then said: "To proceed: By God, O people, if any one of you has censured [me], he has not done so for anything that is unknown to me. I have done nothing unknowingly. But my soul has raised vain hopes within me and lied to me, and my rectitude has slipped away from me. I heard the Messenger of God say, 'Let him who slips repent, and let him who errs turn back and not persist in his own ruin. Verily he who persists in tyranny is very far from the true path.' Now I am the first to take warning. I ask God's forgiveness for what I have done and I turn to Him. A man like me yearns to repent. When I step down [from the pulpit], let your notables (*ashrāf*) come to me and inform me of their opinion. By God, if the truth turns me into a slave, then I shall tread the slave's path, I shall humble myself like a slave, and I shall be like the bondsman. If he is held in servitude, he shows patience; if he is set free, he is grateful. There is no escape from God save by returning to Him.

316. *Wa-yashhadu Allāhu ʿalā mā fī qalbika min ʾl-nuzūʿi waʾl-inābati.*

The best men among you will not fail to draw near me. If my right hand refuses, then my left hand will surely obey me."[317] [2974]

Then the people had pity on him, and some among them wept. Sa'īd b. Zayd stood up before him and said, "O Commander of the Faithful, no one comes to you who does not support you. Fear God, in your soul fear God, and fulfill what you have said!"

When 'Uthmān descended [from the pulpit], he found Marwān (b. al-Ḥakam), Sa'īd (b. al-'Āṣ), and a few of the Banū Umayyah at his home. They had not been present at the sermon, and when ('Uthmān) took his seat, Marwān said, "O Commander of the Faithful, shall I speak or remain silent?" Then Nā'ilah bt. al-Farāfiṣah, 'Uthmān's wife from the Kalb tribe, said, "Nay, be silent, for they will kill him and accuse him of sin; he has made a public statement from which he cannot rightfully withdraw." Then Marwān came up to her and said, "What does this have to do with you? By God, your father died without knowing how to perform the ablutions correctly." "Go easy, Marwān," she responded, "in mentioning our fathers. You speak lies about my absent father. Indeed your father cannot defend himself [against similar charges]. By God, were (your father) not ('Uthmān's) uncle and would (the caliph) not be distressed, I would tell no lies in informing you about (your father)."

Then Marwān turned away from her and said, "O Commander of the Faithful, shall I speak or be silent?" ('Uthmān) answered, "No, speak." Marwān said, "You are as dear to me as my father and my mother! By God, I wish that you had made this statement [before the people] while you were still strong and invincible, and that I had been the first to be satisfied by it and to aid [you] in fulfilling it. However, you have said these things when the girth [2975]
has reached the two teats and the torrent has overflowed the hilltops and when a humiliated man has submitted to humiliation.[318] By God, to persist in an error for which you must seek God's forgiveness is better than to repent because you are afraid.

---

317. The meaning is that he will force himself to submit to their judgment, however bitter he may find it to do so.

318. The first two clauses are proverbial, meaning that the affair had become distressing and surpassed normal limits. See Freytag, *Arabum Proverbia*, I, 151, 293; Lane, *Lexicon*, III, 1215; V, 1830. The last clause is explained in de Goeje, *Introductio*, ccclxvii.

If you so will, you may seek repentance without acknowledging error. The people have piled up at the gate against you like a mountain." 'Uthmān said, "Go out and speak to them, for I am ashamed to do so."

So Marwān went to the gate, where the people were clambering on top of one another. He said, "Why have you gathered here like looters? Your faces are deformed, and every man is holding the ear of his confederate! Whom are you after? You have come to snatch our power (*mulk*)[319] from us. Go! By God, if you mean us [any harm], you will encounter something distasteful from us,[320] and you will not praise the result of your opinions. Return to your homes, for by God we are not men to be robbed of our possessions."

[2976] The people retreated, and one of them went to see 'Alī and informed him of the news. Then 'Alī came in a rage to 'Uthmān and said, "Surely you have satisfied Marwān, but he is satisfied with you only if you deviate from your religion and reason, like a camel carrying a litter that is led around at will. By God, Marwān is devoid of sense in regard to his religion and his soul. I swear by God, I think he will bring you in and then not send you out again. After this visit I will not come again to chide you. You have destroyed your own honor and you have been robbed of your authority (*amr*)."

When 'Alī departed, ('Uthmān's) wife Nā'ilah bt. al-Farāfiṣah entered and said, "Shall I speak or remain silent?" "Speak," he replied. She said, "I have heard what 'Alī said to you, that he will not return to you, and that you have obeyed Marwān, who leads you wherever he wishes." ('Uthmān) said, "What shall I do?" She responded, "You should fear God alone, Who has no partner, and you should adhere to the practice of your two predecessors [namely, Abū Bakr and 'Umar]. For if you obey Marwān he will kill you. Marwān enjoys no prestige among the people and inspires neither awe nor love. The people have only abandoned you due to Marwān's place [in your councils]. Send to 'Alī, then, and

---

319. Or, "our possessions." But "kingship, rulership" seems to fit the context a bit better.

320. *Amā wa'llāhi la-in rumtumūnā la-yamurranna 'alaykum minnā amrun lā yasurrukum.*

trust in his honesty and uprightness. He is related to you, and he is not a man whom people disobey." So ʿUthmān sent to ʿAlī, but he refused to come, saying, "I told him I would not return."

Having learned of Nā'ilah's comments about him, Marwān came to ʿUthmān and took a seat before him. He said, "Shall I speak or remain silent?" "Speak," replied (ʿUthmān). (Marwān) began, "The daughter of al-Farāfiṣah. . . ." ʿUthmān said, "You [2977]
are not to say a thing about her! How evil is your countenance! By God, she is a better adviser to me than you are." With this Marwān desisted.

According to Muḥammad b. ʿUmar (al-Wāqidī)—Shuraḥbīl b. Abī ʿAwn—his father: I heard ʿAbd al-Raḥmān b. al-Aswad b. ʿAbd Yaghūth mention Marwān b. al-Ḥakam. He said: May God disfigure Marwān! ʿUthmān went out to the people and gave them satisfaction. He wept as he stood on the pulpit, and the people wept also, until I saw his beard soaked with tears. He was saying, "O God, I turn to Thee in repentance. O God, I repent, I repent! By God, if it is right for me to become a mere slave, I will be content with that. When I enter my house, all of you come before me, and by God I will not seclude myself from you. On the contrary, I will give you satisfaction in full measure and more, and I will send Marwān and his kin away."

When (ʿUthmān) entered [his house], he commanded that the gate be thrown open. When he went into his house, Marwān came to him and worked ceaselessly to delude him, until at last he beguiled him from his better judgment and eradicated his original intentions. For three days ʿUthmān stayed inside and would not go out, for he was ashamed to face the people. Then Marwān went out to the people and said, "May your faces be deformed! Whom are you after? Go back to your homes. If the Commander of the Faithful needs any of you, he will send for him. Otherwise, he will remain in his house."

ʿAbd al-Raḥmān continues: So I came to ʿAlī, and found him [in the mosque] between the [Prophet's] grave and the pulpit.[321] With

321. The principal mosque of Medina was originally the courtyard of the Prophet's own dwelling. When he died he was buried in one corner of the structure. The pulpit stands more or less in the middle on the same side of the mosque. See J. Sauvaget, *La mosquée omeyyade de Médine* (Paris, 1947).

[2978] him were ʿAmmār b. Yāsir and Muḥammad b. Abī Bakr, and they were saying, "Marwān has acted badly toward the people." ʿAlī came over to me and asked, "Were you present at ʿUthmān's sermon?" "Yes," I said. ʿAlī went on, "And were you present when Marwān spoke to the people?" "Yes," I answered. ʿAlī said, "God forbid, O Muslims, that if I remain in my house, he should accuse me of abandoning him in spite of his kinship [with me] and his rights. And God forbid that if I speak [to him] and things turn out as he desires, Marwān would trick him[322] and he would become like a captured beast driven by him at will—[all this] despite his advanced age and his having been a Companion of the Messenger of God."

ʿAbd al-Raḥmān b. al-Aswad continues: (ʿAlī) kept on until ʿUthmān's envoy arrived and said, "Come with me." ʿAlī responded in a loud, angry voice, "Tell him that I will not come before him again."The messenger departed. I tried without success to meet with ʿUthmān two nights later. I asked his servant where the Commander of the Faithful had been, and he said, "He was with ʿAlī."

ʿAbd al-Raḥmān b. al-Aswad continues: So I took my leave and paid a visit to ʿAlī. He said to me, "ʿUthmān came to me yesterday and began to accuse me of refusing to see him again and of working [against him]. So I said to him, 'After what you said on the pulpit of the Messenger of God, and after [the promises] you gave
[2979] of your own free will, you entered your house, and Marwān went out before the people, reviling and insulting them at your gate.' "

"(ʿUthmān) responded, saying, 'You have severed the bonds of kinship with me. You have abandoned me and emboldened the people against me.' I [that is, ʿAlī] replied, 'By God, I am your strongest defender against the people. But whenever I have brought to you any matter that I think you will find agreeable, (Marwān) brings another. You have heard Marwān speak against me and have invited him to enter your presence.' " Then he left and went home.

ʿAbd al-Raḥmān b. al-Aswad continues: I constantly saw ʿAlī avoiding (ʿUthmān) and not acting as he formerly had. However, I

---

322. The reading of this passage is uncertain: *In takallamtu fa-jāʾa mā yurīdu yalʿab bihi Marwānu.*

know that he spoke with Ṭalḥah when ('Uthmān) was under siege, to the effect that waterskins should be taken to him. ('Alī) was extremely upset about that, until at last waterskins were brought in to 'Uthmān.

According to Muḥammad b. 'Umar (al-Wāqidī)—'Abdallāh b. Ja'far—Ismā'īl b. Muḥammad: 'Uthmān stood upon the pulpit on Friday, and praised and extolled God. Then a man stood up and said, "Carry out the Book of God." 'Uthmān said, "Sit down." He did so. Three times he stood up, 'Uthmān ordered him to sit down, and he did so. Then they began throwing pebbles until the sky could not be seen. ('Uthmān) fell from the pulpit and was carried off unconscious to his house. One of 'Uthmān's chamberlains (*ḥujjāb*) went out carrying a copy of the Qur'ān and crying out, "Those who have made divisions in their religion and become sects, I am not of them in anything; their affair is unto God."[323] Then 'Alī b. Abī Ṭālib entered 'Uthmān's presence while he was still unconscious and the Banū Umayyah were around him. ('Alī) said, "Why, O Commander of the Faithful, have the Banū Umayyah drawn round you like a belt?" They responded, "O 'Alī, you have destroyed us and have brought ill to the Commander of the Faithful. Yea, by God, if you achieve your aims, [2980
then this world will surely become a bitter place for you." Then 'Alī rose up full of anger.

In this year, 'Uthmān b. 'Affān was killed.

The Account of the Murder [of 'Uthmān]

According to Abū Ja'far (al-Ṭabarī): In this year, 'Uthmān b. 'Affān was killed. We have mentioned many of the reasons that his murderers cited as an excuse for killing him, and we have avoided mentioning many others that should not be included here. We will now describe how he was killed, how and through whom it began, and who was the first to treat him audaciously before he was murdered.

According to Muḥammad b. 'Umār al-Wāqidī—'Abdallāh b. Ja'far—Umm Bakr bt. al-Miswar b. Makhramah—her father:

323. A variant version of Qur'ān 6:160. The text is usually read "thou [that is, Muḥammad] art not of them in anything."

Some camels were brought to 'Uthmān as legal alms (*ṣadaqah*), and he made a gift of them to one of the Banū al-Ḥakam.[324] Having learned of this, 'Abd al-Raḥmān b. 'Awf sent to al-Miswar b. Makhramah and 'Abd al-Raḥmān b. al-Aswad b. 'Abd Yaghūth. They took the camels, and 'Abd al-Raḥmān (b. 'Awf) then distributed them among the people while 'Uthmān stayed at home.

According to Muḥammad b. 'Umar (al-Wāqidī)—Muḥammad b. Ṣāliḥ—'Ubaydallāh b. Rāfi' b. Naqākhah[325]—'Uthmān b. al-
[2981] Sharīd: 'Uthmān passed Jabalah b. 'Amr al-Sā'idī as he sat in his courtyard holding a rope. Jabalah said, "You hyena. By God, I shall kill you. I shall carry you off on a scab-covered camel and send you to blazing fire." Another time, when 'Uthmān was standing on the pulpit, Jabalah forced him to get off.

It was related to me by Muḥammad (al-Wāqidī)[326]—Abū Bakr b. Ismā'īl—his father—'Āmir b. Sa'd: The first man who dared to insult 'Uthmān was Jabalah b. 'Amr al-Sā'idī. Once while he was sitting among his kinsmen holding a rope in his hand, 'Uthmān passed by him. 'Uthmān greeted them as he was passing by, and they greeted him in return. Then Jabalah said, "Why do you answer a man who did such-and-such a thing?" Jabalah then approached 'Uthmān and said, "By God, I will throw this rope around your neck unless you abandon your personal entourage (*biṭānah*)." "What entourage," asked 'Uthmān? "By God, I do not choose favorites among the people." (Jabalah) answered, "Marwān, and Mu'āwiyah, and 'Abdallāh b. 'Āmir b. Kurayz, and 'Abdallāh b. Sa'd—all of these you have favored. Among them are men who are condemned in the Qur'ān, men whose blood the Messenger of God has declared lawful." 'Uthmān departed, and the people have continued to talk spitefully about him to this day.

According to Muḥammad b. 'Umar (al-Wāqidī)—Ibn Abī al-

---

324. The Banū al-Ḥakam (the clan from which Marwān stemmed) were of course among the most obdurate opponents of the Prophet. Their association with any act is usually enough to taint it in the eyes of the pious.

325. Perhaps "Nafākhah" or Nuffākhah." See text, 2980, note f.

326. *Ḥaddathanī Muḥammadun*. Presumably he means al-Wāqidī, but there is a difficulty. The term *ḥaddathanī* normally indicates direct oral transmission. However, al-Wāqidī died in 207/823 and so could not have passed this anecdote on to Ṭabarī in that manner.

Zinād—Mūsā b. ʿUqbah—Abū Ḥabībah: One day ʿUthmān was preaching to the people when ʿAmr b. al-ʿĀṣ said, "O Commander of the Faithful, you have incurred grave dangers, and we have incurred them with you. Repent, and we shall repent." ʿUthmān turned in the direction of Mecca and raised his arms in supplication. Abū Ḥabībah states: I have never seen more men and women weeping than on that day. Afterwards, as ʿUthmān preached to the people, Jahjāh al-Ghifārī came up to him and cried, "ʿUthmān, we have brought this old she-camel, and on it there are a robe and a rope. Get down! We will dress you in the robe, throw the rope around your neck, carry you off on the camel, and then throw you into the mountain of smoke." ʿUthmān replied, "May God disfigure you and reveal the ugliness of your deeds." Abū Ḥabībah states: All this happened in front of the people.[327] Then ʿUthmān's favorites and partisans among the Banū Umayyah came up to him and took him home. Abū Ḥabībah states: It was the last I saw of him. [2982]

According to Muḥammad (al-Wāqidī)—Usāmah b. Zayd al-Laythī—Yaḥyā b. ʿAbd al-Raḥmān b. Ḥāṭib—his father: I was watching ʿUthmān as he preached leaning on the Prophet's staff—the staff on which (the Prophet), Abū Bakr, and ʿUmar used to lean while they preached. Jahjāh said to him, "You hyena, get down off this pulpit!" Seizing the staff, Jahjāh broke it over his right knee. A wood splinter pierced (the knee), and the wound remained open for so long that it became infected with gangrene, [2983] and I saw it swarming with maggots. ʿUthmān descended from the pulpit and was taken away. He ordered the staff to be repaired, and it was bound together with a strip of iron. From that day until he was besieged and killed, ʿUthmān went out only one or two times.

It was related to me by Aḥmad b. Ibrāhīm—ʿAbdallāh b. Idrīs—ʿUbaydallāh b. ʿUmar—Nāfiʿ: Jahjāh al-Ghifārī seized a staff that ʿUthmān was holding and broke it over his knee, and (Jahjāh) was stricken with gangrene in that place.

It was related to me by Jaʿfar b. ʿAbdallāh al-Muḥammadī—ʿAmr—Muḥammad b. Isḥāq b. Yasār al-Madanī[328]—his paternal

327. *Wa-lam yakun dhālika minhu illā ʿan mala'in min 'l-nāsi.*

328. Ibn Isḥāq is of course most famous for his *Sīrat Rasūl Allāh,* but he also

uncle ʿAbd al-Raḥmān b. Yasār: When the people saw what ʿUthmān was doing, the Companions of the Prophet in Medina wrote to the Companions who were scattered throughout the frontier provinces: "You have gone forth but to struggle in the path of Almighty God, for the sake of Muḥammad's religion. In your absence the religion of Muḥammad has been corrupted and forsaken. Come then and reestablish Muḥammad's religion." Thus, they came from every direction until they killed (ʿUthmān). When the people turned around to go back after ʿUthmān claimed he had repented, he wrote a letter to ʿAbdallāh b. Saʿd b. Abī Sarḥ, his governor (*ʿāmil*) in Egypt, concerning those who had come from Egypt, for they were the most hostile to him of all the provincial garrisons: "To proceed: Look for so-and-so and so-and-so, and behead them if they come to you. Look also for certain
[2984] other men, and punish them in such-and-such a way." These persons included a few of the Companions of the Messenger of God as well as a body of the Successors. His envoy on this occasion was Abū al-Aʿwar b. Sufyān al-Sulamī. ʿUthmān mounted him on one of his camels and ordered him to get to Egypt before the dissidents (*al-qawm*) arrived. Abū al-Aʿwar overtook the Egyptians along the road, and they asked him where he was going. "To Egypt," he replied, and he was accompanied by a Syrian from Khawlān. When they saw him on ʿUthmān's camel, they said, "Are you carrying a letter?" "No," he said. "Why were you sent," they asked. "I don't know," he responded. "You are not carrying a letter," they said, "and you do not know why you were sent. Your situation is suspicious." Then they searched him and found a letter in an empty waterskin. Upon examining the letter, they discovered that some of them were to be executed and others were to be punished in their persons and property. When they saw this they returned to Medina. The people learned about their return and what had happened to them. They came back from all the provinces, and the Medinese rose up in rebellion.

It was related to me by Jaʿfar—ʿAmr and ʿAlī—Ḥusayn—his

composed a *Ta'rīkh al-Khulafā'*. Ṭabarī cites it only rarely, but a papyrus fragment—dealing with the murder of ʿUmar and the appointment of the electoral council—does survive. This fragment has been studied by Nabia Abbott, *Studies in Arabic Literary Papyri, I: Historical Texts* (Chicago: 1957), pp. 80–99. See also J. M. B. Jones, "Ibn Isḥāḳ," *EI*², III, 810–11.

father—Muḥammad b. Sā'ib al-Kalbī: The Egyptians returned to ʿUthmān after having departed from him because a slave (*ghulām*) of his, riding one of his camels, overtook them carrying a letter to the governor (*amīr*) of Egypt [with orders] to kill some of them and crucify others. When they came back to ʿUthmān they said, "This is your slave." He said, "My slave went without my knowledge." They said, "[It is] your camel." He responded, "He took it from the house without my orders." They said, "[This is] your seal." "It was forged," he said.

When the Egyptians arrived, ʿAbd al-Raḥmān b. ʿUdays al-Tujībī said:

They [fem.][329] came from Bilbays and Upper Egypt,
long-necked, their eyes squinting like bows,
Their flanks covered in chain mail. [2985]
They [fem.] demand God's due from al-Walīd, from
ʿUthmān and from Saʿīd.
O Lord, send us back with what we seek!

When ʿUthmān saw what had happened to him and how many of the people had been sent against him, he wrote Muʿāwiyah b. Abī Sufyān in Syria: "In the name of God, the Merciful, the Compassionate. To proceed: The Medinese have become unbelievers; they have abandoned obedience and renounced their oath of allegiance. Therefore send to me the Syrian soldiers who are at your disposal, on every camel you have, whether docile or stubborn." When Muʿāwiyah got the letter, he delayed action on it, for he did not wish to differ openly with the Companions of the Messenger of God, since he knew that they concurred [on this matter]. When ʿUthmān became aware of the delay, he wrote to seek aid from Yazīd b. Asad b. Kurz and the Syrians; he stressed his rightful claims upon them, and mentioned Almighty God's commandment to obey the caliphs, to give them sincere counsel, and to promise them the support of an army or personal entourage (*biṭānah*) against the people (as a whole). He reminded them of what he had endured with them and his good treatment of them. [He said:] "If you can aid me, then hurry, hurry. For the dissidents (*qawm*) are making haste against me." When his letter was read

329. Camels are meant.

out to them, Yazīd b. Asad b. Kurz, of the clan of Qasr in the tribe of Bajīlah, stood up. He praised and extolled God, and then spoke about ʿUthmān, stressing his rightful claims [upon them] and urging them to go to his aid. He commanded them to set out, and a great number heeded him and went with him until, having learned at Wādī al-Qurā[330] of ʿUthmān's murder, they returned.

ʿUthmān also wrote ʿAbdallāh b. ʿĀmir a copy of his letter to the Syrians, commanding him to send the Baṣrans to him. ʿAbdallāh b. ʿĀmir assembled the people and read ʿUthmān's letter to them. Speakers from among the Baṣrans stood up, urging him to go to
[2986] ʿUthmān's aid. The first among them who spoke was Mujāshiʿ b. Masʿūd al-Sulamī, at that time the chief (*sayyid*) of the Qays tribe in Baṣrah. Qays b. al-Haytham al-Sulamī also arose and exhorted the people to support ʿUthmān. The people hastened to do that, and ʿAbdallāh b. ʿĀmir put Mujāshiʿ b. Masʿūd in command of them. Mujāshiʿ led them out, but when the people made camp at al-Rabadhah—the vanguard having located in a district of Medina named Ṣirār—they learned of ʿUthmān's murder.

It was related to me by Jaʿfar—ʿAmr and ʿAlī—Ḥusayn —his father—Muḥammad b. Isḥāq b. Yasār al-Madanī—Yaḥyā b. ʿAbbād b. ʿAbdallāh b. al-Zubayr[331]—his father: The Egyptians in al-Suqyā or Dhū Khushub wrote a letter to ʿUthmān. One of them brought it to ʿUthmān, who did not reply in any way, but ordered him to be ejected from the house. Then six hundred Egyptians marched on ʿUthmān. They were divided into four brigades, and the commander of each carried a banner. The overall command was in the hands of ʿAmr b. Budayl b. Warqāʾ al-Khuzāʿī, one of the Companions of the Prophet, and ʿAbd al-Raḥmān b. ʿUdays al-Tujībī. Their letter to (ʿUthmān) contained [the following statements]:

"In the name of God, the Merciful, the Compassionate. To proceed: Know that 'God changes not what is in a people, until

330. Wādī al-Qurā ("The Valley of Towns") is a long depression stretching northwest from Medina, roughly parallel to the Red Sea coast. As the name implies, several major oasis settlements of the Ḥijāz are located there, and the principal trade route to Syria likewise traversed it.

331. The text reads *Yaḥyā b. ʿAbbād ʿan ʿAbdallāh b. al-Zubayr*. I have followed de Goeje's emendation: *Introductio*, dcxxix.

they change what is in themselves.'[332] So fear God, fear God! You are in a transitory world, and you must seek its fulfillment in a world to come. Do not forget your share in the world to come, and be not tempted by this present life. Know, by God, that we have [2987]
been angered for God's sake, and that we find satisfaction in God. Know that we will not remove our swords from our shoulders until you come to us either with frank and unambiguous repentance or with outright falsehood. This is our statement to you, and this is our case against you. God will excuse us for our actions against you. Peace."

The Medinese wrote to ʿUthmān, calling on him to repent, and swearing by God that they would not desist until they killed him or he fulfilled his God-ordained obligations to them.

When (ʿUthmān) feared he would be killed, he consulted his advisers and the members of his family (*ahl baytihi*) and said, "You see what the dissidents (*qawm*) have done. What is the way out?" They counseled him to send for ʿAlī b. Abī Ṭālib and to ask him to turn the people away by granting their requests in order to stall them until reinforcements could get to him. ʿUthmān replied, "The dissidents will not be put off. My promises were empty and I did nothing the first time they came.[333] If I give them my promise again they will demand that I fulfill it." Marwān b. al-Ḥakam said, "O Commander of the Faithful, dealing discreetly with them until you gain strength is preferable to struggling with them at close range. Give them what they ask and put them off so long as they delay in regard to you. They rebelled against you, so they possess no binding commitment [from you]."

ʿUthmān sent for ʿAlī, and when ʿAlī arrived he said to him, "Abū Ḥasan, you see what the people have done and you know what I have done. I fear they may kill me. Send them away from me, and I swear to God that I shall requite them for everything they detest, and I will grant them justice against me or anyone else, even if my own blood be shed thereby." ʿAlī said, "The people desire your justice more than your death. I see a band of

---

332. Qur'an 13:12.

333. *Wahā maḥmilī ʿahdan wa-qad kāna minnī fī qadmatihim 'l-ūlā mā kāna.* See de Goeje, *Introductio*, ccii, sub verbo *ḥamala*; and dcxxix.

men (*qawm*) who will be content only with full satisfaction.
[2988] When they first came to you, you gave them your promise in God's name that you would turn back from everything that they denounced, and thus you [were able to] send them away. Then you failed to carry out any of that. Do not tempt me with anything this time, for I will give them justice against you." "Yes," said ʿUthmān. "Give them justice, and by God I will carry it out in full."

So ʿAlī went out to the people and said, "O people, you have demanded justice and [now] it is granted to you. ʿUthmān claims that he will do you justice, whether it be against himself or anyone else, and that he will abandon everything that you detest. Accept this from him and affirm it." The people answered, "We accept it. Make a compact with him for us, for by God, we will not be content with words instead of deeds." ʿAlī said to them, "You will have it." Then he entered ʿUthmān's presence and told him the news.

ʿUthmān said, "Arrange a delay between them and me so that I will have time to act, for I cannot do away with the things they detest in one day." ʿAlī responded, "There can be no delay concerning matters here in Medina. As to matters elsewhere, you may delay as long as it takes your orders to get there." ʿUthmān said, "All right, but give me a delay of three days for affairs in Medina." ʿAlī agreed. Then he went to the people and informed them of this. He wrote out a document between (the people) and ʿUthmān that gave him a three-day grace period to do away with every injustice and remove every governor whom they disliked. Then he bound him in this document as tightly as God had ever bound one of His creatures by compact or covenant. (ʿAlī) had (the document) witnessed by a body of the leading Emigrants and Helpers.

Thus, the people turned back from (ʿUthmān) and withdrew until he should fulfill the promises that he had freely given them. But (ʿUthmān) began preparing for war and gathering arms. He had already formed a strong army from among the slaves acquired as part of the caliph's one-fifth share.[334] When the three days had

334. *Wa-qad ittakhadha jundan ʿaẓīman min raqīqi 'l-khums.* On the one-fifth share of booty paid to the caliph, see above, note 30.

passed and he had done nothing to alter anything which was hateful to the people or to remove any governor, they revolted against him.

'Amr b. Ḥazm al-Anṣārī went out to the Egyptians in Dhū Khushub and informed them of the situation. He proceeded with them to Medina, where they sent to 'Uthmān and said, "Did we not leave you when you claimed that you had repented of your unlawful innovations (*aḥdāth*) and turned away from things hateful to us? Have you not given us a compact and covenant before God?" He answered, "I have indeed, and I hold to that." Then ('Amr b. Ḥazm) said, "So what is this letter that we found in the possession of your messenger, written by you to your governor?" ('Uthmān) responded, "I did not write it, and I don't know what you are talking about." They said, "It was your messenger on your camel, a letter [written] by your secretary and bearing your seal."[335] ('Uthmān) replied, "As for the camel, it was stolen. [One man's] handwriting may resemble [another's]. As to the seal, it was forged." [2989]

They said, "We will not act precipitously even though we suspect you. Remove from us your sinful governors and appoint others over us who are not accused [of taking] our lives and property. Respond to our grievances." 'Uthmān said, "How do I look if I name officials whom you desire and remove those hateful to you? Authority (*al-amr*) would then belong to you." They said, "By God, you must either do [what you promised], abdicate, or be killed. See to things yourself or leave [them to us]." But he refused, saying, "I am not one to remove a robe that God has placed upon me." So they besieged him for forty nights, and in the meantime Ṭalḥah led the people in worship.

It was related to me by Ya'qūb b. Ibrāhīm—Ismā'īl b. Ibrāhīm—Ibn 'Awn—al-Ḥasan—Waththāb. According to (al-Ḥasan): (Waththāb) was one of those manumitted by the Commander of the Faithful 'Umar, and I saw on his throat the scars of two stab wounds, like a pair of leather thongs, which he had suffered on the Day of the House. According to (Waththāb): 'Uthmān sent me to summon al-Ashtar and he came.[336]

---

335. In other reports, 'Uthmān's secretary is identified as Marwān b. al-Ḥakam. For *barīd* as "messenger," see above, note 289.

336. Mālik b. al-Ḥārith al-Nakha'ī, nicknamed al-Ashtar. See L. Veccia Vaglieri,

Ibn ʿAwn thinks that Waththāb went on as follows: I laid down a cushion for the Commander of the Faithful and another for (al-Ashtar). Then (ʿUthmān) said, "Ashtar, what do the people want from me?" "You cannot avoid doing one of three things," he said. "What are they?" asked (ʿUthmān). (Al-Ashtar) said, "They ask
[2990] you to choose between [the following]. You may turn their affairs over to them and say, 'This is your affair; choose whomever you will for it.' Second, you may have yourself punished. If you reject these two choices, then this band of men (*qawm*) will kill you." (ʿUthmān) replied, "As for my turning their affairs over to them, I am not one to remove a robe that Almighty God has placed upon me."

According to (Ibn ʿAwn), other authorities beside (Waththāb) report [the following statement]: "By God, I would rather be brought out and beheaded than remove a shirt that God has placed upon me. I would be abandoning Muḥammad's Community to civil war." According to Ibn ʿAwn, this more closely resembles what he said. [Continuing ʿUthmān's statement:] "As for having myself punished, by God, you know that two of my associates were punished before me, and my body cannot endure punishment.[337] As for your killing me, by God, if you kill me you will never again have love for one another, nor will you ever pray together again, nor will you ever be united in fighting an enemy."

Al-Ashtar rose and hurried away, while we remained there for some days. Then a little man came like a wolf, peered in through the door, and then left. Muḥammad b. Abī Bakr came with thirteen men and went up to ʿUthmān. He seized his beard and shook it[338] until I heard his teeth chattering. (Muḥammad b. Abī Bakr) said, "Muʿāwiyah was no help to you, nor was Ibn ʿĀmir nor your letters." (ʿUthmān) said, "Let go of my beard, son of my brother! Let go of my beard!" Then I saw (Ibn Abī Bakr) signaling with his

---

"Al-Ashtar," *EI*², I, 704. He was a tribal leader in Kūfah, and one of the bitterest opponents of the governor Saʿīd b. al-ʿĀṣ. See above: pp. 112–21, 125, 132–35 (text, I, 2907–2917, 2921, 2927–2931). He was one of ʿAlī's most ardent supporters until his death in 37/658.

337. Presumably he refers to al-Walīd b. ʿUqbah and someone else. See above, pp. 53–55 (text, I, 2848–2849). Cf. the longer account in Balādhurī, *Ansāb*, V, 29–35, based largely on the testimony of Abū Mikhnaf and (to a lesser degree) al-Wāqidī.

338. *Fa-qāla bihā*. See de Goeje, *Introductio*, cdxxxviii, sub verbo *qāla*.

eye to one of the rebels (*qawm*). He came over to him with a broad iron-headed arrow and stabbed him in the head with it. I [that is, [2991] Ibn ʿAwn] asked, "Then what happened?" (Waththāb) replied, "They gathered round him and killed him."

According to al-Wāqidī—Yaḥyā b. ʿAbd al-ʿAzīz—Jaʿfar b. Maḥmūd—Muḥammad b. Maslamah: I set out with a band of my fellow tribesmen (*qawmī*) to meet the Egyptians. They were led by four chiefs: ʿAbd al-Raḥmān b. ʿUdays al-Balawī, Sūdān b. Ḥumrān al-Murādī, ʿAmr b. al-Ḥamiq al-Khuzāʿī—whose name became so dominant that (the force) was called "the army of Ibn al-Ḥamiq"[339]—and Ibn al-Nibāʿ. I entered their presence as the four of them were in a tent, and I saw that the people (*al-nās*) were following them. I stressed ʿUthmān's rights and the oath of allegiance that lay upon their necks. I filled them with a dread of civil war (*fitnah*), and informed them that (ʿUthmān's) murder was a grave matter, concerning which there was much dissension. "Do not be the first to open the gate of discord.[340] He will turn away from those practices for which you have criticized him, and I will be the guarantor of that." The dissidents said, "And what if he does not desist?" I answered, "Then the matter is up to you." They went away satisfied, and I returned to ʿUthmān and said, "Grant me a private audience." He did so. I said, "Fear God, ʿUthmān, fear God for your life! Verily these people have only come seeking your blood, and you see how your associates have abandoned you. Worse, they are going over to your enemy." He expressed his consent and asked God to requite me.

Then I departed from him, but remained [in Medina] so long as God willed. ʿUthmān had spoken [to me] about the Egyptians' return [to Dhū Khushub]; he mentioned that they had come for one thing but had obtained something else and then departed. I [2992] wanted to come and rebuke him, but I kept silent. Suddenly someone said, "The Egyptians have arrived and are in al-Suwaydāʾ." I said, "Is it true, what you say?" "Yes," he replied. ʿUthmān sent to me, for the news had reached him, and the dissi-

---

339. Here I follow Caetani, *Annali,* VIII, 175. As emended the sentence would read: *wa-qad kāna hādhā 'l-ismu ghalaba ḥattā kāna yuqālu jayshu 'bni 'l-Ḥamiqi.*

340. Cf. p. 2921, note g.

dents (*qawm*) had made camp in Dhū Khushub at that very moment. ('Uthmān) said, "Abū 'Abd al-Raḥmān, these dissidents have returned. What should be done about them?" I responded, "By God, I do not know, but I do not think they have come back for any good purpose." ('Uthmān) said, "Go out to them and send them away." "No, by God, I will not," I said. "Why?" he asked. I said, "Because I assured them that you would desist from certain matters, and you have not desisted from a single letter of them." He said, "God is the one whose aid we seek." I went out, while the dissidents came and established themselves in al-Aswāf and laid siege to 'Uthmān.

'Abd al-Raḥmān b. 'Udays came to me, accompanied by Sūdān b. Ḥumrān and his two comrades. They said, "Abū 'Abd al-Raḥmān, do you not know that you spoke to us and sent us away? And you claimed that our companion [that is, 'Uthmān] would cease his reprehensible acts?" "Yes indeed," I said. Then they showed a short letter to me; there was a lead tube, and they were saying, "We found one of the alms-tax camels being ridden by 'Uthmān's slave. We seized his belongings and searched him, and we found this letter on him. It contains the following: 'In the name of God, the Merciful, the Compassionate. To proceed: If 'Abd al-Raḥmān b. 'Udays comes to you, give him a hundred lashes. Shave his head and beard, and keep him in confinement until my orders reach you. Do the same with 'Amr b. al-Ḥamiq, Sūdān b. Ḥumrān, and 'Urwah b. al-Nibā' al-Laythī.'" I said, "How do you know that 'Uthmān wrote this?" They responded, "Suppose Marwān has done this without 'Uthmān's knowledge. That would be worse,
[2993] and he must remove himself from office." They added, "Hurry to him with us. We have spoken to 'Alī, and he has promised us that he will speak with him at the noon prayer."

We came to Sa'd b. Abī Waqqāṣ, but he said, "I will not intervene in your affair." We came to Sa'īd b. Zayd b. 'Amr b. Nufayl, and he said the same thing. Muḥammad (b. Maslamah) asked, "Where did 'Alī promise you [he would act]?" "He promised us that he would go and see ('Uthmān) at the noon prayer," they answered.

According to Muḥammad (b. Maslamah): I performed the prayer with 'Alī; then he and I entered ('Uthmān's) presence and said, "These Egyptians are at the door, so give them leave [to come in]." Now Marwān was sitting with him, and he said, "May I be thy ransom. Permit me to speak to them." ʿUthmān responded, "May God leave you openmouthed! Get away from me. You have nothing to say about this matter." So Marwān went out, and ʿAlī came in to see him. The Egyptians had told him what they had told me, and ʿAlī began to inform (ʿUthmān) what they had discovered in the letter. (ʿUthmān) started to swear by God that he had not written or known about or sought advice concerning (this letter). Muḥammad b. Maslamah [that is, the narrator of this incident] said, "By God he is telling the truth. This is Marwān's doing." ʿAlī said, "Then have them come in and hear your excuse." ʿUthmān went up to ʿAlī and said, "We are kinsmen through the female lineage.[341] By God, if you were in this situation I would extricate you from it. Go out and speak to them, for they will listen to you." But ʿAlī replied, "I will not do it. Rather, have them enter so that you may present your excuses to them." (ʿUthmān) said, "Have them come in."

According to Muḥammad b. Maslamah: So at that point they entered, but they did not give him the greeting appropriate to a caliph. Then I knew that this was evil itself. We exchanged the usual greetings, and then Ibn ʿUdays stepped forward as spokesman for the dissidents. He mentioned what Ibn Saʿd had done in Egypt, recalling his unjust treatment of the Muslims and the protected peoples, and noting his appropriation of the Muslims' booty for himself alone. And when he was told about that, [2994]
he said, "These are the written orders of the Commander of the Faithful." Then they mentioned innovations which (ʿUthmān) had instituted in Medina—things opposed by his two predecessors.

(Ibn ʿUdays) said, "We journeyed from Egypt seeking nothing but your blood or an end [to these abuses], but ʿAlī and Muḥammad b. Maslamah sent us back, and Muḥammad assured us that everything we had complained about would be ended." Then they turned toward Muḥammad b. Maslamah and asked, "Did you tell us that?" According to Muḥammad, "I said that I had." [Ibn ʿUdays continued:] "Then we returned to our country, calling

341. *Inna lī qarābatan wa-raḥiman.*

upon Almighty God for help against you, because we had overwhelming proof [for our claims]. Then when we were in al-Buwayb[342] we apprehended your slave and seized the letter under your seal to ʿAbdallāh b. Saʿd, in which you order him to flog us, to disfigure us by cutting off our hair, and to imprison us for long terms. Here is your letter."

ʿUthmān praised and extolled God. Then he said, "By God I did not write it, I did not order it [to be written], I did not take counsel about it, I did not know about it." According to Muḥammad (b. Maslamah): ʿAlī and I both said, "He is telling the truth." ʿUthmān was relieved at this.

The Egyptians asked, "So who wrote it?" (ʿUthmān) responded, "I don't know." (Ibn ʿUdays) continued, "Can anyone treat you so audaciously that your slave is sent on a camel paid by the Muslims as alms tax, your seal is forged, and your governor is written to concerning these grave matters, while you know nothing?" "Yes," he replied. They said, "A man like you should not govern. Remove yourself from this office (*amr*), as God has removed you from it." (ʿUthmān) replied, "I shall not remove a shirt that Almighty God has placed upon me." The shouting and noise grew louder, and I [that is, the narrator, Muḥammad b. Maslamah] thought that they would not leave without attacking him. Then
[2995] ʿAlī arose and went out, and when he stood up I did the same. He told the Egyptians to go and they did so. ʿAlī and I each returned to our own homes, but they broke off their siege of (ʿUthmān) only when they had killed him.

According to Muḥammad b. ʿUmar (al-Wāqidī)—ʿAbdallāh b. al-Ḥārith b. al-Fuḍayl—his father—Sufyān b. Abī al-ʿAwjāʾ: When the Egyptians came the first time, ʿUthmān spoke to Muḥammad b. Maslamah, and he set out with fifty horsemen from among the Helpers. Having reached them at Dhū Khushub, (Muḥammad) sent them away. The dissidents (*qawm*) went as far as al-Buwayb, where they came upon a slave of ʿUthmān carrying a letter to ʿAbdallāh b. Saʿd. They turned round and went back to Medina, where al-Ashtar and Ḥukaym b. Jabalah had stayed behind. They

342. "*Buwayb* is the diminutive of *bāb*, meaning a cleft between two mountains. According to Yaʿqūb, al-Buwayb is the place where the Ḥijāzīs enter Egypt." (Yāqūt, *Muʿjam al-Buldān*, I, 764).

presented the letter, but ʿUthmān denied that he had written it. "This is a forgery," he said. "The letter is written by your scribe," they replied. "Indeed," said (ʿUthmān), "but he did not write it on my orders." They said, "The messenger on whom we discovered the letter is your slave." "That is so," he said, "but he set out without my permission." "The camel is your camel," they said. "Yes," he replied, "but it was taken without my knowledge."

They said, "You are either truthful or a liar. If you are lying, you deserve to be deposed because you have unjustly ordered our blood to be shed. If you are telling the truth you deserve to be deposed because of your weakness and neglect, as well as the wickedness of your entourage. It is not right that we allow someone whose commands are ignored due to his weakness and neglect to have authority over us."[343] They continued, "You have beaten some of the Prophet's Companions and others when, in denouncing various acts of yours, they have admonished you and commanded you to return to righteousness. Have yourself chastised, then, in recompense for those whom you have wrongfully beaten." He answered, "The imām both errs and acts rightly. I shall not have myself chastised, because if I accepted retaliation for everyone against whom I have acted in error, I would be [2996]
destroyed."

They said, "You have introduced grave innovations, and for them you deserve to be deposed. When people spoke to you about them, you declared your repentance, but then you did the same things again. Then we came to you and you claimed that you would repent and return to righteousness. Muḥammad b. Maslamah remonstrated with us on your behalf and gave us guarantees as to what would happen. But you betrayed him, and he declared that he would have nothing more to do with you. We returned [to Egypt] the first time in order to deprive you of any pretext and to give you every possible excuse, even as we sought the aid of Almighty God against you. Then we intercepted a letter from you to your governor over us, in which you ordered him to kill and mutilate and crucify us. You allege that (this letter) was written without your knowledge. But it was carried by your slave

343. *Lā yanbaghī lanā an natrūka ʿalā riqābinā man yuqtaṭaʿu mithlu ʾl-amri dūnahu li-ḍuʿfihi wa-ghaflatihi.*

on your camel, it was written in the hand of your scribe, and it bore your seal. All this has aroused ugly suspicions against you, together with what we already knew about your tyrannical rule, your selfishness in sharing out [booty], your freehanded punishments against the people, and your feigned repentance followed by reversion to error. We went away, but we should not have gone before deposing you and replacing you with a Companion of the Messenger of God—a man who had not introduced the innovations that we have endured from you, and who is not subject to the suspicion that falls upon you. Give back our caliphate and abdicate, for that is our surest recourse against you and your surest recourse against us."

'Uthmān said, "Have you said everything you wanted to say?" "Yes," they answered. He said, "Praise be to God! I praise Him and seek His aid. I believe in Him, I place my trust in Him, and I bear witness that there is no deity save God alone, Who has no partner, and that Muḥammad is His servant and messenger. 'He sent him with guidance and the religion of truth, that he may uplift it above every religion, though the unbelievers be averse.'[344] To proceed: You have struck the balance neither in speech nor in
[2997] judgment. As for your telling me to abdicate, I shall not remove a shirt that Almighty God has placed upon me, and by which He has honored me and set me apart from others. However, I will repent and desist [from sin], and I will never again do anything that the Muslims find blameworthy. By God, I am a man who needs God and fears Him."

They said, "Were this the first innovation that you had introduced, and had you then repented and not repeated it, we would have to accept [your repentance] and depart from you. But you know of previous innovations on your part. When we departed from you the first time, neither we nor the man through whom you had excused your conduct [namely, Muḥammad b. Maslamah] suspected that you would write the things that we found in the letter carried by your slave. How can we accept your repentance when we know by experience that as soon as you display repentance for a sin, you do it again? We shall not depart

344. Qur'ān 9:33.

from you [now] until we have deposed you and replaced you. If your supporters—fellow tribesmen (*min qawmika*), kinsmen, or men devoted to you—choose battle, then we shall fight them until we reach you and kill you, or until you dispatch our souls to God."

'Uthmān responded, "As for surrendering my office (*imārah*), I would rather be crucified than give up the mandate (*amr*) of Almighty God and His caliphate (*khilāfatuhu*). As for your statement that you will fight whoever defends me, I shall not order anyone to fight you. Whoever fights for me will not do so on my orders. By my life, if I wished to fight you, I would have written to the commanders of the garrisons,[345] and they would have brought troops and dispatched men [to my aid]. I might also have linked up with my supporters[346] in Egypt or Iraq. Fear God, fear God and save yourselves. If you do not spare my life, if you kill me, you will bring about bloodshed by this affair." Then they departed [2998]
from him, warning him that war would come. He sent to Muḥammad b. Maslamah and told him to send them away. [Muḥammad] replied, "By God, I do not lie to God twice in one year."

According to Muḥammad b. 'Umar [al-Wāqidī]—Muḥammad b. Muslim—Mūsā b. 'Uqbah—Abū Ḥabībah: On the day 'Uthmān was killed, I saw Sa'd b. Abī Waqqāṣ go in to him. Then he came out, saying "To God we belong and to Him we shall return," on account of what he saw at ('Uthmān's) door. Marwān said to him, "Now you are sorry, but you have slain him." I [that is, the narrator Abū Ḥabībah] heard Sa'd say, "I beg God's forgiveness. I did not imagine that the people would dare to demand his blood. I came before him just now, and he made a statement that neither you nor your comrades heard. He renounced all his reprehensible actions and manifested repentance. He said, 'I will not keep on toward ruin, for he who persists in tyranny is very far from the [true] path. I shall repent and desist from evil.'" Marwān said, "If you mean to defend ('Uthmān), you must get Ibn Abī Ṭālib, but he has secluded himself and will not be spoken to."

Sa'd left and went to 'Alī, who was [in the mosque] between the [Prophet's] tomb and the pulpit. He said, "Get up, Abū Ḥasan.

345. Following the proposed emendation, 2997, note f.
346. *Aṭrāfī:* see de Goeje, *Introductio*, cccxxxix.

May my father and mother be your ransom. By God, I bring you the best news anyone has ever received. Take care of your cousin, deal kindly with him, spare his blood, and the situation will again be as we desire. Your caliph has given [us] satisfaction of his own free will." ʿAlī responded, "May God hear him, Abū Isḥāq. By God, I have persisted in defending him until I am filled with shame. But Marwān, Muʿāwiyah, ʿAbdallāh b. ʿĀmir, and Saʿīd b. al-ʿĀṣ have dealt with him as you see. When I gave him sincere
[2999] counsel and directed him to send them away, he became suspicious of me, until what you now see has happened." While (Saʿd and ʿAlī) were thus engaged, Muḥammad b. Abī Bakr came and whispered to ʿAlī. Then ʿAlī took my hand and arose, saying, "What good is his repentance now?" And by God, I [that is, the narrator Abū Ḥabībah] no sooner reached my house than I heard the cry that ʿUthmān had been killed. And by God, we have remained in an evil state down to this day."

According to Muḥammad b. ʿUmar (al-Wāqidī)—Shuraḥbīl b. Abī ʿAwn[347]—Yazīd b. Abī Ḥabīb—Abū al-Khayr:[348] When the Egyptians set out against ʿUthmān, ʿAbdallāh b. Saʿd sent a messenger posthaste to inform him of their departure and to tell him that they were pretending to undertake the Lesser Pilgrimage. The messenger having reached ʿUthmān b. ʿAffān with this news, ʿUthmān in turn sent to the Meccans to warn them against these Egyptians and to inform them that (the Egyptians) had slandered their imam. Then ʿAbdallāh b. Saʿd set out toward ʿUthmān on the heels of the Egyptians, having sought and received his permission to come to him. Upon reaching Aylah,[349] Ibn Saʿd learned that the Egyptians had returned against ʿUthmān and put him under siege.

Now Muḥammad b. Abī Ḥudhayfah was in Egypt; when he heard that ʿUthmān was under siege and that ʿAbdallāh b. Saʿd had left (the country), he seized power in Egypt, and (the Egyptians)

---

347. Emended in accordance with de Goeje. *Introductio*, dcxxix.

348. Marthad b. ʿAbdallāh al-Yazanī. See de Goeje, *Introductio*, dcxxix.

349. Aylah: Biblical Elath, modern al-ʿAqabah. A small port located at the head of the Gulf of ʿAqabah. In ancient and early Islamic times, it was a prosperous center for the Red Sea trade with Syria, as well as the crossroads of the Pilgrimage caravans from Egypt and Damascus. See H. W. Glidden, "al-ʿAḳaba," "Ayla," *EI*², I, 314–15, 783–84. There are now important excavations at this site by the Oriental Institute, University of Chicago.

submitted to his authority. ʿAbdallāh b. Saʿd turned back toward Egypt, but Ibn Abī Ḥudhayfah fended him off. Thus, he made his way to Palestine and resided there until ʿUthmān was murdered.

The Egyptians advanced and made camp at al-Aswāf, and laid siege to ʿUthmān. Ḥukaym b. Jabalah came from Baṣrah with a troop of horsemen, and al-Ashtar arrived with the Kūfans. [All three parties] met in Medina, then al-Ashtar and Ḥukaym b. Jabalah withdrew, so that Ibn ʿUdays and his comrades, numbering 500 men, were the ones besieging ʿUthmān. They sustained the [3000] siege for forty-nine days, until at last he was killed on Friday, eighteen nights having passed in Dhū al-Ḥijjah, in the year 35 (17 June 656).

According to Muḥammad (b. ʿUmar al-Wāqidī)—Ibrāhīm b. Sālim—his father—Busr b. Saʿīd—ʿAbdallāh b. ʿAyyāsh b. Abī Rabīʿah:[350] I entered ʿUthmān's presence and talked with him for an hour. He said, "Come, Ibn ʿAyyāsh," and he took me by the hand and had me listen to what the people at his door were saying. We heard some say, "What are you waiting for," while others were saying, "Wait, perhaps he will repent." While the two of us were standing there, Ṭalḥah b. ʿUbaydallāh passed by; he stopped and said, "Where is Ibn ʿUdays?" He was told, "He is over there." Ibn ʿUdays came over to (Ṭalḥah) and whispered something to him, then he went back to his comrades and said, "Do not let anyone go in to see this man or leave his house."

ʿUthmān said to me, "These are Ṭalḥah b. ʿUbaydallāh's orders." He continued: "O God, protect me from Ṭalḥah b. ʿUbaydallāh, for he has incited all these people against me. By God, I hope nothing will come of it and that his blood will be shed. He has abused me unlawfully. I heard the Messenger of God say, 'The blood of a Muslim is lawful only in three cases: a man who disbelieves after having professed Islam is put to death; a man who commits adultery is stoned; a man who kills except in legitimate retaliation for another is put to death.'[351] So why should I be killed?" Then ʿUthmān went back [into the house].

---

350. Reading "Busr" instead of "Bishr," and "ʿAyyāsh" instead of "ʿAbbās," in accordance with de Goeje, *Introductio*, dcxxix.

351. The last clause is quoted from Qur'ān 5:35. The context is significant in view of the charges laid against ʿUthmān by his opponents (see also below, I,

According to Ibn ʿAyyāsh: I wanted to leave, but they blocked my path until Muḥammad b. Abī Bakr passed by and said, "Let him go." They did so.

According to Muḥammad (b. ʿUmar al-Wāqidī)—Yaʿqūb b. ʿAbdallāh al-Ashʿarī—Jaʿfar b. Abī al-Mughīrah—Saʿīd b. ʿAbd al-
[3001] Raḥmān b. Abzay—his father: I witnessed the day they went in against ʿUthmān. They entered the house through an opening in the residence of ʿAmr b. Ḥazm. There was some skirmishing and then they got in. By God, I have not forgotten that Sūdān b. Ḥumrān came out and I heard him say, "Where is Ṭalḥah b. ʿUbaydallāh? We have killed Ibn ʿAffān!"

According to Muḥammad b. ʿUmar (al-Wāqidī)—Shuraḥbīl b. Abī ʿAwn—his father—Abū Ḥafṣah al-Yamāni: I used to belong to a Bedouin. Marwān liked me and purchased me along with my wife and son, and then freed us all. I used to accompany him. When ʿUthmān was put under siege, the Banū Umayyah prepared to defend him, and Marwān entered the [caliph's] residence [and stayed] with him. I too was there. By God, I initiated the fighting among the people by throwing [a stone] from the roof of the house at a man of [the tribe of] Aslam named Niyār and killed him. Then fighting broke out and I descended. The people battled at the door, and Marwān fought until he fell down. I carried him off and brought him into the house of an old woman and locked him in. The people set fires at the doors of ʿUthmān's residence, and one of them was set ablaze. ʿUthmān said, "The burning door only signals something more terrible.[352] None of you must raise his hand [to resist them]. For by God if I were the furthest of you all from them, they would walk over you to kill me, and if I were the closest of you to them, they would not go past me. I will endure patiently, as the Messenger of God enjoined upon me. I shall suffer the death that Almighty God has decreed for me (*kataba lī*)."

Marwān said, "By God, you shall not be killed while I yet hear!" Then, sword in hand, he went toward the door reciting this poem as a proverb:

3023): "Whosoever slays a soul not to retaliate for a soul slain, nor for corruption done in the land, shall be as if he had slain mankind altogether."

352. *Mā iḥtaraqa 'l-bābu illā limā huwa aʿẓamu minhu.*

The woman with the flowing hair,
 the soft palm and fingertips,
Knows that I strike fear in the vanguard, [3002]
 on a steed quick as the *qaṭā*-bird in the well-watered valley.[353]

According to Muḥammad (b. ʿUmar al-Wāqidī)—ʿAbdallāh b. al-Ḥārith b. al-Fuḍayl—his father—Abū Ḥafṣah: On Thursday I dropped a stone from the roof of the house and killed a man of [the tribe of] Aslam named Niyār. They sent to ʿUthmān and demanded his murderer. (ʿUthmān) responded, "I do not know who killed him." They spent the night before Friday [that is, Thursday evening] berating us like fire. In the morning they attacked, and the first one to climb onto our roofs was Kinānah b. ʿAttāb, holding a torch. They way had been opened for him through the house of the Ḥazm clan. Then naphtha-soaked firebrands penetrated [the compound] right behind him. We fought them for a hour, standing on blazing wood. I heard ʿUthmān say to his companions, "After the fire there will be nothing. The wood has burned, the doors have burned. Whoever still obeys me must cling to his own house. The rebels (*qawm*) are only after me. They will repent of killing me. By God, even if they left me alone, I believe I would not wish to live. My health is ruined; my teeth have fallen out and my bones have weakened."

Then he said to Marwān, "Sit down. Do not go out." But Marwān disobeyed him and said, "By God, you will not be killed and no one will get to you while I can yet hear." Then he went out against the people. I said, "I cannot abandon my master," and I went out alongside him to defend him. We were only a few men, and I heard Marwān reciting:

The woman with the flowing hair,
 the soft palm and fingertips knows.

Then he shouted, "Who will step forth [against me]?" He raised [3003]
the bottom of his mailed shirt (*dirʿ*) and tucked it in his belt. Ibn al-Nibāʿ jumped on him and struck him down from behind with a

353. Not an easy verse; cf. Caetani, *Annali*, VIII, 182. De Goeje's proposed emendation of *azūʿu* ("I urge on") instead of *arūʿu* ("I frighten") is doubtful, since Balādhurī, *Ansāb*, V, 79, cites the same lines with *arūʿu*.

blow on his neck. No pulse could be detected, and I brought him into the house of Fāṭimah bt. Aws, the grandmother of Ibrāhīm b. al-ʿAdī. ʿAbd al-Malik and the Banū Umayyah always remembered the clan of al-ʿAdī for that.

It was related to me by Aḥmad b. ʿUthmān b. Ḥakīm—ʿAbd al-Raḥmān b. Sharīk—his father—Muḥammad b. Isḥāq—Yaʿqūb b. ʿUtbah b. al-Akhnas—Ibn al-Ḥārith b. Abī Bakr—his father, Abū Bakr b. al-Ḥārith b. Hishām: I can still see[354] ʿAbd al-Raḥmān b. ʿUdays al-Balawī as he was leaning with his back against the mosque of God's Prophet, while ʿUthmān lay besieged. Marwān b. al-Ḥakam emerged and said, "Who will step forth [against me]?" ʿAbd al-Raḥmān b. ʿUdays said to some son of ʿUrwah, "Go fight this man." A tall young slave rose to fight him, seized the edge of his mailed shirt, and stabbed him in his girdle. His thigh was unprotected, and Marwān lunged at him, but ʿUrwah's son struck him on the neck. I can still see him twisting around, and ʿUbayd b. Rifāʿah al-Zuraqī rose up to finish him off. But Fāṭimah bt. Aws, the grandmother of Ibrāhīm b. ʿAdī (*sic*), leaped on him. She had nursed Marwān and his children, and she said, "If you only want to kill the man, he has already been killed. But if you mean to toy
[3004] with his flesh, that is shameful." So he left him alone, and (the Banū Umayyah) were grateful to her ever after. Later on, they appointed her son Ibrāhīm a governor.

According to Ibn Isḥāq: When ʿAbd al-Raḥmān b. ʿUdays al-Balawī set out from Egypt for Medina, he said:

From Bilbays and Upper Egypt (the she-camels) came,
 their flanks covered in chain mail,
Demanding God's due against Saʿīd
 until they brought back what we sought for.

It was related to me by Jaʿfar b. ʿAbdallāh al-Muḥammadī—ʿAmr b. Ḥammād and ʿAlī b. Ḥusayn—Ḥusayn b. ʿĪsā—his father: When the three days following the Feast of Sacrifice[355] had passed

---

354. *Ka-annī anẓuru ilā ʿAbda 'l-Raḥmāni*: lit., "[It is] as if I were looking at ʿAbd al-Raḥmān."

355. *Ayyām al-Tashrīq*, the three days from 11 to 13 Dhū al-Ḥijjah following the ritual sacrifice (ʿĪd al-Aḍḥā), which takes place on 10 Dhū al-Ḥijjah. These days represent the holiday at the conclusion of the Pilgrimage rites proper. See A. J. Wensinck and J. Jomier, "Ḥadjdj," *EI*², III, 36.

(the rebels) surrounded 'Uthmān's house, but he insisted on retaining his office, and sent to assemble his retainers and close associates (*ḥashamuhu wa-khāṣṣatuhu*). One of the Prophet's Companions, a venerable old man named Niyār b. 'Iyāḍ, arose and called out, "'Uthmān!" ('Uthmān) looked down at him from the roof of his house. (Niyār) reminded him of God and implored him in God's name to dissociate himself from (his evil associates).[356] And while he was speaking, one of 'Uthmān's associates shot and killed him with an arrow. ('Uthmān's opponents) claimed that the man who shot him was Kathīr b. al-Ṣalt al-Kindī, and at this they said to 'Uthmān, "Turn the murderer of Niyār b. 'Iyāḍ over to us that we may kill him in retaliation." He replied, "I will not kill a man who has defended me while you intend to murder me." When they perceived this they rushed at ('Uthmān's) door and set it ablaze. Marwān b. al-Ḥakam emerged from 'Uthmān's residence leading a band of men against them. Sa'īd b. al-'Āṣ and al-Mughīrah b. al-Akhnas b. Sharīq al-Thaqafī, the ally of the Banū Zuhrah, both did the same, and the fighting raged fiercely.

They were driven to fight by the news that reinforcements from [3005]
Baṣrah had made camp in Ṣirār, a night's journey from Medina, while the Syrians were approaching as well. Thus, they fought bitterly at the door of the house, and al-Mughīrah b. al-Akhnas al-Thaqafī attacked the rebels (*qawm*), reciting:

A lovely serving girl,
    Adorned with necklace and anklets,
Knows my skill with the sword blade.

He was assailed in turn by 'Abdallāh b. Budayl b. Warqā' al-Khuzā'ī, who was saying:

If you wield the sword as you say,
    stand fast against a noble opponent who attacks
Bearing a Mashrafī sword with polished edge.

'Abdallāh struck and killed (al-Mughīrah), and Rifā'ah b. Rāfi', of the clan of Zurayq among the Anṣār,[357] charged Marwān b. al-

356. *fa-nashadahu 'llāha wa-dhakkarahu 'llāha lammā i'tazalahum.* For this idiom see Wright, *Arabic Grammar,* II, 339D–340A. See also de Goeje, *Introductio,* dcxxix.

357. Zurayq was a clan in the tribe of Khazraj, one of the two main Medinese

Ḥakam and struck him down. He drew back from him, thinking he had killed him. ʿAbdallāh b. al-Zubayr suffered numerous wounds. ʿUthmān's supporters (*al-qawm*) were routed and retreated toward the palace (*qaṣr*). At the door they held fast and fought a fierce battle there.

In the battle at the door, Ziyād b. Nuʿaym al-Fihrī was killed, along with several other companions of ʿUthmān. The people continued to fight until ʿAmr b. Ḥazm al-Anṣārī opened the door of his residence, which lay adjacent to ʿUthmān b. ʿAffān's. He shouted to the people, and they advanced through his house against (the defenders of ʿUthmān), fighting them in the courtyard of [ʿUthmān's] house until they fled and the door was abandoned to (the rebels). (The defenders) fled into the streets of Medina, while ʿUthmān remained behind with a few associates and members of his household. ʿUthmān was killed, and they were killed along with him.

[3006] It was related to me by Yaʿqūb b. Ibrāhīm—Muʿtamir b. Sulaymān al-Taymī—his father—Abū Naḍrah—Abū Saʿīd, the client (*mawlā*) of Abū Usayd al-Anṣārī: One day ʿUthmān gazed down upon them [from his rooftop] and said, "Peace be upon you." But he heard no reply from any of the people, unless someone perchance responded silently. (ʿUthmān) said, "I adjure you by God, do you know that with my own money I purchased [the well] of Rūmah, highly esteemed for its sweet water, and that I made it available to every Muslim.[358] "Yes," they answered. He said, "Why am I kept from drinking from it, so that I have to break my fasting with salt water? I adjure you by God, do you know that I bought such-and-such a piece of land and added it to the [Prophet's] mosque?" "Yes," they said. He went on, "And do you know anyone among the people except me who is prevented from worshipping there? I adjure you by God, did you hear the Prophet of God mention such things concerning it, or did God mention the like in His clear Book?" Calls for restraint spread, and the people began to say, "Let us go easy with the Commander

---

tribes from whom the *Anṣār* were drawn. See Watt, *Muhammad at Medina*, 154, 169–70.

358. *Fa-jaʿaltu rishāʾi minhā ka-rishāʾi rajulin min ʾl-muslimīna*. Lit., "I made my rope from it like the rope of any man among the Muslims."

of the Faithful." Then al-Ashtar arose—I do not know whether it was that day or another—and said, "Perhaps ('Uthmān) has deceived you." The people trampled him underfoot and he encountered rough treatment.[359]

Another time I [that is, Abū Sa'īd] saw him looking down at (his opponents). He exhorted and admonished them, but his exhortations made no impression on them. [His] preaching used to affect the people the first time they heard it, but when it was repeated it had no impact. Then ('Uthmān) opened the door and placed the Qur'ān before him. He did this, having dreamed during the night that God's Prophet was saying [to him], "Break the fast with us tonight."[360]

According to Abū al-Mu'tamir—al-Ḥasan: Muḥammad b. Abī Bakr went up to him and seized his beard, saying, "You have behaved toward us in a manner which Abū Bakr would not have done." Then he went out and left him. Another man, named the Black Death, entered ('Uthmān's) presence and throttled him and slapped him.[361] Then he went out and said, "By God, I have never seen anything softer than his throat. By God, I throttled him until I saw his soul shaking in his body like the soul of a jinn." Then he went out.

According to Abū Sa'īd's account: A certain man went in to [3007]
'Uthmān, in front of whom lay the Qur'ān, and he said, "The Book of God is between you and me." (The intruder) went for him with his sword; ('Uthmān) protected himself with his hand and it was cut. I do not know whether he sliced (the hand) clear off or cut it without severing it. Then he said, "Yea, by God, this is the first palm which has crossed the Qur'ān."

According to an account besides that of Abū Sa'īd: Al-Tujībī went in to ('Uthmān) and wounded him with a broad iron-tipped arrow, and his blood dripped on this verse: "God will suffice you for them; He is the All-Hearing, the All-Knowing."[362] (The blood)

---

359. *Fa-waṭi'ahu 'l-nāsu ḥattā laqiya kādhā wa-kādhā.*

360. The motif of 'Uthmān's dream is developed more fully in Balādhurī, *Ansāb*, V, 82.

361. Caetani (*Annali*, VIII, 188) translates: "e strangolato il Califfo, lo spacciò con la spada." But in my judgment he is reading too much into the second verb (*khafaqahu*); 'Uthmān is not done away with just yet.

362. Qur'ān 2:131. In the present context the whole verse is significant: "And if

is still on that copy of the Qur'ān and has not been scraped off. According to Abū Sa'īd's account, the daughter of al-Farāfiṣah [that is, 'Uthmān's wife] took her jewelry and placed it in her bosom before he was killed. When he was wounded, or perhaps killed, she wailed over him. One of (the assassins) said, "God fight her! How heavy her buttocks are!" And so I knew that the enemy of God desired only the things of this world.

The version of Sayf (b. 'Umar) is as follows: It was transmitted
[3008] to me in writing by al-Sarī—Shu'ayb—Sayf—Badr b. 'Uthmān—his paternal uncle: The last sermon preached by 'Uthmān before a congregation (*jamā'ah*) was this: "Verily, Almighty God has only given you this world so that through it you might seek the next. He did not give it to you as something to rely on. Verily this world will vanish and the next will endure. Perishable things must not make you heedless and distract you from things everlasting. Prefer that which endures to that which perishes, for this world will pass away, and God is the goal of our journey. Fear Almighty God, for fear of Him is a shield against His evil and a means to dwell with Him. Beware lest God's [favor toward you] be altered; cling to your community (*jamā'ah*) and do not be divided into factions. 'Remember God's blessing upon you when you were enemies, and He brought your hearts together, so that by his blessing you became brothers.' "[363]

It was transmitted to me in writing by al-Sarī—Shu'ayb—Sayf—Muḥammad and Talḥah and Abū Ḥārithah and Abū 'Uthmān: When 'Uthmān had accomplished his aims at that gathering, and he and the Muslims had resolved to endure patiently and to resist (the rebels) through God's power, he said, "May God have mercy on you. Go to the door and have those who have been barred from me join you." He sent to Ṭalḥah, al-Zubayr, 'Alī, and a number [of others] and ordered them to draw near. They gathered together, and he looked down at them and said, "O people, be seated." So they sat down together, both newly arrived rebels and loyal established residents.[364] Then he said,

they believe in the like of that you believe in, then they are truly guided; but if they turn away, then they are clearly in schism; God will suffice you for them; He is the All-Hearing, the All-Knowing."

363. Qur'ān 3:98.

364. *Fa-jalasū jamī'an 'l-muḥāribu 'l-ṭāri'u wa'l-musālimu 'l-muqīmu.* Caetani

"O men of Medina, I commend you to God, and I ask Him to restore the caliphate for you after me. Now, by God, I will not go to see anyone after today, until God has carried out His judgment in my regard. I will certainly leave those outside my door alone, [3009] giving them no pretext that they can use against you to damage God's religion or [the affairs of] this world, until Almighty God disposes of all this as He wishes." He commanded and entreated the Medinese to return [to their homes]. They all went away, save for al-Ḥasan, Muḥammad (b. Ṭalḥah), Ibn al-Zubayr, and others like them. These took their place at [the caliph's] door in accordance with their fathers' command. Many people returned to join them, while ʿUthmān stayed in his house.

It was transmitted to me in writing by al-Sarī—Shuʿayb—Sayf—Abū Ḥārithah and Abū ʿUthmān and Muḥammad and Ṭalḥah: The siege itself lasted forty nights, while (the rebels) stayed [in Medina] for seventy altogether.[365] Eighteen days after the siege had begun, a band of horsemen made up of tribal leaders (*rukbān min al-wujūh*) arrived and stated that some men from the provinces had prepared to move against (the besiegers)—Ḥabīb from Syria, Muʿāwiyah from Egypt [*sic*], al-Qaʿqāʿ from Kūfah, and Mujāshiʿ from Baṣrah. On this news, they cut ʿUthmān off from the people and denied him everything, even water. ʿAlī had been bringing some of what he wanted.

(The attackers) sought for pretexts [to justify their acts] but none were offered them. During the night, they launched stones into (ʿUthmān's) house, in the hope that stones would be thrown at them and they could say, "We have been attacked." ʿUthmān called out to them, "Do you not fear God? Do you not know that there are others besides me in the house?" They replied, "No, by God, we did not throw [anything] at you." "Who threw [stones] at us?" he said. "It was God," they answered. "You lie," he said. "If Almighty God had thrown [stones] at us, He would not have missed us, but you did."

(*Annali*, VIII, 209) translates: "E tutti sederono tanto i recenti ribelli, che i fedeli costanti." But in my opinion the distinction intended is between outsiders and Medinese, not between newly aroused rebels and loyalists of long standing.

365. *Kāna 'l-ḥasru arbaʿīna laylatan wa-'l-nuzūlu sabʿīna.* Caetani (*Annali*, VIII, 209) translates: "L'assedio dura 40 giorni, e gli abitanti della casa erano 70."

ʿUthmān looked down [from his rooftop] onto the clan of Ḥazm, who were his neighbors, and dispatched one of ʿAmr's sons to ʿAlī [with this message]: "They have denied us water. If you can send
[3010] us some, do so." [He sent the same message] to Ṭalḥah and al-Zubayr, and to ʿĀ'ishah and the other wives of the Prophet. The first to come to his aid were ʿAlī and Umm Ḥabībah. ʿAli came shortly before dawn and said, "O people, neither Believers nor unbelievers act like this. Do not cut off supplies from this man. The Romans and Persians give food and drink to their captives. This man did not resist you, so how can you think it lawful to besiege and kill him?" "No, by God, we will show no mercy,"[366] they answered. "We will not let him eat or drink." Then (ʿAlī) threw down his turban in the house [and said], "I have done what you asked me to do." He went home.

Then Umm Ḥabībah came on a mule of hers with a saddle containing a waterskin. They said, "This is the Mother of the Faithful, Umm Ḥabībah,"[367] and struck her mule on the face.[367] She said, "The wills of the Banū Umayyah are with this man; I want to meet with him and ask him about this, so that the property of orphans and widows will not be lost." "She is lying," they said. They lunged at her and severed the mule's rope with a sword. The mule ran away with Umm Ḥabībah. Its saddle slipped, but the people got to her and held her [on the animal]. She had almost been killed, and they brought her to her house.

ʿĀ'ishah prepared to flee by going on the Pilgrimage. She asked her brother (Muḥammad b. Abī Bakr) to accompany her, but he refused. She said, "By God, if I can make it so that God will frustrate their efforts, I will surely do so." Ḥanẓalah the scribe
[3011] came up to Muḥammad b. Abī Bakr and said, "Muḥammad, the Mother of the Believers asks you to accompany her and you do not. Then Bedouin wolves invite you to do unlawful things and you go along with them." (Muḥammad) replied, "What is that to you, son of the woman of Tamīm?" (Ḥanẓalah) replied, "Son of the woman of Khathʿam, if there is a struggle over this affair, the

---

366. *Wa-lā nuʿmata ʿaynin*—an idiomatic phrase. See Goeje, *Introductio*, dxxi.

367. The usual appellation for the wives of the Prophet; it is given Qur'ānic sanction in 33:6.

clan of ʿAbd Manāf[368] will overpower you in it." Then he departed, saying:

I am astonished at the depths into which the people plunge,
desirous of the Caliphate's end.
Should it disappear, all good would pass from them as well,
and thereafter they would suffer shameful humiliation.
They would be as the Jews or Christians—
they would all alike have lost their way.

He proceeded to Kūfah, and ʿĀ'ishah was filled with rancor against the Egyptians. Marwān b. al-Ḥakam came to her and said, "Mother of the Faithful, if you remained [in Medina] they would be more likely to show respect to this man." She responded, "Do you want me to be treated as Umm Ḥabībah was? I find no one who will defend me. No, by God, I am not to be blamed. I do not know what the actions of these people will lead to."[369]

When Ṭalḥah and al-Zubayr heard what had happened to ʿAlī and Umm Ḥabībah, they stayed in their homes. The clan of Ḥazm[370] continued to bring water to ʿUthmān whenever the guards appointed to maintain surveillance over them were careless.

ʿUthmān looked down at the people [from his rooftop] and called to ʿAbdallāh b. ʿAbbās. He was summoned, and (ʿUthmān) said, "Go. You will command the Pilgrimage this year." Now ʿAbdallāh b. ʿAbbās was among those stationed at the door, and he responded, "O Commander of the Faithful, I prefer the struggle (*jihād*) against these people to the Pilgrimage." But (ʿUthmān) entreated him to go, so Ibn ʿAbbās departed and commanded the Pilgrimage that year.

---

368. ʿAbd Manāf comprises both ʿAbd Shams (the clan to which the Umayyads belonged) and Hāshim (the Prophet's clan). These two lineages were of course hostile to each other during the Prophet's lifetime, as well as during the succession struggles after ʿUthmān. Here, however Ḥanẓalah asserts that ʿUthmān can count on the combined support of both lineages against the rebels. Cf. note 251 above.

369. *Wa-lā adrī ilā mā yuslimu amru hā'ulā'i.* See de Goeje, *Introductio,* ccxcvi, sub verbo *salima.*

370. In contrast to all previous citations, the Ḥazm clan is here presented as a defender of the embattled Caliph.

ʿUthmān turned his will over to al-Zubayr, and he left [the house] with it. Concerning al-Zubayr, there is disagreement over whether he was present at (ʿUthmān's) murder or had already
[3012] departed. ʿUthmān said, "'O my people, let not the breach with me move you, so that there smite you the like of what smote the people of Noah.'[371] O God, 'set a barrier between these factions and what they hope for, as was done with the likes of them aforetime.' "[372]

It was transmitted to me in writing by al-Sarī—Shuʿayb—Sayf—ʿAmr b. Muḥammad: Laylā bt. ʿUmays sent to Muḥammad b. Abī Bakr and Muḥammad b. Jaʿfar and said, "Verily the lamp consumes itself as it gives light to the people. Do not sin in a matter that you may bring on to someone who has not sinned against you. This matter that you are pursuing today will affect someone else tomorrow. Beware lest your deeds today become a source of grief to you." But they were obstinate and went off in anger, saying, "We will not forget what ʿUthmān has done to us." She was saying, "He did nothing to you except to compel you to obey God."

Saʿīd b. al-ʿĀṣ encountered the two men. There was some hostility between him and Muḥammad b. Abī Bakr, and he ignored the latter as he was leaving Laylā's house. At that (Muḥammad) recited the following verse to him:

Be quick to show your love for a friend;
be not a shadow stubbornly clinging
to one who betrays [friendship].[373]

Saʿīd responded in kind:

You shall see a well-placed blow from one
exposed to attack and averse to violence.

It was transmitted to me in writing by al-Sarī—Shuʿayb—Sayf—Muḥammad and Ṭalḥah and Abū Ḥārithah and Abū

371. Qur'an 11:91.
372. Qur'ān 34:52, but with the initial verb changed from the perfect to the imperative.
373. Cf. Lane, *Lexicon*, I, 2069, sub verbo *ʿaḍḍa*.

'Uthmān:[374] The people (*al-nās*) learned that the members of the Pilgrimage caravan all meant to attack the Egyptians and their allies, and to combine this [meritorious act] with the Pilgrimage. [3013] When (the rebels) heard this and learned of the disgust [felt for them] by the men of the garrison towns, Satan gripped them and they said, "Our only way out of this situation is to kill this man. The people will be too preoccupied with that to pay attention to us."

Their only hope of escape was to kill him. They assaulted the door but were held off by al-Ḥasan, Ibn al-Zubayr, Muḥammad b. Ṭalḥah, Marwān b. al-Ḥakam, Saʿīd b. al-ʿĀṣ, and the sons of the Companions who had stayed with them. As they fought with swords, 'Uthmān cried out, "Fear God, fear God! You are absolved from defending me." When they refused [to lay down their arms], he opened the door and went out with shield and sword to hold them back. When the Egyptians saw him they retreated. ('Uthmān's supporters) chased after them, but he restrained them and they withdrew. The situation was distressing for both sides. ('Uthmān) entreated the Companions not to reenter [his residence], but they refused to leave and came back in, and he bolted the door against the Egyptians.

Al-Mughīrah b. al-Akhnas b. Sharīq had been one of those who made the Pilgrimage, then he hastened [back to Medina] with a number of his fellow pilgrims and reached 'Uthmān before he was killed. He participated in the skirmish, entered the house with the others, and took his place inside the door. "How would we find any excuse before God," he said, "if we abandoned you while we could prevent them [from killing you] until we ourselves die?"

During those days 'Uthmān took up the Qur'ān in tears, praying and keeping the text beside him. When he became fatigued he would sit up and read in it, for people used to regard reciting the Qur'ān as a form of worship. Meantime his defenders (*qawm*), whom he had restrained, were between him and the door. When the Egyptians remained unable to break in though no one was keeping them away from the door, they brought fire and set the

374. Several words seem to be missing in the next two lines. I have followed the paraphrase of this passage in Ibn al-Athīr, *Kāmil* (Beirut), III, 174.

door and portico (*saqīfah*) ablaze. The door and portico burned until, as the wood blazed, the portico collapsed onto the door. Then, as 'Uthmān prayed, the men in the house rose up and
[3014] fended off (the assailants). The first to go out against them was al-Mughīrah b. al-Akhnas, chanting:

A lovely serving girl,
    Adorned with jeweled necklaces,
Knows my skill with the sword blade.
    I will surely defend my friend from you all
With a hard unnicked blade.

Al-Ḥasan b. 'Alī went forth, saying:

Their religion is not my religion, and I am not one of them,
    until I journey to the heights of Shamām.

Muḥammad b. Ṭalḥah went forth, saying:

I am the son of the man who defended him at Uḥud
    and drove off bands of men in spite of Ma'add.[375]

Sa'īd b. al-'Āṣ went forth, saying:

We endured patiently on the Day of the House, as Death approached,
    smiting with our swords to defend the son of Arwā.[376]
On the day of terror in the House we came to his aid;
    our sword blows spoke to them for us as Death pierced within.

The last to go out was 'Abdallāh b. al-Zubayr. 'Uthmān ordered him to take his [namely, 'Uthmān's] will to his father, and to go to the people in the house and command them to go home. So 'Abdallāh b. al-Zubayr was the last of them to leave, and he never

375. The battle of Uḥud, fought against Qurashi forces on the outskirts of Medina in 3/625, was a serious setback for the Muslims, and very nearly a disastrous one, since the Prophet was wounded there. However, Ṭalḥah (along with various others) was able to get him to safety. See Ibn Isḥāq, *Sīrah*, pp. 574–77; transl. Guillaume, pp. 381–83. Ma'add is the ancestor of the Northern Arabs, to whom Quraysh belonged; here it refers to the latter tribe only.

376. 'Uthmān's mother was Arwā bt. Kurayz. See above, note 251, and Balādhurī, *Ansāb*, V, 1.

ceased to laud his own conduct[377] or to tell the people about the final circumstances of 'Uthmān's death.

It was transmitted to me in writing by al-Sarī—Shu'ayb—Sayf—Muḥammad and Ṭalḥah and Abū Ḥārithah and Abū 'Uthmān: (The rebels) set the door ablaze as 'Uthmān performed the prayer. He had begun with the verse, "Ṭā Hā. We have not [3015]
sent down the Qur'ān upon thee for thee to be unprosperous."[378] He recited quickly and was not distressed by the noise. He proceeded without making an error or stuttering until he completed (his recitation) before they could get to him. Then he returned, sat down in front of the sacred text (*muṣḥaf*), and recited, "Those to whom the people said, 'The people have gathered against you, therefore fear them.' But it increased them in faith, and they said, 'God is sufficient for us; an excellent Guardian is He.' "[379]

Al-Mughīrah b. al-Akhnas, outside the house with his comrades, chanted these verses:

The woman with the flowing hair,
  The jewels and soft fingertips knows
My oath to my friend is sincere,
  Secured by a glittering sharp-edged blade.
I shall not seek pardon if I break my word.[380]

Abū Hurayrah came up as the people were withdrawing from the house, save for that band that had courted death in a fierce assault. He stood up among them and said, "I am your leader." Speaking in the Himyarite tongue, he said, "*Hādhā yawm ṭāba 'mḍarbu*"—which means, "Now it is lawful and good to fight."[381] And (Abū Hurayrah) called out, "O my people, how is it with me that I call you to salvation and you call me to the Fire?"[382]

---

377. *Fa-mā zāla yadda'i bihā.* See de Goeje, *Introductio,* ccxl, sub verbo *da'ā.*

378. Qur'an 20:1.

379. Qur'ān 3:167. This is part of a section that discusses the battle of Uḥud.

380. *Lā astaqīlu in aqaltu qīlī.* A difficult line, which Caetani (*Annali,* VIII, 214) renders as follows: "[in tale cosa] non mi dichiaro sciolto da obbligo, seppure in altre circostanze io rescinda qualche patto."

381. *Innahu min 'l-qitāli wa-ṭāba.* I have followed de Goeje (*Introductio,* dcxxix) in reading *ḥalla* in place of *min.*

382. Qur'ān 40:44. One of Pharaoh's subjects, converted by the signs of Moses, is trying (in vain) to persuade the king and his counselors to heed the prophet.

On that day Marwān rushed out, shouting, "Which man will oppose me?" A man of the Banū Layth called al-Nibāʿ stepped forward against him. They traded two blows; Marwān struck him on his lower leg, while his opponent struck him at the base of the neck and threw him down. Marwān fell and lay prostrate and
[3016] each man's comrades dragged him away. The Egyptians said [to ʿUthmān's defenders], "By God, were it not that you would be a decisive proof (*ḥujjah*) against us within the Community (*ummah*), we would kill you, for we gave due warning."[383]

Al-Mughīrah said, "Who will come forth against me?" A man came forward and they set to, as (al-Mughīrah) said:

With the hard sword I smite them,
As the brave youth smites
Who despairs of life.

His opponent responded: [*lacuna*].

The people said, "Al-Mughīrah b. al-Akhnas has been killed." The man who had killed him said, "Verily we belong to God!" "What is wrong with you?" asked ʿAbd al-Raḥmān b. ʿUdays. He replied, "While I was asleep, I dreamt that someone came to me and said, 'Announce to the killer of al-Mughīrah b. al-Akhnas [that he will be] in the Fire,' and (that deed) has been visited upon me."

Qabāth al-Kinānī killed Niyār b. ʿAbdallāh al-Aslamī. The people (*al-nās*) stormed the house from the houses around it and occupied it without those stationed at the door having noticed them. The tribesmen (*al-qabāʾil*) fell upon their own members [who were defending ʿUthmān] and carried them off after they had been overpowered in trying to defend their caliph (*amīr*). They delegated a man to kill (ʿUthmān). Having been appointed for the deed, he entered the house and went in before him. "Abdicate and we will spare you," he said. "Woe to you," replied (ʿUthmān). "I have not violated a woman, either in the Time of Ignorance or in Islam. Nor have I sung songs or expressed carnal desires or touched my genitals with my right hand since I swore allegiance to the Messenger of God. I shall not remove a shirt that Almighty God has placed upon me. I shall remain in my appointed place until God bestows honor upon the virtuous (*ahl al-saʿādah*) and

383. See 3016, note a, and de Goeje, *Introductio*, dcxxx.

abases the sinners." (The would-be assassin) went out, and they said, "What did you do?" "We are trapped," he responded. "By God, only his murder can save us from the people, but it is not lawful for us to murder him."

Then they sent in a second man, from the Banū Layth. "What tribe does this man belong to?" said ʿUthmān. "[I am] from Layth," he responded. "You are not my companion in death (*ṣāḥibī*)," said (ʿUthmān). "How is that?" asked the other. (ʿUthmān) said, "Are you not among those persons for whose safety the [3017]
Prophet prayed in such-and-such a battle?" "Indeed I was," he answered. "Then you will not lose your way," said (ʿUthmān). (The man) went back out and departed from the rebels (*al-qawm*).

Then they sent in a third man, from Quraysh. He said, "ʿUthmān, I am your murderer." He answered, "No, such-and-such, you will not kill me." "How is that?" asked (the intruder). He replied, "The Messenger of God sought forgiveness for you in such-and-such a battle. You will not be tempted to sin against forbidden blood." (The man) sought God's forgiveness, went back out, and departed from his comrades.

ʿAbdallāh b. Salām came forth and stood at the door of the house, forbidding them to kill (ʿUthmān). "O my people," he said, "Do not unsheathe God's sword against yourselves. By God, if you draw it you will not put it back in its scabbard. Woe to you! Your government today is based on the whip, and if you kill him it will rest only on the sword.[384] Woe to you! Your city is surrounded by God's angels. By God, if you kill him they will surely forsake it." "What is this to you, son of a Jewess?" they said, and he withdrew.

The last one to go in to (ʿUthmān) and then come back to the rebels was Muḥammad b. Abī Bakr. ʿUthmān said to him, "Woe to you. Are you angry at God? Have I done you any injury, save to uphold His rightful claims on you?" At this he recoiled and went away.

When Muḥammad b. Abī Bakr came out and they learned that he had failed, Qutayrah al-Sakūnī, Sūdān b. Ḥumrān al-Sakūnī,

384. *Inna sulṭānakum 'l-yawma yaqūmu bi'l-dirrati fa-in qataltumūhu lā yaqum illā bi'l-sayfi.* That is, the existing political order is based on the Caliph's legitimate right to demand obedience and punish malefactors; if he is overthrown, however, government will be rooted solely in violence and terror.

and al-Ghāfiqī rose up and attacked [ʿUthmān]. Al-Ghāfiqī struck
[3018] him with an iron tool he was carrying and kicked the Qurʾān with his foot. The sacred text flew over, dropping into (ʿUthmān's) hands, and his blood flowed upon it. Sūdān b. Ḥumrān came up to strike him, and Nāʾilah bt. al-Farāfiṣah bent over him and warded off the sword with her hand. He aimed at her and struck off her fingers. As she turned to flee, he fondled her hips and said, "How large her buttocks are!" Then he struck ʿUthmān and killed him. Some of ʿUthmān's slaves entered alongside the rebels (*qawm*) to defend him. ʿUthmān had manumitted certain of them, and when they saw that Sūdān had struck him, one of them fell on him and cut off his head. Qutayrah jumped on the slave and killed him. (The rebels) pillaged the house and drove out those who lived there, then they locked the three dead men inside.

When they went out into the courtyard of the house, another of ʿUthmān's slaves jumped on Qutayrah and killed him. The rebels coursed through the house taking everything they found, even what was on the women. One man, named Kulthūm b. Tujīb, snatched Nāʾilah's head wrap. Nāʾilah turned away, and he said, "Woe to your mother! How full your buttocks are!" A slave of ʿUthmān saw him and killed him, then was killed himself. The rebels shouted to one another: "Every man should keep an eye on his comrades."[385] Within the house they cried out, "Seize the Public Treasury! No one must get there ahead of you!" The guards of the Public Treasury—in which there were but two sacks—heard their voices and said, "Run! These people are only after worldly goods." They fled, while (the rebels) came to the Treasury and pillaged it.

[3019] The people (*al-nās*) were of different minds about the matter.[386] The residents [of Medina] lamented, "We belong to God and to Him we shall return," while the outsiders rejoiced. The rebels (*al-*

385. *Wa-tanādā 'l-qawmu abṣir rajulun man ṣāḥibuhu.* Caetani (*Annali*, VIII, 216) reads the second verb as *abṣara* and translates: "Il popolo si disse, l'un l'altro: 'Uno ha avuto soddisfazione dell'altro.'" However, I can find no warrant for rendering *abṣara* in this manner.

386. *Wa-māja 'l-nāsu fīhi.* See de Goeje, *Introductio*, cdxcvi, sub verbo *mawj*, and Caetani, *Annali*, VIII, 216. On the key words *tāniʾ* ("resident") and *ṭāri* ("outsider") in the following sentence, cf. Caetani, *loc. cit.*; and note 364 above (text, I, 2008, ll. 15–16).

qawm) now regretted [their acts]. Al-Zubayr had already left Medina and made camp on the road to Mecca so that he would not witness ('Uthmān's) murder. The news of 'Uthmān's murder having reached him while he was there, he said, "Verily we belong to God and to Him we shall return. May God have mercy on 'Uthmān and avenge him." "The rebels regret their deeds," he was told. (Al-Zubayr) replied, "They planned this and brought it about. 'And a barrier is set up between them and what they desire.' "[387]

The news reached Ṭalḥah, and he said, "May God have mercy on 'Uthmān, and may He avenge both him and Islam." He was told, "The rebels regret their deeds." "May they perish!" he replied, and recited the verse, "They will not be able to make any testament, nor will they return to their people."[388]

'Alī came and was told of 'Uthmān's murder. "May God have mercy on 'Uthmān," he said, "and replace [the evil we have suffered] with good." When he was told, "The rebels regret their deeds," he recited the verse: "Like Satan, when he said to man, 'Disbelieve.' "[389]

Sa'd (b. Abī Waqqāṣ) was sought out while he was in his garden. He had said, "I will not witness his murder." When he learned of his death, he said, "We have taken refuge in something contemptible, and have become contemptible thereby."[390] Then he recited, "Those whose striving goes astray in the present life, while they think that they are working good deeds,"[391] and said, "O God, make them regret this, and seize them."

It was transmitted to me in writing by al-Sarī—Shu'ayb—Sayf—al-Mujālid—al-Sha'bī—al-Mughīrah b. al-Shu'bah: I said to 'Alī, "This man is going to be murdered, and if he is killed while you are in Medina, they will hold you responsible. Go and stay in such-and-such a place. If you do this, the people will seek you out, even if you are in a cave in Yemen." But ('Alī) refused.

---

387. Qur'ān 34:53.
388. Qur'ān 36:50.
389. Qur'ān 59:16. The whole verse reads: "Like Satan, when he said to man, 'Disbelieve'; then, when he disbelieved, he said, 'Surely I am quit of you. Surely I fear God, the Lord of all Being.' "
390. See de Goeje, *Introductio*, ccxlv, sub verbo *danā*.
391. Qur'ān 18:104.

When ʿUthmān had been under siege for twenty-two days, they set fire to the door. Many people were in the house, among them
[3020] ʿAbdallāh b. al-Zubayr and Marwān. "Permit us [to fight]," they said, but he responded, "The Messenger of God has laid an obligation (*ʿahd*) on me, and I will suffer it patiently. The rebels would not have set fire to the door of the house unless they were after something more important. I forbid any man to court death in battle." Then all the people left, and he called for the Qur'ān to be brought. Al-Ḥasan was with him as he recited from it, and he said, "Your father is in a grave situation now. I beg of you to leave."

ʿUthmān ordered Abū Karib—a man of [the tribe of] Hamdān—and one of the Helpers to stand guard at the door to the Public Treasury, which contained just two sacks of silver coin. When the fire was eventually extinguished,[392] Ibn al-Zubayr and Marwān skirmished with (the assailants). The two men were threatened by Muḥammad b. Abī Bakr, and when he entered ʿUthmān's presence they both fled. (Muḥammad b. Abī Bakr) seized (ʿUthmān's) beard, and he said, "Let go of my beard! Your father would not have grabbed it." So he let go. Then (the rebels) came in and attacked (ʿUthmān); one was striking him with the iron tip of his scabbard and another was beating him with his fists. A man with broad iron-tipped arrows came and stabbed him in the throat, and the blood flowed down on the Qur'ān. Even as they did this they were afraid to kill him, but he was old and lost consciousness. Still others came in, and when they saw that he was unconscious, they dragged him away by the leg. Nā'ilah and her daughters screamed. Al-Tujībī drew his sword to plunge it into (ʿUthmān's) belly. Nā'ilah shielded him, but (al-Tujībī) cut her hand, then leaned on (ʿUthmān's) chest with his sword. ʿUthmān—may God be pleased with him—was murdered before sunset. Someone cried out, "How is it that his blood is lawful and his property forbidden?" So they pillaged everything, and then broke into the Public Treasury. The two guards threw down the keys and fled for their lives, shouting, "Flee! Flee! This is what the rebels (*al-qawm*) are after."

---

392. Some words are missing at this point. See text, I, 3020, note d.

According to Muḥammad b. 'Umar (al-Wāqidī)—'Abd al-Raḥmān b. 'Abd al-'Azīz—'Abd al-Raḥmān b. Muḥammad: Muḥammad b. Abī Bakr, accompanied by Kinānah b. Bishr b. 'Attāb, Sūdān b. Ḥumrān, and 'Amr b. al-Ḥamiq, reached 'Uthmān by climbing over the wall from the house of 'Amr b. Ḥazm. They found 'Uthmān, with his wife Nā'ilah, reading the Sūrah of the Cow from the Qur'ān. Muḥammad b. Abī Bakr came up to them and seized 'Uthmān's beard. "May God disgrace you, you hyena," he said. 'Uthmān replied, "I am no hyena. I am God's servant and the Commander of the Faithful." Muḥammad said, "Neither Mu'āwiyah nor anyone else has been of any use to you." 'Uthmān said, "Son of my brother, let go of my beard. Your father would not have gripped it like this." Muḥammad replied, "Had my father seen you doing these things, he would have denounced you for them, and I mean to do worse to you than grab your beard." 'Uthmān said, "I seek God's help and support against you." Then (Muḥammad) pierced his forehead with a broad iron-tipped arrow that he was holding. Kinānah b. Bishr raised some arrows of the same kind that he was holding, and plunged them from the base of 'Uthmān's ear down to his throat. Then he fell on him with his sword until he killed him. [3021]

According to 'Abd al-Raḥmān—Abū 'Awn: Kinānah b. Bishr struck his forehead with an iron bar. He pitched forward, face down, and Sūdān b. Ḥumrān al-Murādī beat him after he had fallen and killed him.

According to Muḥammad b. 'Umar (al-Wāqidī)—'Abd al-Raḥmān b. Abī al-Zinād—'Abd al-Raḥmān b. al-Ḥārith: The one who killed him was Kinānah b. Bishr b. 'Attāb al-Tujībī. The wife of Manẓūr b. Sayyār al-Fazārī used to say: We had gone on the Pilgrimage, and we did not learn of 'Uthmān's murder until, while [3022]
we were at al-'Arj[393], we heard a man singing in the darkness:

Yea, the best of the people, save three,
is the one murdered by al-Tujībī who came from Egypt.

---

393. Al-'Arj: "A mountain pass between Mecca and Medina, on the Pilgrimage road, mentioned along with al-Suqyā by al-Ḥāzimī.: (Yāqūt, *Mu'jam al-Buldān*, III, 637). Yāqūt mentions another al-'Arj, near al-Ṭā'if, some 78 miles from Medina, but the former seems to be the place intended here.

As to ʿAmr b. al-Ḥamiq, he jumped on ʿUthmān and sat on his chest—he was still barely alive—and stabbed him nine times. ʿAmr said, "I stabbed him three times for God's sake, and six times because of the anger in my breast against him."

According to Muḥammad (b. ʿUmar al-Wāqidī)—Isḥāq b. Yaḥyā—Mūsā b. Ṭalḥah: I saw ʿUrwah b. Shīyam strike Marwān's neck with his sword on the Day of the House, and he severed one of his neck muscles. Marwān survived, but with a bent neck. Marwān is the one who used to say:

On the Day of the House I did not say to [my] people, "Hold back.
Go easy. Prefer life to death."
Rather I said to them, "Smite
with your swords so that they reach even the man in his prime."[394]

According to Muḥammad al-Wāqidī—Yūsuf b. Yaʿqūb—ʿUthmān b. Muḥammad al-Akhnasī: ʿUthmān was under siege
[3023] before the Egyptians' arrival. The Egyptians arrived on one Friday and killed him on the following Friday.

It was related to me by ʿAbdallāh b. Aḥmad al-Marwazī—his father—Sulaymān—ʿAbdallāh—Ḥarmalah b. ʿImrān— Yazīd b. Abī Ḥabīb: Nahrān[395] al-Aṣbaḥī was responsible for ʿUthmān's murder, and he was the one who killed ʿAbdallāh b. Busrah. He belonged to the tribe of ʿAbd al-Dār.

According to Muḥammad b. ʿUmar (al-Wāqidī)—al-Ḥakam b. al-Qāsim—Abū ʿAwn, the client (*mawlā*) of al-Miswar b. Makhramah: the Egyptians steadfastly abstained from shedding (ʿUthmān's) blood and from fighting until [ʿUthmān's] reinforcements from Baṣrah and Kūfah in Iraq and from Syria approached. Their coming encouraged the rebels (*al-qawm*) to attack. They learned that detachments had departed from Iraq and from Egypt, the latter sent by Ibn Saʿd. Previously Ibn Saʿd had not been in

394. The last hemistich reads: *bi-asyāfikum kaymā yaṣilna ilā 'l-kahli.* Caetani (*Annali*, VIII, 185) translates: "Battete tanto forte con le vostre spade da giungere fino in mezzo alle spalle." However, *kahl* normally means "in the prime of life," while the word for "the base of the neck" is *kāhil.*

395. The first letter of this name is uncertain: I have followed Ibrāhīm's reading.

Egypt, having fled to Syria. They said, "We must deal quickly with ('Uthmān), before the reinforcements arrive."

According to Muḥammad (b. 'Umar al-Wāqidī)—al-Zubayr b. 'Abdallāh—Yūsuf b. 'Abdallāh b. Salām: While he was under siege, and (the rebels) had surrounded the house on every side, 'Uthmān looked down upon them and said, "I adjure you by Almighty God, do you know that when the Commander of the Faithful 'Umar b. al-Khaṭṭāb was struck down, you beseeched God to bless you and to unite you [in choosing] the best among you [to succeed 'Umar]? What is your opinion of God, then? Do you say that He did not answer you, and that you were of no importance to him, even though at that time you were the [only] adherents of the truth among his creatures and were of one mind in all your affairs? Or do you say that His religion was of no account to God and He did not care to whom He gave authority over it, even though God was worshipped through this religion, [3024] and its adherents had not yet fallen into schism? [If you say this], then you are turning your responsibilities over to someone else or even neglecting them altogether, and you will be punished [for that].[396] Or do you say that I was chosen without consultation? [If that is so] you are rebellious indeed—and God will abandon the Community (*al-ummah*) if it disobeys Him—for you did not consult among yourselves concerning the imām nor make an effort to discover his reprehensible traits. Or do you say that God did not know what my conduct would be? In some things I have done well and satisfied men of sound religion (*ahl al-dīn*). I have not yet committed any act offensive either to God or to you which God—glory be to Him!—did not know of on the day He chose me and attired me with the garment of His grace. I adjure you by God, do you know of the good actions which God long ago conferred upon me, and through which He has caused me to bear witness to His rights? The struggle against His enemy is [one of His] rights, and it will be the duty of all those who succeed me to undertake what still remains [of this struggle].[397] No, do not kill me, for a

396. See de Goeje, *Introductio*, ccclxix, sub verbo *'aqaba;* and *ibid.*, dlxv, sub verbo *wakala.*

397. *Wa-anshudukum bi-'llāhi hal ta'lamūna lī min sābiqati khayrin wa-salafi khayrin qaddamahu 'llāhu lī wa-ashhadanīhi min ḥaqqihi wa-jihādu 'aduwwihi*

man may be put to death only in three cases: when he commits adultery, when he disbelieves after accepting Islam, or when he takes another's life except in legitimate retaliation.[398] Verily, if you kill me, you will place the sword upon your own necks, and Almighty God will not lift it from you until the Day of Resurrection. Do not kill me, for if you do, you will never pray together again, nor will you ever join together in sharing out booty (*fay'*), nor will God ever remove dissension from among you."

They replied to him, "You say that after 'Umar, the people asked Almighty God for guidance in choosing someone to rule over them, and having sought God's guidance, they chose you. Truly all God's acts are the best acts, but God—glory be to Him!—has made your case a test for His servants. You refer to your long-standing ties and priority with the Messenger of God. You did indeed possess ties of long-standing and precedence, and you were worthy of authority (*wilāyah*), but since then you have changed and brought about innovations that you are well aware
[3025] of. You mention the trials that will afflict us if we kill you. But it is not right to fail to uphold the truth against you out of fear of discord (*fitnah*) sometime in the future. You say that it is lawful to kill a man only in three cases. But in the Book of God, we find that other men are put to death besides the three named by you. [We find that] the man who spreads corruption in the land is put to death,[399] and likewise the oppressor who fights to continue his oppression and the man who prevents justice (*al-ḥaqq*) in any way and resists it, then scornfully battles against it. You have committed oppression. You have scorned justice, resisting it and preventing it from being carried out. You refuse to exact punishment against yourself for those whom you willfully wronged. You have clung tenaciously to the caliphate (*imārah*) over us, and you have been tyrannical in your legal judgments and in the allocation of booty. If you allege that you were not arrogant towards us, and that those who have risen up to defend you from us are fighting without orders from you,[we say that] they fight only

---

ḥaqqun 'alā kulli man jā'a min ba'dī an ya'rifū lī faḍlahā. The text is quite difficult to interpret; cf. Caetani, (*Annali*, VIII, 171), who in fact omits a segment of it.

398. Cf. above, p. 199 (text, I, 3000) and note 351.

399. Qur'ān 5:37.

because you maintain your grip on the caliphate. Were you to abdicate, they would depart without fighting on your behalf."

The Conduct of 'Uthmān b. 'Affān—May God Be Pleased with Him

It was related to me by Ziyād b. Ayyūb—Hushaym—Abū al-Miqdām—al-Ḥasan b. Abī al-Ḥasan: I entered the mosque, and there was 'Uthmān b. 'Affān reclining upon his cloak. Then two water carriers came to him with a dispute, and he judged between them [on the spot].

It was transmitted to me in writing by al-Sarī—Shu'ayb—Sayf—'Umārah b. al-Qa'qā'—al-Ḥasan al-Baṣrī: 'Umar b. al-Khaṭṭāb had forbidden the notables of Quraysh (*a'lām Quraysh*) who were Emigrants to go out into the conquered territories (*al-buldān*) except with his permission, and [then only] for a set period of time. People complained [that 'Uthmān did not restrain them likewise.] Having heard this, he arose and said: "Verily I have tended Islam carefully, like a camel. It makes its appearance and grows into a young animal ready to ride. Then it passes through its sixth, seventh, and eighth years, and finally becomes a fully mature nine-year-old. Now, do we expect anything but declining vigor from a mature camel? Now surely Islam has reached [3026]
maturity, and the Quraysh wish to usurp God's wealth for their own benefit to the exclusion of His [other] servants. Is Ibn al-Khaṭṭāb alive? He is not. I shall stand outside the pass of al-Ḥarrah[400] and grip the throats and waist-wrappers of Quraysh so that they tumble into Hellfire."[401]

It was transmitted to me in writing by al-Sarī—Shu'ayb—Sayf—Muḥammad and Ṭalḥah: When 'Uthmān ruled, he did not treat (the notables of Quraysh) as 'Umar had, and thus they traveled throughout the conquered territories. As they observed (these lands) and the things of this world (*al-dunyā*), and as the

400. Shi'b al-Ḥarrah. The Ḥarrah is a broken lava field northeast of Medina, through which one must pass to get to Syria, Egypt, or Iraq. It was the site of the famous battle in 63/683 between the Medinese and an expeditionary force sent by Yazīd b. Mu'āwiyah. See L. Veccia Vaglieri, "Ḥarra," *EI*², III, 226–27.

401. The text is obscure; cf. the version in Caetani, *Annali*, VIII, 61.

people in turn saw them, those who were obscure and without power or privilege in Islam attached themselves to (the notables of Quraysh), forming into factions around them.[402] The (Qurashīs) aroused their hopes, and in this manner they acquired precedence. Then they said, "(The Quraysh) are powerful, and we will become known to them and acquire precedence by gaining access to them and attaching ourselves exclusively to them." That was the first flaw to enter Islam, and the first discord (*fitnah*) to appear among the common people (*al-ʿāmmah*) was none other than this.

It was transmitted to me in writing by al-Sarī—Shuʿayb—Sayf—ʿAmr—al-Shaʿbī: No sooner had ʿUmar died than the Quraysh were weary of him. He had penned them up in Medina and put restraints on them, saying: "The thing I most fear for this Community is that you will scatter throughout the conquered territories." If one of the Emigrants confined to Medina sought his permission to go on campaign—and (ʿUmar) had not restricted other Meccans in this manner—he would say: "You have obtained your reward by your campaigns with the Messenger of God. It is better for you to avoid entanglement in worldly affairs than to go on campaign now."[403] Now when ʿUthmān took power, he freed them from such restrictions. They betook themselves to the conquered territories, where the people attached themselves to them. Therefore (the Quraysh) preferred (ʿUthmān) to ʿUmar.

It was transmitted to me in writing by al-Sarī—Shuʿayb—Sayf—Mubashshir b. al-Fuḍayl—Sālim b. Abdallāh: When ʿUthmān was caliph, he made the Pilgrimage every year of his
[3027] reign except for the final Pilgrimage. He made the Pilgrimage with the wives of the Messenger of God, as ʿUmar used to do. ʿAbd al-Raḥmān b. ʿAwf was in his place, and he put Saʿīd b. Zayd in his own place, one at the head of the caravan and the other at its rear, and the people were secure.[404]

402. See de Goeje, *Introductio*, dcxxx.

403. *Wa-khayrun laka min 'l-ghazwi 'l-yawma allā tarā 'l-dunyā wa-lā taraka.*

404. This meaning of this sentence is obscure; presumably it is a vestige of a longer anecdote. On ʿAbd al-Raḥmān b. ʿAwf's role as a critic of ʿUthmān's religious practices, see above pp. 38–40 (text, I, 2833–2835).

('Uthmān) wrote to the garrison towns that the Pilgrimage should be performed every year by the governors and by those who had complaints to lodge against them. He wrote to the people of the garrison towns [as follows]: "Command one another to do good and forbid one another to do evil. The believer should not humble himself, for, God willing, I will side with the weak against the strong as long as he suffers oppression." And things continued in this way, until certain factions (*aqwām*) used ('Uthmān) as a means to create schism within the Community (*ummah*).

It was transmitted to me in writing by al-Sarī—Shu'ayb—Sayf—Muḥammad and Ṭalḥah: 'Uthmān had not been caliph a year before certain men of Quraysh took over various properties (*amwāl*) in the garrison towns and the people attached themselves to them. This state of things continued for seven years, with every faction (*qawm*) desiring that its leader (*ṣāḥib*) should rule. Then Ibn al-Sawdā' converted to Islam and engaged in theological speculation. Through him the world fell into chaos and baneful innovations arose, and (his followers) claimed that 'Umar was superior to 'Uthmān.[405]

It was transmitted to me in writing by al-Sarī—Shu'ayb—Sayf—'Uthmān b. Ḥakīm b. 'Abbād b. Ḥunayf—his father: When the world fell into chaos and the ability of the people [to act rightly] came to an end, the first forbidden thing to appear in Medina was [the obtaining of auguries by observing] the flight of pigeons and [by] shooting clay pellets. In the eighth year [of his caliphate], 'Uthmān gave authority over these matters to a man from the tribe of Layth, and he clipped their wings and smashed the pellets.[406]

It was transmitted to me in writing by al-Sarī—Shu'ayb— [3028]

405. Again Ibn al-Sawdā'—that is, 'Abdallāh b. Sabā'—emerges as the malign *deus ex machina* in Sayf's narrative. See above, pp. 64–65, 145–47 and note 107 (text, I, 2858–2859, 2942–2943).

406. Another obscure passage. I have adopted the general interpretation of Caetani (*Annali*, VIII, 63), though he admits he cannot find any external evidence for soothsaying practices of this kind. His translation of the phrase *sanata thamānin* as "per otto anni" must be rejected, since it contradicts both Arabic grammar and Sayf's theme that the community was troubled by unlawful practices only *after* the "conversion" of 'Abdallāh b. Sabā'.

Sayf—Muḥammad b. ʿAbdallāh[407]—ʿAmr b. Shuʿayb: ʿUthmān was the first to put a stop to [divining the future by observing] pigeons in flight and [by shooting] pellets. When (these practices) appeared in Medina, he put a certain man in charge of them, and he prohibited (the people) from performing them.

It was transmitted to me in writing by al-Sarī—Shuʿayb—Sayf—Sahl b. Yūsuf—al-Qāsim b. Muḥammad—his father: An account similar to the above. Then he added the following: Drunkenness began to occur among the people. ʿUthmān dispatched a patrol armed with staffs to make the rounds among them, and thus he prevented (such behavior) among them. Afterwards (drunkenness) intensified, and ʿUthmān publicly proclaimed the divinely prescribed punishments and protested to the people about (their behavior). They agreed that they should be flogged in cases of wine drinking, and a certain number of them were arrested and flogged.

It was transmitted to me in writing by al-Sarī—Shuʿayb—Sayf—Mubashshir b. al-Fuḍayl—Sālim b. ʿAbdallāh: When unlawful innovations made their appearance in Medina, certain men left to go to the garrison towns as fighters in the Holy War and to be close to the Arabs [who dwelt there]. Some of (these men) came to Baṣrah, others to Kūfah, still others to Syria. (These newcomers) all denounced the sons of the (warriors) who had settled in the garrison towns (*abnāʾ al-muhājirīn bi'l-amṣār*) for evils like those that had arisen among the Medinese. Only the Syrians were exempt from their strictures. They returned in a body to Medina, save for those residing in Syria, and informed ʿUthmān about what they had discovered. Then ʿUthmān stood up in the midst of the people to give the Friday sermon, saying: "O people of Medina, you are the very root of Islam. The people sow corruption only if you do, and they are upright only if you are. By God, by God, by God! If I learn of any innovation on the part of anyone of you, I shall send him into exile without fail. Verily, I do not mean to learn about anyone who has made any statement or demand apart from those [who have already come to my attention]. As to your predecessors, their members used to be

407. Not Muḥammad b. ʿUbaydallāh, as in Prym's text. See de Goeje, *Introductio*, dcxxx.

cut off without any of them being able to say a word about the evidence for or against him." Henceforth, whenever ʿUthmān [3029] found any of them committing an evil deed or drawing a weapon—whether a staff or something more lethal—he would send him into exile. Their fathers raised a hue and cry over this, until he learned that they were saying, "What an unlawful innovation exile is, albeit that the Messenger of God exiled al-Ḥakam b. Abī al-ʿĀṣ." (ʿUthmān) replied, "Al-Ḥakam was a Meccan, and the Messenger of God exiled him from there to al-Ṭā'if, and afterwards brought him back to his native town.[408] The Messenger of God exiled him for his crimes, and brought him back after having pardoned him. (The Prophet's) successor [namely, Abū Bakr] sent men into exile, as did ʿUmar after him. I swear by God, I shall accept pardon from you, and on my part I shall freely extend it to you. [Fearful] things are close at hand, and I desire them to befall neither us nor you. I stand watch anxiously; be yourselves on guard and consider [what may happen]."

It was transmitted to me in writing by al-Sarī—Shuʿayb—Sayf—ʿAbdallāh b. Saʿīd b. Thābit and Yaḥyā b. Saʿīd: Someone asked Saʿīd b. al-Musayyab what had impelled Muḥammad b. Abī Ḥudhayfah to rebel against ʿUthmān. (Saʿīd) replied: "He was an orphan under the guardianship of ʿUthmān, for ʿUthmān was responsible for the orphans among his kinsfolk and took care of all of them. Then (Muḥammad) asked ʿUthmān to appoint him as a governor when the latter became caliph. ʿUthmān responded, "My son, if I thought you were well-suited for office and you had asked me for a governorship, I would appoint you.[409] But that is not the case." (Muḥammad) said, "Then give me leave to go and find some way to support myself." (ʿUthmān) replied, "Go wherever you wish." He outfitted him out of his own possessions, provided him with sustenance, and gave him gifts. Now when (Muḥammad) reached Egypt he became one of those who were

---

408. Al-Ḥakam b. Abī al-ʿĀṣ was the father of Marwān; he was exiled as punishment for his obdurate opposition to the Prophet. The hill town of al-Ṭā'if, better watered and cooler than Mecca, was a common summer residence of the Meccan elite.

409. *Law kunta riḍan thumma sa'altanī 'l-ʿamala la-'staʿmaltuka.* Caetani (*Annali*, VIII, 65) translates as follows: "Se tu fossi stato facile a contentare e m'avessi chiesto una provincia, io te l'avrei data."

angry with ('Uthmān) because he had refused to appoint them to office.

In regard to 'Ammār b. Yāsir, (Sa'īd b. al-Musayyab) states: Words were exchanged between ('Ammār b. Yāsir) and 'Abbās b. 'Utbah b. Abī Lahab.[410] 'Uthmān had both of them beaten. That incident—that is, the affair on account of which they were beaten—has caused bad feeling between the families of 'Ammār and 'Utbah up until the present.

[3030] It was transmitted to me in writing by al-Sarī—Shu'ayb—Sayf—'Abdallāh b. Sa'īd b. Thābit: I asked Ibn Sulaymān b. Abī Ḥathmah [about this incident], and he informed me that it consisted of an exchange of calumnies.

It was transmitted to me in writing by al-Sarī—Shu'ayb—Sayf—Mubashshir: I asked Sālim b. 'Abdallāh what had impelled Muḥammad b. Abī Bakr to rebel against 'Uthmān. He responded, "Anger and greed." "How is that," I said? He replied, "(Muḥammad) held his place in Islam, but various parties (*aqwām*) deluded him and he coveted [even more]. He had a bold manner and a certain right [to the caliphate] attached to him, but 'Uthmān was contemptuous of him and made no effort to conciliate him.[411] So one thing was added to another, and he became a man despised (*mudhammam*) after having been highly praised (*muḥammad*)."

It was transmitted to me in writing by al-Sarī—Shu'ayb—Sayf—Mubashshir—Sālim b. 'Abdallāh: When 'Uthmān ruled he was lenient with (the people). He contested claims vigorously but did not void a single rightful claim. So they loved him for his leniency, and that induced them to submit to the commandments of Almighty God.

It was transmitted to me in writing by al-Sarī—Shu'ayb—Sayf—Sahl—al-Qāsim: Among 'Uthmān's novel acts—and he was regarded with approval for it—is that he struck a man during a quarrel in which the latter had belittled al-'Abbās b. 'Abd al-Muṭṭalib. When people brought this up to him, he said, "So, if the Messenger of God shows honor to his uncle, shall I allow con-

---

410. 'Abbās is perhaps the grandson of the infamous uncle of the Prophet cursed in Qur'ān 111.

411. A very obscure passage, *Wa-kānat lahu dāllatun fa-lazimahu ḥaqqun fa-akhadhahu 'Uthmānu min ẓahrihi wa-lam yudhin.*

tempt for him? Anyone who does that is an opponent of the Messenger of God, as is anyone who approves of such an act."

It was transmitted to me in writing by al-Sarī—Shuʿayb—Sayf—Ruzayq b. ʿAbdallāh al-Rāzī—ʿAlqamah b. Marthad—Ḥumrān b. Abān: ʿUthmān sent me to al-ʿAbbās after he had received the oath of allegiance, and I summoned (al-ʿAbbās) before him. He said, "Why have you called me to your service?" (ʿUthmān) replied, "I have never needed you more than I do today." (Al-ʿAbbās) said, "So long as you adhere to five things, the Community will not jerk its nose rings [from your grasp]." "What [3031] are they," asked (ʿUthmān)? (Al-ʿAbbās) said, "Abstention from killing, showing affection, pardoning offences, affability, and keeping secrets."

According to Muḥammad b. ʿUmar (al-Wāqidī)—Ibn Abī Sabrah—ʿAmr b. Umayyah al-Ḍamrī: The older men of Quraysh were passionately fond of *khazīrah*.[412] I was having a supper of *khazīrah* with ʿUthmān, made from some of the best cooked meat I had ever seen. It contained sheep's stomachs, and the broth was made of milk and fat. ʿUthmān said, "What do you think of this food?" "It is the finest I have ever eaten," I replied. He continued, "God have mercy upon Ibn al-Khaṭṭāb! Did you ever eat *khazīrah* with him?" "Yes," I said, "and the morsel almost dissolved in my hand when I went to put it in my mouth. There was no meat in it, and its broth was made of fat without milk." ʿUthmān said, "You are right. By God, ʿUmar fatigued those who followed him, and he would seek to turn them away from these things and towards austerity. No, by God, I do not eat from public funds (*māl al-muslimīn*) but only from my own. You know that I was the wealthiest man of Quraysh and the most single-minded merchant among them. I have never ceased eating soft and delicate foods. I have attained a great age, and it is the most delicate food that I like best. I know of no accusation that anyone can bring against me on account of this."

According to Muḥammad (al-Wāqidī)—Ibn Abī Sabrah—ʿĀṣim b. ʿUbaydallāh—ʿAbdallāh b. ʿĀmir:[413] During Ramaḍān, I used to

412. *Khazīrah* is a staple dish among the bedouin, a sort of stew consisting of cooking broth and pieces of meat, to which salt and flour have been added.

413. The *isnād* is corrected in accordance with de Goeje, *Introductio*, dcxxx.

break my fast with 'Uthmān, and he would serve us food of finer quality than 'Umar used to. Every night, I saw on 'Uthmān's table lamb and things made with fine flour. I never saw 'Umar eat
[3032] anything made of sifted flour, nor any sheep save old mutton. I spoke to 'Uthmān about this, and he replied, "God be merciful to 'Umar and to those who endure what 'Umar used to endure."

According to Muḥammad (al-Wāqidī)—'Abd al-Malik b. Yazīd b. al-Sā'ib—'Abdallāh b. al-Sā'ib—his father: The first tent I ever saw in Minā was one belonging to 'Uthmān, along with another belonging to 'Abdallāh b. 'Āmir b. Kurayz. 'Uthmān was the first to add the third call to prayer on Fridays, which was declaimed from al-Zawrā'. 'Uthmān was the first caliph who used sifted flour.[414]

It was transmitted to me in writing by al-Sarī—Shu'ayb—Sayf—Muḥammad and Ṭalḥah: 'Uthmān heard that Ibn Dhī al-Ḥabakah al-Nahdī was performing magical spells (*nīranj*). According to Muḥammad b. Salamah: Verily, it was a spell. So ('Uthmān) sent to al-Walīd b. 'Uqbah [in Kufah] to ask him about this. If it was the case, (al-Walīd) was ordered to punish him. Thus, (al-Walīd) summoned (Ibn Dhī al-Ḥabakah) and interrogated him. The latter said, "This is just sleight-of-hand, something to amuse people." Then (al-Walīd) ordered him to be severely chastised. He informed the people about him and read out 'Uthmān's letter to them: "You have all been dealt with earnestly, and you are obligated to be earnest in your conduct, so beware of those who act in jest." Then the people turned against 'Uthmān and wondered at his concern for matters of this kind.

(Ibn Dhī al-Ḥabakah) was angered, and he was one of those who rebelled [against 'Uthmān] and struck him down. Letters were
[3033] written to 'Uthmān about him, and when ('Uthmān) exiled certain persons to Syria, he also exiled Ka'b b. Dhī al-Ḥabakah and Mālik b. 'Abdallāh, who were alike in their religious thought and conduct, to Dunbāwand, because it was a land of sorcery.[415] In regard to this, Ka'b b. Dhī al-Ḥabakah said to al-Walīd:

---

414. This paragraph recalls 'Uthmān's liturgical innovations as well as his taste for luxury. Al-Zawrā' was the name of the Caliph's residence; see above, pp. 31–32, 70 and note 121 (text, I, 2827, 2864).

415. Dunbāwand means Damāvand, the great mountain north of Tehran. To its

By my life, if you expel me you will find no path
leading to the downfall which you covet for me.
I have long hoped to return, O son of Arwā,
to come back to what is rightfully mine—a calamity has snatched that away.
My exile in these lands and my bitter reviling
of God Himself will be brief;
My imprecations against you will be long,
every day and night, in this Dunbāwand of yours.

When Saʿīd (b. al-ʿĀṣ) became governor, he brought (Kaʿb) back [to Kūfah]. He treated him well and wished to help him, but (Kaʿb) was ungrateful to him and responded only with evil.

In the time of al-Walīd b. ʿUqbah, Ḍābiʾ b. al-Ḥārith al-Burjumī borrowed a dog called Qurḥān from a band of the Helpers in order to hunt gazelles. When he failed to return it, the Helpers were disgusted and sought the aid of his fellow tribesmen (*qawmuhu*) against him. These latter banded together against him, snatched the dog from him and returned it to the Helpers. He derided them about this affair in the following words:

The deputation of Qurḥān, not I, has imposed
upon itself a task at which the broad-cheeked woman perseveres, burdened with fatigue.[416]
They have passed the night in comfort, amply fed, as though
an amir had given them the marzubān's house.
Do not abandon your dog! For it is your mother,
and disrespect to mothers is a grave sin indeed.

On this account they complained about him to ʿUthmān. He [3034] sent for him, chastised him severely, and threw him in prison, as he was accustomed to do with the Muslims. That was too much for (Ḍābiʾ), and he stayed in prison until he died there. In regard to

---

flank the tyrant Zohhak (al-Ḍaḥḥāq) was chained, and it was also the home of the wonderful *sīmurgh,* the bird which nurtured the infant Zal, Rustam's father. Finally, sorcerers were believed to reside there. Le Strange, *Eastern Caliphate,* 371. On the Syrian exiles, see above, pp. 112–29 (text, I, 2907–2926).

416. A rather puzzling line, even with de Goeje's proposed reading of *taẓallu* instead of *taḍillu* (*Introductio,* dcxxx): *Tajashshama dūnī wafdu Qurḥāna khuṭ-ṭatan / taẓallu lahā 'l-wajnāʾu wa-hya ḥasīru.*

['Uthmān's] assassination, he excused himself to his companions in these words:

I resolved but did not act, though I was on the verge.
Would that I had acted, that I had fled leaving his wives in tears.[417]
By her who speaks, Ḍābi' has died in prison.
Who then opposes him? He has found no one to dispute him.
By her who speaks, God must not send Ḍābi' away.
How excellent is the youth whom you forsake and to whom you contrive excuses!

Because of these events [his son] 'Umayr b. Ḍābi' became an adherent of Ibn Sabā'.

It was transmitted to me in writing by al-Sarī—Shu'ayb—Sayf—al-Mustanīr—his brother: I know of no one who rode forth to war against 'Uthmān who was not [eventually] killed. A few individuals banded together in Kūfah—among them al-Ashtar, Zayd b. Ṣūḥān, Ka'b b. Dhī al-Ḥabakah, Abū Zaynab, Abū Muwarri', Kumayl b. Ziyād, and 'Umayr b. Ḍābi'—and they stated: "No, by God, no man can hold his head high[418] so long as 'Uthmān has authority over the people." Then 'Umayr b. Ḍābi' and Kumayl b. Ziyād said, "We shall kill him," and rode forth to Medina. As for
[3035] 'Umayr, he shrank back, but Kumayl b. Ziyād dared to assault ('Uthmān). He was sitting, waiting for [the right moment to strike], when 'Uthmān came up to him and slapped his face. (Kumayl) fell back on his buttocks and exclaimed, "You hurt me, Commander of the Faithful!" ('Uthmān) said, "Are you not a murderer?" "No, by God—apart from Whom there is no god," replied (Kumayl), and he swore [he was telling the truth]. The people gathered around him and said, "We will examine him, O Commander of the Faithful." ('Uthmān) responded, "No, for God has bestowed forgiveness, and I do not wish to learn anything

417. *Hamamtu wa-lam af'al wa-kidtu wa-laytanī / fa'altu wa-wallaytu 'l-bukā'a ḥalā'iluh.* Ibn al-Athīr, *Kāmil* (Beirut), III, 183, gives a variant of this line: *Hamamtu wa-lam af'al wa-kidtu wa-laytanī / taraktu 'alā 'Uthmāna tabkī ḥalā'iluh.*

418. *Lā wa'llāhi lā yarfu'u ra'sun.*

contradicting what he has said." He continued, "If things are as you say, Kumayl, then submit to me"—and he knelt down—"for by God, I can only think that you have designs against me. If you are telling the truth, then may God reward [you] abundantly. But if you are lying, may He abase [you]." (Kumayl) sat up in front of him and said, "Beware!" ('Uthmān) said, "I leave [you to your own devices]."

(Kumayl and 'Umayr) lived on until their longevity was much talked about among the people.[419] Now when al-Ḥajjāj arrived [in Kūfah] he said, "Those enlisted for the expedition of al-Muhallab b. Abī Ṣufrah should report to their posts; let no one neglect his duty."[420] So 'Umayr (b. Ḍābi') stood up before him and said, "I am but a frail old man, but I have two strong sons. Send one or both of them in my place." "Who are you," asked al-Ḥajjāj? "I am 'Umayr b. Ḍābi'," he answered. Then (al-Ḥajjāj) said, "By God, forty years ago you rebelled against Almighty God, and I shall make an example of you to the Muslims. You wrongfully defended the man who stole the dog. Your father, when he was in chains, determined [to take revenge against 'Uthmān], and you resolved [to do the same] but then shrank back. Now I am determined to act, and I will not shrink back." And so ('Umayr's) head was struck off.

It was transmitted to me in writing by al-Sarī—Shu'ayb—Sayf—a man of the Banū Asad: It is told of ('Umayr b. Ḍābi') that he had attacked 'Uthmān along with the other assailants. When al-Ḥajjāj came [to Kūfah] and announced [the campaign against the Khārijites], a certain man presented something to him in order to purchase his exemption from military service, and (al-Ḥajjāj) accepted it from him.[421] Now when (al-Ḥajjāj) was named

---

419. *Fa-baqiya ḥattā akthara 'l-nāsu fī najā'ihimā.* Caetani (*Annali*, VIII, 68) translates: "E restarono i due [i.e., Kumayl and 'Uthmān], finchè la gente s'affollo meravigliata del colloquio." However, I can find no warrant for rendering *najā'* in this manner. My version is suggested by Ibn al-Athīr's loose paraphrase (*Kāmil* [Beirut], III, 183): *Wa-baqiya ilā ayyāmi 'l-Ḥajjāji fa-qatalahumā.*

420. Sayf b. 'Umar's taste for unexpected chronological leaps shows up here. Al-Ḥajjāj b. Yūsuf was made governor of Iraq by 'Abd al-Malik in 75/694, in order to pursue the struggle against the Kharijites. Al-Ḥajjāj at once mounted a massive and ultimately successful campaign for this purpose under the command of al-Muhallab b. Abī Ṣufrah. See Wellhausen, *Arab Kingdom*, 227–31; Hawting, *First Islamic Dynasty*, 66–67.

421. *Lammā qadima 'l-Ḥajjāju wa-nādā bimā nādā bihi 'araḍa rajulun 'alayhi*

[3036] governor, Asmā' b. Khārijah said, "The matter of ʿUmayr has been one of the things worrying me." (Al-Ḥajjāj) asked, "And who is ʿUmayr?" "This old man here," he replied. (Al-Ḥajjāj) said, "You have reminded me of the assault, which I had forgotten. Is he not one of those who rebelled against ʿUthmān?" (Asmā') replied, "He is indeed." (Al-Ḥajjāj) continued, "And is there someone else in Kūfah [who was also implicated]?" "Yes," said (Asmā'), "Kumayl." (Al-Ḥajjāj) said, "Bring ʿUmayr before me," and he struck off his head. He demanded Kumayl also, but he had fled, so he held the tribe of al-Nakhaʿ responsible in his stead. Al-Aswad b. al-Haytham said to him, "What do you want with an old man? His old age should be enough for you." "Verily, by God," replied (al-Ḥajjāj), "you should hold your tongue with me, or else I will certainly slice off your head." He said, "Go ahead!"

When Kumayl perceived the anguish suffered by his fellow tribesmen, even though they numbered two thousand warriors, he said, "Death is better than fear when two thousand are filled with fear because of me and have been denied [their stipends]." Then he set out and presented himself before al-Ḥajjāj. The latter said to him, "You are a man who harbored evil designs; the Commander of the Faithful did not find you out, and you were not satisfied until you made him subject to reprisal when he fended you off." (Kumayl) answered, "On what grounds will you put me to death? Will you kill me because he was forgiving or because I am yet in good health?" (Al-Ḥajjāj) said, "Adham b. Muḥriz, kill him!" (Adham) said, "Is the reward [for this deed] to be shared between you and me?" "Yes," said (al-Ḥajjāj). Adham replied, "Nay. Rather, you will obtain the reward, while whatever sin there may be will fall upon me." Mālik b. ʿAbdallāh, who had been one of those exiled [to Syria],[422] said these words:

The son of Arwā did an injustice to Kumayl;
 he pardoned him for it, for the one who seeks to avenge himself is blameworthy.

---

mā ʿiwaḍa nafsihi. I have followed Caetani's interpretation of this elliptical passage (*Annali*, VIII, 68).

422. See above, pp. 120–29 text, I, 2916 ff.).

(Kumayl) said to him, "I shall not vilify you today for such a
thing,
O Abū ʿAmr, while you are still imām.
Go easy! By Him Whom Quraysh worships with us [3037]
my head is unlawful to the great man.
In forgiveness there is security
whose excellence is well known among the people, though
for retaliation we incur no sin.
Had the Just One [ʿUmar] known what you do,
he would have forbidden it to you, brooking no dispute."

It was related to me by ʿUmar b. Shabbah—ʿAlī b. Muḥammad (al-Madāʾinī)—Suḥaym b. Ḥafṣ: Rabīʿah b. al-Ḥārith b. ʿAbd al-Muṭṭalib was ʿUthmān's business partner (*sharīk*) during the Time of Ignorance. Al-ʿAbbās b. Rabīʿah said to ʿUthmān, "Write to Ibn ʿĀmir on my behalf and ask him to lend me 100,000 [dirhams]." He did write, and (Ibn ʿĀmir) gave that sum to him outright. (Ibn ʿĀmir) also assigned his house to him, [and it is known as] the House of al-ʿAbbās b. Rabīʿah nowadays.

It was related to me by ʿUmar (b. Shabbah)—ʿAlī—Isḥāq b. Yaḥyā—Mūsā b. Ṭalḥah: Ṭalḥah owed 50,000 [dirhams] to ʿUthmān. When ʿUthmān went to the mosque one day, Ṭalḥah said to him, "Your money is ready, so take it." (ʿUthmān) replied, "It is yours, Abū Muḥammad, to support you in fulfilling the manly virtues."

It was related to me by ʿUmar (b. Shabbah)—ʿAlī—ʿAbd Rabbihi b. Nāfiʿ—Ismāʿīl b. Abī Khālid—Ḥakīm b. Jābir: ʿAlī said to Ṭalḥah, "I adjure you by God, send the people away from ʿUthmān."[423] (Ṭalḥah) replied, "No, by God, not until the Banū Umayyah voluntarily submit to what is right."

It was related to me by ʿUmar (b. Shabbah)—ʿAlī—Abū Bakr al-Bakrī—Hishām b. Ḥassān—al-Ḥasan: Ṭalḥah b. ʿUbaydallāh sold ʿUthmān a property of his for 700,000 [dirhams], and (ʿUthmān) brought (the money) over to him. Then Ṭalḥah said, "Surely a

---

423. *Anshuduka ʾllāha illā radadta ʾl-nāsa ʿan ʿUthmāna.* Caetani (*Annali*, VIII, 69) has misconstrued the meaning of this phrase, for which see Wright, *Arabic Grammar*, II, 339D–340A.

man who possesses so much wealth and stores it in his own house, in ignorance of what may befall him by the command of
[3038] Almighty God—God, Glory be to Him, has made that man a fool!" That night his messenger plied the streets of Medina dividing up the cash until morning. By morning, (Ṭalḥah) did not have a single dirham left. Al-Ḥasan said: "He came here seeking the dinar and the dirham"—or, according to other reports: "the yellow and the white."

In this year—that is, 35 (656)—ʿAbdallāh b. ʿAbbās led the people on the Pilgrimage at ʿUthmān's command. This was related to me by Aḥmad b. Thābit al-Rāzī—one who related [it] to him—Isḥāq b. ʿĪsā—Abū Maʿshar.

The Reason Why ʿUthmān Ordered ʿAbdallāh b. ʿAbbās to Lead the Pilgrimage in This Year

According to Muḥammad b. ʿUmar al-Wāqidī—Usāmah b. Zayd—Dāwūd b. al-Ḥuṣayn—ʿIkrimah—(ʿAbdallāh) b. ʿAbbās: [This took place] when ʿUthmān was under siege for the last time. ʿIkrimah states: I asked Ibn ʿAbbās, "Were there two sieges?" Ibn ʿAbbās replied, "There were." The first siege lasted for twelve [days]. When the Egyptians appeared, ʿAlī met them at Dhū Khushub and induced them to leave. By God, ʿAlī was a sincere friend to (ʿUthmān), until he aroused ʿAlī's anger against him. Marwān, Saʿīd, and their kinsmen began to incite him against ʿAlī, so that he would be eager to take offence.[424] They would say, "Had (ʿAlī) so desired, no one would have spoken to you [as the rebels have]." This refers to the fact that ʿAlī used to advise and counsel him and to speak very harshly about Marwān and his kin. The latter used to tell ʿUthmān, "(ʿAlī) treats you like this even though you are his imam, his brother-in-law, the son of his paternal uncle and aunt. What do you suppose he has hidden from you?" Their criticism of ʿAlī was so relentless that (ʿUthmān) decided to conduct affairs without him.

I [that is, ʿAbdallāh b. ʿAbbās] entered (ʿAlī's) presence on the day I set out for Mecca and mentioned to him that ʿUthmān had called on me to go there. (ʿAlī) said, "ʿUthmān does not seek

424. *Fa-yataḥammala.* See de Goeje, *Introductio,* cciii–cciv, sub verbo *ḥamala.*

honest counsel from anyone. He has surrounded himself with a circle of perfidious advisers. There is not one among them who has not taken possession of some district, devouring its revenues and treating its inhabitants shamefully." I replied to him: "He has ties of kinship [to you] and a claim [to your support]. If you think it right to act independently of him, you should do so, for otherwise you will not absolve yourself [from the consequences of his acts]." [3039]

Ibn ʿAbbās says, "Now God knows that I saw (ʿAlī) relent and become gentle toward ʿUthmān, then I would see him greatly distressed."

According to ʿIkrimah—Ibn ʿAbbās: ʿUthmān said to me, "Ibn ʿAbbās, go to Khālid b. al-ʿĀṣ in Mecca and tell him that the Commander of the Faithful sends his greetings and says: 'I have been under siege every day since such-and-such a date. I cannot drink except from the brackish water in my house, and I am barred from using a well that I purchased with my own money at Rūmah. Only the people drink there, while I get nothing from it. I can eat only what is in my own house; I am prevented from obtaining anything in the marketplace. As you see, I am under siege.' Command (Khālid b. al-ʿĀṣ) to lead the people on the Pilgrimage, for there is no one to do it. If he refuses, then you will lead the Pilgrimage."

I reached the Pilgrimage caravan[425] on the tenth, eleventh, and twelfth days [of Dhū al-Ḥijjah]. I came to Khālid b. al-ʿĀṣ and told him what ʿUthmān had said to me. He replied, "Is that possible in view of the hostility of those whom you see here?" He refused to lead the Pilgrimage and said, "You lead the people on the Pilgrimage, for you are the son of ʿAlī's paternal uncle, and this responsibility belongs only to him. You are more worthy [than I] to carry it out on his behalf."

Thus, I led the people on that Pilgrimage. Then at the end of the month I returned to Medina. There I discovered that ʿUthmān had been killed and the people were thronging around ʿAlī b. Abī Ṭālib. When ʿAlī saw me he got away from the people and came up to me. Whispering, he said, "What do you think about what has happened? A terrible thing indeed has taken place, as you see,

---

425. I follow the emendation of de Goeje, *Introductio,* dcxxx.

something that no one can control." I responded, "In my opinion the people must inevitably turn to you today. I also think that no [3040] one can receive the oath of allegiance today without being suspected of the murder of this man." However, (ʿAlī) refused not to have the oath of allegiance sworn to him, and thus he was suspected of (ʿUthmān's) blood.[426]

According to Muḥammad (al-Wāqidī)—Ibn Abī Sabrah—ʿAbd al-Majīd b. Suhayl—ʿIkrimah: Ibn ʿAbbās recounts: ʿUthmān said to me, "I have named Khālid b. al-ʿĀṣ b. Hishām to be governor in Mecca. The Meccans have heard about what the people have done [here in Medina], and I fear that they will bar him from office. He will refuse [to accept that] and will fight them in the Sanctuary of Almighty God, in which He has established His peace—both (the Meccans) and those people 'who have come from every deep ravine that they may witness things profitable to them.'[427] Therefore I have thought it best to give you authority over the Pilgrimage." Along with all this, (ʿUthmān) wrote a letter to the pilgrims, asking them to uphold his rights against those who were besieging him.

Ibn ʿAbbās set out and encountered ʿĀ'ishah in al-Ṣulṣul.[428] She said, "Ibn ʿAbbās, I entreat you by God: abandon this man, sow doubt about him among the people, for you have been given a sharp tongue. Their powers of discernment have been clarified, the beacon light is raised high to guide them, and (the Caliph's associates) have milked the lands that once abounded in good things.[429] I have seen Ṭalḥah b. ʿUbaydallāh take possession of the keys to the public treasuries and storehouses. If he becomes caliph, he will follow in the path of his paternal cousin Abū Bakr."

According to (Ibn ʿAbbās): I said, "O Mother (of the Believers), if

---

426. *Fa-abā illā an yubāʿaya fa'ttuhima bi-damihi.* Caetani (*Annali*, VIII, 263) translates: "Egli rifiuto il califfato, e fu sospettato (ugualmente)."

427. Qur'ān 22:28–29. The reference is to those performing the Pilgrimage in obedience to God's commandment. Presumably ʿUthmān fears that innocent and pious pilgrims would be caught up in the conflict between Khālid and the Meccans.

428. Al-Ṣulṣul: a locality near Medina, some seven miles south on the road toward Mecca. See Yāqūt, *Muʿjam al-Buldān*, III, 413.

429. *Wa-taḥallabū min 'l-buldāni li-amrin qad jamma.* A very puzzling passage, in part because the subject of the first verb is not identified.

some evil were to befall that man [namely, ʿUthmān], the people would seek asylum only with our companion [namely, ʿAlī]." She replied, "Be quiet! I have no desire to defy or quarrel with you."

According to Ibn Abī Sabrah: ʿAbd al-Majīd b. Suhayl informed me that he had made a copy from ʿIkrimah of the letter written by ʿUthmān. Here it is:

> In the name of God, the Merciful, the Compassionate. From God's servant ʿUthmān, Commander of the Faithful, to the Believers and Muslims. Peace be with you, and to you I praise God—there is no god but He.
>
> To proceed: Verily I call on you to remember Almighty God, who has bestowed benefits upon you, taught you [3041] Islam, guided you away from error, delivered you from unbelief, shown you clear proofs, lavished sustenance upon you, and given you victory over the enemy. "And He has lavished on you His blessings."[430] For verily Almighty God says, and His saying is the truth, "If you count God's blessing, you will never number it; surely man is sinful, unthankful."[431]
>
> The Almighty also says, "O Believers, fear God as He should be feared, and see you do not die save in surrender [that is, as Muslims]. And hold you fast to God's bond, together, [and do not scatter; remember God's blessing upon you when you were enemies, and He brought your hearts together, so that by His blessing you became brothers. You were on the brink of a pit of Fire, and He delivered you from it; even so God makes clear to you His signs; haply so you will be guided. Let there be one nation of you, calling to good, and bidding to honor, and forbidding dishonor; those are the prosperers. Be not as those who scattered and fell into variance after the clear signs came to them;] those there awaits a mighty chastisement."[432]

---

430. Qur'ān 32:19.
431. Qur'ān 14:37.
432. Qur'ān 3:97–101. In many of the Qur'ānic citations in this letter, only the opening and closing words are quoted in the text. Ṭabarī's readers, of course, would have been able to supply the missing lines from memory. In certain cases,

He has also said, and His saying is the truth, "O Believers, remember God's blessing upon you, and His compact (*mīthāq*) which he made with you, when you said, 'We have heard and we obey.' "[433]

He has also said, and His saying is the truth, "O Believers, if an ungodly man comes to you with a tiding, [make clear, lest you afflict a people unwittingly, and then repent of what you have done. And know that the Messenger of God is among you. If he obeyed you in much of the affair, you would suffer; but God has endeared to you belief, decking it fair in your hearts, and He has made detestable to you unbelief and ungodliness and disobedience. Those—they are the right-minded,] by God's favor and blessing; God is All-Knowing, All-Wise."[434]

[Remember also] the saying of the Almighty, "Those that sell God's covenant (*'ahd Allāh*) and their oaths for a little price . . . for them awaits a painful chastisement."[435]

He has also said, and His saying is the truth, "So fear God as far as you are able, [and give ear, and obey, and expend well for yourselves. And whosoever is guarded against the avarice of his own soul,] those—they are the prosperers."[436]

He has also said, and His saying is the truth, "Break not the oaths after they have been confirmed [and you have made God your surety; surely God knows the things you do. And be not as a woman who breaks her thread, after it is firmly spun, into fibres, by taking your oaths as mere mutual deceit, one nation being more numerous than another nation. God only tries you thereby; and certainly He will make clear to you upon the Day of Resurrection that whereon you were at variance. If God had willed, He would have made you one nation; but He leads

---

therefore, I have supplied the omitted passages [in square brackets] so as to clarify 'Uthmān's meaning.

433. Qur'ān 5:10.
434. Qur'ān 49:6–8.
435. Qur'ān 3:71.
436. Qur'ān 64:16.

astray whom He will and guides whom He will; and you will surely be questioned about the things you wrought. Take not your oaths as mere mutual deceit, lest any foot should slip after it has stood firm and you should taste evil, for that you barred from the way of God, and lest there should await you a mighty chastisement. And do not sell the covenant of God for a small price; surely what is with God—that is better for you, did you but know. What is with you comes to an end, but what is with God abides,] and surely we shall recompense those who were patient their wage, according to the best of what they did."[437]

He has also said, and His saying is the truth, "Obey God, and obey the Messenger and those in authority among you. [If you should quarrel on anything, refer it to God and the Messenger, if you believe in God and the Last Day; that is better,] and fairer in the issue."[438]

He has also said, and His saying is the truth, "God has [3042]
promised those of you who believe and do righteous deeds [that He will surely make you successors in the land, even as He made those who were before them successors, and that He will surely establish their religion for them that He has approved for them, and will give them in exchange, after their fear, security: 'They shall serve Me, not associating with Me anything.'] Whoso disbelieves after that, those—they are the ungodly."[439]

He has also said, and His saying is the truth, "Those who swear obedience to thee swear obedience in truth to God; [God's hand is over their hands. Then whosoever breaks his oath breaks it but to his own hurt; and whosoever fulfills his covenant made with God,] God will give him a mighty wage."[440]

To continue. Almighty God desired for you absolute obedience and unity (*al-samʿ wa'l-ṭāʿah wa'l-jamāʿah*),

437. Qur'ān 16:93–98.
438. Qur'ān 4:31.
439. Qur'ān 24:54.
440. Qur'ān 48:10.

and warned you against rebellion, schism, and discord. He informed you about what your predecessors had done, presenting it to you so that He might have it as proof against you. If you rebel against Him, then accept the counsel of Almighty God and beware of His punishment, for you will never find a community (*ummah*) that has been destroyed save after it has fallen into discord. [Such a community can be saved] only if it has a head who can unite it. If ever you do that, you will not perform the prayer together, your enemy will be given power over you, and you will disagree as to what is lawful or forbidden. If you do that, no true religion (*dīn*) will remain before God—glory be to Him—and you will be divided into sects. Now Almighty God has said to His Messenger, "Those who have made divisions in their religion and become sects, thou art not of them in anything; their affair is unto God, then He will tell them what they have been doing."[441] Verily I enjoin upon you what God has enjoined, and I warn you of His chastisement. For Shu'ayb said to his people (*qawm*), "O my people, let not the breach with me move you, so that there smite you the like of what smote the people of Noah . . . [And ask forgiveness of your Lord, then repent to Him; surely my Lord is] All-Compassionate, All-Loving."[442]

To continue: Verily certain groups (*aqwām*) among those who have been talking in this way have maintained to the people that they but summon [them] to the Book of Almighty God and to the truth, and that they desire neither this world nor any conflict over it. When the truth was presented to them, behold the people were at variance concerning it: among them are those who accept the truth when it is presented to them and [then] turn away from it, and among them are those who abandon the truth and renounce it in this matter, desiring to snatch it without any right. My life has seemed long to them and their

441. Qur'ān 6:160.
442. Qur'ān 11:91–92.

hopes of governing have been deferred, and so they seek to hasten [God's] decree [by murdering me.]

They have written you that they returned [to their homes] on the basis of (certain promises) which I gave them; I am not aware that I have neglected any of my [3043]
promises to them. They have been seeking, so they allege, [the enforcement of] the divinely authorized punishments (*al-ḥudūd*).[443] I said, "Inflict them upon those whom you know to have violated any one of them. Inflict them upon anyone near or far who has wronged you." They said, "The Book of God is to be recited aloud." I replied, "Then let him who recites do this, except for one who inserts something that God has not revealed in the Book." They said, "The deprived man ought to be provided for, and the public wealth (*al-māl*) should be expended in such a way that sound custom (*al-sunnah al-ḥasanah*) may be followed thereby. The [caliph's] one-fifth share and the [fixed] alms tax should not be exceeded. Capable and trustworthy men should be placed in authority. The wrongs [suffered by] the people should be charged against those who have committed them." Now I am content with this and have persevered in doing it. I came to the Prophet's wives to speak with them, saying, "What do you command me?" They answered, "You should assign governorships (*tu'ammirū*) to ʿAmr b. al-ʿĀṣ and ʿAbdallāh b. Qays [namely, Abū Mūsā al-Ashʿarī] and leave Muʿāwiyah [in office]. An amir [ʿUmar?] made him governor before you; he sees to the well-being of his province and his army is content with him. Send ʿAmr back [to Egypt], for his army is content with him. Make him governor and he will restore good order in his territory." Now I did all that, and (ʿAmr) has since then transgressed against me and violated right conduct.

I have written to you and to my associates who have made allegations concerning the matter. They have

443. Emended in accord with de Goeje, *Introductio*, dcxxx.

sought to hasten God's decree, barred me from the prayer, and kept me from the mosque. They have stolen what they could in Medina. I have written this letter to you at a time when they are giving me one of three choices. First, they may retaliate against me for every man whom I have struck, rightly or wrongly, except that some portion of it will be forgone. Alternatively, I may resign my office (*al-amr*) and they will assign it to someone else. Or finally, they may send to the provincial garrisons (*al-ajnād*) and to the inhabitants of Medina who obey them, and thus declare themselves free of the absolute obedience to me that God has enjoined upon them.

To them I have replied [as follows]. As for my exacting retaliation against myself, caliphs before me used to strike [men] in error and retaliation was not demanded against any of them, and I know that they are aiming only
[3044] against me. As for my abdicating the caliphate (*al-imārah*), I would rather they rage against me than to resign from the work of Almighty God and His caliphate. As for your statement—"they will send to the provincial garrisons and the inhabitants of Medina and thus be quit of obedience to me"—I am not an agent of yours, nor did I compel them to obey beforehand. Rather, they voluntarily accepted (obedience to me), seeking to please Almighty God and to resolve discord. As to him among you who desires only this world, he shall obtain of it only what Almighty God has prescribed for him. He who desires only God's face, the Abode hereafter, the well-being of the Community (*al-ummah*), the seeking of Almighty God's pleasure, and the sound custom (*al-sunnah al-ḥasanah*) laid down by the Messenger of God and the two caliphs after him, (that man) shall surely be rewarded for that by God.

Your reward is not in my hands. If I bestowed upon you the whole world, it would neither be a fair price for your religion nor would it compensate you in any way. So fear God and take into account His reward. I am not content—nor will God (Glory be to Him!) be content—that anyone among you should violate His covenant (*'ahd*). As for what (the rebels) will force me to choose between, it adds up simply to deposing [me] and naming a new caliph (*al-naz' wa'l-ta'mīr*). I have been master of myself and those with me, I have seen to [the enforcement of] God's judgment (*ḥukm*) and [avoided] altering the benefits [bestowed] by God—Glory be to Him. I have hated evil custom, division within the Community, and the shedding of blood. I adjure you by God and by Islam to take only what is right—and you will be given that by me—and to abandon wrongdoing against those with rightful claims. Deal justly between us, as Almighty God has commanded you. I adjure you by God—Glory be to Him—who has appointed for you the covenant and mutual support in God's affair—for God has said, and His saying is true, "Fulfill the covenant (*'ahd*); surely the covenant shall be asked of."[444] This is an excuse before God; perhaps you will be mindful. [3045]

To continue: "Yet I claim not that my soul was innocent—surely the soul of man incites to evil—except inasmuch as my Lord had mercy; truly my Lord is All-Forgiving, All-Compassionate."[445] If I have chastised certain groups (*aqwām*), I have desired only good thereby, and I turn in repentance to Almighty God from every [evil] deed I have committed and seek His forgiveness. Verily none forgives sins but He. Surely the mercy of my Lord comprehends everything. Only the nation (*al-qawm*) that has gone astray despairs of God's mercy, and He accepts repentance from His servants and pardons evil deeds and knows what they do. I ask Almighty God to forgive me and you, to reconcile the hearts of this Community to what is good, and to make sin hateful to it.

Peace be upon you and the mercy of God and His blessings, O Believers and Muslims.

Ibn 'Abbās states: I read this letter out to them in Mecca, one day before the Day of Watering.[446]

---

444. Qur'ān 17:36.
445. Qur'ān 12:53.
446. *Yawm al-tarwiyah,* "the Day of Watering," falls on 8 Dhū al-Ḥijjah. It

According to (al-Wāqidī)—Ibn Abī Sabrah—ʿAbd al-Majīd b. Suhayl—ʿUbaydallāh b. ʿAbdallāh b. ʿUtbah—Ibn ʿAbbās: ʿUthmān summoned me and put me in charge of the Pilgrimage. I went to Mecca, where I led the people in the Pilgrimage rites and read ʿUthmān's letter out to them. Then I arrived back in Medina, and the oath of allegiance had been rendered to ʿAlī.

ʿUthmān's Burial Place, and Those Who Led the Prayer for Him and Took Charge of His Funeral Rites

[3046] It was related to me by Jaʿfar b. ʿAbdallāh al-Muḥammadī—ʿAmr b. Ḥammād and ʿAlī b. Ḥusayn—Ḥusayn b. ʿĪsā—his father—Abū Maymūnah—Abū Bashīr al-ʿĀbidī: ʿUthmān['s corpse] was thrown aside and left unburied for three days. Then Ḥakīm b. Ḥizām al-Qurashī, who was a member of the clan of Asad b. ʿAbd al-ʿUzzā, and Jubayr b. Muṭʿim b. ʿAdī b. Nawfal b. ʿAbd Manāf spoke to ʿAlī about his burial, seeking his permission for (ʿUthmān's) family to see to that. ʿAlī granted them his permission, but when news of this spread, people lay in wait for (ʿUthmān's body) by the road, armed with stones. A few members of his family set out with (his body), intending to take him to an enclosure in Medina named Ḥashsh Kawkab, where the Jews used to bury their dead. Now when (ʿUthmān's body) was brought out before the people, they stoned his bier and were bent on throwing him to the ground. When ʿAlī heard that, he sent and demanded that they leave him alone. They did so, and (ʿUthmān's body) was hurried along and interred in Ḥashsh Kawkab. When Muʿāwiyah b. Abī Sufyān gained supremacy over the Muslims (*al-nās*), he ordered that enclosure to be razed and transferred (ʿUthmān's body) to al-Baqīʿ.[447] Then he commanded the people to bury their dead around his grave, until ultimately (those graves) adjoined the cemetery of the Muslims.

---

marks the day on which the pilgrims leave Mecca for the pilgrimage station of ʿArafāt. Muslim commentators explain the name by saying that on this day the pilgrims collect water to supply themselves and their animals during the forthcoming rites. See A. J. Wensinck and J. Jomier, "Ḥadjdj," *EI*², III, 35.

447. Al-Baqīʿ or Baqīʿ al-Gharqad is the principal cemetery area in Medina, some 150 meters due east of the Prophet's Mosque. The name implies that it was

It was related to me by Ja'far—'Amr and 'Alī—Ḥusayn[448]—his father—al-Mujālid b. Sa'īd al-Hamdānī—Yasār b. Abī Karib—his father Abū Karib, who had been an official in charge of 'Uthmān's treasury: 'Uthmān was buried at twilight. Only Marwān b. al-Ḥakam, three of his freedmen (*mawālī*), and his fifth daughter were present at his funeral. His daughter wailed in mourning and raised her voice in lament for him. The people took stones and hooted "Long-bearded old idiot!" She was nearly stoned.[449] Then [3047] they said, "(Go to) the compound, the compound." And thus he was interred in a compound outside [Medina].

According to al-Wāqidī—Sa'd b. Rāshid—Ṣāliḥ b. Kaysān: When 'Uthmān was killed, a certain man said, "He will be buried at Dayr Sal', the Jewish cemetery." Ḥakīm b. Ḥizām replied, "That will never be, so long as one member of the lineage of Quṣayy remains alive."[450] Things almost came to blows, and Ibn 'Udays al-Balawī said, "Old man, what harm does it do you where he is buried?" Ḥakīm b. Ḥizām responded, "He will be buried nowhere but at Baqī' al-Gharqad, where his brother-in-law and his young son are buried." And so Ḥakīm b. Ḥizām, along with twelve men including al-Zubayr, set out with ('Uthmān's body), and Ḥakīm b. Ḥizām led the funeral prayer for him.

According to al-Wāqidī: In our judgment, the best-attested testimony is that Jubayr b. Muṭ'im led the funeral prayer for him.

According to Muḥammad b. 'Umar (al-Wāqidī)—al-Ḍaḥḥāk b. 'Uthmān—Makhramah b. Sulaymān al-Wālibī: 'Uthmān was killed on Friday morning. (His kin and supporters) could not bury him, and Nā'ilah bt. al-Farāfiṣah sent to Ḥuwayṭib b. 'Abd al-'Uzzā, Jubayr b. Muṭ'im, Abū Jahm b. Ḥudhayfah, Ḥakīm b. Ḥizām, and Niyār al-Aslamī. They all responded, "We cannot

---

originally marked by a stand of thorn trees. See W. C. Brice, *Historical Atlas of Islam,* 23; al-Harawi, *Guide des lieux de pèlerinage,* 211–16.

448. Instead of "Ḥasan"; emended in accordance with de Goeje, *Introductio,* dcxxx.

449. *Na'thal* was a common epithet flung at 'Uthmān by his enemies; see de Goeje, *Introductio,* cccxliv, sub verbo *ṭūl.*

450. Quṣayy was the eponymous ancestor of several of the most influential clans of Quraysh in Mecca, including 'Abd Manāf (the common ancestor of the Prophet and 'Uthmān). His prestige was based on his control of the cult of the Ka'bah and his welding the various clans of Quraysh into an effective tribal unit. See G. Levi della Vida, "Ḳuṣayy," *EI*[2], V, 519–20.

take (his body) in the daytime with these Egyptians at the gate." Thus, they held off until the evening. Then these men (*qawm*) entered ['Uthmān's house], but they were barred from him. Abū Jahm said, "By God, no one will keep me from him unless I die along with him. Bear him away!" And so ('Uthmān's body) was carried to al-Baqī'.

Nā'ilah followed behind them with a slave of 'Uthmān's and a lamp, which she lighted at al-Baqī'. At length they came to a stand of date palms in an enclosure. They broke through the wall and then buried him among those date palms, with Jubayr b. Muṭ'im leading the funeral prayer for him. Nā'ilah left intending to talk [about 'Uthmān's burial place], but the mourners (*qawm*) scolded
[3048] her, saying, "We are afraid that this rabble may go dig him up." And so Nā'ilah returned to her home.

According to Muḥammad (al-Wāqidī)—'Abdallāh b. Yazīd al-Hudhalī—'Abdallāh b. Sā'idah: For two nights after he was killed, 'Uthmān remained [where he had fallen] and they were unable to bury him. Then four men bore (his body) away—Ḥakīm b. Ḥizām, Jubayr b. Muṭ'im, Niyār b. Mukram, and Abū Jahm b. Ḥudhayfah. When he was laid down so that the funeral prayer could be performed for him, a band of the Helpers came and forbade them to perform the prayer. These included Aslam b. Aws b. Bajrah al-Sā'idī and Abū Ḥayyah al-Māzinī among several others. They forbade ('Uthmān's supporters) to bury him at al-Baqī'. Abū Jahm said, "Bury him, for God and His angels have blessed him." "No, by God," they said, "he will never be buried in the Muslims' cemetery." So they buried him in Ḥashsh Kawkab. When the Banū Umayyah reigned, they had that garden[451] included in al-Baqī', and it is today the cemetery of the Banū Umayyah.

According to Muḥammad (al-Wāqidī)—'Abdallāh b. Mūsā al-Makhzūmī: When 'Uthmān was killed, (his assassins) tried to cut off his head, but Nā'ilah and Umm al-Banīn[452] fell upon him and stopped them. The two women screamed and beat [their] faces and rent their clothing. In the face of this, Ibn 'Udays said, "Leave

---

451. *Ḥashsh.* The narrator may intend a pun, since *ḥashsh* means not only "garden" but also "privy."

452. Another of 'Uthmān's wives, the daughter of 'Uyaynah b. Ḥiṣn b. Ḥudhayfah b. Badr al-Fazārī. See Caetani, *Annali,* VIII, 300–1, and below, p. 254 (text, I, 3056).

him." And thus ʿUthmān, his corpse still unwashed, was taken out and brought to al-Baqīʿ. (The mourners) wanted to perform the funeral prayer for him in the place set aside for funerals, but the Helpers refused [to allow that]. ʿUmayr b. Ḍābiʾ appeared while ʿUthmān was stretched out upon a door. (ʿUmayr) jumped on him and broke one of his ribs, saying, "You left Ḍābiʾ in prison until he died there."

It was related to me by al-Ḥārith—Ibn Saʿd—Abū Bakr b. ʿAbdallāh b. Abī Uways—his grandfather's paternal uncle, al-Rabīʿ b. Mālik b. Abī ʿĀmir—(Al-Rabīʿ's) father: I was one of ʿUthmān's pallbearers when he was killed. We carried him upon a door, and his head was bumping up and down on the door because we were walking so fast. We were possessed with fear until we [3049] interred him in his grave in Ḥashsh Kawkab.

As for Sayf (b. ʿUmar's) account, it was transmitted to me in writing by al-Sarī—Shuʿayb—Sayf—Abū Ḥārithah and Abū ʿUthmān and Muḥammad and Ṭalḥah: When ʿUthmān was killed, Nāʾilah sent for ʿAbd al-Raḥmān b. ʿUdays and said to him, "You are the closest of the rebels (*qawm*) in kinship and the best suited of them to deal with my situation. Have these corpses removed from me." But he abused and reviled her until, in the depths of the night, Marwān went out and came to ʿUthmān's house. He was joined by Zayd b. Thābit, Ṭalḥah b. ʿUbaydallāh, ʿAlī, al-Ḥasan, Kaʿb b. Mālik, and most of the Companions who were present [in Medina]. Meantime boys and women assembled in the place set aside for funerals. They had ʿUthmān brought there, and Marwān led the prayer for him. Afterwards they took him to al-Baqīʿ and buried him there, in the part adjacent to Ḥashsh Kawkab.

The next morning, they came [to collect the bodies of] ʿUthmān's slaves who been killed with him and brought them out [for burial]. When (the rebels) saw them, they stopped them from burying (the slaves). So (the mourners) took them into Ḥashsh Kawkab. That evening, they brought out two of the dead slaves and buried them beside ʿUthmān. Each (corpse) was accompanied by five persons and a woman, Fāṭimah, the mother of Ibrāhīm b. ʿAdī.[453] Then they returned [to Medina] and came to Kinānah b.

453. On Fāṭimah see above, p. 202 (text, I, 3003–3004).

Bishr. They said to him, "You are the most closely related to us among the rebels. Order these two corpses in ('Uthmān's) house to be taken out." (Kinānah) spoke to (the other rebels) about this, but they refused. He said, "I am a protected neighbor of the members of 'Uthmān's clan living in Egypt and of those allied with them. Bring these two out. Throw them out!" So (the two corpses) were dragged by their feet and thrown onto the pavement, where
[3050] the dogs devoured them. The two slaves who were killed on the Day of the House were called Nujayḥ and Ṣubayḥ, and their names were paramount among the slaves because of their merit and bravery. The people did not remember the name of the third slave [who had been killed in that event].

'Uthmān was not ritually washed, and was wrapped [for burial] in his garments, still bloody. Nor were his two slaves ritually washed.

It was transmitted to me in writing by al-Sarī—Shu'ayb—Sayf—Mujālid—al-Sha'bī: 'Uthmān was buried at night, and Marwān b. al-Ḥakam led the funeral prayer for him. His daughter and Nā'ilah bt. al-Farāfiṣah went out wailing behind him.

The Date of 'Uthmān's Murder

All authorities agree that he was killed in Dhū al-Ḥijjah, but they differ as to the year. Some say that he was killed on 18 Dhū al-Ḥijjah in the year 36 (7 June 657), but the great majority say that he was killed on 18 Dhū al-Ḥijjah in the year 35 (17 June 656).

(The following) was related to me by al-Ḥārith b. Muḥammad—Ibn Sa'd—Muḥammad b. 'Umar (al-Wāqidī)—Abū Bakr b. Ismā'īl b. Muḥammad b. Sa'd b. Abī Waqqāṣ—'Uthmān b. Muḥammad al-Akhnasī. It is also stated on the authority of al-Ḥārith—Ibn Sa'd—Muḥammad b. 'Umar—Abū Bakr b. 'Abdallāh b. Abī Sabrah—Ya'qūb b. Zayd—his father: 'Uthmān was killed on Friday afternoon, 18 Dhū al-Ḥijjah, in the year 36. His caliphate lasted for twelve years, less twelve days, and he was eighty-two years old.

[3051] According to Abū Bakr—Muṣ'ab b. 'Abdallāh: 'Uthmān was killed on Friday afternoon, 18 Dhū al-Ḥijjah, in the year 36.

According to others, he was killed on 18 Dhū al-Ḥijjah in the year 35.

It was related to me by Ja'far b. 'Abdallāh (al-Muḥammadī)—'Amr b. Ḥammād and 'Alī—Ḥusayn[454]—his father—al-Mujālid b. Sa'īd al-Hamdānī—'Āmir al-Sha'bī: 'Uthmān was besieged in the house for twenty-two nights, and he was killed early on the morning of 18 Dhū al-Ḥijjah, in the year 25 dating from the death of the Messenger of God.

It was related to me by Aḥmad b. Thābit al-Rāzī—one who related it to him—Isḥāq b. 'Īsā—Abū Ma'shar: 'Uthmān was killed on Friday, 18 Dhū al-Ḥijjah, in the year 35. His caliphate lasted twelve years, less twelve days.

It was transmitted to me in writing by al-Sarī—Shu'ayb—Sayf—Muḥammad and Ṭalḥah and Abū Ḥārithah and Abū 'Uthmān: 'Uthmān was killed on Friday, 18 Dhū al-Ḥijjah in the year 35, at precisely eleven years, eleven months, and twenty-three days since the assassination of 'Umar.

According to Zakariyā' b. 'Adī—'Ubaydallāh b. 'Amr—Ibn 'Aqīl: 'Uthmān was killed in the year 35.

It was transmitted to me in writing by al-Sarī—Shu'ayb—Sayf—Abū Ḥārithah and Abū 'Uthmān and Muḥammad and Ṭalḥah: 'Uthmān was killed on Friday, 18 Dhū al-Ḥijjah, in the last [3052]
hour [before sunset].

According to others, he was killed on Friday morning.

According to Hishām b. al-Kalbī: 'Uthmān was killed on Friday morning, 18 Dhū al-Ḥijjah in the year 35. His caliphate lasted twelve years less eight days.

It was related to us by al-Ḥārith (b. Muḥammad)—Ibn Sa'd—Muḥammad b. 'Umar (al-Wāqidī)—al-Ḍaḥḥāk b. 'Uthmān—Makhramah b. Sulaymān al-Wālibī: 'Uthmān was killed on Friday morning, 18 Dhū al-Ḥijjah, in the year 35.

According to others, he was killed during the *ayyām al-tashrīq*.[455]

It was related to me by Aḥmad b. Zuhayr—his father, Abū Khaythamah—Wahb b. Jarīr—his father—Yūnus b. Yazīd al-Aylī—al-Zuhrī: Some authorities claim that 'Uthmān was killed during the *ayyām al-tashrīq*, while others state that he was killed on Friday, 18 Dhū al-Ḥijjah.

---

454. See above, note 448.
455. On the *ayyām al-tashrīq* (11–13 Dhū al-Ḥijjah), see above, note 355.

'Uthmān's Life Span

The early scholars (*al-salaf*) who preceded us differ on this, some saying that he lived eighty-two years.

[3053] It was related to me by al-Ḥārith—Ibn Sa'd—Muḥammad b. 'Umar (al-Wāqidī): When 'Uthmān was killed, he was eighty-two years old.

According to Muḥammad b. 'Umar—al-Ḍaḥḥāk b. 'Uthmān—Makhramah b. Sulaymān al-Wālibī: 'Uthmān was killed at the age of eighty-two.

According to Muḥammad (b. 'Umar)—Sa'd b. Rāshid—Ṣāliḥ b. Kaysān: 'Uthmān was killed when he was eighty-two years and some months old.

Others state that he was ninety or eighty-nine.

According to al-Ḥasan b. Mūsā al-Ashyab—Abū Hilāl—Qatādah: 'Uthmān was killed at the age of eighty-nine or ninety.

Others state that he was killed when he was seventy-five, and this figure is given on the authority of Hishām b. Muḥammad (b. Sā'ib al-Kalbī).

According to some authorities, he was killed at the age of sixty-three; this statement is linked by Sayf b. 'Umar to a body of informants. It was transmitted to me in writing by al-Sarī—Shu'ayb—Sayf—Abū Ḥārithah and Abū 'Uthmān and Muḥammad and Ṭalḥah: 'Uthmān was killed when he was sixty-three years old.

According to others, he was killed at the age of eighty-six.

It was related to me by Muḥammad b. Mūsā al-Ḥarashī—
[3054] Mu'ādh b. Hishām—his father—Qatādah: 'Uthmān was killed when he was eighty-six.

'Uthmān's Personal Appearance

It was related to me by Ziyād b. Ayyūb—Hushaym—Abū al-Miqdām—al-Ḥasan b. Abī al-Ḥasan: I entered the mosque and saw 'Uthmān reclining on his cloak. I looked closely at him. He possessed a handsome face, though it had pockmarks left by smallpox, and his arms were covered with hair.

It was related to me by al-Ḥārith (b. Muḥammad)—Ibn Sa'd—Muḥammad b. 'Umar (al-Wāqidī): I asked 'Amr b. 'Abdallāh b.

ʿAnbasah and ʿUrwah b. Khālid b. ʿAbdallāh b. ʿAmr b. ʿUthmān and ʿAbd al-Raḥmān b. Abī al-Zinād about ʿUthmān's personal appearance, and I discerned no difference of opinion among them. According to them, he was a man neither short nor tall, with a handsome face and fine skin. He had a full beard, reddish-brown in color. He was strong-boned and broad-shouldered. He possessed a thick head of hair, and used to saffron his beard.

It was related to me by Aḥmad b. Zuhayr—his father—Wahb b. Jarīr b. Ḥāzim—his father—Yūnus b. Yazīd al-Aylī—al-Zuhrī: ʿUthmān was a man of medium stature, with much hair and a handsome face. He was bald on the front, and walked bowlegged.

The Date of His Conversion to Islam and of His Seeking Refuge

It was related to me by al-Ḥārith—Ibn Saʿd—Muḥammad b. ʿUmar: ʿUthmān's conversion to Islam was of long-standing, having taken place before the Messenger of God entered the house of al-Arqam. He was among those who left Mecca and sought refuge in Abyssinia, both the first and second time. He was accompanied on both occasions by his wife Ruqayyah, the daughter of the Messenger of God.[456] [3055]

The Kunyah of ʿUthmān b. ʿAffān

It was related to me by al-Ḥārith b. Muḥammad—Ibn Saʿd—Muḥammad b. ʿUmar (al-Wāqidī): In the Time of Ignorance, ʿUthmān b. ʿAffān bore the *kunyah* Abū ʿAmr. But after the coming of Islam, a son was borne to him by Ruqayyah, the daughter of the Messenger of God, and he named him ʿAbdallāh. He took his *kunyah* from him, and the Muslims now called him Abū ʿAbdallāh. ʿAbdallāh was six years old when a rooster pecked him on the eye, and he fell ill and died in Jumādā I in the year 4 of the Hijrah (October–November 625). The Messenger of God led the funeral prayer for him, and ʿUthmān placed (his body) in the grave.

456. On these events see Watt, *Muhammad at Mecca*, pp. 109–17.

'Uthmān's Lineage

He is 'Uthmān b. 'Affān b. Abī al-'Āṣ b. Umayyah b. 'Abd Shams b. 'Abd Manāf b. Quṣayy. His mother is Arwā bt. Kurayz b. Rabī'ah b. Ḥabīb b. 'Abd Shams b. 'Abd Manāf b. Quṣayy; her mother in turn was Umm Ḥakīm bt. 'Abd al-Muṭṭalib.

His Children and Wives

1. Ruqayyah and Umm Kulthūm, both daughters of the Messenger of God. Ruqayyah bore him 'Abdallāh.

[3056] 2. Fākhitah bt. Ghazwān b. Jābir b. Nusayb b. Wuhayb b. Zayd b. Mālik b. 'Abd [sic] b. 'Awf b. al-Ḥārith b. Māzin b. Manṣūr b. 'Ikrimah b. Khaṣafah b. Qays b. 'Aylān b. Muḍar. She bore him a son and he named him 'Abdallah—that is, 'Abdallāh the Younger (*al-Aṣghar*), who died at an early age.

3. Umm 'Amr bt. Jundab b. 'Amr b. Ḥumamah b. al-Ḥārith b. Rifā'ah b. Sa'd b. Tha'labah b. Lu'ayy b. 'Āmir b. Ghanm b. Duhmān b. Munhib b. Daws, of [the tribe of] Azd. She bore him 'Amr, Khālid, Abān, 'Umar, and Maryam.

4. Fāṭimah bt. al-Walīd b. 'Abd Shams b. al-Mughīrah b. 'Abdallāh b. 'Umar b. Makhzūm. She bore him al-Walīd, Sa'īd, and Umm Sa'īd.

5. Umm al-Banīn bt. 'Uyaynah b. Ḥiṣn b. Ḥudhayfah b. Badr al-Fazārī. She bore him 'Abd al-Malik, who died at an early age.

6. Ramlah bt. Shaybah b. Rabī'ah b. 'Abd Shams b. 'Abd Manāf b. Quṣayy. She bore him 'Ā'ishah, Umm Abān, and Umm 'Amr.

7. Nā'ilah bt. al-Farāfiṣah b. al-Aḥwaṣ b. 'Amr b. Tha'labah b. al-Ḥārith b. Ḥiṣn b. Ḍamḍam b. 'Adī b. Janāb b. Kalb. She bore him Maryam.

According to Hishām b. al-Kalbī: Umm al-Banīn bt. 'Uyaynah b. Ḥiṣn bore 'Abd al-Malik and 'Utbah to 'Uthmān. Likewise, Nā'ilah bore 'Anbasah.

According to al-Wāqidī: By Nā'ilah, 'Uthmān had a daughter
[3057] named Umm al-Banīn. She is the one who was married to 'Abdallāh b. Yazīd b. Abī Sufyān. When 'Uthmān was killed, [his wives] Ramlah bt. Shaybah, Nā'ilah, Umm al-Banīn bt. 'Uyaynah, and Fākhitah bt. Ghazwān were all living in his household. However,

ʿAlī b. Muḥammad (al-Madāʾinī) claims that he had divorced Umm al-Banīn even while he lay besieged.

These are the wives whom he took, both in the Time of Ignorance and in Islam, and his male and female children.

The Names of ʿUthmān's Provincial Governors during This Year

According to Muḥammad b. ʿUmar (al-Wāqidī)—ʿAbd al-Raḥmān b. Abī al-Zinād: When ʿUthmān was killed, his provincial governors were as follows:

1. in Mecca, ʿAbdallāh b. al-Ḥaḍramī;
2. in al-Ṭāʾif, al-Qāsim b. Rabīʿah al-Thaqafī;
3. in Ṣanʿāʾ, Yaʿlā b. Munyah;
4. in al-Janad, ʿAbdallāh b. Abī Rabīʿah;[457]
5. in Baṣrah, ʿAbdallāh b. ʿĀmir b. Kurayz—he had left his post, but ʿUthmān had appointed no one to replace him;
6. in Kūfah, Saʿīd b. al-ʿĀṣ—he had been driven out and was not permitted to reenter the city;
7. in Egypt, ʿAbdallāh b. Saʿd b. Abī Sarḥ—when he came to [consult with] ʿUthmān, Muḥammad b. Abī Ḥudhayfah had usurped power there; ʿAbdallāh b. Saʿd had named al-Sāʾib b. Hishām b. ʿAmr al-ʿĀmirī as his deputy in Egypt, but Muḥammad b. Abī Ḥudhayfah drove him out;
8. in Syria, Muʿāwiyah b. Abī Sufyān.

It was transmitted to me in writing by al-Sarī—Shuʿayb—Sayf—Abū Ḥārithah and Abū ʿUthmān: When ʿUthmān died, Muʿāwiyah held authority in Syria. Muʿāwiyah's lieutenants were as follows: in Ḥimṣ, ʿAbd al-Raḥmān b. Khālid b. al-Walīd; in Qinnasrīn, Ḥabīb b. Maslamah; in Transjordan, Abū al-Aʿwar b. Sufyān; in Palestine, ʿAlqamah b. Ḥakīm al-Kinānī; in command [3058] of naval forces (*ʿalā al-baḥr*), ʿAbdallāh b. Qays al-Fazārī; in charge of justice, Abū al-Dardāʾ.

457. Instead of "b. Rabīʿah"; see de Goeje, *Introductio*, dcxxx.

It was transmitted to me in writing by al-Sarī—Shu'ayb—Sayf—'Aṭiyyah: When 'Uthmān died, his officials in Kūfah were as follows: in charge of public worship was Abū Mūsā (al-Ash'arī); in charge of tax revenues from the Sawād were Jābir b. 'Amr al-Muzanī[458]—who was also superintendant of the dike (*ṣāḥib al-musannāt*) beside Kūfah—and Simāk al-Anṣārī; in command of the army was al-Qa'qā' b. 'Amr. [The subgovernors of the districts attached to Kūfah were as follows:]

1. in Qarqīsiyā', Jarīr b. 'Abdallāh;
2. in Ādharbayjān, al-Ash'ath b. Qays;
3. in Ḥulwān, 'Utaybah b. al-Nahhās;
4. in Māh, Mālik b. Ḥabīb;
5. in Hamadan, al-Nusayr;
6. in al-Rayy, Sa'īd b. Qays;
7. in Iṣfahān, al-Sā'ib b. al-Aqra';
8. in Māsabadhān, Ḥubaysh;[459]

The public treasury was under 'Uqbah b. 'Amr, and at the time of 'Uthmān's death, Zayd b. Thābit executed justice on his behalf.

Citations from 'Uthmān's Sermons

It was transmitted to me in writing by al-Sarī—Shu'ayb—Sayf—al-Qāsim b. Muḥammad—'Awn b. 'Abdallāh b. 'Utbah:[460] After the oath of allegiance had been rendered to him, 'Uthmān preached to the people in these words: "To proceed: I have been burdened [with a heavy load], and I have accepted it. Verily I will be a follower, not an innovator. Verily, you may demand three things from me, beyond [obedience to] the Book of Almighty God and the way (*sunnah*) established by His prophet. [First,] that I follow those who preceded me in matters that you have agreed upon and established. [Second,] that I adhere to the path laid out by pious and virtuous men (*ahl al-khayr*) in matters that you have

458. Instead of Jābir b. Fulān; see de Goeje, *Introductio*, dcxxx.
459. Māsabadhān (Middle Persian, Masptan) is a district in the central Zagros mountains about 300 km. northeast of Kūfah. See Morony, *Iraq after the Muslim Conquest*, 127, 142, 154.
460. Instead of *'an 'Utbah*; see de Goeje, *Introductio*, dcxxx.

not established by general consensus. [Third,] that I avoid coercion against you save in cases where you have deemed it necessary. Verily, this world is a verdant meadow that has been made [3059] to seem desirable to the people and toward which many among them incline. Do not rely on this world and put no trust in it, for it is not a thing to be trusted. Know that it leaves nothing behind save him who has left it behind."

It was transmitted to me in writing by al-Sarī—Shuʿayb—Sayf—Badr b. ʿUthmān—his paternal uncle: The last sermon that ʿUthmān preached before an assembled congregation was [as follows]: "Almighty God has given you this world only so that you may seek thereby the world to come. He did not give it to you that you should rely upon it. Verily this world perishes, while the world to come endures, so be certain that things perishable do not make you heedless or distract you from things everlasting. Prefer that which endures to that which passes away, for this world will be cut off and [our] journey is toward God. Fear Almighty God, for the fear of Him is a shield against his terrible power and a means of access to Him. Beware of the Divine wrath. Adhere to your community (*jamāʿah*); do not divide into hostile sects. 'Remember God's blessing upon you when you were enemies, and He brought your hearts together, so that by His blessing you became brothers.'"[461]

Those Who Led the People in Prayer in the Mosque of the Messenger of God while ʿUthmān Was under Siege

According to Muḥammad b. ʿUmar (al-Wāqidī)—Rabīʿah b. ʿUthmān: The muezzin Saʿd al-Qaraẓ came to ʿAlī b. Abī Ṭālib on that day and asked, "Who will lead the people in prayer?" ʿAlī responded, "Summon Khālid b. Zayd." (Saʿd) did so, and Khālid b. Zayd led the people in prayer. That was the first day it was known that the name of Abū Ayyūb al-Anṣārī was Khālid b. Zayd.[462] He led them in prayer for some days, then ʿAlī took over this office thereafter.

461. Qur'ān 3:98.
462. I follow the fuller reading in Ibn al-Athīr, *Kāmil* (Beirut), III, 187.

[3060] According to Muḥammad (al-Wāqidī)—ʿAbd al-Raḥmān b. ʿAbd al-ʿAzīz—ʿAbdallāh b. Abī Bakr b. Ḥazm: The muezzin came to ʿUthmān and called him to the prayer. But (ʿUthmān) said, "I am not coming out to pray. Go to someone who is." The muezzin came to ʿAlī, and he commanded Sahl b. Ḥunayf [to lead the prayer]. (Sahl) thus led the prayer on the day when the final siege of ʿUthmān commenced. This was the night on which the new moon [signaling the beginning of Dhū al-Ḥijjah] was sighted. (Sahl) led them in prayer until the Feast of Sacrifice,[463] when ʿAlī led the festival prayer. Then he [continued to] lead them in prayer until (ʿUthmān) was killed.

According to (al-Wāqidī)—ʿAbdallāh b. Nāfiʿ—his father—Ibn ʿUmar: When ʿUthmān was besieged, Abū Ayyūb led the people in prayer for some days, then ʿAlī led them in the Friday and festival prayers until (ʿUthmān) was killed.

The Threnodies Composed for ʿUthmān

After his murder the poets spoke about him—some in praise, some in derision, some in tearful lamentation, some in gleeful joy. Those who lauded him included Ḥassān b. Thābit al-Anṣārī, Kaʿb b. Mālik al-Anṣārī, and Tamīm b. Ubayy b. Muqbil, as well as others.

Ḥassān praised and lamented him and derided his murderer, in these words:

Have you abandoned your campaigns on the roads [leading to the frontier]?
    And do you now make war against us at Muḥammad's grave?
How evil the guidance which you give the Muslims!
[3061]   How evil the willful sinner's command!
If you advance [against us], we shall make
    the hospitality all mild and gentle offered to your chiefs around Medina, into a spear.
Or if you turn back, what an evil thing is the purpose for which you have traveled [here];

463. That is, 10 Dhū al-Ḥijjah.

the like of your amir's command was ill guided.
It is as though the Prophet's Companions were fattened
animals
to be slaughtered at eventide by the mosque gate.
I weep for Abū ʿAmr as befits his virtuous conduct;
he has made his dwelling in Baqīʿ al-Gharqad.

He also says:

If the house of Ibn Arwā stands desolate—
one door beaten down, another burnt and shattered—
Then he who seeks the good may encounter what he desires
therein, and fame and good repute may strive [to enter] it.
O people, display your true selves!
For sincerity and falsehood are not equal in God's sight.
Uphold the rights of the people's lord, and you will learn of [3062]
bands of horsemen [coming to your aid], and behind them
yet other bands.
Leading them is Ḥabīb,[464] the meteor of death,
wearing a breastplate, with anger displayed upon his face.

(Ḥassān) composed many verses about (ʿUthmān). Kaʿb b. Mālik al-Anṣārī spoke in these words:

Woe, O men, for thy life, robbed by force [from thee, ʿUthmān],
and for thine overflowing tears, now dry!
Alas for a fearful thing which has befallen me,
which has crushed the mountains, so that in vast
convulsions they have fallen.
The caliph's murder was a thing atrocious;
a terrifying calamity has arisen thereby.
Before the murder of the Imām the very stars bow down;
and because of it the sun is in eclipse.
Ah, how grief burdened my soul, when at early morn
they hoisted the bier onto their shoulders.

---

464. Instead of *khabīth,* "a vicious man," in accordance with Ibrāhīm's text (IV, 424, n. 5). Ibrāhīm explains this as an allusion to Ḥabīb b. Maslamah al-Fihrī, placed by Muʿāwiyah in command of the Syrian troops whom he had dispatched (too little and too late) to aid ʿUthmān.

They brought their brother and lowered him into the grave.
 What does his grave, covered over, conceal—
What benefit, what sovereignty and sense of duty,
 wherein he led the way among the people, what meritorious deed?
How many an orphan did he support;[465]
 the wretched would visit his house time and again.
Without cease he would receive them and mend their wrongs,
 until I heard the sound of anxious sighing.
He has made his dwelling in al-Baqīʿ, and (his assassins)
 have scattered, resolved to flee.
The Fire is their rendezvous for having murdered their Imam,
 honest ʿUthmān, in his palace.[466]
To dignified forbearance he added duty,
 and the good in him was manifest and known to all.
[3063] O Kaʿb, cease not to weep for a lord,
 so long as you shall live and travel throughout the lands.
Even as an old man I shall mourn Abū ʿAmr,
 and lament their perverted deed, since he was no fool.
Let the horsemen mourn him as they defend [us] against calamity
 between mountain defiles and soldiers in serried ranks.
They have murdered you, ʿUthmān—by thy life,
 the murder of a man undefiled [by sin], in the shelter [of his own home].

Ḥassān composed these lines:

He whom death gladdens with unmixed joy,
 let him come into a den of savage lions[467] in the house of ʿUthmān—
[Let him come against] men clad in iron mail, wearing
 helmets fitted with nose guards to adorn their bodies.
By patience you will be redeemed, O my mother and (the children) whom she bore.

465. Lit., "Of how many an orphan would he set the bones."
466. See de Goeje (*Introductio*, dcxxx), who suggests *al-balāṭ* in place of *al-tilād* (text) or *al-bilād* (ms.).
467. The lions are ʿUthmān's assassins.

Patient suffering in the face of something hateful may at
times bring [us] benefit.
We were well-pleased with the Syrians as they made haste [to
aid us],
and with the amir [Muʿāwiyah] and [our] brothers.
Verily I will be among them, whether they are absent or
present.
So long as I live and am called Ḥassān,
Very soon you will hear in their lands,
"God is most great! Vengeance for ʿUthmān!" [3064]
Would that I knew, would that the birds would inform me,
what went on between ʿAlī and Ibn ʿAffān.

Al-Walīd b. ʿUqbah b. Abī Muʿayṭ spoke these words in urging on ʿUmārah b. ʿUqbah:[468]

Yea, the best of men save three[469]
has been killed by al-Tujībī, who came from Egypt.
If my opinion of my mother's son is sound,
ʿUmārah will not seek vengeance.
He will pass the night, mulling revenge for Ibn ʿAffān,
encamped between Khawarnaq and the Castle.[470]

To this al-Faḍl b. ʿAbbās added the following verses: [3065]

Do you seek a vengeance to which you have no right?
What is Ibn Dhakwān al-Ṣafūrī next to ʿAmr?"[471]
Just as the ass's foal claims descent from her mother (the horse)
and forgets her father (the ass) when she vies with those
possessing rightful pride.
Verily the best of men after Muḥammad [i.e., ʿAlī], is

---

468. Al-Walīd had been ʿUthmān's governor in Kūfah; ʿUmārah is his reluctant brother. Al-Walīd and ʿUthmān were half-brothers, since both had the same mother; it is this fact that gives the second line in the following poem its sting.

469. That is, Muḥammad, Abū Bakr, and ʿUmar.

470. Khawarnaq was a famous, almost legendary palace near al-Ḥīrah erected for Bahram Gur (420–438) by the Lakhmid king al-Nuʿmān al-Aʿwar. Presumably the "Castle" (*al-qaṣr*) refers to another such palace (perhaps the one named Sadīr) in al-Ḥīrah. See L. Massignon, "Khawarnaḳ," *EI*², IV, 1133.

471. The point of this line is a bit obscure. ʿAmr was ʿUthmān's eldest son (born before he became a Muslim). Ibn Dhakwān seems to have been a son of ʿUthmān's half-brother al-Walīd b. ʿUqbah by a Jewish woman from Sepphoris (al-Ṣaf-

the executor of the Chosen Prophet
in the sight of God,
The first who prayed, the twin to His prophet,
and the first to strike down the sinners at Badr.
Had the Helpers seen wrong done to your cousin,
they would have brought him aid against his wrong.
It is shame enough [for him] that they advised his death
and surrendered him to the Egyptian mobs.

Al-Ḥubāb b. Yazīd al-Mujāshiʿ, the paternal uncle of al-Farazdaq,[472] spoke these words:

By my father's life, you must not mourn.
The best man, save only a few, has perished.
The people have become fools in their religion,
and behind him Ibn ʿAffān has left enduring evil.
You who reproach [him]: every man perishes,
so follow the path of virtue to God.

---

fūriyyah], a village near Nazareth. A man of such dubious descent could hardly claim to be the avenger of his lineage.

472. The famous Umayyad court poet, d. ca. 110/728. See R. Blachère, "al-Farazdaḳ," *EI*², II, 788–89.

Bibliography of Cited Works

Abbott, Nabia. *Studies in Arabic Literary Papyri.* I: *Historical Texts.* Oriental Institute Publications, LXXV. Chicago: University of Chicago Press, 1957.

Ahsan, M. M. *Social Life under the Abbasids.* London and New York: Longmans, 1979.

al-Balādhurī, Aḥmad b. Yaḥyā. *Ansāb al-Ashrāf.* Vol. V. Edited by S. D. Goitein. Jerusalem: Hebrew University Press, 1936.

———. *Futūḥ al-Buldān.* Edited by M. J. de Goeje. Leiden: E. J. Brill, 1866. Translated by P. K. Hitti and F. Murgotten as *The Origins of the Islamic State.* Columbia University Publications in History, Economics, and Public Law. Vol. LXVIII, nos. 163–163a. New York: 1916–1924.

Barthold, W. *An Historical Geography of Iran.* Translated by Svat Soucek. Princeton: Princeton University Press, 1984.

———. *Turkestan down to the Mongol Invasion.* E. J. W. Gibb Memorial Series, N. S. 5. 3rd ed. Edited by C. E. Bosworth. London: Luzac, 1968.

Biberstein Kazimirski, A. de. *Dictionnaire arabe-français.* 2 vols. Paris: Maisonneuve, 1860.

Bosworth, C. E. "The Concept of Dhimma in Early Islam." In *Christians and Jews in the Ottoman Empire.* Edited by Benjamin Braude and Bernard Lewis. 2 vols. New York: Holmes and Meier, 1982. Vol. I, 37–51.

Brice, W. C. *An Historical Atlas of Islam.* Leiden: E. J. Brill, 1981.

Caetani, Leone. *Annali dell Islam.* 10 vols. Milan: Ulrico Hoepli, 1905–1926. Vols. VII–VIII.

Cameron, A. J. *Abū Dharr al-Ghifārī: An Examination of His Image in the Hagiography of Islam.* London: Royal Asiatic Society, 1973.

Conrad, Lawrence J. "The Plague in the Early Medieval Near East." Ph.D. Dissertation, Princeton University, 1981.
Donner, F. M. *The Early Islamic Conquests.* Princeton: Princeton University Press, 1981.
Encyclopaedia of Islam. New Edition. 6 vols. Leiden: E. J. Brill, 1954–.
Freytag, G. W. F., ed. and transl. *Arabum Proverbia.* 3 vols. in 4. Bonn: A. Marcus, 1838–1843.
Gibb, H. A. R. *The Arab Conquests in Central Asia.* London: Royal Asiatic Society, 1923.
al-Harawī, Abū al-Ḥasan ʿAlī. *Guide des lieux de pèlerinage.* Translated by Janine Sourdel-Thomine. Damascus: Institut Français de Damas, 1957.
Hawting, G. R. *The First Dynasty of Islam: The Umayyad Caliphate, A.D. 661–750.* Carbondale: Southern Illinois University Press, 1987.
Hinds, Martin. "Kûfan Political Alignments and Their Background in the Mid-Seventh Century A.D." *International Journal of Middle East Studies,* II (1971), 346–67.
———. "The Murder of the Caliph ʿUthmān." *International Journal of Middle East Studies,* III (1972), 450–69.
———. "Sayf b. ʿUmar's Sources on Arabia." in *Studies in the History of Arabia,* I, part 2. Riyad: Riyad University Press, 1979. Pp. 3–16.
———. "The Siffin Arbitration Agreement." *Journal of Semitic Studies,* XVII (1972), 93–129.
Hinz, Walther. *Islamische Masse und Gewichte, umgerechnet ins metrische System.* In *Handbuch der Orientalistik,* Ergänzungsband I, 1955; 2nd ed., 1970.
Humphreys, R. S. *Islamic History: A Framework for Inquiry.* Minneapolis: Bibliotheca Islamica, 1988.
Ibn al-Athīr, ʿIzz al-Dīn ʿAlī. *al-Kāmil fī al-Taʾrīkh.* 13 vols. Beirut: Dār Sader and Dār Beyrouth, 1965–1967.
Ibn Isḥāq, Muḥammad. *Sīrat Rasūl Allāh.* Edited by F. Wüstenfeld. 2 vols. Göttingen: Dieterichsche Buchhandlung, 1858–1860. Translated by Alfred Guillaume as *The Life of Muhammad.* London: Oxford University Press, 1955.
Juynboll, G. H. A. *Muslim Tradition: Studies in Chronology, Provenance and Authorship of Early Hadith.* Cambridge: Cambridge University Press, 1983.
Lane, E. W. *An Arabic-English Lexicon.* One volume in 8 parts. London and Edinburgh: Williams and Norgate, 1863–1893.
Le Strange, Guy. *The Lands of the Eastern Caliphate.* Cambridge: Cambridge University Press, 1905.

———. *Palestine under the Moslems.* London: Palestine Exploration Fund, 1890.

al-Masʿūdī, ʿAlī b. al-Ḥusayn. *Murūj al-Dhahab wa-Maʿādin al-Jawhar.* Edited and translated by C. Barbier de Meynard and Pavet de Courteille as *Les prairies d'or;* revised by Charles Pellat. 7 vols. Beirut: al-Jāmiʿah al-Lubnāniyyah, 1965–1979.

Morony, Michael G. *Iraq after the Muslim Conquest.* Princeton: Princeton University Press, 1984.

Noth, Albrecht. *Quellenkritische Studien zu Themen, Formen, und Tendenzen frühislamischen Geschichtsüberlieferung.* Bonn: Selbstverlag der Universität Bonn, 1973.

Ostrogorsky, George. *History of the Byzantine State.* Translated by Joan Hussey. 2nd ed. New Brunswick, N.J.: Rutgers University Press, 1969.

Petersen, E. L. "ʿAlī and Muʿāwiya: the Rise of the Umayyad Caliphate, 656–661." *Acta Orientalia,* XXIII (1959), 157–96.

———. *ʿAlī and Muʿāwiya in Early Arabic Tradition: Studies on the Genesis and Growth of Islamic Historical Writing until the End of the Ninth Century.* Copenhagen: Munksgaard, 1964.

al-Qadi, Wadad. "The Development of the Term *Ghulāt* in Muslim Literature with Special reference to the Kaysaniyya." *Akten des VII Kongresses für Arabistik und Islamwissenschaften.* Göttingen, 1976. Pp. 295–319.

al-Qur'an. Translated by A. J. Arberry as *The Koran Interpreted.* 2 vols. London: George Allen and Unwin, 1955.

Rotter, Gernot. *Die Umayyaden und der zweite Bürgerkrieg (680–692).* Wiesbaden: F. Steiner for the Deutsche Morgenländische Gesellschaft, 1982.

Sachedina, Abdulaziz. *Islamic Messianism: The Idea of the Mahdi in Twelver Shiʿism.* Albany: State University of New York Press, 1981.

Sauvaget, Jean. *La mosquée omeyyade de Médine: Étude sur les origines architecturales de la mosquée et de la basilique.* Paris: Vanoest for the Institut Français de Damas, 1947.

Serjeant, R. B. "Ḥaram and Ḥawṭah, the Sacred Enclave in Arabia." In *Mélanges Taha Husain,* edited by A. R. Badawi. Cairo, 1962. Pp. 41–58.

———. "The *Sunnah Jāmiʿah,* Pacts with the Yathrib Jews, and the *Taḥrīm* of Yathrib. Analysis and Translation of the Documents Comprised in the So-called 'Constitution of Medina.'" *Bulletin of the School of Oriental and African Studies,* XLI (1978), 1–42.

Shaban, M. A. *The ʿAbbāsid Revolution.* Cambridge: Cambridge University Press, 1970.

———. *Islamic History, a New Interpretation.* I: *A.D.* 600–750. Cambridge: Cambridge University Press, 1971.

Shorter Encyclopaedia of Islam. Edited by H. A. R. Gibb and J. H. Kramers. Leiden: E. J. Brill, 1953.

Shoufani, Elias. *Al-Riddah and the Muslim Conquest of Arabia.* Toronto: University of Toronto Press, 1973.

Stratos, Andreas. *Byzantium in the Seventh Century.* Various translators. 5 Volumes. Amsterdam: Adolf Hakkert, 1968–1980.

Watt, W. M. *Muhammad at Mecca.* Oxford: Clarendon Press, 1953.

———. *Muhammad at Medina.* Oxford: Clarendon Press, 1956.

Wellhausen, Julius. *The Arab Kingdom and Its Fall.* Translated by M. G. Weir. Calcutta: University of Calcutta, 1927.

———. *Prolegomena zur ältesten Geschichte des Islams. Skizzen und Vorarbeiten,* VI. Berlin: Georg Reimer, 1899.

Wörterbuch der klassischen arabischen Sprache. Wiesbaden: Otto Harrassowitz, for the Deutsche Morgenländische Gesellschaft, 1957–.

Wright, William A. *A Grammar of the Arabic Language.* 3rd ed. 2 vols. Cambridge: Cambridge University Press, 1896–1898.

al-Ya'qūbī, Aḥmad b. Abī Ya'qūb. *al-Ta'rīkh.* Edited by T. H. Houtsma. 2 vols. Leiden: E. J. Brill, 1883.

Yāqūt al-Ḥamawī. *Mu'jam al-Buldān.* Edited by F. Wüstenfeld. 6 vols. Leipzig: F. A. Brockhaus for the Deutsche Morgenländische Gesellschaft, 1866–73.

Index

Included are names of persons, groups, and places, as well as Arabic words that recur often in the text or are discussed in the footnotes; the protagonist of this volume, the caliph ʿUthmān b. ʿAffān, is, however, omitted, as his name is found on almost every page. An asterisk (*) indicates one of the transmitters listed in the isnāds *preceding the reports or a medieval historian cited in the footnotes. When part of a name is given in parentheses, the enclosed segment has been supplied from sources other than the present text. Entries that are mentioned in both text and footnotes on the same page are listed by page number only. Finally, the Arabic definite article* al- *and the abbreviations* b. (ibn) *and* bt. (bint) *have been disregarded in the alphabetizing of entries.*

A

Abān b. ʿUthmān b. ʿAffān 254
* ʿAbbād b. ʿAbdallāh b. al-Zubayr 186
al-ʿAbbās b. ʿAbd al-Muṭṭalib 99, 228
al-ʿAbbās b. Rabīʿah 235
ʿAbbās b. ʿUtbah b. Abī Lahab 155, 228
Abbasid dynasty 20 n. 33
ʿAbd al-Dār (clan) 220
* ʿAbd al-Majīd b. Suhayl 238–39, 246
* ʿAbd al-Malik 72
ʿAbd al-Malik b. ʿAmr b. Abī Sufyān al-Thaqafī 38
ʿAbd al-Malik b. Marwān (Umayyad caliph) 50 n. 81, 202, 233 n. 420
ʿAbd al-Malik b. ʿUmayr al-Zuhrī 137
ʿAbd al-Malik b. ʿUthmān b. ʿAffān 254
* ʿAbd al-Malik b. Yazīd b. al-Sāʾib 230
ʿAbd Manāf (section of Quraysh) 209, 247 n. 450
ʿAbd al-Muṭṭalib b. Hāshim 141 n. 251
ʿAbd al-Qays (tribe) 36, 69, 125
* ʿAbd Rabbihi b. Nāfiʿ 235
* ʿAbd al-Raḥmān b. ʿAbd al-ʿAzīz 219, 258
*ʿAbd al-Raḥmān b. Abī al-Zinād 219, 253, 255
ʿAbd al-Raḥmān b. ʿAlqamah al-Kinānī 74

'Abd al-Raḥmān b. al-Aswad b. 'Abd Yaghūth 179–80, 182
'Abd al-Raḥmān b. 'Attāb b. Asīd 174
'Abd al-Raḥmān b. 'Awf 3 n. 5, 11, 39–40, 57, 99, 182, 224
'Abd al-Raḥmān b. Ghanm 165
'Abd al-Raḥmān b. Ghubays 34
* 'Abd al-Raḥmān b. al-Ḥārith 219
'Abd al-Raḥmān b. Ḥubaysh al-Asadī 113–14, 121
'Abd al-Raḥmān b. Khālid b. al-'Āṣ 119–20
'Abd al-Raḥmān b. Khālid b. al-Walīd 119, 125, 132–33, 255
'Abd al-Raḥmān b. Muḥammad 219
'Abd al-Raḥmān b. Rabī'ah al-Bāhilī 50, 62, 95–96, 98
'Abd al-Raḥmān b. Samurah 36
* 'Abd al-Raḥmān b. Sharīk 202
'Abd al-Raḥmān b. 'Udays al-Balawī, also al-Tujībī 159, 172, 175, 185–86, 191–94, 199, 202, 214, 247–49
* 'Abd al-Raḥmān b. Yasār 184
'Abd Shams b. 'Abd Manāf (clan of Quraysh) 141 n. 251, 159 n. 282, 209 n. 368; see also Umayyah, Banū
* 'Abdallāh 152, 220
'Abdallāh b. 'Abbās 38, 42–43, 62, 66, 209, 236–38, 245–46
'Abdallāh b. Abī Awfā 164
* 'Abdallāh b. Abī Bakr b. Ḥazm 258
'Abdallāh b. Abī Rabī'ah 255
* 'Abdallāh b. Abī Sufyān 74
* 'Abdallāh b. Aḥmad b. Shabbawayh al-Marwazī 152, 220
'Abdallāh b. 'Āmir b. Kurayz 6, 33–37, 42, 69, 77, 90–93, 102, 104, 107–10, 111, 125–26, 128, 136–38, 142, 157, 173, 182, 186, 190, 198, 229, 230, 235, 255
'Abdallāh b. 'Amr b. al-'Āṣ 42–43, 171
'Abdallāh b. al-Aṣamm 159–61
'Abdallāh b. Budayl b. Warqā' al-Khuzā'ī 203
'Abdallāh b. Busrah 220
'Abdallāh b. al-Ḥaḍramī 255
* 'Abdallāh b. al-Ḥārith b. al-Fuḍayl 194, 201
* 'Abdallāh b. Idrīs 183
* 'Abdallāh b. Ja'far 99, 170, 181
'Abdallāh b. Khālid b. Asīd 15, 153
'Abdallāh b. Khāzim al-Sulamī 36–37, 91–92, 108–10
'Abdallāh b. Mas'ūd 15–17, 40, 45, 47, 50–51, 99, 100–1, 164
* 'Abdallāh b. Muḥammad 140, 172, 175
* 'Abdallāh b. Mūsā al-Makhzūmī 248
'Abdallāh b. Nāfi' b. 'Abd al-Qays al-Fihrī 19, 22
'Abdallāh b. Nāfi' b. al-Ḥuṣayn al-Fihrī 19, 22, 258
'Abdallāh b. Qays, see Abū Mūsā al-Ash'arī
'Abdallāh b. Qays al-Jāsī, also al-Fazārī 29–30, 255
'Abdallāh b. Sabā' (= Ibn al-Sawdā') xvi, 64–65, 126, 133, 145–46, 148, 154, 159, 225, 232
'Abdallāh b. Sa'd b. Abī Sarḥ 12, 18–20, 22–24, 31, 74–77, 111, 136–38, 148–50, 157, 164, 170, 172, 182, 184, 193–94, 198–99, 220, 255
* 'Abdallāh b. al-Sā'ib 230
* 'Abdallāh b. Sa'īd b. Thābit 46, 227, 228
* 'Abdallāh b. Sā'idah 248
'Abdallāh b. Salām 215
'Abdallāh b. Shubayl b. 'Awf al-Aḥmasī 8–9
'Abdallāh b. 'Ukaym 16, 164
'Abdallāh b. 'Umar b. al-Khaṭṭāb 42–43, 147, 149–50, 258
* 'Abdallāh b. 'Umayr al-Ashja'ī 140
'Abdallāh b. 'Umayr al-Laythī 34
'Abdallāh b. 'Uthmān, al-Aṣghar 254

'Abdallāh b. 'Uthmān b. 'Affān 253
'Abdallāh b. Yazīd b. Abī Sufyān 254
* 'Abdallāh b. Yazīd al-Hudhalī 248
'Abdallāh b. Zayd b. 'Abd Rabbih 99
'Abdallāh b. al-Zubayr 42–43, 161, 204, 207, 211–12, 218
Abīward 90, 92
Abraham, lineage of 127
al-Abrash, chamberlain of the caliph Hishām 21
Abrashahr 42, 90–92, 111; see also Nishapur
Abraz 93; see also Barāz; Māhawayh
Abū 'Abs b. Jābir 144
* Abū 'Amr 166
Abū 'Aqīl, daughter of 53–54
* Abū al-'Arīf 54
Abū al-'Āṣ, Banū (clan of the Banū Umayyah) 158
* Abū al-Ashhab al-Sa'dī 105
Abū al-A'war b. Sufyān al-Sulamī 184, 255
* Abū 'Awn, *mawlā* of al-Miswar b. Makhramah 170, 219, 220
Abū Ayyūb al-Anṣārī 257–58
Abū al-Bakhtarī al-Ṭā'ī 139
* Abū Bakr 250
* Abū Bakr b. 'Abdallāh b. Abī Sabrah 1, 250
* Abū Bakr b. 'Abdallāh b. Abī Uways 249
Abū Bakr b. Abī Quḥāfah (first caliph) 38–39, 63, 77, 118, 141, 157, 163, 178, 183, 205, 227, 238
* Abū Bakr al-Bakrī 235
* Abū Bakr b. al-Ḥārith b. Hishām 202
* Abū Bakr al-Hudhalī 36–37
* Abū Bakr b. Ismā'īl b. Muḥammad b. Sa'd b. Abī Waqqāṣ 1, 120, 182, 250
Abū Barāz, see Māhawayh
* Abū Bashīr al-'Ābidī 246
Abū al-Dardā' al-Khazrajī 25, 31, 65, 165, 255
Abū Dharr al-Ghifārī 25, 64–68, 100–1
* Abū al-Dhayyāl Zuhayr b. Hunayd al-'Adawī 92–93
* Abū Ghassān Sakan b. 'Abd al-Raḥmān b. Ḥubaysh 52
* Abū Ḥabībah 183, 197
* Abū Ḥafṣ al-Azdī 92
Abū Ḥafṣah al-Yamānī 200–1
* Abū Ḥārithāh (Muḥriz al-'Abshamī) 18, 26, 27–28, 30, 72–73, 128, 151, 159, 166, 206–7, 210, 213, 249, 251–52, 255
Abū Ḥayyah al-Māzinī 248
* Abū Hilāl 252
Abū Hurayrah 96, 166, 213
* Abū Isḥāq al-Hamdānī 125
Abū Jahm b. Ḥudhayfah al-'Adawī 174, 247–48
Abū Karib al-Hamdānī 218, 247
* Abū Khalaf 'Abdallāh b. 'Īsā al-Khazzāz 62
* Abū al-Khayr Marthad b. 'Abdallāh al-Yazanī 198
* Abū Khaythamah 251
Abū Khushshah al-Ghifārī 52, 57
* Abū Kibrān 55
* Abū Manṣūr 4
* Abū Ma'shar 2, 11, 12, 14, 18, 25, 37, 41, 71, 94, 111–12, 130, 131, 145, 236, 251
* Abū Maymūnah 246
* Abū Mikhnaf, Lūṭ b. Yaḥyā 8, 9, 10, 91, 95 n. 166
* Abū al-Miqdām 69–70, 223, 252
Abū Mufazzir al-Tamīmī 97, 101
* Abū al-Mujālid Jarād b. 'Amr 26, 27, 72
Abū Mūsā al-Ash'arī 5, 33–37, 135, 139–40, 154, 243, 256
Abū Muṣ'ab b. Jaththāmah 57
Abū Muslim al-Khawlānī 165
* Abū al-Mu'tamir 205
Abū Muwarri' b. Fulān al-Asadī 49, 52–54, 232
* Abū Naḍrah 167–68, 204
Abū Rāfi' al-Muzanī 102
* Abū Sa'īd 31, 46

* Abū Sa'īd, *mawlā* of Abū Usayd al-Anṣārī 167–68, 204–6
Abū al-Ṣalt b. Kanārā 91
Abū Sammāl al-Asadī 47–48
* Abū al-Sarī al-Marwazī 92
Abū Shurayḥ al-Khuzā'ī 46
Abū Sufyān b. Ḥarb 73, 77, 122, 138 n. 246
Abū Ṭalḥah 100
Abū Thawr al-Ḥadā'ī 139
* Abū 'Ubaydah al-Iyādī 54
Abū 'Ubaydah b. al-Jarrāḥ 72, 73 n. 126
Abū Umāmah 165
Abū Usayd al-Sā'idī 141, 174
* Abū 'Uthmān (Yazīd b. Asīd al-Ghassānī) 18, 26, 27, 30, 72, 73, 128, 151, 159, 166, 206–7, 210–11, 213, 249, 251–52, 255
* Abū Yaḥyā 'Umayr b. Sa'd al-Nakha'ī 139
Abū Zaynab b. 'Awf al-Azdī 49, 52–54, 232
Abū Zubayd 48–49
Abyssinia 253
Adham b. Muḥriz 234
Ādharbayjān 8, 62, 132, 256
al-'Adī, Banū (tribe) 92, 144, 202
'Adī b. Suhayl b. 'Adī 34
'Affān b. Abī al-'Āṣ (father of 'Uthmān) 170
Africa Proconsularis 12 n. 21, 74; see also Ifrīqiyah
'ahd 111, 218, 240, 244–45
aḥdāth 136, 189
Aḥjār al-Zayt (locale near Medina) 161
ahl 2 n. 3
ahl al-ayyām 112
ahl al-qiblah 139
ahl al-sābiqah wa'l-qudmah 57–58
* Aḥmad b. Ibrāhīm 183
* Aḥmad b. Thābit al-Rāzī 2, 12, 18, 25, 37, 41, 71, 94, 111, 131, 145, 236, 251
* Aḥmad b. 'Uthmān b. Ḥakīm 202
* Aḥmad b. Zuhayr 251, 253
al-Aḥnaf b. Qays 36, 70, 90–91, 102–7, 111
al-Ahwāz 34, 89
'A'ishah bt. Abī Bakr 141 n. 251, 208–9, 238
'A'ishah bt. 'Uthmān b. 'Affān 254
al-Ajall 19–20
'Ajlā, mother of 'Abdallāh b. Khāzim 37
al-'Ajlān 171
'Ajrūd 172
* al-'Alā' b. 'Abdallāh b. Zayd al-'Anbarī 135
al-'Alā' b. al-Ḥaḍramī 27
a'lām 147
Alexandria 12
'Alī b. Abī Ṭālib 3 n. 5, 28, 37, 38, 54–55, 109 n. 188, 141–43, 146, 150–52, 160–62, 169, 173–76, 178–81, 187–88, 192–94, 197–98, 206–9, 217, 235–39, 246, 249, 257–58, 261
* 'Alī b. Ḥusayn b. 'Īsā 135, 137, 139, 184, 186, 202, 246–47, 251
* 'Alī b. Muḥammad, see al-Madā'inī
* 'Alī b. Mujāhid 36, 42–43, 91
* 'Alī b. Sahl 30
* 'Alī b. 'Umar 176
'Alqamah b. Ḥakīm al-Kinānī 255
* 'Alqamah b. Marthad 229
'Alqamah b. Mujazziz al-Mudlifī 71 n. 122, 73
'Alqamah b. Qays al-Nakha'ī 96–98, 102, 120
'amal 72, 73, 123, 127, 135
'āmil/'ummāl 5, 6, 15, 17, 45, 73, 136, 140, 148, 170, 184
amīr/umarā' 17, 125, 126, 135, 137, 140, 146, 148, 185, 214
'Āmir b. 'Abd Qays, see 'Āmir b. 'Abdallāh
'Āmir b. 'Abdallāh al-Tamīmī al-'Anbarī 92, 126–28, 136
* 'Āmir b. Sa'd 120, 182
'Āmir b. Ṣa'ṣa'ah (tribe) 159
'āmmah/'awāmm 5, 54, 147, 154, 224

'Ammār b. Yāsir 100, 147–48, 155, 165, 173–74, 180, 228
* 'Amr b. 'Abdallāh b. 'Anbasah 252–53
* 'Amr b. Abī al-Miqdām 137
'Amr b. al-'Āṣ b. Wā'il al-Sahmī 12, 18–19, 23–24, 26–27, 73–74, 136–38, 149, 170–72, 175–76, 183, 243
'Amr b. al-Aṣamm 159
'Amr b. 'Āṣim al-Tamīmī 46
'Amr b. Budayl b. Warqā' al-Khuzā'ī 186
'Amr b. al-Ḥamiq al-Khuzā'ī 125, 191–92, 219–20
* 'Amr b. Ḥammād b. Ṭalḥah 135, 137, 139, 183–84, 186, 202, 246–47, 251
'Amr b. Ḥazm al-Anṣārī 189, 200, 204, 208, 219; see also Ḥazm
'Amr b. Ḥurayth 134–35
'Amr b. Ma'dīkarib 106
* 'Amr b. Muḥammad 3, 15, 210
* 'Amr b. Muḥammad al-Murrī 107
* 'Amr b. Murrah al-Jamalī 139
* 'Amr b. Shu'ayb 226
* 'Amr b. Umayyah al-Ḍamrī 229
'Amr b. 'Utbah b. Farqad al-Sulamī 97–98, 102
'Amr b. 'Uthmān b. 'Affān 254, 261
amṣār 3
Anas b. Mālik 165
'Anbasah b. 'Uthmān b. 'Affān 254
Anṣār, see Helpers
al-'Aqabah 198 n. 349
'Aqīl 47
'Aqīl b. Abī al-Bukayr 144
al-Aqra' b. Ḥābis 106
Arabia xiii, 61, 158
Arabs 81–84, 87, 90, 102, 115–17, 119, 156, 172, 226
'Arafah 38
Ardashīr b. Bābak (Sasanian emperor) 69 n. 117, 90
Ardashīr-Khurrah 69
al-'Arj 219
Armenia 8–10, 78
'arrādah 95
Arwā bt. Kurayz 141 n. 251, 212, 231, 234, 254, 259
al-'Āṣ, Banū (clan of the Banū Umayyah) 159
Asad, Banū (tribe) 114, 151, 233
Asad b. 'Abd al-'Uzzā (clan of Quraysh) 246
asāwirah 80, 103
al-Ash'ath 60
al-Ash'ath b. Qays 132, 256
* al-Ash'ath b. Ṣiwār 67
ashrāf xiii, 114, 125, 134, 176
al-Ashtar, see Mālik b. al-Ḥārith
al-'Āṣī b. Wā'il 171
Asīd b. al-Mutashammis 106
'Āṣim b. 'Amr 34–35
* 'Āṣim b. Kulayb 68
* 'Āṣim b. Sulaymān 7
* 'Āṣim b. 'Ubaydallāh 229
* 'Āṣim b. 'Umar b. Qatādah 72, 174
Aslam b. Aws b. Bajrah al-Sā'idī 248
Asmā' b. Khārijah 234
al-Aswad b. al-Haytham 234
al-Aswad b. Kulthūm al-'Adawī 92–93
al-Aswad b. Yazīd al-Nakha'ī 101, 114, 164
al-Aswāf (locale in Medina) 192, 199
'Ātikah bt. Qurṭah b. 'Abd 'Amr b. Nawfal b. 'Abd Manāf 94
Atil 95 n. 167
* 'Aṭiyyah (b. al-Ḥārith, Abū Rawq) 54, 64, 100, 125, 145, 148, 256
al-A'waṣ (locale near Medina) 160–62
* 'Awf al-A'rābī 33
* 'Awn b. 'Abdallāh b. 'Utbah 47, 50, 256
'Awn Abū 'Abdallāh b. 'Awn al-Faqīh 109
Aws b. Jābir al-Tamīmī al-Jushamī; see also al-Aḥnaf 90
Aws b. Maghrā' 98
Aylah 198
Azd (tribe) 45 n. 74, 109 n. 188

B

al-Bāb, see Bāb al-Abwāb
Bāb al-Abwāb 62, 94 n. 166, 95–96, 99, 132, 140
al-Babar 8
Babūnaj 92
Bādghīs 107–8
Bādhān 103
Badr, battle of 15 n. 26, 144
* Badr b. al-Khalīl b. 'Uthmān b. Quṭbah al-Asadī 151
* Badr b. 'Uthmān 3, 206, 257
Baḥrayn 27 n. 45, 37, 117
Bakr b. 'Abdallāh al-Tamīmī 101
Bakr b. Wā'il (tribe) 69
* al-Balādhurī, Aḥmad b. Yaḥyā xix–xx, 2 n. 1, 35 n. 57, 64 n. 106, 85 n. 147, 87 n. 155, 100 n. 174, 113 n. 199, 156 n. 273, 190 n. 337, 201 n. 353, 205 n. 360, 212 n. 375
Balanjar 94–95, 97, 99 n. 173
Balanjar, Day of 98
Balkh 36, 106–7
al-Balqā' 157 n. 278
al-Baqī', Baqī' al-Gharqad (cemetery in Medina) 246–49, 259–60
Barāz 83, 88
barīd 28, 162 n. 289
Baṣrah xiii, 5 n. 12, 33–35, 42, 45 n. 74, 69, 90, 92, 109–10, 112, 125–29, 145, 147, 154, 157, 162, 165, 176, 186, 199, 203, 207, 220, 226, 255
Baṭn Nakhl 38
Bā'y Bābān 87
Bayhaq 92
Berbers 19 n. 31, 20 n. 32, 22–23
bid'ah 142
Bilbays 185
Bīmand 69
Bishr b. Mutashammis 107
Bishr b. Shurayḥ al-Ḥuṭam b. Ḍubay'ah al-Qaysī 160
biṭānah 182, 185
Bosphorus 94
al-Buḥayrah 45
al-Buqay' 99
Buwayb, battle of 113 n. 197, 194
Byzantine Emperor 23, 27–28
Byzantine Empress 28
Byzantines 9–11, 23, 26, 29–31, 71, 74, 76, 95 n. 167, 111
Byzantium xiii, 13

C

Caesar 61
Camel, battle of the 109
Carthage 23 n. 39
Caspian Sea 42
Caucasus 95 n. 167
China 83
Chosroes 61; see also Kisrā
Christians 89, 209
Cilicia 30 n. 49, 125
Circesium, see Qarqīsiyā'
Companions of the Prophet xiii, xvii, 16, 25, 42, 46, 77, 96 n. 169, 140–41, 152, 155, 164–65, 168, 174, 180, 184–86, 195–96, 203, 211, 249, 259
Constans II Pogonatus (Constantine; Byzantine emperor) 74–76
Constantinople 22, 23 n. 39, 99
Copts 131
Córdoba 24 n. 41
Ctesiphon 60
Cyprus 25–26, 30–31, 111–12, 130

D

Ḍabbah (tribal confederation), 92
Ḍābi' b. al-Ḥārith al-Burjumī 231–32, 249
al-Ḍaḥḥāk b. Qays al-Fihrī 11
* al-Ḍaḥḥāk b. 'Uthmān 247, 251, 252
dā'ī/du'āt 20 n. 33, 146
Dajjājah bt. al-Asmā' al-Sulamī 34

Damascus 24 n. 41, 30, 56, 65 n. 109, 73, 119
Darband, see Bāb al-Abwāb
al-Dārūm 157 n. 278
Dastabā 43
* Dāwūd 69, 107
* Dāwūd b. Abī Hind 62
* Dāwūd b. al-Ḥuṣayn 236
* Dāwūd b. Khālid 38
* Dāwūd b. Yazīd 96, 98
Dayr Salʿ (Jewish cemetery in Medina) 247
dhimmah, ahl al-dhimmah 6 n. 13, 28, 104, 126
Dhū al-Khimār, daughter of 53–54
Dhū Khushub (locale near Medina) 145, 160–62, 170, 172–75, 186, 189, 191–92, 194, 236
Dhū al-Marwah (locale near Medina) 145, 160–62
Dhū al-Nūr, see ʿAbd al-Raḥmān b. Rabīʿah
Dhū al-Ṣawārī, see Masts
Dhurayḥ b. ʿAbbād al-ʿAbdī 160
Dihistān 45
dihqān 81
Diḥyah b. Khalīfah al-Kalbī 63
Dunbāwand (Mt. Demavand) 230–31
Dvin 10 n. 19

E

Egypt xiii, 18–19, 20 n. 32, 23–24, 31, 73–74, 126, 129, 145, 147–49, 165, 168–70, 172, 175, 184–85, 193, 195, 197–99, 207, 219–21, 227, 243, 250, 255
Emigrants *(al-Muhājirūn)* 23, 158, 173–74, 223–24
Euphrates River 134

F

al-Faḍl b. ʿAbbās 261
* al-Faḍl al-Kirmānī 69
Fākhitah, see ʿĀtikah
Fākhitah bt. Ghazwān 254
al-Farazdaq 262
Farghānah 34, 83
Farrūkhzād 82–84
Fārs 32, 34–37, 44, 68–69, 78, 82, 90, 107, 126
farsakh 60
* Farwah b. Laqīṭ al-Azdī al-Ghāmidī 8, 9
al-Faryāb 102, 104–5
Fāṭimah bt. Aws 202, 249
Fāṭimah bt. al-Walīd b. ʿAbd Shams 254
fay' 7, 61, 134, 222
* Fayḍ b. Muḥammad 49
Fayrūz Abū Lu'lu'ah 4
Fazārah, Banū (tribe) 29
firqah 160
Fīrūzābād, see Jūr
fitnah/fitan 57, 59, 110, 118, 124, 140, 150, 172, 191, 222, 224
al-Fusṭāṭ xiii

G

Gabriel (angel) 62
Gaza 157 n. 278
al-Ghāfiqī b. Ḥarb al-ʿAkkī 159, 166
ghāshiyah 114
Ghaylān b. Kharashah al-Ḍabbī 33, 35–36
* Ghiyāth b. Ibrāhīm 78
ghulāt 146
* al-Ghuṣn b. al-Qāsim 47, 50, 56, 96
Gregory, Patrician of Ifrīqiyah 23

H

Ḥabīb b. ʿAbd Shams (clan of Quraysh) 33–34, 36
Ḥabīb b. Maslamah b. Khālid al-Fihrī 10–11, 31, 78, 94, 98–99, 164, 207, 255, 259

Ḥabīb b. Qurrah al-Yarbū'ī 36
Ḥadā' (section of Murād tribe) 139
ḥadd/ḥudūd 51, 150, 155, 243
al-Ḥadīthah 9
Ḥaḍramawt 60, 61
al-Ḥajjāj b. Yūsuf 79, 233–34
al-Ḥakam b. Abī al-'Āṣ 24, 156–58, 182, 227
* al-Ḥakam b. al-Qāsim 220
Ḥakīm b. Ḥizām al-Qurashī 174, 246–48
* Ḥakīm b. Jābir 235
al-Ḥalḥāl b. Dhurrī al-Ḍabbī 97, 101–2
ḥalīf 144
Hamadhān 8 n. 16, 43 n. 72, 132, 256
Ḥamzah b. 'Abd al-Muṭṭalib 153 n. 269
Ḥamzah b. al-Hirmās al-Māzinī 104
* Ḥanash b. 'Abdallāh al-Ṣan'ānī 75
* Ḥanash b. Mālik al-Taghlibī 42–43
Ḥanẓalah b. al-Rabī' al-Tamīmī 164, 208, 209 n. 368
ḥaqq/ḥuqūq 155, 222
ḥaram 14 n. 24
Ḥarb (clan of the Banū Umayyah) 159
Harim b. Ḥassān al-Yashkurī 36, 69
Harim b. Ḥayyān al-'Abdī 36, 69, 165
* al-Ḥārith b. al-Fuḍayl 194
* al-Ḥārith b. Muḥammad 1, 249, 250, 251, 252, 253
al-Ḥārith b. Suwayd al-Taymī 102
* al-Ḥarmalah b. 'Imrān 220
al-Ḥarrah 223
Ḥarrān 119
* Hārūn b. Sa'd 135, 139
* al-Ḥasan 189, 205, 235–36
* al-Ḥasan b. Abī al-Ḥasan 223, 252
al-Ḥasan b. 'Alī b. Abī Ṭālib 42, 161, 166, 207, 211–12, 218, 249
* al-Ḥasan al-Baṣrī 223
* al-Ḥasan b. Mūsā al-Ashyab 252
* al-Ḥasan b. Rashīd 37, 107, 110
Hāshim b. 'Abd Manāf (clan of Quraysh) 209 n. 368
Hāshim b. 'Utbah 16
ḥāshiyah 159
Ḥashsh Kawkab (cemetery in Medina) 246, 248–49
Ḥassān b. Thābit xx, 141, 174, 258–59, 260–61
Ḥātim b. al-Nu'mān al-Bāhilī 91–92, 93
al-Hayāṭilah, see Hephthalites
al-Ḥayy (tribe) 70
Ḥazm (clan) 208–9
Helpers *(al-Anṣār)* 23, 158, 173–74, 194, 218, 231, 248–49, 262
Hephthalites 91
Heraclius (Byzantine emperor) 23 n. 39, 28, 63
Herāt 36, 91, 107–8
Ḥijāz 60–61, 145, 186 n. 330
Ḥimṣ 26, 73, 119, 125, 255
Hind bt. 'Utbah 152 n. 269
Hishām b. 'Abd al-Malik b. Marwān (Umayyad caliph) 20–23, 43 n. 71
Hishām b. 'Āmir 32, 165
* Hishām b. Ḥassān 235
* Hishām b. Muḥammad b. Sā'ib al-Kalbī 8, 9, 81, 95 n. 166, 251, 252, 254
* Hishām b. Sa'd 75
* Hishām b. 'Urwah 59
Ḥiṣn al-Mar'ah 111
al-Ḥubāb b. Yazīd al-Mujāshi' 262
Ḥubaysh 256
Ḥubaysh al-Asadī 112–14
Ḥudhayfah b. al-Yamān 8, 42, 62, 98–99, 139, 140
Hudhayl (tribe) 15 n. 26, 16, 47–48
Ḥukaym b. Jabalah al-'Abdī 126, 159–60, 165, 194, 199
Ḥukaym b. Salāmah al-Ḥizāmī 132
Ḥulsidān 85
Ḥulwān 132 n. 236, 135, 256
Ḥumayd b. Khiyār al-Māzinī 104
Ḥumrān 92
Ḥumrān b. Abān 126–27, 229
al-Hurmuzān 3–4
Ḥurqūṣ b. Zubayr al-Sa'dī 160
al-Ḥuṣayn b. Abī al-Ḥurr 34, 127

al-Ḥusayn b. ʿAlī b. Abī Ṭālib 13 n. 22, 42
* Ḥusayn b. ʿĪsā 135, 137, 139 n. 247, 184, 186, 202, 246–47, 251
Ḥuṣayn b. al-Mundhir 106
* Hushaym 223
Ḥuwayṭib b. ʿAbd al-ʿUzzā 247

I

Ibn ʿAbbās, see ʿAbdallāh b. ʿAbbās
Ibn Abī ʿAwn, see Shuraḥbīl
* Ibn Abī Mulaykah 3
* Ibn Abī Sabrah 23, 229, 238–39, 246
Ibn Abī Sarḥ, see ʿAbdallāh b. Saʿd
* Ibn Abī al-Zinād 182–83
Ibn ʿĀmir, see ʿAbdallāh b. ʿĀmir
* Ibn ʿAqīl 251
* Ibn al-Athīr, ʿIzz al-Dīn xiii, 5 n. 11, 35 n. 57, 99 n. 173, 106 n. 182, 113 n. 198, 115 n. 205, 150 nn. 267–68, 211 n. 374, 232 n. 417, 233 n. 419, 257 n. 462
* Ibn ʿAwn 189–91
Ibn ʿAyyāsh 200
Ibn Dhakwān al-Ṣafūrī 261
Ibn Habbār 47
Ibn al-Ḥaḍramī 109
Ibn al-Ḥamiq, see ʿAmr b. al-Ḥamiq
* Ibn al-Ḥārith b. Abī Bakr 202
Ibn Ḥassān al-Yashkurī, see Harim b. Ḥassān
Ibn al-Ḥaysumān al-Khuzāʿī 45–46
* Ibn Ḥubaysh, ʿAbd al-Raḥmān b. Muḥammad xx, 104 n. 179
* Ibn Isḥāq, see Muḥammad b. Isḥāq
Ibn Juʿayyah al-Aʿrajī 105
* Ibn Jurayj 3
* Ibn Kaʿb 23
* Ibn al-Kalbī, see Hishām b. Muḥammad
Ibn al-Kawwāʾ 113, 125, 129
Ibn Kindīr al-Qushayrī 36
Ibn Kuthayyir al-Nahshalī 106
Ibn Masʿūd, see ʿAbdallāh b. Masʿūd
Ibn al-Muḥarrish b. ʿAbd ʿAmr al-Ḥanafī 160
Ibn al-Nābighah, see ʿAmr b. al-ʿĀṣ
Ibn al-Nibāʿ, see ʿUrwah b. al-Nibāʿ
Ibn Rabīʿah al-Sulamī 102
Ibn Sabāʾ, see ʿAbdallāh b. Sabāʾ
Ibn Saʿd, see ʿAbdallāh b. Saʿd
* Ibn Saʿd, Muḥammad 1, 3, 249, 250, 251, 252, 253
Ibn Sahlah 155
Ibn al-Sawdāʾ, see ʿAbdallāh b. Sabāʾ
Ibn Sīrīn, see Muḥammad b. Sīrīn
* Ibn Sulaymān b. Abī Ḥathmah 228
Ibn ʿUdays, see ʿAbd al-Raḥmān b. ʿUdays
Ibn Wathīmah al-Naṣrī 20
Ibrāhīm b. ʿAdī 202, 249
Īdhaj 34
* Idrīs b. Ḥanẓalah al-ʿAmmī 44, 92
Ifranjah 22
Ifrīqiyah 12, 18–23, 111, 157
ijtihād 151
* ʿIkrimah 62, 66, 236–39
Iliyā, metropolitan of Marw 89
imām 6, 115, 124, 140, 142, 155, 175, 195, 221, 235, 259
imārah 197, 222, 244
ʿImrān b. al-Faṣīl al-Burjumī 35, 36
ʿImrān b. Ḥuṣayn 165
Iran xiii, xv
Iraq xiii, 41 n. 66, 45 n. 74, 58–61, 73, 92, 112, 115, 119, 126, 132, 150, 197, 220, 233 n. 420
al-ʿĪṣ, Banū (clan of the Banū Umayyah) 159
* ʿĪsā b. ʿAbd al-Raḥmān 125
* ʿĪsā b. ʿAlqamah 74
Iṣfahān 81, 132, 256
* Isḥāq b. ʿĪsā 2, 12, 18, 25, 37, 41, 71, 94, 111, 131, 145, 236, 251
* Isḥāq b. Rabīʿah 235
* Isḥāq b. Yaḥyā 152, 220
* Ismāʿīl b. Abī Khālid 16, 235
* Ismāʿīl b. Ibrāhīm 189
* Ismāʿīl b. Muḥammad 181
* Ismāʿīl b. Muslim 102

ispabadh 41, 78 n. 135, 82
Iṣṭakhr 24, 32, 35–36, 79, 81, 90
'Iyāḍ b. Ghanm 72
'Iyāḍ b. Warqā' al-Usaydī 104
* Iyās b. al-Muhallab 106

J

Jabalah b. 'Amr al-Sā'idī 182
* Jābir 67
Jābir b. 'Amr al-Muzanī 256
* Ja'far b. 'Abdallāh al-Muḥammadī 135, 137, 139, 183–84, 186, 202, 246–47, 251
* Ja'far b. Abī al-Mughīrah 200
* Ja'far b. Maḥmūd 191
Jahjāh al-Ghifārī 183
jamā'ah 118, 122, 129, 135, 154, 161, 168, 206, 241, 257
al-Janad 255
jār/jīrān 117
al-Jara'ah 135, 139, 154
al-Jara'ah, Day of 131, 139
Jarīr b. 'Abdallāh 132, 135, 256
Jaththāmah b. Ṣa'b b. Jaththāmah 52
Jaz' b. Mu'āwiyah al-Sa'dī 104
Jazīrah 17, 45, 48, 72, 119, 132, 133
Jesus (prophet) 146
Jews 64, 67, 145, 209
al-Jibāl 132 n. 233
jihād 21, 35, 77, 136, 140, 209
Jīlān 95–96
jizyah 30
Jordan 73
Jubayr b. Muṭ'im b. 'Adī b. Nawfal b. 'Abd Manāf 57, 174, 246–48
* Jubayr b. Nufayr 31
* Junādah b. Abī Umayyah al-Azdī 26–27
jund 19, 20 n. 32, 21
Jundub 113
Jundub b. 'Abdallāh 49–52, 57
Jundub b. Ka'b al-Azdī 125
Jundub b. Zuhayr al-Ghāmidī 125
Jūr 69
Jurjān 42–45, 91, 95–96
al-Jūzajān 102, 104–6

K

Ka'b al-Aḥbār 22, 66–67, 151
Ka'b b. Dhī al-Ḥabakah al-Nahdī 113, 230–32
Ka'b b. Ju'ayl 43
Ka'b b. Mālik al-Anṣārī 141, 174, 249, 258–60
Ka'b b. Sūr 165
Ka'bah 13 n. 22, 14 n. 24, 38 n. 63, 100, 247 n. 450
Kābul 6, 34, 83
Kalb (tribe) 47, 133
Kanārā 91–92
Karbalā' 13 n. 22
Kathīr b. al-Ṣalt al-Kindī 174, 203
Kaysān, *mawlā* of Banū Tha'labah 104
Khabīṣ 91
Khālid b. 'Abdallāh b. Zuhayr 36
* Khālid b. Abī 'Imrān 75
Khālid b. al-'Āṣ b. Hishām 237–38
* Khālid b. Ma'dān 26, 28, 31, 73
Khālid b. Muljam 148
Khālid b. Rabī'ah 97
Khālid b. 'Uthmān b. 'Affān 254
Khālid b. al-Walīd 72, 119
Khālid b. Zayd, see Abū Ayyūb
khalīfah 134
kharāj 6, 24, 45, 103, 170
Khārijah b. Ḥudhāfah al-Sahmī 18, 165
Kharijites 20 nn. 32–33, 45 n. 74, 233
khāṣṣah/khawāṣṣ 54, 84, 122, 154, 203
al-Khaṭṭ 117
Khawarnaq 261
Khawlān 184
Khaybar 60
Khazars 83, 94 n. 166, 95–96, 99
khazīrah 229
khilāfah 116, 197
al-Khirrīt b. Rāshid 36
Khulayd b. 'Abdallāh al-Ḥanafī 107

* Khulayd b. Dhafarah 2
Khunays al-Asadī, see Ḥubaysh al-Asadī
Khurāsān 6, 34–37, 42, 44, 45 n. 74, 68–69, 79, 82, 90–91, 107–10, 111
* Khurdādhbih al-Rāzī 79
Khurrazādh-Mihr 79
Khusraw Anushirvan (Sasanian emperor) 41 n. 66, 78 n. 135
Khusraw Parviz (Sasanian emperor) 42 n. 66, 63
Khūṭ 106
Khūzistān 37
Khwārazm 106
Khwāst 91
Kinānah (tribe) 34, 96
Kinānah b. Bishr b. ʿAttāb al-Tujībī 148, 159, 201, 219, 249–50
Kirmān 34–35, 44, 69, 78, 82, 87, 90, 107
Kisrā 71, 103; see also Chosroes
Kisrā b. Hurmuz, see Khusraw Parviz
Kūfah xiii, 5, 8–9, 15–17, 42–43, 45–46, 48–50, 56–59, 62, 91, 94, 97–100, 112–15, 119–21, 124–26, 128–29, 131–33, 135, 139–40, 145, 147, 149, 154, 162, 164, 176, 190 n. 336, 199, 207, 209, 220, 226, 230–34, 255–56
* Kulayb b. al-Ḥalḥāl 101
* Kulayb b. Khalaf al-ʿAmmī 44
Kulthūm b. Tujīb 216
Kumayl b. Ziyād al-Nakhaʿī 113, 121, 125, 232–35
Kunāsah (locale in Kūfah) 48
* Kurayb 23
Kurds 34

L

Laylā bt. ʿUmays 210
Layth, Banū (tribe) 214–15, 225
* al-Layth b. Saʿd 30

M

Maʿadd (tribal confederation) 212
* al-Madāʾinī, ʿAlī b. Muḥammad xv, 33, 36, 41–44, 69–70, 78–79, 90–93, 102–10, 235, 255
Madhḥij (tribe) 123 n. 221
Maghrib 12
Magians 85
Māh al-Kūfah 132, 256
Māhak 103
Māhawayh b. Māfanāh b. Fayd 79–80, 83–87
* Maḥmūd b. Labīd 174–75
Mājān 87
majlis/majālis 149, 164
* Makhramah b. Sulaymān al-Wālibī 247, 251, 252
Makhzūm (clan of Quraysh) 141 n. 251, 154
Makrān 34, 36
Māl-Amīr 34 n. 56
malaʾ 114
Malaṭyah 111
Mālik b. ʿAbdallāh 234
* Mālik b. Aws b. al-Ḥadathān 74
Mālik b. Ḥabīb al-Yarbūʿī 132, 256
Mālik b. al-Ḥārith al-Nakhaʿī al-Ashtar 57, 113–14, 119–21, 125, 132–33, 135, 139, 159, 189–90, 194, 199, 205, 232
Mālik b. Kaʿb al-Arḥabī 120
* Maʿmar b. Rāshid 77
manjanīq 95
Manẓūr b. Sayyār al-Fazārī 219
* al-Maqrīzī, Taqī al-Dīn Aḥmad 113 n. 199
Marw 36, 78–90, 92–93, 105, 107, 111
Marw al-Rūdh, Marwarūdh 36, 85, 102–6, 111
Marwān b. al-Ḥakam b. Abī al-ʿĀṣ 24 n. 41, 60, 144, 153, 171, 173–75, 177–80, 182, 187, 192–93, 197–98, 200–4, 209, 211, 214, 218, 220, 227 n. 408, 236, 247, 249–50
Mary (mother of Jesus) 115

Maryam bt. 'Uthmān b. 'Affān 254
marzubān 78
Māsabadhān 256
al-masjid al-ḥarām 14 n. 24
Maslamah b. 'Abd al-Malik 50
* Maslamah b. Muḥārib 34, 69, 90, 107–9
Masrūq b. al-Ajda' 164
Masts, battle of the 71–72, 76–77, 131
Mas'ūd b. Nu'aym al-Nahshalī 57
Maṭyār 81–82
mawlā 135
al-Mawriyān al-Rūmī 10–11
Maysarah 21
Mecca 9 n. 17, 13 n. 22, 14, 16 n. 27, 38 nn. 62–63, 39, 57, 60–61, 100–1, 156–57, 183, 217, 219 n. 393, 227 n. 408, 237–38, 245–46, 247 n. 450, 253, 255
Medina 4, 5, 13, 23 n. 38, 24, 37, 39, 46, 48, 53, 56–57, 59–60, 62–66, 68, 101, 119, 127, 129, 135, 139, 144, 147, 151, 153–56, 159–60, 162–63, 164 n. 295, 168–72, 184, 186, 188–89, 191, 193, 199, 203–4, 207, 211, 212 n. 375, 216–17, 219 n. 393, 224–26, 236–38, 244, 246–47, 249, 258
Mediterranean Sea 27
Messenger of God, see Muḥammad
Mi'ḍad al-Shaybānī 95, 96–98, 102
Mihrgān 106–7
millah 103
al-Milṭāṭ 113
Minā 38, 70, 230
al-Minjāb b. Rāshid 36
al-Miqdād 25
Mirbad (locale in Baṣrah) 48 n. 78
Mismar al-Qurashī 107
Misṭaḥ b. Uthāthah 144
al-Miswar b. Makhramah 181–82
mīthāq 168, 240
Mosul 9, 132
* Mu'ādh b. Hishām 252
Mu'āwiyah b. Abī Sufyān 6, 9–11, 13, 24, 25–31, 55–56, 64–65, 67, 72–74, 94, 109 n. 188, 111, 114–19, 121–24, 128–29, 131–32, 136–38, 143, 149–53, 164, 173, 182, 185, 190, 198, 207, 219, 243, 246, 255, 259, 261
Mu'āwiyah b. Ḥudayj al-Sakūnī 164
* Mubashshir b. al-Fuḍayl 67, 73, 224, 226, 228
* al-Mufaḍḍal al-Ḍabbī 105
* al-Mufaḍḍal al-Kirmānī 90
al-Mughīrah b. al-Akhnas b. Sharīq al-Thaqafī 203, 211–14
* al-Mughīrah b. Muqsim 48
al-Mughīrah b. Shu'bah 5, 15, 142, 217
Muhājirūn, see Emigrants
al-Muhallab b. Abī Ṣufrah 233
Muḥammad, the Prophet xvi–xvii, 3, 7, 9 n. 17, 23 n. 38, 24 n. 41, 38–39, 42, 62–63, 66 n. 113, 68, 77, 96 n. 169, 99, 100, 103, 116, 117, 118, 122–23, 138 n. 246, 139–40, 141 n. 251, 142, 146, 151, 153, 155, 157, 160–61, 163, 165, 174, 176, 182–84, 199–200, 204–5, 208, 214–15, 218, 222, 224, 227, 228–29, 240–44, 247 n. 450, 253–54, 256, 258, 261–62
Muḥammad b. 'Abd al-Malik b. Marwān 50
* Muḥammad b. 'Abdallāh (b. Sawād) 5, 17–18, 22, 34, 37, 45, 48, 51, 56, 61–62, 95, 98, 112, 126–27, 140, 147–48, 159, 166, 206–7, 210, 213, 223, 226, 230, 249, 251, 252
Muḥammad b. Abī Bakr 77, 155, 165, 172, 180, 190, 198, 200, 205, 208, 210, 215, 218–19, 228
* Muḥammad b. Abī Ḥarmalah 23
Muḥammad b. Abī Ḥudhayfah 75–77, 165, 172–73, 198–99, 227, 255
Muḥammad b. Abī Qutayrah 165
Muḥammad b. 'Amr b. al-'Āṣ 171
Muḥammad b. 'Amr b. al-Walīd b. 'Uqbah 50
* Muḥammad b. 'Awn 66

Muḥammad b. al-Ḥakam b. Abī 'Aqīl al-Thaqafī 43
* Muḥammad b. Isḥāq b. Yasār al-Madanī 78, 143 n. 269, 157 n. 278, 183, 186, 202, 212 n. 375
Muḥammad b. Ja'far 210
* Muḥammad b. Kurayb 47, 55
Muḥammad b. Maslamah 147, 165, 174–75, 191–97
* Muḥammad b. Mūsā al-Ḥarashī 62, 252
* Muḥammad b. Muslim 197
* Muḥammad b. Sā'ib al-Kalbī 185
* Muḥammad b. Sa'īd 26
* Muḥammad b. Salamah 230
* Muḥammad b. Ṣāliḥ 72, 174, 182
* Muḥammad b. Sīrīn 67, 92, 102
* Muḥammad b. Sūqah 68
Muḥammad b. Ṭalḥah b. 'Ubaydallāh 207, 211–12
* Muḥammad b. 'Umar, see al-Wāqidī
* Muḥārib 33
* Mujālid b. Sa'īd al-Hamdānī 2, 5, 120, 217, 247, 250, 251
Mujāshi' b. Mas'ūd al-Sulamī 67, 69–70, 90, 186, 207
al-Mukhdaj 79
mulḥid 158
mulk 116, 178
Mūqān 8
* Muqātil b. Ḥayyān 93, 104
Murād (tribe) 139
Murghāb River 36 n. 58, 78–81, 104 n. 180, 105, 107 n. 184
Murrah (tribe) 107
* Mūsā b. 'Abdallāh b. Khāzim 92
* Mūsā b. Ṭalḥah 48, 152, 220, 235
* Mūsā b. 'Uqbah 183, 197
* Muṣ'ab b. 'Abdallāh 250
* Muṣ'ab b. Ḥayyān 93, 104
* al-Musayyab b. 'Abd Khayr 16
* al-Mustanīr b. Yazīd 96, 131, 232
* Mu'tamir b. Sulaymān al-Taymī 167, 204
al-Muthannā 113 n. 197
Muwarri' b. Abī Muwarri' al-Asadī 46

N

* Naḍr b. Isḥāq 70
* Nāfi' (*mawlā* of 'Abdallāh b. 'Umar) 183
* Nāfi' b. Jubayr 47, 55
Nahd, Banū (tribe) 42–43
Nahrān al-Aṣbaḥī 220
Nā'ilah bt. al-Farāfiṣah al-Kalbiyyah 31, 177–79, 206, 216, 218–19, 247–50, 254
Nakha' (tribe) 121 n. 216, 123 n. 221, 234
Nāmiyah 43
nās 2 n. 3
Nasā 90–92
Nashāstaj 60, 113
Nawrūz 107 n. 183
al-Nibā' al-Laythī, see 'Urwah b. al-Nibā'
Nihāwand, battle of 8, 34 n. 56, 42, 81
Nishapur 36, 42 n. 67, 91, 93, 108; see also Abrashahr
Niyār b. 'Abdallāh al-Aslamī 200–1, 214; see also Niyār b. 'Iyāḍ
Niyār b. 'Iyāḍ 203
Niyār b. Mikraz 174
Niyār b. Mukram al-Aslamī 247, 248
Nīzak Ṭarkhān 84–85
Noah (prophet) 210, 242
Nujayḥ 250
al-Nu'mān b. al-Afqam al-Naṣrī 92
* Numayr b. Wa'lah 91
al-Nusayr al-'Ijlī 132, 256
al-Nūshajān 92

P

Palestine 73–74, 171, 176, 255
Persia, Persians 81, 102–3, 117, 208
Prophet, see Muḥammad

Q

qabā' 97
Qabāth al-Kinānī 214

al-Qādisiyyah 112, 139
al-Qādisiyyah, battle of 58, 60, 133 n. 239
Qaḥdham 43
al-Qa'qā' b. 'Amr 132–34, 140, 154, 164, 207, 256
* al-Qa'qā' b. al-Ṣalt 101
qāri'/qurrā' 58, 112, 136
Qārin 107–10
Qarqīsiyā' 132, 135, 256
al-Qartha' al-Ḍabbī 97, 102
qasāmah 46–47
* al-Qāsim b. Muḥammad 226, 228, 256
al-Qāsim b. Rabī'ah al-Thaqafī 255
* al-Qāsim b. Walīd 16
Qaṣr al-Aḥnaf 104
Qaṣr Mujāshi' 69
qāṣṣ/quṣṣāṣ xvii, 129
* Qatādah 252
qawm 2 n. 3
Qayrawān 20
Qays (tribe) 186
* Qays b. Abī Ḥāzim 16
Qays b. al-Haytham al-Sulamī 36–37, 108–10, 186
* Qays b. Yazīd al-Nakha'ī 96, 131
Qinnasrīn 24, 73, 255
qinṭār 23, 24
Quḍā'ah (tribe) 133 n. 238
Quhistān 87, 91, 108
al-Qumādhbān b. al-Hurmuzān 4
Qūmis 42, 44
Quraysh (tribe) 15 n. 26, 16 n. 27, 23, 56, 115–17, 120–22, 134, 138 n. 246, 141 n. 251, 172, 215, 223–25, 229, 235, 247 n. 450
qurrā', see *qāri'/qurrā'*
Quṣayy (ancestor of Quraysh) 247
Qutaybah b. Muslim 44, 45 n. 74, 79
Qutayrah b. Fulān al-Sakūnī 159, 215–16

R

al-Rabadhah 66–68, 101, 186
* al-Rabī' b. Mālik b. Abī 'Âmir 249
* al-Rabī' b. Nu'mān al-Naṣrī 26, 27, 72
Rabī'ah (tribe) 17
Rabī'ah b. al-Ḥārith b. 'Abd al-Muṭṭalib 235
Rabī'ah b. 'Isl 127
* Rabi'ah b. 'Uthmān 257
Rāfi' b. Khadīj 68, 101
ra'īs/ru'asā' 132
ra'iyyah 66, 95, 115, 125, 148
* Rajā' b. al-Ḥaywah al-Kindī 26, 151
raj'ah 146
al-Ramādah (locale in Kūfah) 47
Ramlah bt. Shaybah b. Rabī'ah b. 'Abd Shams 254
al-Raqqah 119
Raskan 105
Rāvar 91
al-rawādif wa'l-lawāḥiq 58 n. 95
* Rawḥ b. 'Abdallāh 79
al-Rayy 8, 43 n. 71, 62, 82, 132, 256
* al-Rāzī, see Aḥmad b. Thābit
Razīq Canal 87; see also Murghāb River
al-riddah xvi, 27 n. 45, 119
Rifā'ah b. Rāfi' al-Anṣārī al-Zuraqī 203
Romans 208
al-Rūm 10 n. 19; see also Byzantines
Rūmah, well of 204, 237
Ruqayyah bt. Muḥammad 141 n. 251, 253, 254
* Ruzayq b. 'Abdallāh al-Rāzī 229

S

al-Sab' (locale in Palestine) 171
al-Sabā'iyyah 154
Sābūr 13, 14
Sa'd b. Abī Waqqāṣ 3 n. 5, 5, 15–17, 45, 73, 132 n. 235, 152, 173–74, 192, 197–98, 217
Sa'd b. Layth, Banū (tribe) 144
Sa'd b. Mālik 166
Sa'd al-Qaraẓ 257
* Sa'd b. Rāshid 247, 252

ṣadaqah 67, 182
* Ṣadaqah b. Ḥumayd 107
al-Saffāḥ, Abū al-ʿAbbās 50 n. 81
al-Sāḥil, Sawāḥil 125
Sahl b. Ḥunayf 258
* Sahl b. Yūsuf 226, 228
al-Sā'ib b. al-Aqraʿ 132, 256
al-Sā'ib b. Hishām b. ʿAmr al-ʿĀmirī 255
* Saʿīd b. ʿAbd al-Raḥmān b. Abzay 200
* Saʿīd b. ʿAbdallāh al-Jumaḥī 59
Saʿīd b. Abī al-ʿArjā' 127
Saʿīd b. al-ʿĀṣ 10–11, 41–45, 52, 54, 56, 57–59, 62, 77, 91, 94–95, 98, 112–14, 118–20, 124–25, 131, 132–40, 149, 151, 154, 173–74, 177, 185, 190 n. 336, 198, 202–3, 210–12, 231, 236, 255
Saʿīd b. Ḥidhyam al-Jumaḥī 72
* Saʿīd b. al-Musayyab 227–28
Saʿīd b. Qays 132, 256
Saʿīd b. ʿUthmān b. ʿAffān 254
Saʿīd b. Zayd b. ʿAmr b. Nufayl 174, 177, 192, 224
* al-Sakan b. Qatādah al-ʿUraynī 90, 108
Ṣakhr b. Qays 103; see also al-Aḥnaf b. Qays
Salʿ (locale in Medina) 65–66
* Salamah b. Nabātah 68
Salāmah b. Rawḥ al-Judhāmī 171–72
* Salamah b. ʿUthmān 69, 102
* Ṣāliḥ, *mawlā* of al-Taw'amah 38
* Ṣāliḥ b. Kaysān 247, 252
* Sālim, the *mawlā* of Umm Muḥammad 75
* Sālim b. ʿAbdallāh (b. ʿUmar) 73, 224, 226, 228
Salmān al-Fārisī 96
Salmān b. Rabīʿah al-Bāhilī 8–11, 94–96, 98–99, 132
* al-Ṣalt b. Dīnār 92
al-Ṣalt b. Ḥurayth 109
Sāmah, Banū (tribe) 36
Ṣanʿā' 145, 255
Sanjān 83–84, 88
Sarakhs 84, 90, 92–93
* al-Sarī (b. Yaḥyā) 2–5, 7, 15–17, 18, 22, 26–28, 30, 34, 37, 45–52, 54–56, 59, 61–62, 64, 66–68, 72–73, 95–96, 98, 100–1, 112, 121, 125–28, 131, 140, 145, 148, 151, 159, 166, 206–7, 210, 213, 217, 223–30, 232–33, 249–50, 251, 252, 255–57
Ṣaʿṣaʿah b. Ṣūḥān al-ʿAbdī 113, 115–16, 121–23, 125, 128
Sasanian dynasty, Sasanian Empire xiii, 41 n. 66, 95 n. 167
Sawād 34, 113, 120, 133, 256
* Sayf b. ʿUmar xv–xvii, 2–5, 7, 15–17, 18, 20 n. 32, 22, 23 n. 39, 26–28, 30, 34, 37, 41, 45–52, 54–56, 59, 61–62, 64, 66–68, 72–73, 94–96, 98, 100–1, 112, 121, 125–28, 131, 140, 145, 148, 151, 153, 159, 166, 167, 206–7, 210, 213, 217, 223–30, 232–33, 249–50, 251, 252, 255–57
Sepphoris 261 n. 471
* al-Shaʿbī, ʿĀmir b. Sharāḥīl 3, 5, 7, 15, 49–50, 91, 96, 120, 217, 250, 251
Shaddād b. Aws 25
Shahriyār b. Khusraw Parviz (Sasanian emperor) 89
Sharīk b. al-Aʿwar al-Ḥārithī 90
Sharīk b. Khubāshah al-Numayrī 165
* Shaybān 120
Shīrīn (Sasanian empress) 89
Shuʿayb (prophet) 242
* Shuʿayb (b. Ibrāhīm) 2–5, 7, 15–17, 18, 22, 26–28, 30, 34, 37, 45–52, 54–56, 59, 61–62, 64, 66–68, 72–73, 95–96, 98, 100–1, 112, 121, 125–28, 131, 140, 145, 148, 151, 159, 166, 206–7, 210, 213, 217, 223–30, 232–33, 249–50, 251, 252, 255–57
Shubayl b. Ubayy al-Azdī 46
shuhūd 147
shūrā 3, 55 n. 92, 163 n. 291

* Shuraḥbīl b. Abī 'Awn 179, 198, 200
Shurayḥ b. al-Ḥārith 164
shurṭah 121
Ṣiffīn, battle of xvi, 55
Sijistān 6, 34–36, 82, 107
Simāk al-Anṣārī 256
al-Sīrajān 69, 90
Ṣirār (locale in Medina) 186, 203
Sogdiana, see al-Ṣughd
Spain 19, 22–23
Ṣubayḥ 250
Successors (*Tābi'ūn*) 164–65
Sūdān b. Ḥumrān al-Sakūnī, also al-Murādī 148, 159, 191–92, 201, 215–16, 219
* Sufyān b. Abī al-'Awjā' 194
Sufyān b. 'Awf al-Azdī 29
Sufyān b. 'Uwayf 57
al-Ṣughd 79
Ṣuhayb al-Rūmī 3
* Suḥaym b. Ḥafṣ 235
Ṣūl 45
* Sulaymān 220
Sulaymān b. 'Abd al-Malik (Umayyad caliph) 44 n. 73
* Sulaymān b. Abī Karīmah 30
Sulaymān b. Kathīr al-Khuzā'ī 110
al-Ṣulṣul (locale near Medina) 238
Sunbīl 109
sunnah 134, 142, 243, 244, 256
al-Suqyā (locale near Medina) 186, 219 n. 393
Sūriyah 31
Suwayd b. Math'abah al-Tamīmī 102
Suwayd b. Muqarrin 41
al-Suwaydā' 191
Syria 9, 10, 26, 30 n. 49, 56, 64, 72–74, 94, 98, 112, 119, 121, 124–25, 127, 129, 132, 138, 145, 147, 153, 165, 186 n. 330, 207, 220–21, 226, 230, 255

T

Ṭabaristān 41, 43, 82
al-Ṭabasayn 87, 91, 108
Taghlib, Banū (tribe) 48
Tahmīj 92
al-Ṭā'if 16 n. 27, 39, 60, 156–57, 227, 255
* Ṭalḥah (b. al-A'lam) 5, 17, 18, 22, 34, 37, 45, 48, 51, 56, 61–62, 95, 98, 112, 126–27, 140, 147–48, 159, 166, 206–7, 210, 213, 223, 230, 249, 251, 252
Ṭalḥah b. 'Ubaydallāh 3 n. 5, 60, 113, 150–52, 160–62, 166, 171, 173, 181, 189, 199–200, 206, 208–9, 217, 235–36, 238, 249
al-Ṭāliqān 102, 104–5
Tamīm (tribe) 90, 109
Tamīm b. Ubayy b. Muqbil 258
Ṭamīsah 42
al-Tarjumān al-Hujaymī 36
Taurus Mts. 30 n. 49
al-Ṭaylasān 8
Taym (clan of Quraysh) 141 n. 251
Thābit b. Qays b. Munqa' al-Nakha'ī 121, 125
* al-Thawr b. Yazīd 31
Tīzanābādh 60
Transjordan 255
* Ṭufayl b. Mirdās al-'Ammī 44
al-Tujībī 205, 218, 261; see also 'Abd al-Raḥmān b. 'Udays; Kinānah b. Bishr
Ṭukhāristān 102, 104
Ṭulayḥah 114
Turks 78–80, 83, 95, 97
Ṭūs 36, 90–92
Tustar 69

U

* 'Ubādah b. Nusayy 26–27
'Ubādah b. al-Ṣāmit 25, 65, 165
'Ubayd b. Rifā'ah al-Zuraqī 202
* 'Ubayd al-Ṭanāfisī 54
* 'Ubaydallāh b. 'Abdallāh b. 'Utbah 246
* 'Ubaydallāh b. 'Amr 251

'Ubaydallāh b. Ma'mar al-Taymī 34–35
* 'Ubaydallāh b. Rāfi' b. Naqākhah 182
'Ubaydallāh b. 'Umar b. al-Khaṭṭāb 3–5, 59, 183 (?)
Uḥud, battle of 15 n. 26, 152 n. 269, 164, 212
'Umān 37, 117
'Umar b. al-Khaṭṭāb 2 n. 4, 3–8, 9 n. 17, 11, 15, 17, 18, 22 n. 36, 26–28, 30, 33, 38–39, 41, 45, 48, 55 n. 92, 56–57, 63, 70, 72–74, 77, 118, 123, 141–43, 150, 155, 157, 158 n. 281, 163, 167, 170, 178, 183, 189, 221–25, 227, 229–30, 235, 243
* 'Umar b. Ṣāliḥ b. Nāfi' 38
* 'Umar b. Shabbah xv, 41–44, 235
'Umar b. 'Uthmān b. 'Affān 254
* 'Umārah b. al-Qa'qā' 223
'Umārah b. 'Uqbah 49, 120, 261
Umayr b. Aḥmar al-Yashkurī 35–36, 92
'Umayr b. Ḍābi' 113, 232–34, 249
'Umayr b. Sa'd al-Anṣārī 72–74
'Umayr b. 'Uthmān b. Sa'd 34–36
Umayyad dynasty 24 n. 41, 43 n. 71, 50 n. 81, 55 n. 93, 94 n. 166; see also Umayyah, Banū
Umayyah, Banū (clan of Quraysh) 120, 138, 158, 168, 177, 181, 183, 200, 202, 208, 235, 248
Umm Abān bt. 'Uthmān b. 'Affān 254
Umm 'Abdallāh bt. Yazīd al-Kalbiyyah 11
Umm 'Amr bt. Jundub al-Azdī 254
Umm 'Amr bt. 'Uthmān b. 'Affān 254
* Umm Bakr bt. al-Miswar b. al-Makhramah 181
Umm al-Banīn bt. 'Uthmān b. 'Affān 254
Umm al-Banīn bt. 'Uyaynah al-Fazārī 248, 254–55
Umm Ḥabībah 208–9
Umm Ḥakīm bt. 'Abd al-Muṭṭalib 254
Umm Ḥarām 25
Umm Kulthūm bt. 'Alī b. Abī Ṭālib (wife of 'Umar) 28
Umm Kulthūm bt. Muḥammad 254
Umm Kulthūm bt. 'Uqbah b. Abī Mu'ayṭ 172
Umm Sa'īd bt. 'Uthmān b. 'Affān 254
ummah 30, 31, 96, 117, 129, 143, 148, 214, 221, 242, 244
'umrah 68, 108
'Uqbah b. 'Amr al-Anṣarı, Abū Mas'ūd 139, 164, 256
'Urwah b. al-Ja'd 125
* 'Urwah b. Khālid b. 'Abdallāh b. 'Amr b. 'Uthmān 253
'Urwah b. al-Nibā' al-Laythī 191–92, 201, 214
'Urwah b. Shīyam 220
* Usāmah b. Zayd b. Aslam al-Laythī 5, 23–24, 183, 236
Usāmah b. Zayd b. Ḥārithah 147, 157
'Utaybah b. al-Nahhās 132, 135, 256
'Utbah b. Ghazwān 142
'Utbah b. 'Uthmān b. 'Affān 254
'Uthmān b. Abī al-'Āṣ al-Thaqafī 24, 35, 37
* 'Uthmān b. Ḥakīm b. 'Abbād b. Ḥunayf 225
* 'Uthmān b. Muḥammad al-Akhnasī 1, 220, 250
* 'Uthmān b. al-Sharīd 182
Uyaynah b. Ḥiṣn b. Ḥudhayfah b. Badr al-Fazārī 248 n. 452, 254

V

Volga River 95 n. 167

W

Wādī al-Qurā 160 n. 285, 186
* Wahb b. Jarīr b. Ḥazm 251, 253
wālī/wulāt 5, 144

al-Walīd b. 'Abd al-Malik (Umayyad caliph) 44 n. 73, 79
* al-Walīd b. Muslim 30
al-Walīd b. 'Uqbah b. Abī Mu'ayṭ 5, 7–10, 15, 17, 45–46, 48–57, 113 n. 199, 120, 185, 190 n. 338, 230–31, 261
al-Walīd b. 'Uthmān b. 'Affān 254
* Wāqid b. 'Abdallāh 140
* al-Wāqidī, Muḥammad b. 'Umar xv–xvi, xix, 1, 3, 5, 10–11, 12–13, 14–15, 18, 23–24, 25, 31–32, 37–38, 40, 41, 71–72, 74–75, 77–78, 94, 99–100, 111–12, 120–21, 125, 140, 145, 170, 172, 174–76, 179, 181–83, 191, 194, 197–98, 200–1, 219–21, 229–30, 236, 238, 246–48, 250, 251, 252, 253, 254–55, 257–58
waṣī 146
Waththāb 189–91
wazīr/wuzarā' 135
wilāyah 222

Y

* Yaḥyā b. 'Abbād b. 'Abdallāh b. al-Zubayr 186
* Yaḥyā b. 'Abd al-'Azīz 191
* Yaḥyā b. 'Abd al-Raḥmān al-Ḥāṭib 183
* Yaḥyā b. Muslim 140
* Yaḥyā b. Sa'īd 227
Ya'lā b. Munyah 255
* Ya'qūb b. 'Abdallāh al-Ash'arī 200
* Ya'qūb b. Ibrāhīm 167, 189, 204
* Ya'qūb b. 'Utbah b. al-Akhnas 99, 202
* Ya'qūb b. Zayd 1, 250
* al-Ya'qūbī, Aḥmad b. Wāḍiḥ 5 n. 11, 52 n. 86
* Yāqūt b. 'Abdallāh al-Rūmī 160 n. 285, 171 n. 308, 194 n. 342, 219 n. 393, 238 n. 428
Yarfa' (slave of 'Umar b. al-Khaṭṭāb) 143
Yarmūk, battle of 15 n. 26
* Yasār b. Abī Karib 247
Yathrib 164 n. 294; see also Medina
Yazd 91
Yazdagird (III) b. Shahriyār (Sasanian emperor) xv, 8 n. 16, 68–69, 71, 78–90
Yazīd (II) b. 'Abd al-Malik (Umayyad caliph) 45 n. 74
* Yazīd b. Abī Ḥabīb 24, 198, 220
Yazīd b. Abī Sufyān 9 n. 17, 73
Yazīd b. Asad b. Kurz al-Bajalī al-Qasrī 185–86
* Yazīd al-Faq'asī 54, 64, 100, 125, 145–46
Yazīd (I) b. Mu'āwiyah b. Abī Sufyān (Umayyad caliph) 13, 223 n. 400
Yazīd b. Mu'āwiyah al-Nakha'ī 96–98
Yazīd b. Muhallab b. Abī Ṣufrah al-Azdī 45, 50 n. 81
Yazīd b. Qays al-Arḥabī 132–35, 140, 154
Yazīd (III) b. al-Walīd, al-Nāqiṣ (Umayyad caliph) 79
Yemen xvi, 60–61, 217
* Yūnis b. 'Ubayd 62
* Yūnis b. Yazīd al-Aylī 251, 253
* Yūsuf b. 'Abdallāh b. Salām 221
Yūsuf b. 'Umar al-Thaqafī 43
* Yūsuf b. Ya'qūb 220

Z

* Zakariyā' b. 'Adī 251
zakāt 66
al-Zawrā' (Uthmān's residence) 32, 70, 230
* Zayd b. Aslam 75
Zayd b. Ṣūḥān al-'Abdī 125, 159, 232
Zayd b. Thābit 141, 156 n. 276, 165–66, 174, 249, 256
Ziyād 90

* Ziyād b. Ayyūb 223, 252
Ziyād b. Mu'āwiyah 102
Ziyād b. al-Naḍr al-Ḥārithī 159–61
Ziyād b. Nu'aym al-Fihrī 204
Ziyād b. al-Rabī' 109
* al-Zubayr b. 'Abdallāh 221
al-Zubayr b. al-'Awāmm 3 n. 5, 150–52, 160–62, 166, 171, 206, 208–10, 217, 247
* Zuhayr b. Hunayd 106
Zuhayr b. Jundub al-Azdī 46
Zuhr (clan of Quraysh) 154
Zuhrah, Banū (tribe) 203
* al-Zuhrī, Ibn Shihāb 77, 251, 253

Printed in Dunstable, United Kingdom

78147313R00178